IN SEARCH OF
MARY SEACOLE

IN SEARCH OF MARY SEACOLE

The Making of a Cultural Icon

HELEN RAPPAPORT

**SIMON &
SCHUSTER**

London · New York · Sydney · Toronto · New Delhi

First published in Great Britain by Simon & Schuster UK Ltd, 2022

Copyright © Helen Rappaport, 2022

1 3 5 7 9 10 8 6 4 2

Simon & Schuster UK Ltd
1st Floor
222 Gray's Inn Road
London WC1X 8HB

www.simonandschuster.co.uk
www.simonandschuster.com.au
www.simonandschuster.co.in

Simon & Schuster Australia, Sydney
Simon & Schuster India, New Delhi

A CIP catalogue record for this book
is available from the British Library

Hardback ISBN: 978-1-3985-0443-1
eBook ISBN: 978-1-3985-0444-8

Typeset in Sabon by M Rules
Printed and bound by CPI Group (UK) Ltd, Croydon, CR0 4YY

'All history is full of locked doors, and of faint glimpses of things that cannot be reached.'
Herbert Butterfield, *The Historical Novel*

'Look at the same things again and again until they themselves begin to speak.'
Jean-Martin Charcot, advice to Sigmund Freud

'Research is formalized curiosity. It is poking and prying with a purpose.'
Zora Neale Hurston

For Lynne Hatwell, with love and thanks
for the 'sheltering tree' of friendship

CONTENTS

PROLOGUE

'A REAL CRIMEAN HEROINE'

The Crimean Plain – spring 1855. Thus far, it had been an arduous, seven-month military campaign since British forces landed with their French allies the previous September. Here they still were, dug in outside Sevastopol, thousands of miles from home on this peninsula at the southernmost tip of the Russian Empire.*

---

* Control of the territory has been disputed intermittently since the Russians annexed it in 1783. After the fall of the USSR in 1991, Crimea was recognised as an Autonomous Republic within the independent state of Ukraine but in 2014 Russia annexed it again and Crimea's status has been disputed ever since.

Having endured three terrible battles the previous autumn the British Army was still reeling after the devastating winter that had followed. Thanks to the scandalous incompetence of the British Commissariat, thousands of men in the rank and file had suffered and died unnecessarily from frostbite, hypothermia, malnutrition and enteric disease. But the New Year had brought hope and the first trickle of much-needed supplies of food, medicines and warm clothes from England.

It also brought something unexpected to cheer the spirits of the beleaguered British Army. On 9 March 1855 a small announcement was made at the very end of a long dispatch by William Howard Russell, special correspondent of *The Times*, who had been embedded throughout with British troops in the camp outside Sevastopol, in which he noted: '*Inter alia*, we are to have an *hotel* at Balaclava. It is to be conducted by "Mrs. Seacole, late of Jamaica."'

When Russell's dispatch was syndicated across the British press, the announcement provoked a degree of bafflement; nearly every paper amended the sex of the entrepreneur in question to 'Mr Seacole'. Russell's 'Mrs Seacole' must have been a misprint, surely? How could any respectable woman possibly entertain setting up a hotel at the seat of war – and alone and unaccompanied at that?

Events would soon show, however, that, yes indeed, one very determined Mrs Mary Seacole was most definitely on a 3,000-mile journey from England all the way to the Black Sea; although there would be no hotel per se, and certainly not at Balaclava.

It was enough of a surprise that *any* woman should undertake such a venture. But no one in 1855 could have anticipated that the lady in question would be Black. The Victorian popular perception of Black people in the 1850s was pretty much confined to anti-slavery literature of the *Uncle Tom's Cabin* variety. Yet against all the odds – of her sex, ethnicity and time – when no Black person in Britain held any public office or position of authority, Mary Seacole would launch herself into the heart of the war effort, and with it earn herself a unique place in the British public's consciousness.

*

That brief notice in March 1855 would be the first of many sightings in the Crimean Peninsula of the Jamaican caregiver and nurse, herbalist, sutler, humanitarian and patriot Mary Seacole over the next sixteen months. By the time British troops left in July 1856 *everybody* in Crimea knew who Mrs Seacole was – or rather, they were much more likely to know her as 'Mother Seacole'. Not only that, but the British people back home knew of her Crimean exploits too. Thanks to extensive press coverage of the war – the result of some fine on-the-ground reporting – and the many letters home from their men, they knew about the efficacy of Mrs Seacole's Jamaican herbal remedies for dysentery and cholera; her skill with stitching a wound, bandaging injuries and dealing with frostbite; her wonderful stews and Christmas puddings; and most important of all – her compassion and absolute devotion to her 'sons' of the British Army.

By the end of the Crimean War 'Mother Seacole' had become the archetype of the loyal colonial subject doing her bit for the British war effort; the embodiment of Christian kindness, compassion and generosity of spirit. Indeed, searching through hundreds of collections of letters, diaries and newspaper accounts of the war, one finds that only one other woman during that time was accorded as much coverage: Mary's white female nursing contemporary, Florence Nightingale. For, in her way, as *Reynolds's Weekly Newspaper* observed on 14 June 1857, Mary, like Florence, was 'A Real Crimean Heroine'.

There is no doubt that from the late 1850s to her death in 1881, Mary Seacole was the most famous Black woman in the British Empire. Indeed, until she was voted Greatest Black Briton in 2004, only the Trinidadian pianist Winifred Atwell and the Welsh mixed-heritage singer Shirley Bassey had enjoyed an equivalent celebrity; but their popularity had not come until after the Second World War. Over the years, when speaking about Mary, I have tried to impress on people just how extraordinary and exceptional her achievements and fame were in the context of nineteenth-century white Victorian Britain. There simply was nobody quite like her. The nearest modern-day equivalent in terms of the national acclaim accorded a woman of colour, who was also of Jamaican heritage, is probably the tremendous reception given to Kelly – now Dame Kelly – Holmes after she returned from the Athens Olympics in 2004 with two gold medals for the women's 800 and 1,500 metres, the first British woman of colour to achieve this double.

Early in 1857, while riding on the crest of her popularity and to get herself out of debt, Mary Seacole sat down to write her memoirs in an attic room in Soho Square in London. She had served Britain with loyalty and diligence and felt that the time had come for her to receive due recognition of that fact. The account she published – *Wonderful Adventures of Mrs Seacole in Many Lands* – was a catchy populist title that became an instant bestseller; but it has also created problems for the biographer. People assume that this is Mary's 'auto-biography', but it is nothing of the sort. Her book reveals virtually no details of its author's life before 1850. To make up for this, one might imagine, given Mary's celebrity in mid-Victorian Britain, that a considerable archive of personal detail has accrued from that period and added to our knowledge beyond that slim book's 200 pages. Sadly, this is not the case: with Mary Seacole, most of her personal story begins and ends with what she tells us in *Wonderful Adventures*. We come away from it knowing next to nothing about her early life – her parents, her siblings and the complex network of friends and family back home in Jamaica. This is because Mary left us no paper trail; evidence of almost all the key landmarks in her life prior to the war is missing, beyond the publicly accessible documents of her marriage, her death, her will and census returns.

So how does one begin to reconstruct a life that is virtually uncharted for the first forty-five years? This has been the enormous challenge of writing Mary Seacole's biography, for even with the republication of the *Wonderful Adventures* – after 127 years – in 1984, Mary's account was still the sole primary source. But it only takes us up to her return to England in July 1856 and is full of gaps, puzzles, faux-modest evasions and glaring omissions. The challenge for the biographer is to penetrate beyond Mary Seacole's carefully constructed and controlled self-image. Her book is a brilliant piece of PR, but it hides so many secrets from us. It therefore comes as something of a surprise to me, still, that, thanks to an insatiable curiosity about Mary, I have been able to unearth as much as I have. But to get to this level of truth and dig out every possible vestige of evidence relating to her life has consumed me at times and still leaves me endlessly wishing 'If only I knew . . .'; 'If only I could verify this . . .'; 'If only there was more.'

It was my discovery of Mary's lost portrait in January 2003 that was the catalyst for what has ended up as a twenty-year pursuit of the Seacole story. That discovery was a moment of pure serendipity, for every biographer dreams of finding a lost manuscript, a cache of letters, or perhaps a painting of their subject. When it happened to me it felt, from the very first moment, as though Fate had taken a hand and that I was *meant* to find it. I had first come upon Mary Seacole in around 2000, when searching for interesting women of colour in the field of nursing for my *Encyclopedia of Women Social Reformers*. I had been so intrigued by her story that I joined the Crimean War Research Society and, discovering early on just how contentious the subject of the medals she claimed to have been awarded for her service during the war was, I began discussing this thorny issue with members of the CWRS and the Orders and Medals Research Society.

It was Norman Gooding of the latter who, having been told of my interest in Mary, emailed just after Christmas 2002 to ask if I could identify a painting of a Black woman wearing medals that had recently come to light. It had turned up, by an absolute miracle, at a boot sale in the upmarket Cotswold town of Burford and was thought to have come from the contents of a recently deceased person's house. Even more extraordinary was the fact that a local dealer had bought it without actually knowing the painting was there. For the portrait, painted on board, had been hidden behind a cheap Victorian print and used to back the frame, with Mary's portrait facing inwards. It was only when he took it home that the dealer became curious about the name – 'A. C. Challen' – he noticed written on the back of the board and unsealed the frame to investigate.[1] Had the portrait been the work of a known artist, then that might well have been the end of the story. It would have gone straight off to a London auction house; but because 'A. C. Challen' was unknown and the sitter was uncertain, it was instead placed in a small local auction, where another dealer, the one who sold it to me, acquired it.

I still vividly recall the moment I first set eyes on the jpeg of the painting. I knew immediately that it was Mary and from that very moment was overtaken by a powerful sense of mission. I was absolutely determined to acquire it and prevent it from disappearing abroad or into a private collection. This was because, as a historian, I felt a great sense of responsibility; I knew that now that this wonderful lost portrait of Mary Seacole had been found after over a century since Mary's death, it had to be put on display in a major museum where it could be accessible to all. As soon as I had acquired the painting, therefore, I loaned it to the National Portrait Gallery. I also set myself the goal of unravelling Mary's story, despite the fact that I had already heard that another writer was busy on her biography. I simply *had* to find out more; but I never thought for one moment that my search for Mary would be so protracted and that I would hit so many dead ends and disappointments. Indeed, the intensity and duration of my search in itself explains why Mary Seacole's life has remained only partially explored till now. There is no quick and easy fix in tracking down this most elusive of subjects; you cannot just pop onto Google for a few hours and think it's all going to be there, at the click of a mouse.

It strikes me as an extraordinary irony in this current age where fact checking is *de rigueur* in the mainstream media that so few of the true facts of Mary's life have actually been uncovered or verified. Indeed, you will see that a great many Internet sources on her turn out to be an almost wholesale repetition of the contents of Mary's *Wonderful Adventures*, or at worst an inaccurate regurgitation of it. Inevitably, so much of what *has* been written about Mary has been all too easily accepted at face value – a version of her life that is more wishful thinking than fact. For the reality is that Mary has made it much too difficult to track her in any linear way and few people have taken on the challenge.

So it was that what began for me as a pet research project all those years ago (at a time when I had no hope of being commissioned to write a rival biography of Mary) evolved into a very determined investigation. In my search for the truth about Mary Seacole I have needed to adopt the frame of mind of a detective opening up a cold case history and treat every clue, however small, forensically, in terms of how it can be interpreted. It has necessitated a lot of lateral thinking and, here and there, some unavoidable leaps of faith (some might say informed guesswork, but I hate the phrase). It has been slow and painstaking, at times agonisingly frustrating, and often exhausting. But there has not been a moment when I have ever wanted to abandon my mission. Maybe that sounds grandiose, but for me it really has been a mission, born of a desire to reconstruct the story of a woman of colour who was obliged by the racial, social and moral attitudes of her time to omit or obfuscate so much of the detail of her personal life, as well as her true attitude to the white establishment that for all too short a time allowed her to take centre stage. To talk of the narrative that follows as a 'journey' through Mary's life is rather a limp cliché. Let us call it instead an 'exploration'; and as we set out together, fully cognisant of its unique difficulties, we must prepare for disappointments, as well as several surprises, and accept that what will reveal itself to us is by no means a straightforward, conventional biography. In a way, that is precisely what, I hope, will make this search for Mary Seacole such a unique and fascinating experience.

CHAPTER 1

'THE ISLE OF SPRINGS'

We begin with Jamaica, Mary Seacole's homeland from which springs her unique and indomitable character. Although in her *Wonderful Adventures* she makes much of being a proud 'Creole' in the Spanish meaning of *criollo* – native to Jamaica – she tells us little of her Jamaican homeland. She shares no sentiments about its beguiling natural beauty – seemingly so lush and beautiful, so welcoming – nor, equally, does she comment on the terrible scars left on the Jamaican landscape and its people by the iniquities of the colonial sugar trade, built there on the labour of thousands of enslaved Africans. These were brutally wrested from their homelands in West Africa and transported to the West Indies on the notorious Middle Passage in the most inhumane conditions. One might have expected Mary to have something to say on the subject, but no: she makes it implicit from the outset that she does not intend to critique the abuses of slavery under British rule in Jamaica in the historic sense. To do so would have turned her self-promotional travelogue into a polemic that might have been perceived as anti-British. She does, however, feel perfectly justified in criticising slavery's persisting presence in the USA, which is at a remove from the British colonial reality.

The Scottish writer Charles Rampini called Jamaica 'the land of streams and woods', but Jamaica had been known as 'the isle of springs' almost since settlers first arrived.[1] It was the Cubans who had named it 'Xamayca' when Columbus first landed there in 1494;

Spanish colonists followed in 1509 and seized the territory from the native Taino Indians and were the first to exploit the sugar cane that grew there in abundance. In the interim, until 8,000 British forces sent by the Lord Protector, Oliver Cromwell, seized control in 1655, the Spanish systematically hounded and exterminated the Tainos. Other nations – French, Dutch, Portuguese – meanwhile had also set their sights on plundering the islands of the West Indies of their natural riches and then, in the mid-sixteenth century, pirate raiders arrived. During British rule the pirates of Jamaica thrived and by 1660 it was the stronghold of buccaneers who terrorised shipping in and around the Caribbean, until a devastating earthquake in 1692 destroyed their stronghold at Port Royal, which was also the principal base of the British Navy in the West Indies.

With the establishment of the navy in Jamaica, more and more travellers had begun venturing there. They frequently waxed lyrical about their first sight of the island; for at first glance, from the sea, it was utterly breathtaking. Indeed, Columbus had been so taken with it that he had written to the King of Spain that 'I had almost come to the resolution of staying here the remainder of my days: for, believe me, Sire, these countries surpass all the rest of the world in beauty.'[2]

Approaching by sea in the soft balmy winds of summer, under a clear and serene sky, a traveller might have thought he or she had arrived in paradise. 'Nothing can be imagined more pleasing than the sweet refreshing gales that waft a ship along to the West Indies' after crossing the Tropic of Cancer. Over the bows one could watch 'the dolphin and the porpoise gamboling around, the flying-fish sporting in air', as the eye took in the diversity of the approaching islands.[3] After many weeks in the 'dreary bosom of the wide Atlantic', the welcome sound of 'Land Ho!' would send every eager passenger scuttling up on deck to spot the approaching landfall of Deseada – the first of the Caribbean islands discovered by Columbus – and, within a few hours, Antigua, Montserrat, Redonda, Nevis, St Christopher's. Then, as the boat ran down the Caribbean Sea, the distant peaks of 'beautiful Jamaica, the richest western jewel in the British crown[,] triumphantly loomed before the eye'.[4]

From the water's edge, the low, flat ground rose gently into soft hills thick with vegetation, separated from each other by 'vallies filled with delightful groves, through the centre of which a stream generally winds along'. Beyond, a chain of cloud-capped mountains covered in dense, dark woods rose up in 'exquisite contrast to the soft tint of the foreground' with its rich, fertile pastures of guinea grass and its fields of sugar cane. These alluring peaks stretched the whole extent of the 146-mile-long island, forming a natural barrier between its north and south sides; and none were more beautiful than the Blue Mountains, with the highest peak at 7,700 feet, the most easterly of them.[5] Exploring this landscape the visitor would see parrots and parakeets, exquisite blue-green hummingbirds, huge and luminous dragonflies, and in the woods 'a thousand undescribed blossoms and wild flowers'.[6] The night sky was magnificent, where 'many stars and constellations invisible in England here appear and shine with great brilliancy' and the light of the moon was 'so exceedingly strong, and so reflected, as frequently to give the ground, and the roofs of houses, the appearance of being slightly covered with snow.'[7]

One of the most romantic features of this island of 'sylvan beauties' was its many fine rivers, plentiful with fish – though only Black River was navigable – and its water cascades and mineral springs, for few countries in the world were 'better watered than Jamaica'.[8] In summer when the land was in full bloom, the air would seem as though 'loaded with a fragrance from a thousand sweet shrubs and trees'; the abundance of tropical fruit was legendary.[9] Visitors could gorge themselves on figs, guavas, pomegranates, pineapples, pawpaws, melons, mangoes, ackee, sweetsop and star apples, though most were not indigenous and had been imported by settlers. Cashew nuts grew in profusion as well as the predominant crops of sugar, coffee, cocoa, ginger and pimento. There were rich varieties too of cassava, maize, rice and pulses. Visitors could enjoy the wild boar, the fine beef and poultry fattened on the lush savannas, crayfish from the rivers, turtle, crab and sea fish. Other indigenous products were widely exported: cotton, indigo, rum, molasses (a side product of sugar refining) and the hard woods: logwood, fustic and mahogany.

In the year of Mary Seacole's birth, sugar was king, the trade was at its peak and Jamaica was the world's leading exporter. But the wealth of the white planters who grew it had been built on the suffering of hundreds of thousands of enslaved people.

The uncertainties about Mary Seacole's early life begin to unfold straightaway, with her opening sentence. It is an extraordinarily reticent one for a woman whose very strong sense of self dominates the story that follows, but it is a clear statement of intent; self-censorship will be her watchword throughout. In the list of contents for Chapter 1 she states that her opening chapter will contain 'My Birth and Parentage'; but she then proceeds to give us a highly censored version of these details:

> I was born in the town of Kingston, in the island of Jamaica, some time in the present century. As a female, and a widow, I may well be excused giving the precise date of this important event.

There is an echo here of the elliptical opening to Charles Dickens's 1850 picaresque novel *David Copperfield*: 'To begin my life with the beginning of my life, I record that I was born (as I have been informed and believe) on a Friday, at twelve o'clock at night.' Such statements of the uncertain beginning of a life were a convention often seen in the narratives of former enslaved people – particularly African Americans – published in the decades before and after Mary's story.[10] The much-celebrated Black abolitionist Frederick Douglass opened his own *Narrative* by telling the reader, 'I have no accurate knowledge of my age, never having seen any authentic record containing it.' He knew who his mother was but his white father – who was probably his mother's master – never acknowledged him and he did not know his date of birth. But then, as he conceded, 'I do not remember to have ever met a slave who could tell of his birthday.'[11] Had Mary seen recorded evidence of her own birth? It seems unlikely, given that she later intimated that she did not know if she had been baptised as a baby. For me, as biographer, this state of not knowing was, perversely, almost better than discovering in 2017 that Mary's full date of birth had suddenly appeared on the World Wide Web. Click on her Wikipedia entry and it will tell you that she was born on 23 November 1805 and that the source for this is the National Library of Jamaica. But the NLJ provides no documentary proof of this date – as displayed on their website – and, when I enquired, could not tell me where the information came from.[12] We are thus presented with a typical example of the unreliability of Internet 'history': a statement that is accepted, without verification in a primary source, and rapidly circulated as fact. In twenty years of concerted searching I haven't found evidence *anywhere* of Mary's full date of birth, although it has now been declared Mary Seacole Day in Jamaica.

We have here the first of numerous examples, as we progress through this story, of how the advent of the World Wide Web has, for historians, been very much a mixed blessing. It has undoubtedly been a force for good in making available a huge range of digitised newspapers and out-of-print books, as well as acting as a forum for the interchange of ideas, for circulating discussion and requests for information, but it has also seriously damaged standards of historical accuracy. The uncontrolled dissemination of misinformation and downright error is one of the bugbears today's historians have to face, and in Mary's case it presents us with several claims about her life that we will need to carefully unpick.

The fact that Mary was vague about her date of birth might in itself explain several wildly varying discrepancies that confront us in the surviving documents relating to her life; for she repeatedly got her age muddled, or chose to fudge it, for whatever reason. Some of it is deliberate coyness, which was of course the prerogative accorded to genteel Victorian ladies wishing to modestly draw a veil over how old they were. But Mary does at least say, '*I do not mind confessing that the century and myself were both young together, and that we have grown side by side into age and consequence.*'

In contrast to her American contemporaries, who have left harrowing accounts of their enslavement and open them starkly, as did Harriet Jacobs, with the bald statement 'I was born a slave',

Mary had been born free.[13] It is therefore a terrible disappointment for any biographer to have to begin their narrative by admitting to the reader that they do not know exactly when that was, or how and under what circumstances her mother was given her freedom. Even worse though is not even being able to identify Mary's mother and father. But this was the problem that I was faced with until very late in the writing of this book, and I was mortified at the thought of having to see it published without being able to crack that particular puzzle.

Several commentators on Mary Seacole since her rediscovery in the early 1980s have tried to break through the protective brick wall she has built around the true identity of her parents. Mary was born long before the introduction of official, mandatory registration of births in Jamaica, so we only have baptismal records to go on, and these are patchy. Researchers before me had examined Jamaican parish registers for Mary's birth around 1805, not just in Kingston but across all the Jamaican parishes, and had failed to find one that was a convincing match.[14] We know from her later marriage that she was 'Mary Grant' and her name at death was registered (by a relative) as 'Mary Jane Seacole'. But where did the 'Jane' come from? Was this the name of her mother, speculated Jane Robinson in her 2005 biography?

This suggestion was jumped on with alacrity across the Internet as well as published sources on Mary and repeated as fact without any substantiation. Jane has till now been set in stone, and as I completed my first draft, I resigned myself to never finding confirmation of whether this was correct. But then, one morning I received a call from my researcher in Jamaica, Ann Marie. Down in the chilly document room of the archives, she had finally found that elusive entry in the baptismal register. After a long and fruitless initial search, she had sensed my bitter disappointment at hearing the bad news. So, refusing to accept defeat, she had returned to Kingston to go further back in the records and there the baptism was, waiting to be found. It turned out that everyone had been looking in the wrong place and the wrong time frame.

We shall come to the actual baptism at a more opportune moment, but one thing is certain: Mary's mother was not called Jane. The names of her parents given on her baptism entry are John Grant and Rebecca Grant. No, not 'John Grant and his wife Rebecca', or 'Mr and Mrs John Grant'; like so many mixed-heritage relationships at that time, this was a common-law partnership. Rebecca would appear to have been a Grant in her own right and had probably been given the surname of the master – named Grant – to whom she had originally been enslaved, as was the common practice.*

What's in a name? Well, when it is Grant, one lets out a huge groan at the prospect of genealogical mountains to climb, especially when there are two of them.

We shall come to John Grant in the next chapter, but first to Rebecca. She must, at the least, have been of mixed heritage – then termed 'mulatto' – for the law in Jamaica deemed that any enslaved person given their freedom had to be 'above the shade of mulatto'. Jamaican manumissions were always heavily weighted in favour of females, and we can only assume that her Grant master had given Rebecca her freedom some time before Mary's birth.[15] As a 'mulatto', she would most likely have been a domestic servant rather than a field worker. Such women were given household jobs – as seam-stresses, cooks, washerwomen, nursemaids – or, more significantly, sick nurses – not just on the plantations but in urban areas like Kingston. It is probable that Rebecca met John Grant in Kingston, but Mary was not born there, contrary to what every source on the World Wide Web asserts.

Kingston as Mary's place of birth is the first of numerous red herrings circulating on Mary Seacole's life. She herself is the source of it and it is a deliberate piece of obfuscation. According to crucial correspondence in the Jamaican *Daily Gleaner* in the 1930s, Mary Grant – as she then was – was born 80 miles west of Kingston at a small hamlet called Haughton, near Lacovia, in the parish of St

---

* The discovery of the baptism was tempered by the fact that, disappointingly, it did not give Mary's date of birth, as baptism entries often do, and which I had been fervently hoping would be the case.

Elizabeth. This was confirmed at first hand 'by a much respected merchant of Black River' who had known Mary.[16] Perhaps she had felt that such an obscure place as Haughton would mean nothing to her Victorian readers with no geographical knowledge of Jamaica. They might, after all, have had some idea of where Kingston the capital was located, for it had been a major British military and naval base since the beginning of the eighteenth century. Perhaps she wanted to deflect from any possible identification of her mother, had she given her true place of birth. It is all part of the smokescreen Mary carefully creates in order to protect the identity of her parents and their common-law relationship from scrutiny.

Another *Gleaner* correspondent in 1938 was delighted to have it confirmed that Mary had come from the Lacovia area and that 'Coby' – as the English locals called it – had 'produced something more than cashew-nuts and bankra baskets'.[17] The town was so named after the large sugar estates there owned by the Haughton and James families. Nearby Lacovia gets its name from the Spanish *la caoba* for the mahogany that grew in profusion all around. Located 7 miles inland from the coast – with little more than a church and two taverns – it alternated with the port of Black River as the capital of St Elizabeth until Black River took over permanently in 1773. Lacovia was a busy transit point for the shipment from the estates of sugar, molasses, rum, mahogany, logwood, pimento and other goods down to Black River and had thus grown prosperous during the eighteenth century. Mary clearly knew this area well, as she chose to go and live at Black River in the 1830s.

With regard to Mary's mixed parentage, in Jamaica at that time there was no stigma attached to being born illegitimate, for so many mixed-heritage children were the product of liaisons between white British planters or transient military men and Jamaican women. The prevalence of such relationships was largely due to the shortage of white women in the colony; few genteel white European women volunteered themselves for the exigencies of the oppressive climate so far away from home and the risk of fever for which Jamaica was notorious. Interracial relationships therefore became common and were widely accepted on the island, although very few such couples married. As Lucille Mathurin Mair explains: 'Marrying white was almost too much for the brown woman to aspire to; she settled for the role of concubine.'[18] In any event, many of these military men already had wives back home and were not free to marry. White men in Jamaica therefore often installed Black and mixed-heritage women in their homes as 'housekeepers', providing for their children and acknowledging them even in their wills. This much was socially acceptable; indeed, many women of colour at the time, rather than marry men within their own Black and mixed-heritage racial group (whom they generally saw as 'too poor or too indolent to support a wife and family'), felt it was 'more genteel to be the kept mistress of a white man', viewing marriage itself as 'an unnecessary restraint'. Certainly, there are no mixed marriages recorded in Kingston before 1814, according to Jamaican historian Aleric Josephs.[19]

When writing her book, Mary Seacole was astute enough to know that, in Victorian Britain, the straitlaced, conventional white audience she was writing for would have been highly disapproving of such irregular relationships and she glosses over whether her parents were actually married. In so doing she also carefully minimises the fact of her own illegitimate 'racial amalgamation' at a time when miscegenation and racial difference were coming increasingly under critical debate. In order to get on in the world, she needed to present a respectable public persona right from her very first sentence that would win her the acceptance she craved.[20]

We do not know Rebecca Grant's reason for choosing to give birth at Lacovia, but it must have been due to some family connection. Perhaps she herself had been born at one of the plantations there and it had been her childhood home. She may have needed to give birth away from Kingston, in secret; she was, after all, only about fifteen at the time, according to her age at death (though, like so many life events in this story, we cannot be sure it is correct). She must have returned to Kingston fairly soon after Mary's birth; one senses that her child's Scottish father John Grant acknowledged his daughter and made provision for her, which would explain why Mary had such sentimental recall of him. White fathers did not necessarily abandon children such as Mary born to them of Black and mixed-heritage women; indeed, they often had loving relationships with them. Such a child would usually receive a Christian baptism during the first six months, since in Jamaican Obeah belief, an unchristened baby might be carried away by ghosts and become a wandering spirit. But in Jamaica a lot of baptisms occurred many years later, or never took place at all.[21] Whereas in Britain an illegitimate child went by the unmarried mother's surname, in Jamaica it was different. The children of unmarried parents were generally given the *father's*, not the mother's, surname. Fortunately for Mary, that problem did not occur, for it would seem that Grant was Rebecca Grant's given name.

In terms of her own ethnicity, Mary did not in fact ever refer to herself as Black.[22] In the racial terms employed in the colonies at the time she would have been classified ethnically as a 'quadroon' (white/mulatto). Today she would more likely be described as mixed-heritage; in Jamaican patois she is often referred to as a 'browning'. When writing her book, she clearly sought to downplay the degree of her 'blackness' – for obvious reasons of acceptance – by emphasising her mixed Scottish-Jamaican heritage. Indeed, in the Crimean section of her narrative she refers to herself as an 'English woman'. As Dr William Lloyd noted in the late 1830s: 'I have remarked in the tropics how much the residents think of England; all classes, even the negroes, calling it "home".' Certainly, in the official sense Mary was a British subject, because Jamaica was a British colony, but she never sought to deny her 'Creole' identity, in which she also took considerable pride; it was rather a case of being determined that her service to Queen and the Mother Country legitimised her status as a kind of honorary Englishwoman.[23]

As Rebecca and her daughter Mary were both seen as 'Free Coloureds', they were given privileges not accorded to those lower down the Jamaican racial hierarchy – for example they were allowed to own property, including enslaved people – and actively sought to distance themselves from any link to Africa in their aspiration to higher status in Jamaican society.[24] More importantly, Rebecca

would have achieved improved social standing through her relationship with a white man and having a half-Scottish daughter. Little
wonder, then, that Mary Seacole makes every effort to capitalise
on the authenticity of her paternal line, in which she takes such
evident pride.

But who was John Grant, the man who had ensured that she had
'good Scotch blood coursing in my veins'?

CHAPTER 2

'MY FATHER WAS A SOLDIER, OF AN OLD SCOTCH FAMILY'

The failure to name or identify parents is not unusual in nineteenth-century narratives of Black people, but usually it is of those who have been enslaved. In her own *History*, dictated in 1829, Mary Prince, a formerly enslaved woman from Bermuda, failed to give the first names of either of the parents from whom she was cruelly taken and sold; and Nancy Prince (no relation), writing her own *Narrative* in 1850, identified her parents only as an unnamed household slave and a sawyer, Thomas Gardner.[1] Harriet Jacobs in her later, 1861 story of her sufferings under slavery, despite speaking of her mother with particular affection, does not name either parent. One would imagine, therefore, given her beaming pride in her Scottish military connection, that Mary Seacole would have wished to proclaim the name of her father loud and clear. This ancestry is, after all, fundamental to her personality and to '*that energy and activity which are not always found in [the] Creole race*'. For from the outset, Mary sets herself apart from the '*lazy Creole*' – as she perceives those of her fellow Jamaicans with a disinclination for hard work – the reason for her difference being her Scottish aptitude for enterprise, for '*I am sure that I do not know what it is to be indolent.*'[2]

In early nineteenth-century Jamaica, many plantation owners, estate managers and overseers, as well as merchants in the seaports,

were from Scotland. The first Scottish immigrants had been depor-
tees, particularly those rounded up after the failed Jacobite rising
and sent to Jamaica during 1745-46. The subsequent exodus of
Scots, many from the Lowlands, during the second half of the eighteenth century brought a considerable influx of adventurous and
well-educated young men with professional qualifications such as in
medicine and the law.[3] Writing in her journal in 1801, Lady Maria
Nugent – American wife of the governor of Jamaica and resident
there 1801-5 – noted how the adaptable Scots dominated many pro-
fessions: 'almost all the agents, attorneys, merchants and shopkeepers
are of that country, and really do deserve to thrive in this, they are
so industrious.'[4]

When it comes to identifying soldier John Grant, we are severely
hamstrung from the outset by the ordinariness of the name. In
Jamaica, Grant is the tenth most common surname, and it is a mercy
that Mary's mother had a less common given name, or I would have
made little progress in tracking her down. Indeed, if Mary had not
told us her father was a soldier, we would be doomed to failure. Even
so, in the British Army there are several John and 'J' Grants listed
in the period we need to consider. And unfortunately the search for
Mary's father has been further complicated by the suggestion, made
in 2005, that he might have been Lieutenant James Grant of the
60th Regiment – then known as the Royal Americans – a possibility
that for years has sent everyone chasing after the wrong man.[5] This
candidacy was heavily swayed by the fact that Mary's sister, Louisa
Grant, was born (according to her death certificate) in around 1815.
Based on the assumption that the same man fathered them both, a
suitable soldier Grant had to be found to fit that time frame.

The only regiments stationed in the West Indies in *both* of the crucial conception periods of 1804-5 and 1814-15 were the 60th, 83rd,
85th and some of the West India regiments. James Grant seemed to
fit the bill and no sooner was he posited as a *possible* father than his
name was disseminated all over the Web. But when I researched this
James Grant of the 60th in detail, I discovered that although the 1st
and 6th battalions were in Jamaica during the period in question,

he was in fact in the *2nd battalion*, which was not based in Jamaica at all, but in Barbados and then Berbice in Guyana.[6] Pending my eleventh-hour discovery of the baptism naming John Grant, my search for Mary's father had hit a brick wall.

So who are the best candidates for the John Grant who fathered Mary (leaving Louisa out of the equation for now)? Mary implies he was in the regular army, and we have to take that on trust. We can therefore discount the local militia composed of volunteer civilians and narrow our field to the Army Lists for Jamaica in the period 1804-5. Once we do this, we are left with really only two choices: Lieutenant John Grant of the 2nd West India Regiment and Captain John (Alexander Francis) Grant of the 85th Regiment.

We are lucky enough to have a good idea of the first John Grant's movements in the period concerned, thanks to the survival of his 'Statement of Service' in War Office files at the National Archives, Kew, submitted by him in February 1810.[7] John had originally joined the army in Scotland as an ensign in March 1793, transferring to the 14th (Bedfordshire) Regiment of Foot the following year. He was promoted to Lieutenant and served with the 14th in the capacity of marines, in and around Brittany and the Channel Islands before the regiment was posted out to the West Indies. From 1794 he was based in the Leeward Islands – probably Martinique – over 1,000 miles southeast of Jamaica.[8] His service there till 1800 saw him in action against the French at Saint Lucia, Saint Vincent, Trinidad and the siege of Pointe-à-Pitre in Guadeloupe.

On 23 December 1800, after being promoted to Captain, John transferred to the 2nd West India regiment based in Kingston. But we now encounter a problem: the muster books show that for much of the ensuing period John Grant was On Command with a detachment in Providence in the Bahamas, 600 miles from Jamaica, *except* for the period May to August 1804, when he was back in Kingston. This means that he could only be Mary's father if her birth date of 23 November 1805 is incorrect. She would need to have been born not much later than April 1805, for after August 1804 John was back in the Bahamas. He returned to Jamaica in 1808 when he was promoted to Major to replace officers sent to Portugal for the Peninsular War, but in the spring of 1809 he was dispatched with the regiment to San Domingo on the island of Dominica, to assist the Spanish there in driving out French invaders. Returning to Jamaica in September, the regiment was then sent off again at the end of the year – back to the Bahamas, to relieve the 7th West India. It is presumably there that John Grant fell sick and died, on 29 August 1810. His death is noted in the Army Lists, but there is no record of his burial in Kingston, nor is there any sign of a will; nor have burial records for the Bahamas at this time survived.[9] This scenario, if correct, means that John Grant of the 2nd West India Regiment probably did not father Mary Seacole, and he was certainly not the father of her sister Louisa.

The other John Grant – of the 85th – came from an Inverness-shire family with a strong military background. He was born on 18 June 1776, probably in Boston or Rhode Island,* where his father, another John, had been sent with 'Campbell's Company' – Highlanders commanded by Captain Archibald Campbell of the 78th Regiment – after the outbreak of the American Revolution the previous year.[10] John senior was later based in the West Indies for seven years, 1793-1800, and all three of his sons followed him into the army.[11] John Alexander joined the regiment of Highland Foot† as an ensign in November 1794 when it was newly formed by the 4th Duke of Gordon with many men drawn from his estates. The following December, at the age of eighteen, he transferred to the 85th as a lieutenant. The 85th was stationed in Jamaica at just the right time in our scenario, 1802-8, for him to have fathered Mary in early 1805, if the 23 November birthdate is correct. But the following year John got married, on 2 March, in St Catherine parish just west of Kingston, to a Mary Elizabeth Correvant, who,

---

*   At this time soldiers were allowed to take wives and even children with them under the military 'on the strength' rules allowing a ratio of seven women to travel with every company of 100 men. The regiment had fifty-seven women with it in 1779.

†   It was renamed the 100th Foot and then the 92nd; it was not till 1881 that it became known as the Gordon Highlanders.

with her brother, were heirs to an estate named Orange Grove in St Catherine parish.[12]

85ᵗ THE BUCKS VOLUNTEERS LIGHT INFANTRY, 1808.

© Anne S.K. Brown Military Collection, Brown University Library

Given the reputation of the British Army in Jamaica at the time, it is more than possible that before settling down to a conventional marriage with a white wife, John Alexander Grant had struck up a relationship with a local free woman of colour – Rebecca Grant. In order for this to happen, Rebecca would have needed to be resident in Kingston, where he was stationed, by 1804. It may be that she took her surname from a family of four Scottish Grant brothers in Kingston for whom she, or even her mother, worked as a domestic servant or nurse. These Grants had, since the mid-eighteenth century, made good as provision merchants supplying to the naval base at Port Royal. The first we have note of is Robert Grant, who in 1787 had been the contractor for supplying provisions to the Royal Navy there; in 1799 Alexander Grant was the agent responsible for the supply of fresh beef to HM ships. Messrs Alexander Grant & Brothers had a wharf and counting house in Kingston and the company went through several incarnations, by 1815 becoming known

as Alexander Grant & Co.[13] In the 1790s and 1800s the Grant brothers were paying the poll tax on properties in Water Lane, East Street
and Sutton Street in Kingston – all locations later associated with
Mary – not far from the harbour where they had their wharf. A John
Grant is listed at Water Lane in 1792 and 1793. He and Robert are
noted in the Kingston Assessment Book as owners of nine enslaved
people in 1793, who probably worked either in their household or
on their wharf.[14]

Just when we think we are on the right track with Mary's father,
alas, we learn that John Alexander Francis Grant's life was cut short,
and with it any chance of proving a connection to Mary. He died
only five months after his marriage, in Spanish Town on 8 August
1806. If he really was Mary Seacole's father, then the sad fact is that
Mary, who was still a baby at the time, never really knew him.

There is one small detail in John Alexander's favour: his mother's
name was Jane, which is the middle name Mary later adopted, perhaps in memory of that elusive Scottish paternal connection.[15] Another
reason for favouring this John is that from 1802 the 85th comprised
a single battalion corps, thus sparing us from any confusion between
battalions and their possible dispersal elsewhere in the West Indies.
This battalion spent six uneventful years in a settled tour of duty in
Jamaica, the first years to 1807 in Kingston and Spanish Town.

It is very tempting to fix on John Alexander Francis Grant as Mary
Seacole's father, but there is of course a catch. If that birthdate of
23 November 1805 turns out to be wrong, then we could be back
to square one and two possible fathers. Such agonising uncertainty
is par for the course in genealogical research, but one of the biggest
frustrations in writing this biography has been my inability to identify Mary's father with absolute certainty. Nor, for that matter, do
I know anything of Rebecca's origins. I wanted so much to restore
this part of Mary's lost story, not just because I hate being defeated
by genealogical puzzles, but more because of my sadness that Mary
had been obliged to conceal the details of her parentage from us. It
is the greatest irony that the man who left such an indelible mark on
her psyche probably played no actual role in her young life.

But one thing does make a lot of sense in the midst of all this
uncertainty: the early demise of Mary's father explains her very
misty and romanticised sense of him, based on probably a very
subliminal, if any, recall at all and only what her mother told her
of him. Nevertheless, the all-too-brief presence in her life of a
white Scottish father had clearly meant a great deal, for in later
years Mary would regularly remind friends and acquaintances of
her Scottish heritage. As Crimean War artist William Simpson
noted, 'She told me that she had Scotch blood in her veins. I must
say she did not look like it, but the old lady spoke proudly of this
point in her genealogy.'[16] No wonder; it was more important to her
almost than her ethnicity, for it legitimised Mary in the eyes of her
Victorian readers and gave her a degree of social cachet. Not long
before her death, the *Eastbourne Gazette* noted her descent 'from
an old Scotch family' and that Mary 'claimed her right to be an
Englishwoman because her father was a Scotchman, and herself a
free-born slave in British dominions.'[17]

As an adjunct to my search for Mary's parents I have also spent many
years trying to find Louisa Grant's baptism, in hopes that in the
absence of Mary's, hers might name them. Once again, very late in
the writing of this book, I found myself adding new information that
I had never expected to find. The discovery of Rebecca Grant opened
up new avenues for research and enabled me to confirm what I had
long suspected but till then could not prove – that Mary and Louisa
did not share the same father. As we have seen, both our John Grant
candidates were dead before Louisa's presumed conception in around
1814/15. While I was engaged in a concerted attempt to pin down John
Grant, Ann Marie, after much scouring of the records, came up with
new information that confirmed how very little we really know about
Mary's early life. Ann Marie's search in the Kingston parish church
baptisms for the period 1800 to 1830 revealed that Mary was in fact
one of *several* children to whom Rebecca Grant gave birth between
1805 and 1820 – all of them by different fathers. This discovery reveals
a complex web of irregular and extended family relationships that,

while they are a genealogist's nightmare in terms of their unravelling, are fascinating. For they indicate the extent to which Mary felt compelled to create an entirely false front about her ancestry. But then, to be fair, she was not writing an autobiography, but an account of her heroic exploits in war, within a very tight time frame. Her Jamaican home and family connections are very consciously omitted as not being part of that story.

If, as I have argued, John Alexander Francis Grant of the 85th was indeed Mary's father, and had disappeared from her life by 1806, then it is no surprise at all to discover that by 1808, two years after his death, Rebecca Grant had entered into a new relationship. This resulted in another illegitimate child, born when she was about twenty. A son – George Seddon Henriques – a 'free mulatto' born on 2 February 1809 to Rebecca Grant and an Abraham Henriques in Kingston, was baptised in March that year.[18] Ann Marie and I checked very carefully for rival Rebecca Grants, but the only other one baptising children in this same period is Rebecca Grant, née Malcolm, of Burnt Savannah, who married a John Grant in 1806 and baptised several children in the years to 1820 in St Elizabeth parish; but none of them were named Mary, or Louisa. I cannot of course be 100 per cent certain about this child called George, except to say that the name Henriques is significant. His father Abraham was almost certainly of Sephardi Jewish heritage and the name will appear again in Mary's story, suggesting that this indeed is our Rebecca.

Within a couple of years or so, another son, Edward, was born to Rebecca; Mary confirms his existence in her *Wonderful Adventures*, though by first name only. In his case too there is no baptism to be found, although it has always been thought that he was born between Mary and Louisa. According to Mary's will, this brother Edward had a son named Edward Ambleton; so we can only assume that an Ambleton had fathered Edward senior. All searches for any Grant connection to Ambletons have, however, drawn a complete blank, although Mary did later stand as godparent to her nephew at his baptism.

More genealogical surprises follow: in 1905 a *Daily Gleaner* source spoke of Mary's *sisters* (plural) and another till now unknown sister, Amelia Campbell, was indeed born – a 'free quadroon' – to Rebecca Grant on 4 October 1815.[19] Without Rebecca's name I could never have found her, but we can be certain of Amelia's half-sister relationship to Mary because of later evidence that we shall come to, even though her father's name is not given in the baptismal entry.

There remains, however, a looming problem with the sister we *do* know about, Louisa, who has her own claim to fame thanks to the writer Anthony Trollope.

For all the years that I have been working on Mary Seacole, Louisa has always seemed a certainty, a fixed point in her story because she had later enjoyed a degree of celebrity in her own right. But since pinpointing Mary's parents, it now would seem that Louisa was only a half-sister, although she chose to adopt Rebecca's surname rather than use that of the man who fathered her. She was in fact born three years later than her age at death suggested (which is no surprise, as it was not registered by a relative), on 24 May 1818, 'a free quadroon', daughter of 'Rebecca Grant and Jacob Delmar'. Louisa was actually baptised on the same day as Amelia Campbell – 22 June 1818. Indeed, they share the same entry in the baptism register, suggesting the girls were baptised together and thus were half-sisters. Two years later, another child was born to Rebecca Grant and Jacob Delmar – James Alexander, a 'free brown', baptised on 29 July 1820 like all his siblings at Kingston parish church. But of George Seddon Henriques and James Alexander Delmar there is, so far, no further record. Perhaps they died young for there is no sign of a marriage or children for either of them.[20] *

Whether Rebecca's children all grew up at home with her or were farmed out to relatives, and how she supported them we simply do not know, and Mary stubbornly refuses to tell us: *'It is not my intention to dwell at any length upon the recollections of my childhood.'*

---

* Jacob Delmar moved on to another partner, Mary Ann King, and had a daughter by her in 1826; it may be that Louisa chose to be known as Grant out of loyalty to her mother.

As regards her own early years, we are presented instead with another obfuscation: '*I was taken by a very old lady, who brought me up in her household among her own children.*'[21]

Having given birth to her so young, Mary's mother was far too immature to cope with rearing a child and would have needed to work to support her. What this statement does suggest, however, is that of all the six half-siblings, the eldest Mary received a degree of preferential treatment, and her father John may well have made provisions for her before his own untimely death. White European men in Jamaica often provided for their illegitimate children's education, and the wealthier ones even sent them to school in England; some even set their common-law partners up in business. Rebecca had clearly wanted her daughter to benefit from a good upbringing, and in this respect, young Mary Grant was exceptionally fortunate. For this elderly lady clearly acted as an unofficial godmother-cum-patroness and may well have been white. This was not strange, according to Jamaican historian Aleric Josephs, 'as it was accepted practice for white ladies to act as godmothers to coloured offsprings of white men.'[22] Mary's upbringing, therefore, would, adds Josephs, have been 'in keeping with the "idlenesss" of white upper- and middle-class girls' in Jamaica. Perhaps her patroness tutored her at home herself or paid others to do so. Certainly, in the *Wonderful Adventures* Mary demonstrates a high degree of literacy and a knowledge of the classics, of poetry, literature, geography and science that goes well beyond the basic reading and writing skills offered to most mixed-heritage children in her position.

Mary does not reveal exactly where her patroness lived; but a little-known 1932 Jamaican source states that 'sometimes Mary was with an aged relative who lived at 57 Water Lane.'[23] Water Lane, as we know, was where the Grant family mentioned earlier owned property, too much perhaps to be a coincidence. It really is the only solid connection we have to date. What is certain is that young Mary enjoyed a degree of protection during those early years that kept her well insulated from the busy and riotous town that Kingston was at the time.

CHAPTER 3

'THE MOST BROILING PLACE IN THE UNIVERSE'

The British mercantile and naval port of Kingston lay in a landlocked bay that was almost like a lagoon, 6 miles long and about 2 miles wide, with Port Royal the naval base located on a spit of land at the far western end. Founded in 1692 to replace the original capital Port Royal that had been destroyed in a violent earthquake, it was considered 'the largest, best built, most opulent, and populous town' in the West Indies.[1]

Despite Jamaica being a British colony for well over a century, at the beginning of the 1800s, Kingston still had a strongly Hispanic atmosphere. Overall, there was quite a divergence in the houses, from noble-looking stone or brick-built colonial buildings to ramshackle wooden hovels. Most were low, to a maximum of two storeys. With many of the wooden houses in close proximity to each other, Kingston suffered serious fires in 1780, 1782, and a third in 1843. The streets were laid out on a grid, with the major thoroughfare being the long, straight King Street of colonnaded houses running due north, crossed east–west by the commercial hub of Harbour Street, where many taverns were located. There was a central square, known as the Parade, in the middle of town complete with a fountain that marked the location of the old colonial administration. Kingston also boasted a theatre, a courthouse, a hospital, a jail and a mental hospital. Aside from its parish church, it provided places of worship for Jews and Catholics (Roman Catholicism having been brought in by refugees from San Domingo), as well as various Nonconformist chapels.

Lady Maria Nugent, who lived at Spanish Town – Jamaica's then capital – thought Kingston a degenerate place when she visited: the 'Resort of all the disorderly and mischievous Part of the Community, both Natives and Foreigners'. She lived in dread of infection from the enslaved people who had fled there from San Domingo and daily anticipated conspiracy and uprising from these 'alien blacks'. Baptist missionary William Knibb was unequivocal when he arrived in 1825. He had, he exclaimed, entered hell on earth: 'I have now reached the land of sin, disease, and death, where Satan reigns with awful power, and carries multitudes captive at his will.' The white population was 'debauched'; the 'sons of Africa' were 'poor, oppressed, benighted and despised'. The 'cursed blast of slavery' had 'like a pestilence, withered almost every moral bloom'. Kingston was without doubt 'the foulest blot under heaven'.[2]

White colonists wilted in its blistering summer heat and were mercilessly felled by tropical disease.[3] Lady Nugent thought it 'the most broiling place in the universe'. Anna Maria Falconbridge found the heat 'much more oppressive than I ever felt it in Africa', complaining that 'before I had been in Kingston a week, I was tan'd almost as brown as a mulatto.'[4] In high summer, clouds of dust from Kingston's narrow, sandy roadways covered everything; but with the onset of the second heavy rainy season in October the heat-baked streets would be inundated with water washed down in torrents from the mountains. 'Flood succeeds to flood, until we are ready to think the days of Noah again appear,' as one resident wrote, for most of the streets were unpaved with no gutters to carry the excess water away.[5]

During the days of slavery, captives brought in from Africa had been sold on the block at the Kingston Sunday Markets and elsewhere, condemned to lives of miserable servitude and hard labour. Back in Britain, public outrage at the abuses of slavery had led to a growing abolitionist campaign. Parliament was repeatedly lobbied both to abolish not just the trade itself, which came in 1807, but also to free enslaved people in all parts of the British Empire. In 1815 there were around 30,000 whites and 261,400 people of colour in Jamaica, of whom 250,000 were enslaved, 10,000 free and the remainder Maroons (Africans who had escaped from their enslavement into wild mountain country during the Spanish occupation). By the 1820s, Kingston was in the heyday of its prosperity and had become the 'great emporium of the foreign commerce'. Its spacious commercial harbour and wharfs were piled high during the busy harvest time with 'puncheons of rum, hogsheads of sugar, tierces of coffee and ginger, bales of cotton, bags of pimento, legs of mahogany and cedar, and immense piles of logwood, fustic, lignum-vitae, and ebony black and green, besides produce of minor import, such as arrow-root, castor oil, tobacco, India corn'. This is not to mention a vast range of supplies arriving at the harbour from England and America – hogsheads of coal, barrels of herrings, salt beef, pork and butter ... vehicles, machinery, barrels of flour, planks, boards, timber and so on.[6] Kingston was at the nexus of the trade east across the Atlantic to Britain and Spain, north to Cuba, San Domingo and the USA; south to Panama and South America beyond.

Passengers arriving at the harbour would land near the fish market at the bottom of town, where they immediately would notice the very diverse mix of people – tradesmen, higglers and street vendors 'of every shade of colour'. Market days – especially the Sunday 'negro market' – brought throngs of people from outlying districts into the town, many carrying their bulky loads of goods such as yams, plantains and bananas in large bamboo baskets on their heads, others with donkeys and mules heavily weighed down with bankra baskets full of produce. The 'free coloureds', as mixed-heritage women were then referred to, were especially striking with their glossy black hair and brilliant dark eyes, as one traveller remarked in 1833. They were noted for their gaudy appearance, in their showy turbans or large panama hats and brightly patterned, ostentatious gowns, with strings of coloured beads round their necks, large gold earrings and bracelets, short petticoats and bare feet.[7] Lady Nugent was dismayed to see the sapping effect on the white man of the seductive charms of free women of colour once it began to work on them: 'In the upper ranks, they become indolent and inactive, regardless of every thing but eating, drinking, and indulging themselves, and are almost entirely under the dominion of their mulatto favourites.'[8]

Many of these women, as another resident noted, had 'received an education which puts them on a level with the middle ranks of England' and it brought them a degree of respect within the community. Indeed, as James Phillippo observed, 'In their houses, dress, personal appearance (complexion excepted), general deportment, wealth, morals, and religion, many of them are on an equality with the most respectable of the whites.'[9] This is the level of social status that Mary aspired to among her white British patrons. Writing in 1823, John Stewart noted that the free women of colour felt 'a kind of pride in being removed some degrees from the negro race, and affect[ed] as much as possible the manners and customs of the white'; they were encouraged to think of themselves as much as British as Jamaicans.[10]

The best opportunity Rebecca Grant and her daughter Mary had for enhancing their status came through Rebecca's business, for, as Mary tells us: '*My mother kept a boarding-house in Kingston.*' Running lodging houses – as they were more commonly referred to in Jamaica – was a profession taken up by numerous enterprising free women of colour; it was indeed 'one of the few means of economic and possibly social independence for women during and after slavery'.[11] Some of these women raised enough money to buy houses to run their own businesses in, or more commonly rented their premises.

In the case of Mary's mother's lodging house, we unfortunately run up against another puzzle. Water Lane where young Mary was in the care of her elderly patroness was only three streets up from the seafront in downtown Kingston, and No. 57 at the junction with Maiden Lane was located in an area full of lodging houses, many of them on the two long streets running north from there – Duke Street and East Street. During this time Mary tells us that she made frequent visits to her mother's lodging house, which must have been fairly close by. But Rebecca Grant was only in her twenties. Could she really have had her own business that young? It seems more likely that initially Rebecca might have been working for someone else. But where? It is time for us to deconstruct one of the most persistent myths in the Seacole story.

CHAPTER 4

THE MYTH OF BLUNDELL HALL

It is all Anthony Trollope's fault: open any published source on Mary Seacole, or access at random one of the numberless Web articles and blogs about her, and one of the first things you will be told is that Mary Seacole ran a lodging house in Kingston named Blundell Hall that had been her mother's before her. This is simply not so. Rebecca Grant never owned or ran Blundell Hall; nor did Mary either. Neither of them appear in the Tax Assessment Rolls for the property. The business was her sister Louisa Grant's enterprise, but even she did not own the premises. She rented them in around 1858 from Henry Franklin, the executor of the estate of a well-known Kingston woman of colour named Grace Blundell, who had died in 1855.[1]

In his popular 1860 travelogue *The West Indies and the Spanish Main*, the English novelist Trollope inadvertently set everyone off on this false trail. For in it he described how he had arrived in Jamaica early in 1859 and 'took up my abode at Blundel [*sic*] Hall, and found that the landlady in whose custody I had placed myself was a sister of good Mrs Seacole'.[2] This, combined with a misreading of something Mary says later in *Wonderful Adventures* when she leaves for Panama (which we shall come to), has prompted many commentators to rush off down the wrong rabbit hole.

In order to fully understand and unpick this part of Mary's story, we need to take a closer look at Grace Blundell. She was born Grace Boyden in 1788, the daughter of Joseph Boyden, a white planter at

Port Royal, and a 'mulatto woman', Rosanna Bullock.[3] In the 1816 *Jamaica Almanac*, Boyden is listed as having sixty-eight enslaved people working on his coffee plantation at Windsor Lodge; as a master, he had an ugly reputation. In 1818 he was prosecuted under the Slave Act for 'cruelly, maliciously, and wantonly maltreating, by flogging and marking in different parts of the body, a Sambo slave, named Amey, his property, jointly with others.' The judge sent him to jail for six months and gave Amey her freedom.[4]

There is no record of Grace's marriage to a man named Blundell; theirs, like Mary's parents', was no doubt a common-law relationship. A William Blundell is listed in the Poll Tax Roll in East Street for 1819-35 who died in the Kingston Public Hospital in 1844, and it may well be him.[5] It is likely he was related to the prominent Liverpool Blundell family of merchants, for in 1774 Jonathon Blundell junior had come to Jamaica and co-founded Rainford, Blundell & Rainford, one of the leading merchant and 'Guinea-Factor'* firms in Kingston. The company advertised auctions of hundreds of 'choice young Quaw, Chamba and Ebo negroes' brought from what is present-day Nigeria on the Middle Passage. In the period 1785-96, Rainford, Blundell & Rainford 'sold 11,698 captives arriving on Liverpool vessels alone, especially those of William Boats, one of Liverpool's premier slaving merchants.'[6]

---

*   Eighteenth-century slave traders were called 'Guinea Factors' because many of the
     enslaved people they brought from Africa were captured and sold in and around the
     Guinea Coast of West Africa.

Blundell Hall was located at the bottom of East Street, near the junction with Water Lane. Jonathon Blundell junior probably built it as his town house in the 1780s, at around the same time as the equally famous Date Tree Hall went up next door.[7] After funding thirty-seven Middle Passage voyages between 1779 and 1793, the Blundells stopped trading in enslaved people.[8] Jonathon Blundell died in Kingston in 1800 but appears to have left descendants. If the property had not already been in the Blundell family, then Grace may well have bought it, because under the Abolition Act of 1833 she was compensated for seven enslaved people to the tune of £408. 7s. 11d. (the equivalent of over £49,000 today). Some time in the 1830s she appears to have turned Blundell Hall into one of Kingston's best-known lodging houses. However, there is no documentary confirmation that the residence had that name until after 1840, when we have three very clear eyewitness sightings of Grace operating it as such and 'Mr Blundell' is specifically listed in the Poll Tax Roll for Blundell Hall in 1844.[9]

Blundell Hall certainly acquired a good reputation by the 1840s; arriving in Kingston in March 1840, Quaker minister Joseph John Gurney wrote of being met at the harbour and being conducted to 'Grace Blundell's Hotel, in East Street, where we found a clean and airy dwelling, with even luxurious accommodation'. In September 1842, Prince Christophe of Haiti was reported in the *Jamaica Morning Journal* as having 'taken up his abode at the lodging house of Mrs Bloundell [*sic*] in lower East Street'. Two years later, other travellers reported being met off the boat and 'conducted to the lodgings kept by Grace Blundell'.[10] What is so important about this evidence is that it comes in the crucial period when her mother was, according to Mary, running her own lodging house, prior to the Kingston fire of 1843.

Let us pause for a moment to take a look at the lodging houses of Kingston, for Mary herself ran a very successful one in the late 1840s – so she tells us – and Blundell Hall, situated at No. 8 East Street, was a typical example of the better-quality ones. Jamaicans referred to them often as 'halls' or occasionally taverns, rather than hotels or inns. The majority in Kingston in the first half of the nineteenth century were conveniently placed close to the waterfront in order to capture the custom of weary passengers from the Post Office steam packets and other commercial and private shipping arriving daily on the island. After enduring long and exhausting sea journeys, visitors were eager to find a comfortable and welcoming place to stay.

In the run-up to the abolition of slavery and then in the immediate post-liberation period, many evangelical visitors, missionaries, colonialists and do-gooders, as well as the curious traveller, had something to say about the lodging houses of Kingston, if only to complain about their high prices (8 shillings a day or 40 shillings a week; wine extra).[11]

By 1844 there were 157 lodging-house keepers in Jamaica, of whom eighty-eight were female.[12] It is rare to find an advertisement for a lodging house of this period but this one on Lower King Street, run by a Mrs Edwards and advertised in the 1843 *Guide to the Madeiras, Azores, British and Foreign West Indies*, would have been a typical example.

MRS. EDWARDS'S
Private Lodging House;
No. 99,
LOWER KING STREET,
KINGSTON, JAMAICA.

IT commands an open, cool, and airy situation; is in the most central part of the city, and within five minutes' walk from the water-side. The Board, Lodging, and Attendance are of the best character; the Wines, Spirits, &c., of the choicest selection; and the charges at the usual city rates.

N.B. As Mr. Duke's Livery Stables adjoin the establishment, Carriages, Gigs, &c., can be had at the shortest notice.

It is the female lodging-house keepers who are frequently named by travellers, rather than the male ones, and many of them accrued considerable wealth in so doing. They were more willing to tolerate the domestic chores that such work entailed and many were excellent cooks as well as being natural care-givers and sick nurses. As traveller Trelawney Wentworth noted in the 1830s, all the 'taverns' he visited 'were conducted by a Miss Somebody which seemed to indicate that the office strictly appertained to the sagacity and intelligence of the fair sex; and experience confirmed us in this deduction.'[13] Indeed, it was the custom for these generally large and forthright ladies to be addressed as the 'Big Missis' and some visitors found them very intimidating. Gothic novelist 'Monk' Lewis had been warned against staying at a lodging house when he first arrived in Jamaica, but the one who took him in at Montego Bay was 'such an obliging smiling landlady, with the whitest of all possible teeth, and the blackest of all possible eyes', that he was completely won over. Indeed, his experience had been a very positive one: 'Inns would be bowers of Paradise,' he declared, 'if they were all rented by mulatto landladies, like Judy James.'[14]

The lodging houses in downtown Kingston had a signature style often described by travellers. Two-storeyed with shingled roofs, their most familiar feature were their jalousies – large-bladed venetian blinds which shaded the sash windows along their first-floor colonnaded verandahs. The more windows the better; indeed, this was the sign of a better-quality residence. These jalousies would be kept tightly shut during the heat of the day, till at least 5 p.m., making the interiors very dark and stifling, before being opened to allow the cooling breeze of evening to circulate. Most of these houses were surrounded at ground level by piazzas 10-14 feet wide, shaded by date, palm and coconut trees, though better still was the tamarind tree, throwing its spacious shade over the houses and balconies during the torrid heat of summer. On the piazzas, guests could take the cooler evening air watching the brilliant green flashes of the fireflies, listening to the perpetual humming of insect life – 'a compound of the buzzing and chirping and whistling and croaking of numberless reptiles and insects, on the earth, in the air and in the water'.[15] They could lounge in a rocking chair or hammock, drinking a cooling glass of sangaree made of cold wine diluted with spiced or lemon-flavoured water and sugar – (it would be one of the officers' favourite tipples at Mrs Seacole's store in Crimea) – and enjoy a Havana cigar. Retiring to their bedrooms at around 9 p.m. – for there was little to do in Kingston at night – visitors slept beneath heavy mosquito nets to protect themselves from being ravaged by insect bites.[16]

The interiors of the lodging houses often centred around a large drawing room or saloon – hence the designation 'hall' – located on the first floor with an arched passage on either side leading from one end of the house to the other. This room featured beautiful, uncarpeted, gleaming floors of native hard woods such as mahogany, cedar, breadnut and wild orange, with sofas and ottomans for seating. The floors were every landlady's pride and joy and 'rubbed so bright, that it is often difficult for the unpractised to walk without a fall.' Irish physician and abolitionist Richard Robert Madden recalled how 'the stranger slides, at the risk of his neck'.[17] He spent a year in Jamaica, 1833-4, as one of six Special Magistrates appointed to oversee the emancipation of its enslaved people. He left a tantalising and witty account of a typical 'first-rate establishment in East Street' in a letter written from there in February 1834.

It was customary, Madden writes, to pay one's respects before dining 'to the lady of the house'. 'On Mohammed's principle of going to the mountain, which will not come to him', he had accordingly presented himself on arrival 'before the figure of a stout young gentlewoman, seated at the end of the gallery' and asked if he was addressing the lady of the house. The young woman 'point[ed] her chin in the direction of an old emaciated brown lady, stalking through the courtyard ... and, in due time, she deliberately articulat[ed] two words: – "My mother".'[18]

What a shame that Dr Madden did not think to name his hosts. Several other landladies *were* identified in travellers' accounts, which makes it all the more puzzling that Mary, who seems so proud of her mother, does not mention Rebecca's name and her business. Instead she frustrates us yet again, keeping things tastefully vague. But she does so with good reason; she is constructing yet another protective shield around her mother's identity. This is because in the early nineteenth century, the female lodging-house keepers of Jamaica had a reputation for loose morals. Most of them were free women of colour, a few were Black and some of course were white, and these women had often been set up in business and maintained by white European sexual partners or clients. While such relationships were acceptable, with the women often referred to euphemistically as 'housekeepers', what wasn't was the way in which the lodging houses were frequented by white men wanting to take advantage of the sexual services of the Black and mixed-heritage women who worked there as servants – a perpetuation of the mores of the old plantocracy. Some lodging-house keepers arranged dances in their halls to which only white men were invited to mix with the local women. Mary knew that what went on in lodging houses did not always remain within the bounds of 'unimpeachable business' and she was very careful to distance her mother and herself from that association.[19]

But where was Rebecca Grant's lodging house located? There are no directories listing them by name as early as the 1830s and 1840s; the only sources are surviving newspapers or the Assessment Books and Capitation Rolls in the archives at Spanish Town which document property owners and their livestock or those occupying it. The first sighting does not come until 1830, when Rebecca was around forty years old, and appears at Duke Street paying rent of £60, and that same year is among those listed in the *Jamaica Courant* for not 'Giving-In their Taxable Property'.[20] By 1836 she is in the Poll Tax assessment at 1 Stanton Street, the same year she received £19. 10s. 10d. compensation for one enslaved person – probably a domestic servant – under the Slave Compensation Act.[21] The most logical sighting of Rebecca in terms of owning a property large enough to be a lodging house accommodating several guests is her listing in 1841 as the owner of a 'brick one-storey house in Stanton Street' – presumably the aforementioned No. 1 – of 11,250 square feet, that was valued at £300 (the equivalent of £31,327 now). The property was certainly large enough, but the records note that it was 'old and delapidated [sic]'.[22] There is a gap before Rebecca reappears – in the Poll Tax Roll from 1844 onwards at 27 Duke Street.[23] One would assume that this means she handed the business in Stanton Street over to Mary some time in the early 1840s, but it is not as simple as that, as we shall see.

Rebecca, like all the other lodging-house keepers, would have cultivated naval and military personnel as clients. From what Mary tells us, it would seem that she developed a reputation at her lodging house for being *an admirable doctress* whose British military clients *held her in high repute*.[24] In effect such lodging houses provided a valuable service to the army, offering convalescent care to sick and recovering military personnel that could not be provided for them in camp by the army doctors. Indeed, many of the lodging-house keepers recognised this lucrative gap in the market and became accomplished nurses and practitioners of alternative medicine, drawing on the doctressing skills that had been developed by Black women on the plantations in the care of sick slaves. As she grew older, Mary learned these same traditional skills and assisted Rebecca in her nursing duties, *very often sharing with her the task of attending upon invalid officers or their wives, who came to her house from the adjacent camp at Up-Park, or the military station at Newcastle*.[25]

There were 500 troops based at Up Park; another 150 in Kingston itself and 300 at Port Royal. The army hill station at Newcastle, which eventually housed 700 men, was, however, 19 miles to the north-east of Kingston in the Blue Mountains.[26] This suggests Rebecca Grant's skills were much sought-after if people travelled in specially from there. But the camp was not created till 1841, in a drive to remove the troops to a more salubrious environment on higher ground, away from the virulent fevers of Kingston. If Rebecca's lodging house was indeed located originally at No. 1 Stanton Street, this was certainly closer to Up Park, for in this period Stanton Street ran from the northern side of Sutton Street beyond

North Parade and in the 1870s was absorbed into Duke Street (which ran south of the Parade for half a mile down to the harbour). An early Jamaican source tells us that soldiers often came to Rebecca's lodging house 'for beer'. Apparently they 'teased Mary and called her "Contrary" after the nursery rhyme'. '"Eee, she'll be a reet good nurse, that she will,"' one north-country war veteran told her, confirming that from a young age Mary Grant was indeed destined to follow in her mother's footsteps.[27]

CHAPTER 5

'AN ADMIRABLE DOCTRESS'

During her childhood Mary Grant had been captivated watching her mother at work preparing her holistic Jamaican medicines; it inspired her to mimic Rebecca's nursing skills when playing with her doll: *'whatever disease was most prevalent in Kingston, be sure my poor doll soon contracted it.'* It was inevitable therefore that before long *'the ambition to become a doctress early took firm root in my mind.'*[1] But an inert and unresponsive a patient as a doll was not enough for her: Mary started doctoring the cats and dogs at home, conceiving whichever complaint they were suffering from and then *'forc[ing] down their reluctant throats the remedies which I deemed most likely to suit their supposed complaints'*. Inevitably, as children do, having concocted her herbal simples, she then tried them out on herself.

There was no opportunity at that time for Mary to seek formal training as a nurse had she wished to, for it didn't exist in Jamaica. In Britain, hospital nurses had only the most rudimentary skills and women were barred from studying medicine. Formal nurses' training as a profession was still a long way off, although there were old established orders of nursing nuns in Europe who had worked among the sick for centuries, as well as other charitable bodies whose female volunteers offered informal nursing in workhouses, asylums and pauper hospitals.[2] In contrast, in the days of slavery Jamaican doctresses had perfected their own brand of holistic skills on the plantations, nursing enslaved Africans who seemed in particular to be prone to the fevers of humid Jamaica after the dry heat of Africa. Other women, as Sir Hans Sloane observed in 1825, learned medical skills from doctors called in to see their sick clients at the lodging houses. This became a useful selling point, he said: 'The more skilled they were at doctoring, the bigger their business and the wealthier and more influential they became. They became well respected and trained others in their healing art.'[3]

We do not know where or when Rebecca Grant acquired her own skills. She may have originally learned them nursing sick slaves on a plantation somewhere out near Haughton or Lacovia before she was given her freedom and had perfected them later by observing conventional doctors at her lodging house in Kingston. But Jamaican doctresses in general trained on the job, in a plantation sick-house or hot-house, so called because rather than being kept light and clean and airy they were often built with 'fewer windows than any other house on the estate' – often with no other aperture than the door. Such buildings became 'infernal dungeons' at night, with the sick crammed in together and locked in by the estate overseers. Some of these doctresses became legendary – 'a most fearful fraternity', in the words of sugar planter Thomas Roughley, who whenever he fell ill took himself first to the doctress and never to a white doctor.[4] (The same would happen in Crimea when men would go to Mary for treatment rather than the army doctors.)

As early as 1774, colonial administrator Edward Long noticed that 'mulattoes' possessed 'for the most part, a tenderness of disposition, which leads them to do many charitable actions . . . and makes them excellent nurses to the sick'.[5] The most celebrated Jamaican doctress next to Mary Seacole is Cubah Cornwallis, who was renowned for saving many naval officers from the dreaded 'yellow jack'. In 1780 she had nursed the young Horatio Nelson back to health at Fort Charles in Port Royal, after he had fallen sick with typhoid fever on his way back from Nicaragua – probably from drinking infected water on board ship.[6] Sometimes referred to as a 'doctor woman' or 'hot-house woman', a doctress such as Cubah was, in the truer sense, a 'general practitioner'.[7] She was multi-skilled, not just able to nurse the sick in the then understanding of 'nursing', but also adept in basic surgery such as stitching wounds and setting broken bones. She was also indispensable as a midwife and – perhaps the greatest and still underrated talent – she was knowledgeable in the use of native herbal and folk remedies based on the indigenous Jamaican pharmacopoeia for the cures of certain disorders. In many ways a Jamaican doctress then was as skilled as any pharmacist in preparing medicines.

Once a plantation doctress was given her freedom, as Mary's mother was, she could have nursed in parish hospitals or private homes, or at the public hospital in Kingston (one of the island's oldest, established in 1776). Many, however, practised at their lodging houses, as did Rebecca Grant and her daughter Mary after her,[8] for they generally provided a level of care far superior to the appalling standards in public hospitals. Their acquaintance with allopathic medicine might have been superficial, and white medical men were in the main hostile to their methods, but the doctresses had links right back to the original Taino Indians who had lived on the island, as well as to healing practices in African Obeah culture brought in by enslaved people. Unfortunately the latter too often has carried an unjustified connotation of witch-doctoring.

The white medical men might have looked upon some of the Jamaican holistic practices of the day as dangerous quackery, but as Professor Alan Eyre observes, medicine in the early Victorian era had a lot to answer for and 'was really a form of benevolent homicide': 'Mercury, opium, arsenic, antimony, copious bleeding, "terrible" purges, blistering, cupping, emetics and sweating: this was the inevitable fate of any patient who consigned his or her body to the "care" of an academically trained physician.'[9]

Mercury was much favoured as a basic ingredient in proprietary medicines, as too morphia. Queen Victoria's personal physician Sir James Clark was heavily reliant on the highly addictive chlorodyne, 'a mixture of chloroform, ganja and morphia', as a sedative to calm her frayed nerves; although it is thanks to his work on 'the sanitive influence of climate' that Clark recommended the 'salubrity' of the Jamaican mountains as a 'safe temporary retreat to invalids in the early stages of consumption'.[10] Thomas Roughley's *Jamaica Planter's Guide* of 1823 recommended that the doctresses should not be allowed access to 'deleterious drugs' but should only need 'a few doses of glauber salts, sulphur, rhubarb, castor-oil, camphorated spirits, bitters and plaisters to dress sores and make blisters of, with two or three lancets, a pair of scissors, and spatula' in order to be able to administer care.[11]

We can find a very clear definition of the qualities required in a good 'hospital matron' on plantations in the *New Jamaica Magazine* for 1799. She must be

> a woman of middling age, of a compassionate disposition, careful and affectionate; of a robust constitution, capable of bearing fatigue and watching. It is required that she have skill to dress ordinary wounds and sores, to deliver pregnant women, which as births are here mostly natural and easy, is an easy matter. ... Long experience, with the practical knowledge of simples, have set some of these women, in many respects, above surgeons too frequently met with in the mountains. I had one, the loss of whom I shall regret all my life.[12]

We might keep these qualities in mind when exploring Mary's nursing skills in Crimea later.

So what were the treatments offered by the Jamaican doctresses? Herbs such as 'Sarsaparilla, Indian arrowroot flour, cowitch and lime water, Peruvian bark, crab's eye weed' were used to treat a range of ailments from yaws to dysentery, vomiting, catarrh, intermittent fever and constipation.[13] Many households grew their own herbs and specifics in the garden – ginger, mint, fever grass and aloe among them.[14] The native herbalists were canny too, they knew, as did Mary, that

> *the simple remedies which are available for the terrible diseases by which foreigners are attacked, and which are found growing under the same circumstances which produce the ills they*

minister to. So true is it that beside the nettle ever grows the cure for its sting.[15]

Some vestiges of this folk logic still survive: growing up in the 1950s in England, we children knew that the antidote to a nasty nettle sting was to rub it with dock leaves – which always seemed to grow nearby.[16]

Mary Seacole's training in African-Jamaican herbal practices was always an important cultural link with home and traditional doctressing skills of which she was truly proud. In Crimea, as we shall see, she would have to adapt to what herbs, fruits and barks she could obtain locally. But in Jamaica she would have used the shavings of logwood and mahogany bark for their bitter tannin in the making of astringents to treat diarrhoea and dysentery, or ground cinnamon bark – which grew wild all over the island – to make astringent drinks, sweetened always by her standby – guava jelly. One of many traditional sayings in Jamaica was 'Guava root a medicine fe cure young gal fever', and Mary Seacole made good use of it as one of the primary ingredients in all her remedies in Crimea.

The important thing was that the Jamaican doctresses eschewed the use of opiates, so heavily relied on in allopathic medicine, and drew instead on a wide and sophisticated range of herbal treatments, handed down over generations, which were first described in detail by the physician and botanist Dr Hans Sloane in 1696, who catalogued nearly 800 plants in the Jamaican flora, and later by Thomas Thistlewood. During eighteen years in Jamaica as a planter and overseer, Thistlewood noted down in his journal numerous 'receipts for a physick', particularly flux or diarrhoea, involving red guava bark – as well as its buds, seeds and roots – cashew bark, and the tough rind of the pomegranate.[17]

Many of these recipes were echoed in Dr Thomas Dancer's classic work, *The Medical Assistant; or Jamaica Practice of Physic.* Published in 1801, it was primarily intended as a recipe book of treatments to be used to nurse sick enslaved people on plantations. It makes for fascinating reading in its astonishingly wide range of often exotically named indigenous plants and barks used in Jamaica simples to treat every conceivable ailment and disease. Many of them are familiar to us from Mary's own account of her practice:

JAMAICA·SIMPLES; *or,*

employed, like that, in stopping Intermittents, but must be given in small Doses, being considerably Emetic. See Dr. *Wright* and Mr. *Lindsay*, *Ph. Tr.*

NEESEBERRY BULLET-TREE (*Achras.*)——The Bark may be given for the Peruvian Bark. *Browne.*

HALBERT WEED (*Calea Jamaicensis.*)——Fresh Herb in Infusion, a good Bitter. *Browne.*

NEESEBERRY (*Achras sapota.*)——Seeds in Emulsion, a fine Bitter. *Martyn.*

Such as are Binding, or Astringent.

GUAVA (*Psidium.*)——The young Leaves, Buds, and Fruit in Decoction.—The half ripe Fruit stewed.—Marmalade of the ripe Fruit excellent in Fluxes.

POMEGRANATE (*Punica granat.*)——The Rind of the Fruit. Boil in Water, with Cinnamon, and add Port Wine and Guava-Jelly. A Conserve may be made of the Flowers or Pulp, with Sugar. See *Pomet.*

MAMMEE SAPOTA (*Achras sapota.*)——Marmalade of the Fruit in Fluxes. *Martyn.*

CASHEW (*Anacardium.*)——Expressed Juice of the Fruit in Red Wine Sangree. Good in Female Weaknesses. Cure also for Dropsy. The Portuguese turn their Dirt-Eating Negroes out in the Cashew season, and force them to live on the Fruit. *Labat, Tom.* II. 233.

MAHOGANY.——Boil an oz. of the Shavings in 2 pints of Water, till one half is wasted. Dose, from 2 to 4 table spoonfuls frequently, in Diarrhœa or Looseness. *Hughes* in *Medical Facts and Observations, Vol.* VI.

LOGWOOD (*Hæmatoxylon.*)——Decoction of the Wood with Cinnamon. Add Guava-Jelly.

OPOPANAX.——Extract of, the same as the Succus Acacia; a strong Astringent. *Barham.*

BIRCH TREE (*Bursera Gumm.*)——Decoction of the Roots. This Tree affords a fine transparent Varnishing Gum.

SEA-SIDE GRAPE (*Coccoloba uvifera.*)——The Fruit is so very Astringent as to cause a degree of Costiveness in some cases dangerous. Of this I have known instances. It may therefore be a very useful Medicine in some Loosenesses *.

HOG GUM (*Hermannia.*)——Made into Pills acts like Balsam Capivi in stopping Gleets.

NICKARS (*Guilandina bonduc.*)——The Powdered Nut in Seminal Weaknesses. *Grainger. Piso* says they are good to throw out the Yaws.

Hog

But Dancer's book is also a wealth of fascinating herbal curiosities: there was yellow thistle for fluxes and belly ache; velvet leaf and cotton tree for coughs and consumption; spikenard and trumpet tree for dropsy; prickly yellow wood for convulsions; barbadoes [sic] pride for 'female obstructions' and hog-gum for 'female weakness'; halbert weed for indigestion; stinking weed for itch; and parrot weed for warts. Even Dancer had to admit that many of these plants were as yet unknown to him.[18]

One of the many components of the doctress's craft was keeping the patient warm and 'rubbing' – or as we now call it: massage. This was a standard procedure for those suffering from fever, as for example applied by Cubah Cornwallis, who placed 'warm bricks' on the feverish Nelson's feet to counteract his shivering, and 'dosed him with her herbal brews'.[19] Similarly, white rum was rubbed on the chest as a preventive against colds. Mary Seacole practised warming and rubbing the extremities of cholera victims in both Panama and Crimea.

When the Jamaican economy declined after the abolition of slavery and planters gave up and sold their estates and went home, so the numbers of British trained physicians dropped off. Indeed the doctresses made an increasingly significant contribution in the period up to 1860 when British medical facilities in Jamaica were very rudimentary, and before an official service was set up.[20] All the time that Jamaica remained an important military and naval base, Rebecca and Mary Grant provided a much-needed service to British officers, who regularly succumbed to illness in Kingston, as too their wives, whose babies they would also have delivered. But nursing and making up her herbal remedies was not the only occupation that the enterprising young Mary Grant pursued at this time. Never one to stand still, she was also extending her horizons and was already proving to be a skilful businesswoman and entrepreneur.

CHAPTER 6

'THAT LONGING FOR TRAVEL WHICH WILL NEVER LEAVE ME'

Aside from her nursing talents, Mary Grant inherited another quality characteristic of female lodging-house keepers: business acumen. There were few restaurants in Kingston at the time, so they needed to be good cooks, as the quality of the food they offered was a strong selling point. Indeed, travellers often complained of the groaningly huge breakfasts they were served in Kingston. Many women diversified into running dry-goods stores or producing baked and bottled goods. As one visitor attested in 1837, the Kingston lodging-house keepers were all extremely enterprising: 'most of them make cakes and sweetmeats, which they send out on large trays for sale. Many of their preserves are excellent; amongst the best are the green tamarind, pine marmalade, and last, not least, Guava jelly.'[1] Mary would have helped her mother produce preserves and pickles, and this cottage industry would prove to be the beginning of a parallel career as an enterprising woman of business. Having such strong commercial instincts and an enormous curiosity about the world, while yet in her teens, she began to look at the world beyond Jamaica: *As I grew into womanhood I began to indulge that longing for travel which will never leave me while I have health and vigour.*[2]

In idle moments, Mary would pore over maps studying the sea

route to England and watch the sailing ships come and go in the harbour, longing for an opportunity to climb on board. Very soon one was presented, but Mary does not clarify: *'circumstances, which I need not explain, enabled me to accompany some relatives to England'*, is all she will say, leaving us to fill in the gaps and speculate whether these might have been members of the Grant family.[3] She does at least tell us that on this first journey to England in around 1820/1 – the first of nine arduous 5,804 nautical-mile Atlantic crossings she made in her lifetime – she had a female companion of her own age. Her two half-sisters, Amelia and Louisa, were much too young, so it could not have been one of them. Were the two young girls simply enjoying the luxury of a trip to the home country at their relatives' expense? If so, who were they? Or was Mary's indulgent and anonymous patroness paying for it?[4]

We can at least infer that Mary and her companion would have sailed to England on a packet boat primarily carrying mail and cargo between the West Indies and England, or, failing that, a commercial merchantman. In the early 1820s, the Post Office ran the packets sailing to Jamaica from the Falmouth station in Cornwall every month; it was not until the 1830s that faster commercially run steamships took over and operated a more regular service.[5] If they were lucky they might have shared one of the twenty or so cabins during the long six to eight weeks at sea – depending on the weather conditions around the Bay of Biscay – rather than having to endure the dark steerage accommodation on the lower deck. Thankfully they had each other's company, for the Atlantic crossing then was not just extremely tedious but also dangerous if the ship hit bad weather.

The packet boat Mary travelled on would have sailed from Port Royal via Grenada, St Vincent and Barbados; the journey to England, assisted by the Gulf Stream, was generally faster than that coming back. The boats followed the north-east trade winds, along the route south of the sub-tropical anti-cyclone, in order to avoid the worst of the Atlantic storms. To be on board a rolling and pitching packet boat in a storm in the middle of the Atlantic, suffering seasickness and bouts of sheer terror, was something Mary plainly became inured to during her many travels. Having taken last sight of land at Barbados, the next would not come until the northern end of the Azores off Portugal, before her ship sailed north up to England.

Whatever Mary's response was to Regency London (and the indications from *Wonderful Adventures* are that the capital was her location for the entire time), she daintily says she is '*not going to bore the reader with them*', but she does at least comment on the racism that she and her friend encountered at the response of '*the London street-boys*' who '*poke[d] fun at my and my companion's complexion*'. At this point Mary is quick to clarify that it was her friend – '*who was very dark*' – who was the main target of the abuse; not her, for '*I am only a little brown – a few shades duskier than the brunettes whom you all admire so much.*'[6] Here we have the first of numerous points in Mary Seacole's account of her life where she seems anxious to metaphorically 'dilute' her own skin tone in order to appear less 'African' than her white Victorian audience might have otherwise perceived her, and thus in some way be more socially acceptable to them. There are several eyewitness accounts of her over the years where she adopts this same strategy of underplaying the darkness of her skin. In London in the early 1820s there were no policemen – or Peelers as they were nicknamed when founded by Sir Robert Peel in 1829 – to protect these two Jamaican visitors from physical or verbal abuse, and Mary's friend, who she says was '*hot-tempered*', clearly suffered. '*Our progress through the London streets was sometimes a rather chequered one,*' Mary concedes rather flatly, again underplaying what must have been a painful and upsetting experience of British racism at first hand.

Around the end of 1823, and now eighteen, Mary ventured to London again, a fact which in itself is extraordinary, given her sex, her youth and at a time when sea travel – by sail – was still hazardous. It cannot be that she travelled alone; but if she had companions, she fails to tell us. Her failure to do so is very much characteristic of the self-starting, intrepid solo traveller image that she projects of herself throughout her narrative. Her visit this time was effectively the first of many business trips that characterised her determined and enterprising personality. Having now become adept at making Jamaican preserves and pickles, she took '*a large stock*' of her goods to the capital. In so doing she was enacting a traditional Caribbean proverb: 'Hard push mek mulatto woman keep saddler shop'. Even relatively privileged unmarried women of colour such as her had to earn a living, and it was time for Mary to go out into the world.[7]

West India preserves such as Mary's were 'far famed and really excellent', and 'so much prized in England' for serving with cold and preserved meats, as the Scottish writer Mrs Carmichael informed readers of her *Domestic Manners ... of the West Indies*.[8] In the City of London Mary would have found any number of traders with whom to negotiate a sale for her goods. But what exactly were they composed of? It is a poetic coincidence that one of the most popular ingredients of Jamaican pickles and sauces was the very hot red or yellow Scotch bonnet pepper (known to the Spanish colonisers as habanero) that got its name from its similarity in shape to a Scottish tam-o'-shanter hat. (These probably arrived in Jamaica worn by Scottish planters at the end of the eighteenth century, the name picked up from a 1790 poem by Robert Burns.)

Scotch bonnet peppers grew in profusion in Jamaica, and were turned into a relish or sauce with added vinegar, sugar, pimento, ginger and garlic, and any combination of pineapple, mango, chayote (a type of gourd), jalapenos (chilli peppers), tamarind, cucumber, onion, garlic and carrot. Every Jamaican cook would, of course, have added his or her own special ingredients. Also popular was lime pickle and ginger preserve and Mary frequently refers to making guava jelly, which was a favourite sweetener. Women of colour such as the beautiful and languid Miss Clara in Andrea Levy's Jamaican novel *The Long Song* – who had been given her freedom by her papa, 'a naval man from Scotch land' – was sure to announce to all and sundry that 'me be a quadroon' and that she had opted for the more decorous occupation of cooking and selling jams and pickles – or rather supervising their production – and did a roaring trade selling them to the servants sent to her by their white 'missis'.[9]

Mary was in London long enough on this second visit to have made more sauces and relishes when she got there, and to have arranged with West India merchants to supply to them on a regular basis when she got back to Kingston. Perhaps she approached one of the many Oil & Italian Warehouses, as they were known, which dealt in a whole range of imported foodstuffs, including pasta, pickles, olive oil and preserves – companies such as William Day & Co's Oil & Sauce Warehouse at 95 Gracechurch Street. Let us, for now, keep a note of the name.

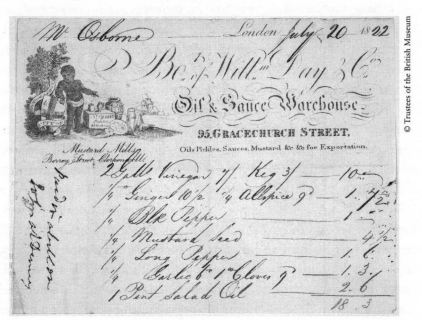

Speculation is risky, but Mary cannot have arrived in London without having some prearranged contacts. She would have needed to know whom to approach in order to make the most of this trip but there is no record anywhere of her business ventures in the capital. One might have hoped that the extraordinary sight of an independently minded woman of business from Jamaica travelling as an 'unprotected female' would have aroused some curiosity or comment in London, but to date, nothing has surfaced. How would Mary have fared, as a lone woman of colour, in finding accommodation? It is likely, given prevailing mistrust of and hostility towards Black people, that many hotel and boarding-house doors would have been closed to her; she might well have needed to already know someone in London who could offer her accommodation.

From our own 21st-century perspective, it would be invaluable to have Mary's take on 1820s England, but if she wrote any letters home to Jamaica they are long since lost. When venturing out in London in the days before the Slavery Abolition Act of 1833, she must have been aware of the presence of Black people as servants attending wealthy Londoners, who often brought them back to England with them after service in the colonies. Some would have been enslaved people who had been sold into domestic service. Those Black people who worked independently tended to live out in the poorer districts of the East End, in and around the docks where work could be found as stevedores and porters. It is estimated that there were about 10,000 Black people living in London – around 1 per cent of the then population – at the beginning of the nineteenth century.

During her visit, Mary surely would have passed some of the many Black beggars and itinerant musicians on the London streets, especially around the richer area of St James's, many of them former soldiers, sailors and bandsmen from Nelson's navy, who had been unceremoniously let go at the end of the Napoleonic Wars. Several Black street musicians became well known around London, men such as the singer Joseph Johnson, a former sailor who wore a model of Nelson's ship on his head, or Billy Waters, a one-legged violinist called the 'King of the Beggars', 'the most facetious fellow, full of fun and whim'.[10] Indeed, she might well have known about – if not witnessed – a landmark event in Black history that occurred in 1825 when she was in London: the English debut of the 17-year-old American actor Ira Aldridge from Harlem, New York. He had appeared under the name 'Mr Keene, the African Roscius' on 11 May at the Royalty Theatre in Covent Garden as the first Black Othello. The whole of London had been agog at the sight of this 'Gentleman of Colour' playing 'that soul-rivetting work of our National Bard'.[11]

Mary Grant set off back to Jamaica in November 1825, just as she reached her twentieth birthday, a journey that was, as she tells us, *very nearly brought to a premature conclusion*.[12] For once we are given a concrete clue: Mary's ship was called the *Volusia* (although she spells it *Velusia*) – a wooden sailing ship, built in Southampton in 1811 and owned by Green & Co., that sailed in and out of Jamaica at Black River in St Elizabeth's. It is described as a 'Jamaica trader' in the *Lloyds List* and with a Captain Raffles in command since around 1818, under whom it often made the crossing in around forty-two days.[13]

The *Volusia* sailed from Gravesend on the Thames Estuary on 23 November 1825, stopping at Portsmouth on the 24th, but somewhere in the Atlantic, just after everyone on board had had a jolly time celebrating Christmas Day, *a fire broke out in the hold*. It must have been a close-run thing, for Mary tells us that had another ship not hoved into sight and its sailors helped put out the fire, this might have been the end of her story. With what will become her typical sangfroid and self-deprecating wit, she describes how, while the fire was still raging, she negotiated her escape and *entered into an arrangement with the ship's cook, whereby, in consideration of two pounds – which I was not, however, to pay until the crisis arrived – he agreed to lash me onto a large hen-coop*.[14] Three months after leaving England, the *Volusia* finally docked in Jamaica on 26 February 1826, having had to stop off to make repairs to its severely damaged deck.

During this second trip to England Mary clearly developed a nose for business and arrived back with new ambitions to diversify her ways of earning a living. She was restless marking time in Kingston and tells us, quite candidly, that before long '*I started upon other trips, many of them undertaken with a view to gain.*'

Respectable ladies never discussed such base matters as making money; but, then, Mary always bucked the system in everything she did. Throughout her memoir she is never coy about her drive to make a good living; hard work for her is a virtue and profiting from her labours is not a sin. With this in mind she boarded a ship for New Providence, the main island in the Bahamas – in her terms a relatively short 500-mile sea journey from Jamaica by schooner – in pursuit of a rather different enterprise: the purchase of exotic seashells to cater to the nineteenth-century craze for shellwork.

© Victorian Picture Library

This had begun in the eighteenth century with the fad for shell grottoes on English country estates and elaborate shellwork centrepieces on grand dining tables. In Jamaica, tortoiseshell-work dates back to Port Royal in the seventeenth century; when the mania for curios and trinkets made of shells took off in Europe, Kingston merchants started importing exotic shells in every shape and size for local women to turn into flower shapes, brooches, earrings, bracelets and necklaces. Sailors would bring in shells from other West Indian islands, too, for turning into curio boxes, frames and mirrors – to sell to passengers and crews of the steamers arriving at Kingston and Port Royal. English merchants were keen to import exotic shells such as the most prized, large orange cowrie, for which they paid high prices, and it must be these that Mary had in mind when she brought back *'a large collection of handsome shells and rare shell-work, which created quite a sensation in Kingston, and had a rapid sale.'*[15] Similar business trips followed to Haiti and Cuba, but their precise nature is unknown, although during this time Mary appears to have acquired the pearls of which she was fond and had them made into necklaces. Back in Kingston, Mary soon had other preoccupations: her primary vocation was calling her. Her kind and now very elderly patroness in Water Lane, to whom she owed so much, was dying, and Mary was needed to nurse her through her last long illness.

CHAPTER 7

'A Certain Arrangement Timidly Proposed by Mr Seacole'

After the loss of her patroness, who, Mary tells us, *'died in my arms'* at her childhood home in Water Lane some time in the early 1830s, she occupied herself increasingly in *'making myself useful in a variety of ways, and learning a great deal of Creole medicinal art.'*[1] Some of the clientele at her mother's lodging house were West India merchants from England travelling back and forth to Jamaica on business. One such gentleman visitor from the City of London appears to have quickly discovered that Miss Mary Grant offered all the domestic and nurturing talents any white, male colonial visitor could desire; for, as the Caribbean song then went: 'Brown girl for cook – for wife – for nurse'.[2]

Any sensible 'Massa Buckra'* in Jamaica knew that 'white lady wery great boder [bother]' if he caught the dreaded fever, for European women had absolutely no nursing skills. It was the Jamaican sick nurses who knew the right physic to give their patients, and Mary Grant clearly impressed, for, without further ado, *'I couldn't find courage to say "no" to a certain arrangement timidly proposed by Mr. Seacole, but married him.'*[3] Such a mixed

---

* Jamaican patois for a white master.

marriage was extremely uncommon in Jamaica at the time, even though the limitations on the civil rights of free people of colour had been removed with Abolition.[4] Not only had Mary found herself the white patron many free women of colour in Kingston craved, but Mr Seacole had – contrary to usual expectations – even offered marriage. But it came at a price. Edwin Seacole was not a well man, most probably succumbing to the climate and the fevers that plagued so many of his fellow countrymen in Jamaica. He clearly needed a nurse rather more than he did a wife, for, as Mary explains, '*before I undertook the charge of him, several doctors had expressed most unfavourable opinions of his health.*'[5] This was clearly no romance, no love match, but a pragmatic business arrangement: the lucky groom does not come across as an object of affection in *Wonderful Adventures*, but rather of pity; and before the reader has got to the bottom of the very same page, Mary has hatched, matched and dispatched him.

What she doesn't, very deliberately, tell her Victorian readers is that Mr Seacole was white. With nothing to identify him, they may well have assumed that he was of mixed heritage too. Poor Edwin Horatio Hamilton of the ostentatious name; he is but a shy, obliging bit player in this story – a complete cypher. But rightly so in Mary's scheme of things, for her *Wonderful Adventures* is by no means a conventional autobiography; as it progresses it becomes more of a picaresque travelogue, and he is pretty much inconsequential to the narrative. However, if we are to know and better understand the fully rounded woman, then we really need to take a look at the fascinating family that gave Mary Seacole the surname that made her famous; for in knowing more about them we can fill in some of the gaps in her life story.

Edwin Horatio Hamilton Seacole's name is not one to be passed over, but to reveal her husband's full name would have necessitated Mary explaining the obvious Nelson connection that goes with it. He was the eighth child and fifth son of Thomas Seacole and his wife Ann, née Akers, and was born in Prittlewell in Essex in around

September 1803 (we only have the record of his baptism). But let's go back to the beginning. Thomas and Ann were married, by licence, at St Dunstan's Church in Stepney, in the East End of London on 25 November 1786. His temporary address for the marriage was given as Ratcliff Back in Mile End Old Town, which was Ann's home – right near the East India Docks. But Thomas was not a local dockside navvy; according to a newspaper notice, he was originally from Rayleigh in Essex.[6] His and Ann's first child, Thomas Fowler Seacole, was born on 19 July 1787 at Prescot Street near St Katharine's Dock (he is the only one of the eight Seacole children for whom we have an actual birth date rather than just a baptism). Thomas senior might well have had a family connection to the East India Company, for Thomas junior subsequently served as a second mate on several ships owned by the company, sailing the routes to Madeira, Bombay, China and Batavia between 1806 and 1820 on the *Georgiana*, *Juliana*, *Thomas Grenville* and the *Alexander*.[7]

By June of 1790 Thomas and Ann had left London for the village of Prittlewell about 6 miles south of his home village of Rayleigh, right near the Essex coast. Here their second child, John Henry, was privately baptised on 27 June at the church of St Mary the Virgin soon after his birth and baptised again publicly the following year. (Such private baptisms were usually done in haste if a baby was weak and not expected to survive, but luckily John Henry did.)[8] Thanks to Overseers Records for the parish in the Essex Record Office, we discover that on Easter Monday 25 April 1791, at a meeting at the Spread Eagle public house, Thomas Seacole was appointed to 'attend all the poor within the bounds of this parish as a Surgeon, Apothecary, a Man Midwife, in all Casualties and women in Labour included, for the sum of Twenty Guineas for the ensuing year'.[9]

But where had Thomas trained in these skills? At the time of his marriage, he was too young to have already learned them as, say, a naval surgeon, because the common age of entry in this capacity was twenty-six. Indeed, he would not necessarily have had any formal medical training. It is more likely that he had been apprenticed to a local Essex apothecary/surgeon. For example, the *Medical Register* for

1783 lists Mr Cooke at Prittlewell and Mr Arnold and Mr W. Smith at Rayleigh as Surgeons & Apothecaries. Apprentices in most trades trained with a relative or family friend, on recommendation; certainly there is no note of Thomas Seacole in either the official Surgeons or Apothecaries records in London. By the time another child – a son, Charles Witton – arrived in around 1793, the Seacoles were prospering and had moved to a fine house, Roots Hall, on West Street.

Not long after their fourth son, Wintringham – a first name that appears to be unique to him – was baptised at Prittlewell on 2 July 1794, they moved again to the tiny hamlet of Milton at the southern end of the parish. In 1796 a daughter joined the family – Anne Fox, baptised on 1 September, followed by a sister, Maria, baptised on 11 August 1799. And then on 18 September 1803 came the baptism of what appears to be twins – Edwin Horatio Hamilton and Elizabeth Caroline Lind. This came just five months after Britain's declaration of war on France; the whole nation would soon be transfixed by the heroic naval victories of Vice-Admiral Horatio Nelson, Thomas Seacole among them. For he undoubtedly already had naval ambitions for his sons at this time of British maritime preeminence; perhaps he himself had once had dreams of a career as a naval surgeon. Thomas Fowler might not have been suitable material for the Royal Navy, but young John Henry entered the service as an Able Seaman at the age of fourteen in 1804. He joined the gun-brig *Hecate* at the Nore station, a sandbank on the River Thames, from which his ship at the time was patrolling the North Sea and the English Channel on the lookout for belligerent French ships.

Thomas Seacole must have been hugely proud to see another son join the Royal Navy in this dramatic period, when on 30 March 1809, Wintringham – who had been named after Sir Clifton Wintringham, physician-in-ordinary to King George III and physician-general to the forces – was taken on to the *Valiant* under Captain John Bligh. The ship was then on duty off Lorient on the Brittany coast and the following month, when Wintringham was not yet fifteen, he saw action in the Battle of the Basque Roads of 11-24 April. On checking their service records, it would appear that he and his older brother were in fact serving on the same ship at this point, for in February 1809, John Henry had been transferred to the *Valiant* from the *Hecate*. Some later accounts of Wintringham confuse his naval history with John Henry's, claiming that one or other of them served under Nelson at the Battle of Trafalgar and was injured during the fighting. But this is not the case; neither son was at that iconic battle, though it would seem that Wintringham suffered some kind of injury during the Basque Roads engagement.

All of this leaves one wondering whether Thomas the surgeon, apothecary and man-midwife might have had personal connections with some of the eminent people after whom he named his children.[10] If Mary Seacole knew, then it is another secret she keeps from us, along with the Nelson legend that won't lie down – that her husband was in fact Nelson's bastard. The claim did not surface in published sources until after her death in 1881 (although Mary might have spoken, of it privately). In a bequest in her will, written in 1876, Mary specified that a diamond ring *'given to my late husband by his Godfather Lord Nelson'* be passed on to one of her eminent military patrons, Lord Rokeby.[11]

Like many such family claims of links with celebrity, the legend began with an amateur genealogist rushing to the wrong conclusion. In 1956 L. F. Matthews published an article in the *Essex Review* claiming descent from the Seacole family, in which he posited this giant leap to Nelson via the confusion of two different Seacole families, his being a quite different Prittlewell group of Seacole agricultural labourers.[12] Since the rediscovery of Mary Seacole in the 1980s, the story has been endlessly cited and repeated, but without any serious substantiation. This is how it goes:

While his two sons were away fighting at sea in Nelson's navy, Thomas Seacole had steadily built a successful practice, drawing in clientele from a new development at the southern end of Prittlewell that was soon to become the fashionable, sea-bathing resort of Southend. In the early 1800s he was the only male practitioner of man-midwifery in the area, at a time when trained male physicians had begun criticising the traditional, exclusive role of women as midwives. As a result, they now began making inroads on the tried and trusted natural birth practices of female midwives going back centuries, introducing, for example, the new, interventionist fad for forceps, and in so doing, they began supplanting them.

In July of 1803 Lord Nelson's married lover, Emma, Lady Hamilton, accepted a long-standing invitation to visit a friend in Norfolk and accompanied her to Southend for a holiday, taking up residence at the recently built Royal Terrace, half a mile from Prittlewell. She had in fact often come to Southend when Nelson's ship had been moored at the Nore. In January of 1801 she had given birth to an illegitimate daughter by Nelson, whom they named Horatia, and it is thought – though opinion differs wildly – that she was now pregnant with a second child by him. Nelson, meanwhile, had gone to rejoin the *Victory* and had sailed to the Mediterranean. The claim is that some time during her stay Emma supposedly went into labour, and that Thomas Seacole, the man-midwife, who lived just down the road at Milton, was called in. The baby, a girl, apparently died within weeks – or did she? Or were there in fact twins born to Emma and did she give them up as foundlings? For in the version linking Edwin Seacole to Nelson, it is claimed that he and his twin

Elizabeth Caroline Lind, baptised at Prittlewell in September 1803, were in fact Nelson and Emma's secret illegitimate offspring, taken in and adopted as their own by Thomas Seacole and his wife Ann, to protect Emma from the scandal.[13]

The story of Emma secretly having twins is not unique to the Seacole legend. Winifred Gérin first posited it in her 1970 biography of Horatia. But having discussed this by email with several Nelson and Emma biographers, the consensus is that there is little evidence to confirm the birth of this second child (or children) to Emma at Southend at that time, beyond an ambiguous secret letter from Nelson that *might* imply that she was pregnant again. In her biography *Beloved Emma*, Flora Fraser suggested Emma was expecting a child at Christmas 1803 – nearly four months after the Seacole twins were baptised – and that a girl was born some time between then and the New Year, who died around six weeks later.[14]

The best explanation of Thomas Seacole's link to Emma and Nelson is that he was indeed called in to treat her while staying at Southend, when she was taken ill during the pregnancy or suffered a miscarriage, and that he named his son Edwin in honour of that personal connection. In response, perhaps Emma – and indeed Nelson himself – had been so grateful for Thomas's care and attention that Emma had agreed to stand proxy for the absent Nelson as godparent. The fact that Thomas Seacole's son John Henry was admitted to the Royal Navy just a year later may well have been a gesture of thanks on Nelson's part.[15] Sadly we can only speculate on a possible scenario, for the register at Prittlewell gives no names of godparents, nor is this normal practice in Anglican baptismal records.

John Henry Seacole did well at sea and was promoted to Master's Mate in 1810. But then in July 1812, while serving in the Mediterranean, he fell sick and was transferred to the Mahon Hospital at Minorca, where he died on 16 September. His obituary appeared in the *London Courier & Evening Gazette* on 16 December, noting that Seacole had been 'a zealous and meritorious young officer, possessing the most amiable qualities, and much regretted by all who knew him.' His brother Wintringham continued to rise through the ranks on a succession of ships, in 1821 serving on the *Christian 7th* and the *Impregnable*. In 1816, Thomas Seacole retired and he and Ann moved back to London, to a rented house at No. 26 Mansion House Street (now Cottington Street) in Kennington, just south of the River Thames. But he died the following year and was buried at St Mary, Lambeth, on 6 September 1817.[16] His widow continued to live in Kennington with her unmarried son Thomas Fowler, who had left East India Company service in 1820 on a pension, and her two daughters Anne and Maria. Or was it three?

It is here that the whole tenuous Seacole–Nelson link may well fall down, for, after much searching, I finally found Edwin Seacole's missing 'twin' Elizabeth, no trace of whom till then had surfaced. She had been hiding in plain sight all along, at Mansion House Street, with her other sisters, doing the only thing respectable young unmarried women could do at that time – teach. During 1826-8 brief advertisements appeared in the *London & Provincial Commercial Directory* and elsewhere for 'Mrs Seacole's Ladies' Academy' at No. 1 Mansion House Street; (the house number had changed from 26). Sadly, all we have of Elizabeth Caroline Lind Seacole's life is the note of her death in 1832, entered as 'Caroline Seacole' in the burial register for 23 July at St Mark's Church, Kennington. But the age given is thirty-two, suggesting a birth year of 1800-01. So if this is correct, then Caroline is not Emma and Nelson's bastard; and if Edwin was indeed her twin, nor was he.

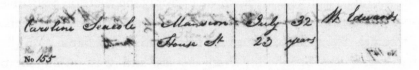

Of the three Seacole sisters, Maria was the only one to marry, in 1823 at the parish church in Newington, Surrey. Her husband was James Kent, a wine merchant based in Mark Lane in the City of London. Mark Lane was occupied mainly by merchant traders, especially wine and spirit dealers, many connected to the West Indies. Which brings us back to the other two Seacole brothers, Edwin and Charles. Neither had opted for maritime careers; Charles was certainly a merchant by the 1820s and may well have been based in Mark Lane or nearby Gracechurch Street, and was known to or had dealings with James Kent and his father William, a distiller. Here, by a roundabout route, we have arrived at the possibility that Mary Seacole might have encountered her future husband Edwin and brother-in-law Charles on her second trip to London on business. If not, she met both of them in Jamaica, for in the early 1820s Charles Witton headed for the West Indies, with aspirations to be a planter. He had applied for and been granted 300 acres of land in an area called The Land of Look Behind in the northeast corner of St Elizabeth parish, close to the border with Trelawny.[17] Since the late eighteenth century the British government had been offering inducements with grants of land to planters to develop Jamaica, and the grant at Look Behind would probably have been cheap because the area was densely forested and mountainous and not suitable for farming. Its major cash crop was the lucrative hardwoods – logwood, fustic and mahogany – cut for export, and coffee.[*18] At this time Black River and Lacovia, the two major towns in St Elizabeth parish, were the centre of the logwood trade, and the demand for this wood brought a brief golden age of economic prosperity.[19]

It's unlikely Charles would have lived up at Look Behind but probably at Black River. He must have been established there by the autumn of 1822, for he quickly left his mark in the form of the birth of an illegitimate 'free mustee' boy, John Gordon Seacole – surely named for his dead brother (Gordon could be the mother's surname). The child was born on 14 July 1823 and baptised at the parish church of St John the Evangelist at Black River on 24 March the following year.[20] But there is no further trace of him. That same year, Charles was co-opted into the local St Elizabeth militia as an

---

* The Land of Look Behind was a favourite Maroon stronghold. British troops were loath to go there in search of the rebels, for the terrain was especially difficult, 'an almost impenetrable region of razor-edged limestone pinnacles, hidden caves and tangled vines' where the Maroons were known to employ guerrilla tactics. The soldiers had to ride in pairs, back to back, constantly looking both forward and behind them for possible attackers, hence the name.

ensign; in November 1827 he was promoted to lieutenant and in 1829 to captain.[21] He also took up an official government post as Harbour Master and Collector of the Transient Tax at Black River, his responsibilities being to assess traders arriving at the port for any taxes payable on their cargoes. Whether he was appointed as such before leaving England is unclear; those who took this post usually had a maritime background. Perhaps Charles had briefly been in the merchant marine before heading for Jamaica.

It is not known whether Charles's brother Edwin travelled out with him or separately, but he seems to have headed for Kingston to set himself up as a West India provision merchant. The assumption has always been that he stayed at Mary's mother's lodging house and that he and Mary met there. Their marriage took place by licence at the Kingston parish church of St Thomas the Apostle and Martyr on 10 November 1836. Conducted by Rev. John MacGrath, who had been recently appointed to the post of curate by the Society for Promoting Christian Knowledge, it was, for its time, one of the first recorded marriages in the city between a white man and a woman of colour.[22] Two years later, Edwin, described as a 'merchant', was admitted to the Freemasons, at the Sussex Lodge, but at some point he and Mary had decided to seek better prospects over in St Elizabeth parish, where she was born and his brother Charles was living. And so, they upped sticks in Kingston and Mary 'took him down to Black River, where we established a store'.

CHAPTER 8

'LEFT ALONE TO BATTLE WITH THE WORLD'

As far as Mary Seacole's time in Black River goes, we are once more reliant on sources written much later. In this case, it is a 1938 letter to the *Daily Gleaner* by Black River resident Sandford Forrest, who told readers that, apparently, when she moved there she 'lived for some time in a stone building on the sea coast, since demolished by hurricanes, at Beach Pen[,] a part of Fullerswood Pen,* within half a mile of the town. At Black River she became famed in the making of cakes and patties.'[1]

Fullerswood was one of the largest pens in the area, comprising 2,104 acres, with Beach Pen an additional forty-two. The land was not good for growing crops and was mainly used for cultivating logwood and fattening livestock for the Black River butchery. It also was close to the Salt Spring River; Edwin was sickly and Mary must have chosen Black River because of this sulpherous spring, located at the western end of town and 'much resembling one of the wells at Cheltenham, in the properties of the water'. Bernard Senior, owner of the Saltspring estate on the river of the same name, claimed that the spring was 'found to be very efficacious in some diseases

---

* In Jamaica, a pen was a farm for breeding livestock – mainly mules, steer, goats, sheep and pigs, but fine-quality horses too.

incidental to the climate.'[2] The Black River spring had been used for many years for treating enslaved people suffering from rheumatism and intestinal troubles, but in 1837, when Mary and Edwin arrived there, the Forrest family, who owned the land, had opened up a commercial spa to the public offering rooms to change in and two pools in which to take the waters.[3]

Black River was also notable for having a greater density of free people of colour. In many ways, the parish of St Elizabeth was one of the most diverse in Jamaica – religiously, politically and economically.[4] The greater tolerance of mixed-heritage marriages saw fourteen such weddings in St Elizabeth between 1780 and 1815.

The seaport of Black River had been established in around 1670 and, much like the island as a whole, at first sight it seemed enchanting. Matthew 'Monk' Lewis was much taken by it when he sailed in from England at the beginning of 1816: 'The beauty of the atmosphere, the dark purple mountains, the shores covered with mangroves of the liveliest green down to the very edge of the water, and the light-coloured houses with their lattices and piazzas completely embowered in trees, altogether made the scenery of the Bay wear a very picturesque appearance.'[5]

But dangers lurked inland, in the Great Morass – an area of unhealthy swampland, where crocodiles hid in the mangroves. It

had prompted the town's original name of Gravesend – an allusion
to the intense, fever-inducing heat that prevailed in summer and all
the insects that thrived in it – flies, ticks, mosquitoes and chigoes
(tropical fleas) being the worst.

In the 1830s, Black River would still have had the look of an
outpost, with only a main High Street running west to east along
the coastline. Here, most of the two-storey wooden houses – with
shops below and living accommodation above – were served by an
unmade carriage road which culminated at the mouth of the Black
River.[6] Mary chose well to set up shop here, for Black River was
an important warehouse area and trading post for logwood. The
timber was brought upriver on flat-bottomed boats from the densely
wooded estates inland, such as that granted to Charles Seacole at
Look Behind. Logwood had long been used in Jamaican holistic
medicine in the form of chippings, but for export the chippings were
sold for the rich dark-blue and black dye the trees produced naturally
that was used in the textile industry.[7]

Packet boats from England and elsewhere in the Caribbean came
and went constantly at Black River, for it was a busy entry and exit
point for passengers as well as goods. But this brings us to a darker
side to Black River's history and to the slave ships that, in the late
eighteenth century, brought thousands of captives from West Africa
to be sold on the Town Wharf. Black River has gone down in history
for its link to the notorious murder in 1781 of African captives on the
Zong. This ship, operated by Liverpool merchants, had been heading
for Black River heavily overloaded with 440 or so enslaved people, but
during the Atlantic crossing many of them had fallen sick and died.
Seeking to claim compensation for the loss of this valuable 'cargo',
the captain had had to reduce the numbers on board as he knew the
insurers would not pay out if he had been carrying too many. In an act
of the most cynical brutality, at least 130 of the African captives were
thrown overboard. The ensuing public outcry and scandal proved to
be a major catalyst in the growing campaign to end the slave trade.*[8]

---

* A monument commemorating this event was erected at Black River in 2013.

The slave trade per se might have long been abolished across the British Empire, but enslaved people were still regularly being bought and sold on the wharf at Black River when the Seacole brothers arrived there. In 1829 Charles Witton Seacole had bought an enslaved 24-year-old, Joe, to serve him as a cook. Indeed, the next we see of Charles is his entering into a business partnership with a Scotsman, Andrew Miller (from whom he had bought Joe), who had also recently been granted 300 acres in St Elizabeth. In the 1832 *Jamaica Almanac*, Miller & Seacole are listed in the Return of Proprietors and Properties as owning ten enslaved people and sixteen livestock.[9]

But two years later came the Abolition Act and Joe was liberated. The official records show that in 1836 Charles Witton received compensation from the British government for a single enslaved person.[10] Did Joe, once free, find employment with Charles's sister-in-law (who later, at her store in Crimea, had two West Indian cooks with her)? Not long after he received his compensation money, Charles Witton Seacole gave up on the rigours of planting, the climate, and Jamaica, and on 22 February 1837 sailed for London via New York, where he picked up the fast new packet ship *Wellington*.[11]

Perhaps the store run by Charles Witton Seacole and Andrew Miller, at which two enslaved men, James Robertson and 'Devonshire', and a woman named Rosey had been sold in 1832 had also been a sales outlet for Mary's patties and pickles.[12] Certainly she would also have offered her skills as a doctress and her herbal remedies to local residents. In around 1821 Andrew Miller had gone into business running a store with another Scottish planter, Matthew Farquharson, whose family owned the Logwood Depot and the Town Wharf, where auctions of enslaved people took place, and whose family were one of the most influential and well known in the region. In 1825 Farquharson had inherited a large estate at Spring Vale, where 160 enslaved people then worked.[13] All these names turn up in the local militia and in various roles in local government in St Elizabeth – along with that of John Salmon, an attorney who handled many of the St Elizabeth compensation claims after the Abolition Act, and whose family owned Fullerswood Pen. Salmon's family, who were related by marriage with the Farquharsons, had by the 1850s, along with several other Black River families, made a fortune out of the logwood trade, until the introduction of synthetic dyes killed their monopoly. The reason for mentioning them all here is that their names will crop up again, for they are an integral, though unspoken, part of Mary Seacole's story. Nor does she tell us in her book of the sad loss back in England of several members of the Seacole family during the 1830s: her sister-in-law Caroline in 1832; her sister-in-law Maria in 1835, leaving three children; and then, on 7 November 1839, Edwin's mother, Ann died at the family home in Mansion House Street.

The loss of his mother was followed barely six weeks later by the horrible murder of Edwin's older brother Wintringham. These last two bereavements must have been very hard for him to cope with so far away from home at Black River. Wintringham had done very well in the Royal Navy, but in 1824 had transferred into the Coastguard.[14] In 1827 he was based at Langstone Harbour, Portsmouth, and by now was clearly on the up and up, for he was presented to King William IV at three Royal Levées and Drawing Rooms in the 1830s. In 1834 came promotion to Chief Officer of the Coastguard, based at Millisle, his role to 'cooperate effectively with the Revenue Police in the suppression of illicit distillation and private malting' in Ireland.[15]

Wintringham was about to transfer to Carrickfergus when, on the night of 31 December 1839, he was attacked and murdered at Donaghadee, near Millisle. Apparently he had just dined there that evening when, returning home with a fellow officer at 11 p.m., 'within a short distance of the watchhouse of the station he was shot through the body, and instantly fell dead'. Reporting this 'most atrocious murder', *The Times* noted that Wintringham had been 'a gentleman of the most estimable character and engaging manners'. The perpetrator turned out to be one of his own men named Daniel Monaghan, who had held a personal grudge against Wintringham 'for having mulcted [fined] him in a portion of his wages, for misconduct'. Wintringham's funeral in Ireland was 'numerously and respectably attended' and his comrades in the Coastguard subsequently erected a monument to him in Donaghadee churchyard.[16]

As for Mary and Edwin Seacole at Black River: to date only one sighting of them has come to light in this period. But it is an important one, for it confirms that in 1840, when Grace Blundell was clearly the proprietress of Blundell Hall, the Seacoles were still out at Black River. On 21 March 1840, the *Royal Jamaica Gazette* reported on an assault on Mr Seacole made by a sailor from the barque *St Mary* anchored at Black River. The man had been clapped in the town jail, upon which the *St Mary*'s mate, 'with a very formidable tail of [six] sailors', had descended on the Seacoles' house demanding Edwin Seacole have the man released. Mary had stepped in 'telling him that it was more than Mr Seacole could do', upon which the mate and his fellow seamen had stomped off to 'pull down the Gaol' and liberate their friend. Soon after, they did so and triumphantly carried him off on their shoulders, he 'being too insensible from the effects of grog and sleep to appreciate their kindness'.[17]

It was typical of the feisty Mary to intervene, but this report suggests that despite her commercial success at Black River, living there had done nothing to ameliorate Edwin Seacole's fragile state of health. '*Poor man! He was very delicate,*' she tells us, pityingly, '*I kept him alive by kind nursing and attention as long as I could; but at last he grew so ill that we left Black River, and returned to my mother's house at Kingston.*'[18] It made sense for Mary to seek her mother's help in nursing Edwin, and she could also help Rebecca once more at her lodging house on Stanton Street. It also meant that, as Sandford Forrest observed, she was able to carry on her production of cakes and patties 'on a much larger scale'.[19]

CHAPTER 9

'THE GRAVEYARD OF EUROPEANS'

The next sequence of events in Mary's account of her early life is obscure, to say the least, for she gets her chronology muddled. She tells us that *'within a month of our arrival there'* – in Kingston from Black River – Edwin Seacole died.[1] The entry in the burial register for 26 October 1844 at the New Burial Ground describes him as 'Edward [*sic*] Horatio Seacole, aged thirty-five, of the Parish of St Elizabeth' and that he was residing at the time of his death at East Queen Street in Kingston. The age is wrong, for Edwin was in fact about forty-two. A page later Mary confuses us by going on to relate how, after this, the great fire of Kingston *'burnt down my poor home'* and that *'I very nearly lost my life, for I would not leave my house until every chance of saving it had gone, and it was wrapped in flames.'*[2] But the devastating fire in Kingston happened in *August 1843* – when Edwin was still alive and the couple were already back in Kingston. We know this for a fact because in 1842 Mary was listed on the Poll Tax Roll at 47 Stanton Street, when she was also judged to be liable for four shillings towards 'church and poor'. The following year, Edwin was a witness at the marriage on 31 March, at the Kingston Wesleyan Church, of Mary's half-sister Amelia Campbell to Arthur James Branigan, a local merchant.[3]

The fire that consumed much of downtown Kingston in 1843

was triggered by an overflow of molten metal at the iron and brass foundry of Messrs James & Co. on Harbour Street that occurred just after midday on 26 August. It spread rapidly across the wooden houses and their dry shingled roofs to the west and the northwest, the flames fanned by a heavy sea breeze. It travelled up East Street, destroying seven houses on one side and ten on the other, although, contrary to what many Seacole sources state, Blundell Hall of the Seacole myth did *not* burn down, which further supports the case for it never having been '*my poor home*', or anything to do with Mary Seacole in the first place.[4]

In Kingston at the time, there was no organised fire brigade of any kind, or any piped water; those fighting the fire frantically fought a losing battle pumping what little water they could from the city's wells. The army sent down a detachment of men from Up Park Camp to help, and naval forces from Port Royal joined in. Army engineers attempted to stop the fire by destroying 114 buildings in the fire's path. To no avail; in all, thirty blocks of houses went up in flames. The fire did not abate until the following morning, by which time 238 build-ings – one tenth of the city – had been turned to ashes.[5] The losses were particularly heavy on the western side, and few owners were insured.[6]

So when Mary refers to the fire having '*burnt down my poor home*' – what is she alluding to? Rebecca's lodging house, or the house where Mary spent most of her first twelve years? What is extremely puzzling, is that there is no record of Rebecca Grant claim-ing relief for the loss of her lodging house in the extensive official list of Sufferers of the Fire; nor is there mention of her in newspaper reports of those people who had lost their businesses. However, there is one source that might help us explain things. Jamaican artist Isaac Belisario left a valuable pictorial record of the 1843 fire that includes a diagram of the streets most affected by it. At the very bottom of Stanton Street, at the junction with Sutton Street, one house is marked as destroyed, and opposite it, another partially so. The Belisario map is too faint to reproduce here, but Hay's 1738 map of Kingston clearly shows where the partially destroyed house may have been – on the site of earlier dwellings numbered 866 and 865.

Beeston ... Street

852	864	876	888	900
851	863	875	887	899
850	862	874	886	898
849	861	873	885	897
848	860	872	884	896
847	859	871	883	895
846	858	870	882	894
845	857	869	881	893
844	856	868	880	892
843	855	867	879	891
842	854	866	878	890
841	853	865	877	889

Blackmore — Stanton — Hospital — East

Sutton

| 696 | 702 | 708 | 714 | 720 |
| 695 | 701 | 707 | 713 | 719 |

Given its state of disrepair, Rebecca Grant's 'old and delapidated [sic]' property mentioned in the tax assessments would have been highly vulnerable to fire. What is more, in the list of Sufferers of the Fire there is only one solitary loss noted for Stanton Street. But here's the rub: the property in question is listed as being occupied/ owned by one 'Maria Campbell'; not Rebecca Grant. But before we throw up our hands in dismay, note the name. Campbell was the birth surname of Mary Seacole's half-sister, Amelia. Did the Campbell family own the lodging house run by Rebecca Grant? Is there a connection here? If so, it is one I have yet to resolve.[7] There is only one other logical possibility for Mary Seacole's *poor home* lost in the Kingston fire. On the list of Sufferers of the Fire there is a claim for No. 57 Water Lane (occupied by an Elizabeth Lawson), which is the house that Mary grew up in and which may have originally belonged to the merchant family of Grants.[8]

From this moment of tragedy, Mary's narrative suddenly leaps for- ward to another, when she tells us that her mother Rebecca died soon after the fire. But again she fudges her timeline. In fact Rebecca Grant lived on for another four years, dying at 27 Duke Street in 1848. She was buried in Kingston West Ground on 8 March;

unfortunately the register does not record her precise date of death. As a '*hot-blooded Creole*', Mary admits to having given full vent to her grief at the loss of Edwin and then her mother; after which '*I was left alone to battle with the world as best I might*'. Well, maybe not. As her own account and other evidence shows, Mary was not without siblings, about whom she makes no mention at all at this point, but who we shall come to soon. For now, however, she knuckled down and little by little recovered from her losses, both material and personal: '*I set to work again in a humbler way, and rebuilt my house by degrees, and restocked it, succeeding better than before.*'[9] It may well be that the partially destroyed house at No. 1 Stanton Street was patched up over a period of time, as suggested here. Mary tells us she was resolute that being happy was more important than financial gain. '*I never thought too exclusively of money,*' she writes. '*Had I done so, I should have mourned over many a promising speculation proving a failure, over many a pan of preserves or guava jelly burnt in the making.*'[10]

She does not tell us where her new lodging house was located, but according to the Tax Relief Rolls for Kingston East Division, in 1846 Mary was charged tax on two properties: at 13 Sutton Street and 13 Stanton Street, but by April 1848 she was 'unable to pay more' tax at Sutton Street and was wrongly taxed for Stanton Street as she was 'not in possession'. In 1850 her name reappears in the Poll Tax Roll for 2 Stanton Street, though heaven knows why the number has changed from 1 to 2.[11] It is highly likely that the street numbering changed after the fire, given the extensive rebuilding that went on, but even so these changes in the house numbering are unbelievably frustrating. Once again we are confounded; the records are more confusing than they are helpful. All we can deduce is that Mary's lodging house was *probably* located in Stanton Street. But one thing really niggles. Had it been as successful as Mary tells us it was, one would have expected to find some mention of it, somewhere – a letter written by a guest who stayed there; a traveller's account; a mention in the Jamaican press – as we have with Grace Blundell at Blundell Hall. But there is not a word.

Nevertheless, sources confirm that, during the second half of the 1840s, Mrs Mary Seacole became one of those legendary, larger-than-life Jamaican figures remembered in the *Daily Gleaner* in 1905 by someone who clearly had known her at that time. Her domineering presence could hardly be missed in Kingston, wrote Resident Magistrate Richard Walcott, for she was very much 'representative of a class of Jamaica women which have almost wholly passed away':

> They usually sat at one of the entrances to their spacious halls, portentous like some Olympic deity, profoundly conscious of their own importance, and English to the backbone. They loved ornaments too, and so Mrs Seacole dressed her hair very gaily and wore earrings of a remarkable size. Her face was broad and good-natured in expression and it was her genuine kindness of heart that won for her so many encomiums.
>
> This class of the old Jamaica hotel-keeper and tradeswoman of independent means, kind heart, questionable morality, genuine patriotism and hearty goodwill have almost entirely, if not indeed, entirely, passed away. They were generous, they were fat, and they now and then partook of the cup which cheers and does inebriate. They kept plenty of what they called 'dumb tings' [chickens], scolded their servants in a loud tone of voice, and drifted through life in a comfortable, contented sort of way.[12]

Such women 'did many acts of kindness while industriously turning an honest penny'. Their servants respectfully addressed them as 'Missis', for women such as Mary made others know their place, as much as she knew hers:

> The best men went to Mrs Seacole's lodgings, and were content with their mahogany beds, were delighted with their dinners, and were satisfied with Mrs Seacole herself ... You could not quarrel with Mrs Seacole, she wouldn't allow you to. She would tell you that if you didn't like what she gave you, you could go

and see if you could get it better elsewhere. She was a merry independent soul. She made money and wasted it, like most Jamaicans.[13]

It was during the late 1840s that Mary built up a strong relationship with British troops in Jamaica – particularly those based at Up Park Camp. It would mean that when she arrived in Crimea in the spring of 1855 several old friends and familiar faces would welcome her. Up Park Camp, located on a 'verdant plain' shaded by lovely trees and a 'great variety of flowering shrubs', with its spacious esplanade and the backdrop of the magnificent Jamaican hills, was, as Captain John Patterson of the Queen's Own Regiment recorded, in reality 'a gilded mausoleum' rife with disease.[14] Since the late 1830s the British government had been increasingly concerned about the high rate of sickness – especially the deadly yellow fever – among the troops in Jamaica. The death rate had been running at around 100 to 300 per 1,000 soldiers, and Up Park Camp had earned the nickname 'the graveyard of Europeans'.[15]

The army had however noted that removing the men to 'even a trifling elevation, or change of climate' – say 300 feet – the scorching temperature dropped considerably and was replaced by a 'delicious atmosphere, the salubrity of which is equal to any part of the world'. For this reason, in London in May 1841 the government had sanctioned the search for a suitable site for a new mountain cantonment. Eventually a coffee plantation 3,800 feet above sea level at Newcastle was chosen, with the primary purpose of 'the saving of life, and the preservation of the health, energy, and efficiency of the European troops', and in particular removing soldiers 'beyond the reach of fever, malaria, and the host of malignant spirits, blue and black devils which poison the air, engender disease, [and] reduce the strong man to the feeble child'.[16]

Once troops were installed at Newcastle, the death rate from fever dropped dramatically, but many of course remained at Up Park. Some officers sought out a lodging house when recovering from fever and in need of nursing back to health. Others preferred such accommodation if they had their wives with them and they found at Mrs Seacole's lodging house not just a warm welcome and wholesome food but also a midwife who could be called in to attend their wives when the time came. One such may well have been Lady Helen Campbell, wife of Lieutenant Colonel Sir John Campbell, commander of the 38th regiment. She gave birth to two sons in Jamaica – in 1846 and 1848 – and she and Sir John caught up with Mary again in Crimea.[17] According to stories of Mary circulating in Kingston, 'she once boasted that she never lost a mother or a child', at a time when such an achievement was 'exceedingly rare'.[18] A steady stream of military and naval clients such as these enabled Mary to recover her business and expand, for, as she tells us, '*I had gained a reputation as a skilful nurse and doctress, and my house was always full of invalid officers and their wives*'.[19]

Of Mary's British Army friends in Jamaica at this time there is one in particular whom we can positively identify. Based at the camp at Newcastle, Captain Hedley Vicars from Mary's favourite regiment, the 97th Earl of Ulster's, had arrived in Jamaica in March 1848, and Mary makes clear in her memoir that she had got to know him during this time. For once the giveaway of his initials, and the regiment number, do not hide him from us. Mary was very taken with Hedley Vicars, as were many who met him: he was '*goodhearted, loveable, noble*' and she never forgot '*the ring of his boyish laughter*'.[20]

It is now, in 1848, that we can at last return to the subject of Mary's missing baptism. The reason others had failed to find it in the Kingston parish registers is that Mary was not baptised into the Church of England, but into the Roman Catholic faith; and she was baptised not as a baby, as is normal practice, but as a mature adult. Back in 2005 it was misguidedly suggested that she had converted to Roman Catholicism after the Crimean War, as a result of her close friendship there with the French chef Alexis Soyer; but he was a Protestant – from a French Huguenot family.[21] However, once made, the suggestion was sufficient to send people off searching in the wrong time frame, on the assumption that Mary's baptism into the Catholic faith had come some time after her return from Crimea in 1856. But no; it was earlier. We are yet to discover what prompted it, other than to assume that Mary's formal adoption of the Catholic faith had been a long-held desire. It is no coincidence, I think, that it came six months after her mother Rebecca's death, which suggests that Mary had deliberately postponed her baptism out of respect for her. I do often wonder whether Rebecca's first name is indicative of a possible Jewish connection, for Lacovia, near to where she gave birth to Mary, was noted for a Sephardi Jewish community that had been present there since Spanish rule in the seventeenth century; and we should remember, too, Rebecca's former Jewish partner, Abraham Henriques.

Mary was about forty-three when the Catholic priest Monsignor Dupont at Holy Trinity Church baptised her on 16 August 1848 as 'Mary Jane Sicole [sic] Grant'. The baptism was noted as being 'conditional', on the understanding that Mary had not known whether she had been baptised at birth, for the Roman Catholic Church does not allow people to be baptised twice. I now doubt she ever received a Church of England baptism, but is it remotely possible that her birth had been recorded in Jewish records at Lacovia? Unfortunately, they have not survived. It is important also to note the name order that Mary gave to Monsignor Dupont, for it signifies a clear reassertion of her Grant heritage over her adopted married name of Seacole. There is also, interestingly, the inclusion of a middle name – 'Jane'; as I suggested earlier, this may have come from the Scottish side of her family. In her choice of sponsors it was typical of Mary to go to the top and enlist an eminent local official, Mr Henry John French, a lieutenant colonel in the 85th Foot,* who at the time was based in Jamaica as Deputy Quartermaster General to the Forces. Also noticeable is that she lied about her age – or was her memory really that faulty? – giving it as thirty-six when in fact

---

* Ah, the 85th! Is that just a coincidence or in fond memory of her father? However, John Alexander Francis Grant does not seem to have come from a Scottish Catholic family.

she was now approaching forty-three. Perhaps it was simple vanity and she had wanted to impress the lieutenant colonel. Her other sponsor was Genevieve Aline Larice, who appears as sponsor at a couple more Roman Catholic baptisms as 'Aline Lerisse'.[22]

Courtesy of Roman Catholic Archives, Kingston

By the end of the 1840s Mary was finding her feet again. Widowhood had given her respectability and elevation to the middle class of her mixed-heritage group in Kingston society. Unlike the typical retiring Victorian widow of the day, who retreated to domesticity, and with it obscurity, she did not actively seek male protection. She was never fearful of being an *'unprotected female'*; indeed, she proudly and wittily declares that *'one of the hardest struggles of my life in Kingston was to resist the pressing candidates for the late Mr Seacole's shoes.'*[23] Mary did not want or need another husband; she wanted to hold on to her independence. Her loyalties lay with her officer friends in the British Army, and even before she left Jamaica, she had already appointed herself as their benign and watchful 'Mother Seacole'.

Mary did not stand still either in further developing her medical skills; she took advantage of the naval and military surgeons who stayed with her, from whom *'I never failed to glean instruction'*; men such as John D. McIlree, surgeon to her favourite regiment the 97th. Another medical friend was Dr Amos Henriques (they may well have been loosely related via Abraham Henriques, the partner by whom Rebecca had a son, George). Born in Jamaica in 1811 of a Sephardi Jewish family, he had trained in London and had had an extraordinary and eventful life in Europe and the Middle East before returning to Jamaica in 1840. He and Mary would certainly have discussed holistic methods in the treatment of cholera, for when Dr Henriques was once more back in London in 1847, he established himself as a homeopath and published medical pamphlets on the nature of cholera. Any expertise Mary had gleaned from him would have been invaluable, for in 1850 a terrible epidemic of Asiatic cholera descended on Jamaica. Surgeon McIlree of the 97th reported that it had first appeared among men of the Royal Navy at Port Royal. Mary insisted that gold prospectors returning from Chagres in Panama had brought it into the port on board a *'steamer from New Orleans'*. It had infected a local washerwoman, 'Dolly Johnson', who had been hired to wash their dirty clothes.[24] The ensuing epidemic killed a quarter of the population in Port Royal and had spread through Kingston at an alarming rate. No wonder, for the town was one great open cesspool without drains or sewers, a dumping ground for filth and garbage that bred cholera, yellow fever and dysentery.

Cholera always lurked in the poorest, unsanitary areas such as the overcrowded dwellings in which many of the Black population lived. Dirty and devoid of fresh air, they were little more than 'wretched sheds, destitute of the most ordinary conveniences', with small courtyards attached containing goats and pigs which were 'invariably the depositories of every species of disgusting filth, such as human ordure, as well as other excrementious matters, stinking fish-guts, and putrid slops'. In fact, as Dr Wingate Johnson concluded, 'everything is there to be found, excepting cleanliness or pure water'. There were no public privies; the 'cleanest' place to relieve oneself was on the beach facing the sea near the church, where the city's night soil was deposited. 'When the sea breeze blows home, this place is directly to windward of the town'. The privies in the barracks were equally 'disgusting', made worse by the large 'miasmas' of potential infection from several vaulted cesspools on site.[25]

The medical belief then was that cholera was transmitted by 'bad air' (its bacterial origins via polluted water were not described till 1855). Extreme measures were taken to try to stop the spread:

'Cannons were fired off, gunpowder exploded, and tar barrels burnt in the streets, whole houses were fumigated with incense. The beds, bedding, and ragged clothes of the dead were taken down to the beach and burnt there or cast into the sea. The thoroughfares, at all times bad, had been made worse by the recent heavy rains ... Carts filled with coffins could hardly be dragged along, and graves could not be dug quickly enough.'[26]

The outbreak had been so severe that visitors were advised not to stay 'at two of the chief lodging-houses in the town, in consequence of the notorious nuisances in their back yards. The landladies of both houses died from the epidemic.'[27] Mary was fortunate – she was able to keep going, but saw the worst: *'I had too many opportunities of watching its nature'*. Even now in the midst of it all she wanted to learn better skills at nursing this deadly disease: *'from a Dr B–– , who was then lodging in my house [I] received many hints as to its treatment which I afterwards found invaluable.'*[28] One must assume she is referring to nursing technique rather than medication, for she had her own holistic medicines to draw on.

At the time numerous quacks and charlatans were actively advertising their 'infallible nostrums'; writing after the event, Dr James C. Phillippo – himself a Jamaican practitioner – commented that he had seen people cured of cholera by cayenne pepper, bitter-bush (a kind of herbal tea) and even doses of sea water.[29] The standard allopathic medication for cholera in 1850 would have been proprietary mixtures such as Battley's Sedative Solution of Opium or twenty drops of laudanum administered in a wine glassful of water with a few drops of Camphorated Spirits; or calomel, designed to purge the system of the infection but serving only to further dehydrate patients. Those who were left to their own resources or could not afford medicines tended to recover.[30]

At its height in the third week, the cholera was carrying off 200 a day; around 4,000 people in all – one eighth of Kingston's population – perished. People fled the town and in so doing spread the disease across the island; in the last weeks of 1850 the cholera advanced west across Jamaica and devastated Black River. In all, some 30,590 had died by December 1851, with mortality particularly high among those of African descent.[31] Yet, in the midst of all this, Mary Seacole had been planning her next business venture. Life in Kingston was too narrow, too limiting for a woman of her ambition and imagination. Unable to check her *'disposition to roam'* any longer, she decided to head off – to a new frontier: that of Panama.* Early in 1850 her brother Edward (though we don't find out his name for several more pages) had gone off to seek his fortune there and *'had established a considerable store and hotel'*. Hearing that there was money to be made providing food and accommodation, not to mention medical care on the Panamanian Isthmus, how could Mary resist the challenge?[32]

---

* The territory now known as Panama was then part of what was called New Granada, composed in the main of modern-day Panama and neighbouring Gran Colombia, which were joined in 1821. But the Panamanians resisted this union and in 1903 Panama separated from Colombia. In the interests of clarity, I shall refer to the territory as Panama throughout.

CHAPTER 10

'A Villainous Looking Little Place'

Mary Seacole's departure for Panama some time in the autumn of 1851 yet again raises the thorny question of the location and name of her Kingston lodging house. For in order to go off on her travels she had, of course, to arrange for someone to take over the running of her business while she was gone. '*I resigned my house into the hands of a cousin*' is what she tells us; the conclusion jumped to has been that the *cousin* here is a veiled reference to her sister Louisa. Perhaps this was indeed the case and Louisa ran Mary's lodging house for a while and then later took over Blundell Hall out of a desire to have her own independent business. But that was not for another seven years or so. We must also bear in mind that we now know that Mary had *two* half-sisters, Amelia and Louisa, and it might well have been Amelia Campbell (now Branigan) who took over for Mary in her absence. Otherwise, if Mary means 'cousin' literally, rather than using it to disguise one of her half-sisters, it might have been one of the three 'cousins' she named in her will: Matilda Symonette and Amelia Kennedy (who were in fact sisters, née Bravo), or Louisa Cochrane.[1]

Before she set off on her new Panamanian adventure, Mary's home was a hive of activity. She was not going to join her brother '*empty handed*', but, with her usual aplomb, she organised the production of a selection of goods to sell when she got there:

My house was full for weeks, of tailors, making up rough coats, trousers etc., and sempstresses cutting out and making shirts. In addition to these, my kitchen was filled with busy people, manufacturing preserves, guava jelly, and other delicacies, while a considerable sum was invested in the purchase of preserved meats, vegetables and eggs.[2]

The discovery of gold in the Sacramento Valley at the foothills of the Sierra Nevada mountains in 1848 had provoked what became known as the Second Gold Rush – a stampede of 'wild-looking gold prospectors' to California, via Panama. Nicknamed 'Forty-Niners', they arrived at Chagres on overcrowded United States Mail Steam Line vessels from New Orleans or New York, and crossed the Isthmus via what they called 'the Yankee Strip' – a 10-mile-wide section of territory that extended 48 miles from coast to coast as the crow flies.[3]

The gold rush had fortuitously coincided with an agreement between American contractors led by W. H. Aspinwall and the government of New Granada – which then controlled the province of Panama – to set up the Panama Railroad Company to construct a quicker and safer crossing. Such an innovation had long been talked about and was much needed, especially after the USA acquired the states of Oregon and California at the end of its war with Mexico in 1848. The railroad across to Panama City would circumvent the long overland trek by wagon train across the American continent to the West Coast, and even more dramatically reduce the arduous 8,000-mile sea voyage via South America around Cape Horn, which then took four or five months. It would also open up access for passengers and freight to ships sailing the Pacific to China, Australia and the East Indies. But in 1850 the Isthmus was a dangerous crossing through 'the most terrible wilderness on the face of the earth', in the view of one early traveller.[4]

A party of American surveyors and engineers had been sent to Panama early in 1849 to survey the most appropriate route for the rail line. It would extend from Navy Bay on the northern, Atlantic coast to the southern port of Panama City, and had originally been planned to take eight years to complete. However, the railroad company soon discovered that the terrain through which the line was to be constructed could not have been more difficult, or inhospitable, or sapping of human strength and endurance. The first thirteen miles out of Navy Bay were the worst: the line would have to be driven through 'a deep morass, covered with the densest jungle, reeking with malaria, and abounding with almost every species of wild beasts, noxious reptiles, and venomous insects known in the tropics'.[5] Further on the route, following trails established by Spanish invaders in the sixteenth century, might have been beautiful – so much so that the natives called it *Paraíso* – but the railway line would have to be blasted and hammered through extremely rugged terrain, 'along steep hill-sides, over wild chasms, spanning turbulent rivers and furious mountain torrents, until the summit-ridge was surmounted, when it descended abruptly to the shores of the Pacific Ocean'.[6]

A considerable workforce would be needed for the task, and soon thousands of workers – many of them formerly enslaved people – were flocking to Panama from all over the West Indies, and especially Jamaica, on the lure of the high wages – 80 cents a day (3s. 2d.) – to be earned building the railroad. Mary's brother Edward was one of the first to leave, though not to work on the railroad but to seek his fortune running a hotel. For by no means all the migrant workers from Jamaica were labourers. At a time when the island was in economic decline, with the Sugar Bill of 1846 putting an end to the preferential treatment of West Indian sugar in the London markets and many plantations being abandoned, a range of professionals, especially craftsmen, were heading to Panama. Carpenters were greatly in demand to make the rail ties and the trestles supporting the rail tracks, but other entrepreneurs and traders also travelled back and forth with comestible goods to sell such as rum, sugar, bananas, yams, plantains and other provisions, and medicines against the prevalent fevers. All of them soon found themselves enduring sultry tropical heat even worse than that in Jamaica, interspersed with endless torrential rain that brought nothing but suffering and disease.

The exodus of Jamaicans became so serious that concerns were raised in the Jamaican government about 'the rapid depopulation of this beautiful island by the increasing outpouring of its agricultural labourers to that house of pestilence and proverbial charnel house Navy Bay'; by January 1855, when the railway was completed and controls on migration had been put in place, 4,000-5,000 had migrated from Jamaica to work there.[7]

Construction of the railroad was begun in May 1850. Till now travellers had docked at Chagres to the west of Navy Bay, but the railroad company decided to create a new freight and passenger terminus at a settlement on the eastern side of the Bay, named

Aspinwall.* But it was excruciatingly slow progress to complete the first 8 miles across swampland to the first stop created at Gatun, which was not operational till September 1851.[8] From there passengers heading for Panama City had to transfer to a boat down the Chagres River until the railroad could be completed. It was soon discovered that the steamboats intended for this purpose could not be used, and only native bongo boats and canoes were suitable for navigating these waters.[9] With hordes of eager gold prospectors from all over America gathering at Gatun, the price of hiring a boat to get south to Gorgona, where they could switch to mules overland, rocketed.

For anyone venturing into the region, the Panamanian Isthmus at this time was a particularly unhealthy area. The marshy riverbanks and swamps bred mosquitoes that carried yellow fever and malaria. But also prevalent were typhoid, dysentery, smallpox and cutaneous infections such as hookworm; and of course, the dreaded cholera too. The Jamaicans – or *antillanos* as the Spanish referred to English-speaking Black people – while seeming more resistant to yellow fever than the Chinese and European workers, succumbed to pulmonary infections, particularly pneumonia, no doubt a result of constantly working in damp conditions and wet clothes. All this contributed to an average death rate of 35-40 per cent of workers.[10] This is not to mention the ever-present threat from a cornucopia of deadly snakes, insects – monstrous spiders and lethal scorpions – as well as alligators lurking under the surface of the waters of the Chagres.

Having taken all these difficulties into consideration, it is hard to imagine a more dangerous, hostile or difficult environment for a middle-aged woman to venture into at that time. Mary Seacole certainly knew that it was a frontier country where the government was '*powerless to control the refuse of every nation which meet together upon its soil*', but she was by no means the only woman to venture across the Isthmus. There were plenty of intrepid American

---

* The original settlement at Aspinwall was known to the locals as Colón, in honour of Christopher Columbus; in 1890 Aspinwall adopted that name.

women prospectors who made the journey, but it nevertheless took a considerable amount of self-possession and courage to undertake such an enterprise, although she would not be travelling alone. Mary took with her a Black cook named Mac, to help in her catering endeavours and '*a little girl*' – a maid-cum-general factotum – whom she names as Mary.[11]

In order to get to her brother Edward's 'Independent Hotel' (a misleading name if ever there was one), Mary had to get herself, her luggage and her supplies to Cruces, halfway between Aspinwall and Panama City – a journey partly by river and partly on mules through the jungle. But at least there was a good Royal Mail steam packet service across the Caribbean Sea from Jamaica to Navy Bay. Established in the mid-1840s, this service operated from Southampton on the 2nd and 17th of the month, and after stopping off at various places in the West Indies, including Jamaica, it sailed on to Panama and even as far south as Peru, or north to San Francisco. A good fast boat could make the crossing in four days.[12]

As the steamer approached land and sailed past Chagres, it seemed to Mary '*an old-world tumbledown town*'. Chagres had been the original port of entry for crossing the Isthmus, but now most boats docked 7 miles further east at Aspinwall. Mary's first impressions of this new settlement as she disembarked in the pouring rain were not good: '*I never thought I had seen a more luckless, dreary spot*'. Built on a coral outcrop called Manzanillo Island, Aspinwall was surrounded by disease-breeding mangrove swamps of stagnant water and comprised ramshackle huts made of bamboo cane with roofs of palm leaves, built on piles. All of the travellers' descriptions concur on its squalid, miserable appearance, especially in the rain and mud. Indeed, one word was regularly used to describe Panama in general at that time, and that was 'pestilential'. Mary's response was therefore typical: '*It seemed as capital a nursery for ague and fever as Death could hit upon anywhere.*' She immediately noticed how '*ghostly and wraith-like*' the white men who met them on the wharf looked; even '*the very negroes seemed pale and wan*'.[13]

The climate might have been draining, but Aspinwall had rapidly become an important trading hub, a transit point for goods from all over South America: the railroad's freight depot was bursting with 'bales of quina bark from the interior, ceroons of indigo and cochineal from San Salvador and Guatemala; coffee from Costa Rica, and cacao from Ecuador; sarsaparilla from Nicaragua, and ivory nuts from Porto Bello; copper ore from Bolivia; silver bars from Chili [*sic*]; boxes of hard dollars from Mexico and gold ore from California; hides from the whole range of the North and South Pacific coast, hundreds of bushels of glistening pearl-oyster shells from the fisheries of Panama'.[14] So many riches, yet all around fever and ague prevailed, and no sooner had she landed than Mary was drawing on the contents of her medicine chest. She only stayed in Aspinwall for one night and had to rough it, as there were as yet no hotels. But even so, she found the time to offer what medical assistance she could to some of the sickly residents, while admitting that *the sufferers wanted remedies which I could not give them – warmth, nourishment, and fresh air.* It was not an encouraging start to her journey, or her new life in Panama *to see men dying from sheer exhaustion*, their only cover from the elements being *leaky tents, damp huts, and ... broken railway wagons*.[15]

Passing through Aspinwall with eight companies of the 4th Infantry in July 1852 en route to the Pacific, regimental quartermaster Ulysses S. Grant (later US president) had had an equally bad experience; he had 'wondered how any person could live many months in Aspinwall, and wondered still more why any one tried'. One minute it was torrential rain; the next 'a blazing, tropical summer's sun'; then back to rain again.[16] Mary made haste the following day to take the new railroad the short 12-mile stretch to the second station of construction at Gatun, a small village on the eastern bank of the Chagres River. She could not have done so until around September 1851 because the line had not been completed till then, which enables us to roughly date her arrival in Panama.[17] Already the construction work had taken its toll on her fellow Jamaicans, with many of the workers already deserting or falling sick. *Every mile of that fatal railway cost the world thousands of lives,* Mary noted, and so many workers had fallen sick and died that the rail-road company had been forced to offer *'unheard-of rates of wages'* to tempt new labourers to the Isthmus to replace them.[18]

At Gatun, Mary and her two companions had had to transfer to river transport: native-made bongo boats. These were often hollowed out of a single log of mahogany and carried four to ten passengers huddled under a canvas canopy against either the teeming rain or the broiling sun, crammed in with pyramids of their luggage while local boatmen poled them up- and downriver.

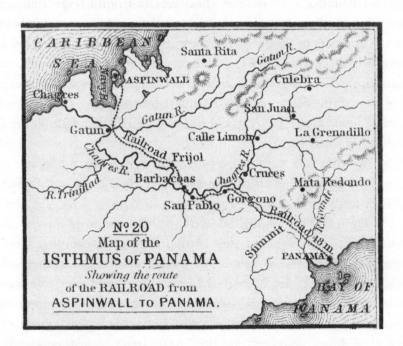

The tropical riverbanks on either side looked so inviting to the uninitiated traveller and rang with the screams of parrots and the chattering of monkeys. Beyond was primeval forest, bursting with rich bright green vegetation, thick creepers and flowering vines, dense canopies of white, scarlet and yellow blossoms among which flitted luminous butterflies, and thick masses of luxuriant foliage 'now towering in the air in bold relief against the sky, now drooping in graceful festoons from the bank, kissing their own reflections in the stream beneath'. But travel was slow and laborious and the heat overpowering.[19] In such a place – as virtually everywhere in Panama – the providers of food, shelter and transport all charged the highest prices they could get away with and travellers were systematically fleeced. The average cost of a bongo to Mary's next stop at Gorgona was £15; baggage was extra, after a fair amount of the prerequisite haggling. Sitting there in the pouring rain with her maid, surrounded by her piles of luggage, while Mac negotiated a price of £10 *'to carry me and my fortunes to Cruces'*, Mary concluded that the two most avaricious *'species of individuals'* she had ever met were *'porters and lawyers'*. On top of which, she was already aware of being an object of curiosity, as she floundered up the slippery, muddy cutting from the train to the riverbank, dressed in her favourite *'delicate light blue dress, a white bonnet prettily trimmed, and an equally chaste shawl'* – hardly the most appropriate clothing for such conditions, but Mary is never reticent about making fun of her own misfortune.[20]

By the time she got to the boat, the wet red clay had stained Mary's lovely dress and the porters had already robbed her of several articles from her luggage.[21] Panama was a lawless place, she could see; it reminded her of Wordsworth's words that *'they should take who have the power, and they should keep who can.'*[22] It would have been cheaper to agree to share a boat with other travellers, but Mary was well aware from past experience that *'Americans (even from the Northern States) are always uncomfortable in the company of coloured people.'* Their *'sour looks'* and *'rude words'* were to be expected. Black people in the USA were, in 1851, still enslaved, a long twelve years away from being liberated. The patent hostility Mary experienced from American travellers towards her as a free and independent woman of colour prompts her first overt reference to slavery and with it a statement of pride in her own colour: *'I have a few shades of deeper brown upon my skin which shows me related – and I am proud of the relationship – to those poor mortals whom you once held enslaved, and whose bodies America still owns.'*

Having failed to say anything at all about the abuses of slavery under the British in Jamaica, this is the closest Mary ever comes in her narrative to pointing the accusatory finger at '*you*' – her white Victorian audience who also once condoned the practice. But she has to keep them on side. This necessitates a clever balancing act, where she criticises the '*airs of superiority which many Americans have endeavoured to assume over me*', as a Black woman, while not applying this to her British readers.[23]

Once on board her bongo Mary gratefully took possession of the hammock strung under the canvas awning, as the *padrone*, a '*fine tall negro*', took the helm and loudly cursed in Spanish at the scantily dressed native Panamanians who poled them downriver. He had promised to deliver Mary and her party to Cruces that evening but the wind rose and then the rain '*came down in torrents*' and they were forced to pull into the shore and take shelter. The following morning they reached Gorgona, to find yet another assemblage of crudely made bamboo huts and wooden houses that was '*indescribably damp, dirty and dull*', where Mary managed to get some food before they continued their journey. Late that afternoon, '*tired, wretched, and out of temper*', Mary Seacole and her companions, along with her pile of damp and dirty luggage, were deposited '*upon the miserable wharf of Cruces*'.[24]

Edward was waiting there to greet them when the three tired and hungry travellers arrived; Mary had been looking forward to at last getting comfortable at his Independent Hotel at the top of the main street, located fortuitously above the flood plain, but her spirits sank when he told her that unfortunately, due to an inrush of travellers from both directions – Panama City *and* Navy Bay – there was sadly no room at the inn. And indeed '*the crowd from the gold-fields of California had just arrived: rude, coarse gold-diggers, in gay coloured shirts, and long, serviceable boots*', as Mary noted.

A contemporary wrote of Cruces in a piece for Charles Dickens's *Household Words* in 1852, describing it as consisting of 'about one hundred huts, arranged along a dirty street, crowded with mules, and steaming with liquid filth'. It was, as another lady traveller noted, 'a villainous looking little place'. Mary writes of how its transient population crowded the streets of the dirty little town, '*lounged in the verandahs*' and vied with the more neat and respectable '*Yankee speculators*' who were also passing through, and had filled up all its hotels.[25] Even they were squalid: 'of the hotels in this town, the best is the American; but the best is bad indeed,' noted *Household Words*. 'Hotel' is certainly a rather generous word to describe any of the makeshift accommodation on offer in this chaotic little shanty town ruled by gun law, where the facilities offered were more often than not a large, leaky tent and even the hotelkeepers had Colts in their belts. The 'American Hotel' was the only one that travellers' accounts ever seem to mention, and it was nothing more than a crude wooden hut 'without any flooring – a horrid hole kept by a true-bred Californian gold-digger, a good specimen of the worst character', as another traveller, Walter Brodie, recalled. Its roof let in the rain perpetually during the rainy season from April to December, for which discomfort guests had to pay about 15 shillings a day. 'Three hundred and fifty of us slept in this *hotel*,' wrote Brodie, 'some in hammocks, some in bunks, and the remainder – the largest number – on the ground in their wet clothes, few of them taking the trouble to change. Five shillings were charged for sleeping on the ground.'[26] Even worse was alternative accommodation offered a mile down the road, where Brodie discovered that the owner 'burned opium, with the intention of sending every one of the travellers to sleep, with the hopes of robbing them of their gold dust'.[27]

Imagine Mary Seacole's dismay, having herself been a lodging-house keeper of good repute in Jamaica, who had prided herself on her high standards, when she finally arrived at her brother's 'hotel' to discover instead that, much like its American counterpart, the Independent Hotel consisted of

> *a long, low hut, built of rough, unhewn, unplanned logs, filled up with mud and split bamboo; a long, sloping roof and a large verandah, already full of visitors. And the interior: a long room, gaily hung with dirty calico, in stripes of red and white; above it another room, in which the guests slept ...*

Edward had his own little room, partitioned off at the end, but even this had been relinquished to three American lady travellers who had coughed up £10 for the privilege. Customers entering the premises paid either in coin or in gold dust for a ticket for their overnight lodgings and a meal. Mary was furious but made the most of it, as she always did on her travels, and soon found herself distracted by observing the travellers who came and went, particularly the 'Yankee' women. She noticed how these *female companions of the successful gold-diggers appeared in no hurry to resume the dress or obligations of their sex*. She couldn't help admiring their pioneer spirit, riding astride in trousers on mules across the Isthmus; but, as one traveller remarked, 'so execrable is the road, that all female passengers have to don male attire, and stick to their mules as best they can', and the spectacle was 'by no means uncommon of lady emigrants'.[28]

There would be many times in the days to come when Mary would wish herself *'safe back in my pleasant home in Kingston'*. But for now, once she had recovered from the journey, she joined in the communal life of the hotel. Everyone ate together at one table the length of the room covered in green oilskin. Meals were a noisy, chaotic affair punctuated by a great deal of shouting and quarrelling in *'Yankee twang'*. The staple appeared to be slapjack; thick pancakes made of flour, salt and water. They *'did not seem particularly tempting'* to Mary, but were followed by copious servings of pork or jerk beef stewed with dumplings, and by rice pudding served with molasses and treacle – all heavily laden with the carbohydrates needed to satisfy hungry prospectors. Eggs were hard to get, and so were chickens, and travellers paid high prices for these luxuries.[29]

In the evenings the sole pursuit in this one-horse town seemed to be gambling, though Edward refused to allow it on his premises as too often it ended in quarrels and violence. These *'hot-brained armed men'* could be very dangerous once provoked and many of them stayed up all night gambling away their gold dust and silver at the faro tables, while local women entertained them singing, dancing the fandango and no doubt offering sexual services too. Mary did not blame the people of Cruces for exploiting the travellers 'while their transitory sun shone', for their arrival was seasonal and they had to make the most of the custom when it was there. But she did reproach herself for allowing 'my rage for change and novelty' to have sent her to Panama so unprepared for the conditions she would have to face there. She was exhausted from having to sleep on a makeshift bed under the long dining table on the hard ground with her little servant girl, and began looking for alternative accommodation.[30]

But worse was to come: had Mary dropped her guard during her progress across the Isthmus and ignored the rumours that there was mucha cólera in the region? She was just beginning to adapt to her life in Cruces when the first signs emerged that those travellers crowding out her brother's hotel en route to Panama from Navy Bay had brought cholera with them on the boats from New Orleans. It was still prevalent in Panama in July 1852 when Ulysses S. Grant's 4th regiment arrived, their surgeon noting that it was by then epidemic in Aspinwall, Cruces and Gorgona and among the labourers on the railroad. Grant lost a third of his men to cholera, either at Cruces or on the way to Panama.[31]

The first victim in Cruces was a Spanish friend of Edward's who died suddenly after a short and intense illness. At first food poisoning – possibly picked up at Edward's hotel – had been suspected, but when Mary went to inspect the corpse 'A single glance at the poor fellow showed me the terrible truth.' The 'distressed face, sunken eyes, cramped limbs and discoloured shrivelled skin' were all so very familiar. There was no doctor in Cruces and so it was down to Mary to pronounce, with absolute conviction, that the man had died from cholera. The citizens of Cruces were far from grateful, as this would severely affect their trade, but soon Mary was called in to attend another victim: 'It was a very obstinate case, but by dint of mustard emetics, warm fomentations, mustard plasters on the stomach and the back, and calomel, at first in large and then in gradually smaller doses, I succeeded in saving my first cholera patient in Cruces.'[32]

Mustard seed ground to a powder in a pestle and mortar was a standard ingredient in any medical practitioner's pharmacy; mixed with water it was commonly used to treat Asiatic cholera, in controlling vomiting and diarrhoea in the first stages of the disease. Fomentations of mustard were one of Mary's go-to remedies for keeping the body warm, as they acted as a rubefacient. The mustard plasters – or poultices – where the mustard seeds were mashed and mixed to a paste with water and vinegar – would be massaged into the pit of the cholera patient's stomach (which swelled and hardened as the disease progressed) and often the soles of the feet to relieve stiffness and cramps. Calomel was a standard mercury-based preparation that was mixed with sugar and given in repeated doses as a sedative to stop vomiting and diarrhoea, and to relieve the acute abdominal pain suffered by patients.* Mary is proud to relate how her devoted nursing during the cholera outbreak in Cruces helped her patients pull through, but nevertheless feels she must apologise for what might appear self-aggrandisement in telling us this. But it is important to her to get her message across now, even before her narrative takes her to Crimea, that what has most mattered to her has been *where I have been enabled to benefit my fellow-creatures suffering from ills [that] my skill could often remedy*. She adds, with unnecessary false modesty, that these charitable acts are the *only claim I have to interest the public ear*. Her goal in life was always to be useful, the words *I love to be of service to those who need a woman's help* were the mantra Mary Seacole lived by, and she would be much called upon in Panama.[33]

---

* Many doctors in Panama advocated people drink quinine as a prophylactic against fever; indeed some of the medics who worked for the Railroad Company swore by it. Mary does not mention using it, but it was derived from the bark of the cinchona tree and was well known as a herbal treatment.

CHAPTER 11

'THE YELLOW WOMAN WITH
THE CHOLERA MEDICINE'

As the cholera made its destructive progress through Cruces, Mary Seacole was struck by the extent to which the locals seemed to lack any fight and capitulated to it. They were *'constitutionally cowardly'* in her view; unwilling and unable to take steps to combat the rate of infection in practical terms; and with no concept of the principle of self-help. They *'never stirred a finger to clean out their close, reeking huts, or rid the damp streets of the rotting accumulation of months'*, she tells us. Instead, all they did was call upon divine intervention by *'making the priests bring out into the streets figures of tawdry dirty saints supposed to possess some miraculous influence'*. For the no-nonsense Mary Seacole, this would never do. This crippling inaction meant that, by default, she soon found the whole community was relying on her for medical assistance. She had quickly become known throughout the town as *'the yellow woman from Jamaica with the cholera medicine'* but only a very few of those Mary treated – mainly the American hotel owners and storekeepers – could afford to pay her. Most of her poor patients, such as the native boatmen and muleteers, *'had nothing better to give their doctress than thanks'*. Mary did her best for them, but even so they *'died by scores'*.[1]

Writing of her experiences six years later, Mary said that even now the sights she witnessed during the cholera epidemic in Cruces haunted her; later she '*saw almost as fearful scenes on the Crimean peninsula among British men*'. She remembered being implored by one of the mule owners in town to go out to his compound and treat several sick men. His head muleteer and most-valued employee was very sick and the owner '*promised me a large remuneration if I should succeed in saving him*'. What she found when she got there appalled and disturbed Mary: the muleteers – '*the strong and the sick together*' – had been herded into one large, damp and muddy hut alongside their hobbled animals, their harnesses and no doubt their ordure, all '*breathing air that nearly choked me*' and that was thick with infection.

The very first thing Mary did on encountering this nightmarish scene was to order doors and shutters to be opened, fires lit and '*every effort made to ventilate the place*'. She spent that long exhausting night trying to do what she could; but '*I was tired to death*'. The rain was relentless and the surrounding fields were a quagmire, but with the help of a couple of women she battled on, putting screens up around the dying. '*But no screens could shut out from the others their awful groans and cries for the aid that no mortal power could give them.*' As the night wore on, silence descended, first behind one screen, then another, as more of her patients died. Mary meanwhile sat in front of the flickering fire cradling her youngest patient – '*a poor, little, brown-faced orphan infant, scarce a year old*' – but having no power to save him. There follows an extraordinary admission. After the child died, the idea came into Mary's mind that '*if it were possible to take this little child and examine it, I should learn more of the terrible disease which was sparing neither young nor old, and should know better how to do battle with it.*'[2]

One might perhaps pause here to remember that Mary, like all sick nurses of that time, had had no *formal* medical training whatsoever; all doors to conventional medical practise, let alone anatomical study and surgical procedures, were utterly closed to her and her sex. Yet she had inherited traditional doctressing skills that were as good as, if not better, than those on offer from ordinary doctors. More to her credit is the fact that she was determined to improve those skills and made the most of every opportunity to do so. It is curious to note that the only woman known (retrospectively) to be practising medicine to a surgical level at this time – albeit disguised as a man – was the Irish military surgeon Dr James Barry, who in 1820 had worked with patients in Mauritius during the first great pandemic of Asiatic cholera of 1817-24; spent time in Jamaica in the 1830s; and dealt with cholera again in Malta in 1850 during the same wave that Mary was encountering in Panama. Much like Mary, Barry saw the key to treating cholera lying in an insistence on cleanliness and ventilation and removing patients from the vicinity of insanitary conditions and noxious open sewers.[*3]

Still exhausted from her night-time vigil, in the *'cold grey dawn'* of the following day, Mary persuaded the man sent to take the dead child away and bury it to *'carry it by an unfrequented path down to the river-side'*, where, having bribed him with silver, she set about performing, with his assistance, a makeshift post mortem so that she might *'learn from this poor little thing the secret inner workings of our common foe'*. It would be her first, and last, such experiment. Afterwards, Mary and her impromptu assistant *'stole back into Cruces like guilty things'*, but, she insists, *'the knowledge I had obtained thus strangely was very valuable to me, and was soon put into practice.'*[4] Through trial and error, Mary developed her own methods and treatments, concluding that *'the simplest remedies were perhaps the best'* and she put them to good use not just in the epidemics in Jamaica and Panama but also in Crimea. Most important of all, and this is something Mary only learned from years of practice, she discovered that *'few constitutions permitted the use of exactly similar remedies'*. What worked for one patient might kill another. Many cholera victims sickened and died

---

* Another pioneer was American Elizabeth Blackwell, who, having managed to train in Geneva in 1847-8, set up her own medical clinic in New York in 1853 against a barrage of hostility from the male medical establishment. Florence Nightingale, whom Mary would encounter at Scutari, had also gone abroad – to Kaiserswerth in Germany for three months in 1851 to receive medical training at the Institution of Protestant Deaconesses. Although Blackwell's and Nightingale's groundbreaking work has been acknowledged in medical histories, that of the gifted nurses and doctresses who learned their holistic skills in the West Indian colonies has not and their achievements remain unsung.

with such horrifying rapidity – within an hour or two – that there was nothing anyone could do for them.[5]

Perhaps one of the regrets we as readers are left with, on reading Mary Seacole's candid appraisal of her own holistic methods, is that she never wrote any kind of treatise on her various treatments and simples for cholera, yellow fever, and the other enteric diseases with which she was so familiar. This is her missing legacy, for had we such documentation and some of her case histories, there would not have been the need to perpetually defend her against detractors who insist that Mary Seacole was merely an enterprising woman of business who did a bit of nursing on the side – nothing more.

As a result of her devoted care of the cholera victims in Cruces and so much daily exposure to the disease, it was inevitable that Mary too would eventually succumb. She sensed the onset shortly after having nursed the wife of a local Spanish 'grandee' on her deathbed. Once again Mary was irritated to find the Spanish response to be one of concerted invocations to God around the sickbed rather than any attempt at practical nursing. '*I had the greatest difficulty to rout the stupid priest and his as stupid worshippers and do what I could for the sufferer.*' It comes as something of a surprise to us, who now know of Mary's Roman Catholic conversion, to discover her undisguised annoyance at the intrusive Catholic rituals conducted around her patients; but then, Mary believed in hands-on intervention as a priority.[6]

Her patient died, and as she sat nursing the moribund child of the dead woman, a group of convicts – the official carriers-away of the dead during the epidemic – took the body away, by which time Mary was already feeling unwell. That telltale pall of chill descended over her and she took to her bed. The locals – both Americans and natives – came offering sympathy and gifts of blankets; '*Air you better, Aunty Seacole, now?*' they asked. Fortunately Mary suffered a relatively mild dose of cholera and recovered quickly, and after a few months the disease receded from Cruces. With almost obscene haste, Mary thought, the dead were quickly replaced; even the Spanish grandee found himself a new wife.[7]

Once the cholera had passed, she could now bask in her medical success and celebrity in the town: '*the reputation I had established founded for me a considerable practice*,' she tells us, and the Americans alone provided her with plenty of business. But she was tired of making do at Edward's hotel and decided it was time to set up her own independent venture. A rather run-down, ramshackle wattle-and-thatch two-roomed house became available across the street and Mary took it on for a rent of £20 a month. She intended to open what she called a *table d'hôte* – effectively a canteen – that would cater for up to fifty customers, with the assistance of Mac, her little maid and a local cook. The meals would be simple – four shillings for dinner, with eggs and chicken extra; though she would have wished her clients had better table manners and refrained from using their hands in preference to knives and forks. She would not offer accommodation but nevertheless grandly named her new business 'The British Hotel'. Handling the often unruly American customers, who indulged in rather too much spitting on the floor, was a challenge for a woman on her own, and she had to be forever on her guard against being robbed and cheated by these clever Yankee travellers – especially the ones who tried to disguise how many eggs they had consumed at eighteen pence a time.[8]

Mary refused to allow gambling in her establishment, but she cannily hired a Black barber named José to offer male guests shaves in a specially constructed outhouse – at a pretty hefty cost of £2 a time. It was as well she made this decision, for in Cruces she had seen at first hand how the gambling establishments bled the gold prospectors of their hard-earned gains, often with violent consequences. An American from San Francisco by the name of 'Dr Casey' – a man known to be '*a reckless and unscrupulous villain*' – ran the most popular gambling den in Cruces but too often card games ended in quarrels and violence. The presence of the Americans undoubtedly boosted the crime rate everywhere, and the knife and the gun ruled in Cruces. Life was cheap, although, if nothing else, dealing with the consequences of violence enhanced Mary's skills in stitching knife wounds and extracting bullets. As for police intervention, this was non-existent; Mary quickly discovered that everywhere on the Isthmus obtaining the protection of the law involved bribery and was *'rather an expensive luxury'*. The local *alcalde* who served as mayor-cum-magistrate and administered Panamanian justice could be found in a *'low bamboo shed'* that served as a courthouse, lounging in a dirty hammock smoking a *cigarito*. On the one occasion Mary appealed to him when she had caught someone stealing from her, she had had to pay him a fee for the privilege.[9]

As such, the *alcalde* represented the pinnacle of the local Panamanian 'aristocracy'. The chances of encountering any people of note in this out-of-the-way place were few. A popular singer, Catherine Hayes – known as 'the Irish nightingale' – passed through the Isthmus in October 1852 while Mary was there but did not deign to come and sing at their town. Nor did the notorious dancer, actress and courtesan Lola Montez – who then was, according to Mary, *'in the full zenith of her evil fame'*. Unfortunately Mary invoked Montez's wrath in her book by describing a supposed overnight visit made by her to Cruces. She enjoys giving us a pen portrait of this flamboyant, confrontational personality, dressed with bravado in men's clothes, complete with spurs and a whip with which she repelled an over-eager American admirer by giving him a cut across the face.[10]

But the problem is, Montez was never in Cruces. True, she did transit the Panama Isthmus in the first week of May 1853 en route to California. But although she stopped off at Gorgona on her way to Panama City, she did not make the detour to Cruces. Perhaps Mary saw Montez in Gorgona, or heard tell of her parading herself in Panama City; perhaps as happens elsewhere in her narrative, Mary gets her dates muddled; there is also the possibility that she was taken in by a Montez impersonator. Montez was furious with the perceived calumny when Mary's *Wonderful Adventures* came out in 1857, and in high dudgeon attacked this account in her own book, *Autobiography and Lectures of Lola Montez*, which was issued by the same publisher, Blackwood, three years later. 'She never was in Cruces in her life,' Montez insisted, 'and she passed many miles from that place.' As a parting shot, Montez levelled a nasty swipe at Mary's reputation: 'The whole story is a base fabrication from beginning to end. It is as false as Mrs Seacole's own name.'[11]

Everywhere Mary went in the Isthmus she witnessed the *'strong prejudice'* of the Yankees towards not just Black people but also the native Panamanians and indeed all people of colour, whom they collectively denigrated as 'niggers'. They were particularly physically aggressive towards the native boatmen and muleteers, always too ready to *'whop all creation abroad as they do their slaves at home'*.[12] But this was Panama, not the Southern states, and for once the natives answered back and refused to be cowed: *'It was wonderful to see how freedom and equality elevate men, and the same negro who perhaps in Tennessee would have cowered like a beaten child or dog beneath an American's uplifted hand, would face him boldly there, and by equal courage and superior physical strength cow his old oppressor.'*[13]

Many fugitive enslaved people from the Southern States had in fact made their way to Panama and elsewhere in Central America and, with the local authorities unwilling to assist in their recapture, had made good there – in local government, the judiciary, the army and the priesthood. In so doing they had garnered the respect of native Panamanians; it delighted Mary to see free Africans succeed in this way, for she was always an admirer of diligence.* In contrast, the hostility towards Americans passing through was palpable, particularly when they were seen to physically punish the enslaved people they brought with them.

An opportunity for Mary to take her own principled stand against American racism was about to come, for in the summer of 1852 she decided she had had enough of Cruces. She tried to persuade Edward to return to Kingston with her, but he was determined to

---

* In contrast, she does not mince her words with regard to the perceived laziness and dishonesty of some of the native Spanish Indians she encounters in Panama, as well as certain Greeks, Maltese and Turks she later had dealings with in Constantinople and Crimea. Mary's benchmark for judging her fellow human beings is consistently based on honesty, integrity and hard work, whatever their race or colour.

stay, and so Mary resolved instead to head 6 miles back along the Chagres River to Gorgona and try her luck there. But before she did so, her fellow Yankee hotel- and storekeepers announced a farewell party for her at Edward's hotel – '*in virtue of my recent services to the community*' – to be held on the anniversary of the United States Declaration of Independence. And so, on 4 July 1852, a substantial meal was enjoyed by all at which champagne at twelve shillings a bottle was quaffed with abandon, after which '*a thin sallow-looking American*' stood up to give the vote of thanks, while simultaneously chewing on a quid of tobacco. He raised his glass to '*Aunty Seacole*', thanking her for all she had done during the cholera epidemic: '*God bless the best yaller woman ... from Jamaica, gentlemen ... from the Isle of Springs.*' He was sure they would all agree there were only two things '*we're vexed for*':

> *the first is, that she ain't one of us – a citizen of the great United States – and the other thing is, gentlemen, that Providence made her a yaller woman. I calculate, gentlemen, you're all as vexed as I am that she's not wholly white, but I du [sic] reckon on your rejoicing with me that she's so many shades removed from being entirely black; and I guess, if we could bleach her by any means we would.*[14]

In what has since become the most-quoted set-piece of *Wonderful Adventures of Mrs Seacole in Many Lands*, Mary rose to her feet, with a gracious but cleverly barbed riposte, which she says would have been much stronger had not Edward urged restraint. Mary reined in her anger but made one thing absolutely clear: she was in no way embarrassed, ashamed or inhibited by the colour of her complexion: '*If it had been as dark as any nigger's, I should have been just as happy and useful, and as much respected by those whose respect I value*,' she declared. She also politely declined the gentleman's '*offer of bleaching me*': '*As to the society which the process might gain me admission into, all I can say is that, judging from the specimens I have met with here and elsewhere, I don't think that I shall lose much by being excluded from it. So, gentlemen, I drink to you and the general reformation of American manners.'*[15]

As things turned out, Mary lingered on in Cruces, still trying to persuade Edward to leave with her, to no avail. She worried about him; he was often ill and seemed vulnerable to the climate there. Eventually, an old Jamaican friend in Gorgona helped Mary find a premises for her new venture – a *'miserable little hut'* which she bought for a hundred dollars. She wasn't the only hotel keeper in town: there was the American-run Union Hotel and the Hotel Francaise, but she managed to obtain permission from the resident *alcalde* to improve and extend the premises with the help of a local labourer, Mac and her maid.[16] Soon *'I found myself in possession of a capital dining-room some thirty feet in length, which was gaily hung with coloured calico.'* She added on a bar and a storeroom and even a small private apartment for lady travellers and made clear the kind of business she was prepared to accept was *'principally ladies, and the care of those who might fall ill on the route'*.

Despite this, and the fact that *'the speculation paid well,'* Mary's heart was no longer in her Panamanian adventure. Her *'old roving inclination'* resurfaced and she wished for better, female company – of the kind that respected her colour, not these women from the Southern States who were always so hostile towards her. True, while she despised them for their racism *'I made money out of their wants'*, and if they came to her sick and suffering, then that was quite a different matter.[17]

The move to Gorgona proved to be a failure; the town proved to be yet another accumulation of crude bamboo shanties and canvas-tented 'hotels'. Life there was no different and palled very quickly. Gorgona was full of gold prospectors on their way back from the California goldfields. They all seemed thin, and sickly, as one traveller noted at the time: 'disappointed-looking men, poorly dressed, some suffering from rheumatism, crippled limbs, and broken constitutions and wasted by fever'. All the rude swagger they had displayed on their outward journey had evaporated and they seemed worn out.[18] Mary was depressed by her surroundings: nothing but a succession of '*hangers-on, idlers, and thieves, gamblers and dancing women*'. And then came the flood and the town turned into a quag-mire; closely followed by a serious fire. This was the last straw: Mary handed over the running of her hotel to Edward and with Mac and her maid took the first steamer out of Navy Bay for Kingston that she could.[19] Unfortunately it was an American one, and she soon dis-covered that her crossing would be uncomfortable. Having bought her ticket, Mary installed herself in the saloon only to be surrounded by a large group of American women who asked what she thought she was doing: '*Guess a nigger woman don't go along with us in this saloon,*' said one of them and another even '*spat in poor little Mary's frightened yellow face*'. An older American woman advised her quietly to retreat; a female stewardess reiterated the advice: '*you can't expect to stay with the white people.*' When an Englishman intervened on Mary's behalf, the women rounded on him: '*If the Britishers is so took up with coloured people, that's their business; but it won't do here.*' Mary became so enraged that she went to the captain, demanded her money back and despite the fact it was now midnight, removed herself, Mac, her maid and all her bags and bag-gage back onto the wharf at Navy Bay. The disconsolate party were stranded there for two days before the welcome sight of the Royal Mail steam packet *The Eagle* hove into view. At the helm was an old familiar friend from the service, Captain Edward George Baynton, who soon had Mary and her companions safely back in Kingston.[20]

CHAPTER 12

'A WILD AND UNPROFITABLE SPECULATION'

Mary Seacole had not long been back in Kingston when her medical services were once more urgently required. The next few months would be yet another time of *'suffering and gloom'* in Jamaica's history, hot on the heels of the cholera of 1850-1. This time, yellow fever had broken out in June among the men of the 3rd West India Regiment at Up Park Camp. Many of the white officers of the largely Black regiment fell victim, as too did newly arrived European visitors. It had already been noted that the Black population of Jamaica was far less susceptible to the fever; they seemed to have a natural immunity, or only experienced mild infections (in contrast, they were extremely vulnerable to pulmonary disease such as TB). The first cases had been seen in the Kingston public hospital the previous November among the crews of vessels in port. The hospital's Principal Medical Officer had noted how highly infectious it was and that he had 'never before seen so fatal a form as the present one'.[1] The epidemic gathered speed from March 1853 and was at its height in June/July; Mary noted with dismay that *'the yellow fever never made a more determined effort to exterminate the English in Jamaica than it did in that dreadful year.'* So virulent was it that even some of her own team of Black nurses succumbed.[2]

Mosquitoes that bred around stagnant water transmitted the

highly malignant yellow fever. The illness came on very rapidly, first with an intense chill, followed by feverishness, severe headache, heaviness and pain in the back and legs, culminating in necrosis of the liver. But the most telltale sign was the black vomit – the Spanish called the disease *vomito negro* – produced by the sufferer. This was triggered by bleeding in the mouth, nose, eyes and gastrointestinal tract; it left the patient totally prostrate and brought delirium and then death soon after. Bleeding and purges, plus heavy doses of calomel, were the standard response of allopathic medicine; the doctresses of Jamaica such as Mary would have had their own simples with which to treat patients. But, fundamentally, Mary would have followed the same nursing principles she had for cholera patients – using her simple herbal remedies (the juice of vervain – verbena – in the form of a tea was a popular plant used in the West Indies for treating yellow fever).[3] She would also have ensured good ventilation and cleanliness, giving patients plenty of fluids, and keeping them warm with her mustard poultices and massage. Once more calomel would have been her only proprietary standby drug.

In an effort to control the spread of the disease, the chief army surgeon at Up Park Camp recommended that the sick men be moved out of the poorly ventilated barracks and put under canvas on the parade ground, which at once arrested the spread of the disease. But patients were also farmed out to the lodging houses; Mary tells us that her own was *'full of sufferers – officers, their wives and children'*. Some were brought to her straight from the harbour, having fallen sick as soon as they arrived by sea. Despite all the terrible suffering she had seen during the previous cholera epidemics in Jamaica and Panama, Mary found the ravaging effects of the yellow fever that she witnessed in 1853 *'more difficult to bear than any I had previously borne a part in'*. Time and time again she found herself not only nursing the dying but then having to comfort the bereaved. And it was not just the officers who died; many of their wives, and children, perished too. *'It was a terrible thing to see young people in the youth and bloom of life suddenly stricken down,'* Mary writes. All the more so, as these young soldiers were not dying in war, but *'in vain contest with a climate that refused to adopt them'*. This observation allows her an opportunity to slip in a covert swipe at the system that exposed British soldiers to such unnecessary suffering: *'the mother country pays a dear price for the possession of her colonies.'*[4] The British press concurred and advised that 'In consequence of the disastrous effects of this fearful disease we think it really advisable, at least for the present, that Europeans should not risk their lives by coming out to the West Indies.'[5]

In describing the impact of the yellow fever Mary pauses to reflect on how her entire *'life's experience'* has been shaped by witnessing sickness, suffering and death. It had often been a humbling experience, for each patient confronted death in their own way, some with more courage than others: *'I have seen some brave men, who have smiled at the cruellest amputation, die trembling like children; while others, whose lives have been spent in avoidance of the least danger or trouble, have drawn their last painful breath like heroes, striking at their foe to the last, robbing him of his victory, and making their defeat a triumph.'*[6]

In a moment of quiet compassion and a homiletic affirmation of her Christian faith, Mary offers the story of the death of one particular young soldier in her care during the epidemic, of how deeply she was affected by it and how he taught her the true nature of courage. She promises us a revelation; only to immediately disappoint us by saying: *'I must not tell you his name, for his friends live yet, and have been kind to me in many ways.'* Why? Such false modesty and evasiveness is disappointing for the reader, let alone the frustrated biographer sighing about yet another dead end.

But to continue: Mary tells us her patient was a young surgeon – *'as busy, light-hearted, and joyous as a good man should be'*. When he went down with yellow fever, he was brought to Mary's lodging house to be nursed. She grew very fond of him, as though she were his own mother, calling him *'My son, my dear child'*, and she fervently hoped for his recovery. But then those *'terrible symptoms'* – the black vomit – came, and the young surgeon knew he would die. Yet even now he thought only of those he would leave behind – his parents and siblings back home. Mary helped support him as he wrote a final letter to them, his hands trembling uncontrollably. He dictated his simple will to a fellow officer – 'his dog to one friend, his ring to another, his books to a third, his love and kind wishes to all'.[7]

Mary held the young man in her arms as he died, 'a child in all save a man's calm courage'. She could not hold back the tears as he whispered, 'Let me lay my head upon your breast ... It's only that I miss my mother; but Heaven's will be done.'[8] His was a deathbed worthy in its pathos of the pen of Charles Dickens, and Mary demonstrates real empathy and literary skill in its telling, knowing that such an account of Christian resignation and faith would play well to her church-going Victorian audience. Perhaps she had subliminal recall of The Old Curiosity Shop serialised in 1840-1 and the death of Little Nell?[9] We have here one of those moments in her narrative where the mere storytelling of this autobiographical travelogue reveals the compassionate heart of Mary Seacole. It is also the perfect example of that Victorian archetype – the 'angel in the house': in other words, woman as wife, mother and caregiver. Mary Seacole the intrepid traveller and businesswoman is now ceding centre stage to Mary Seacole the Mother of the Army, and heroine of the Crimean War, who will dominate the remainder of her narrative.

After the young surgeon's death, Mary sent her condolences to his mother back home. Some months later, she received in response a mark of her gratitude – 'a little gold brooch with his hair in it' and a note thanking her for soothing her son's last moments 'by your kindness'. It was signed 'Your ever sincere and obliged M–– S––.'[10] It is tiny clues such as this that can enable the diligent historian with luck to make a connection. Thus: in October 1853 a couple of London papers noted the deaths of officers during the yellow fever epidemic in Kingston: Lieutenant [John Maryon] Wilson of the 3rd West India regiment on 13 August (closely followed by his wife Eliza who had been on the point of leaving Jamaica for her own safety). Dr Andrew Ferguson, surgeon of the Army Medical Department in Kingston, succumbed not long after arriving to take up his post and had suffered terribly for fifteen days before the fever finally took him.

Assistant Surgeon Walter W. Harris of the 1st West India Regiment
died on 4 August; and then another doctor from the 3rd West India
Regiment: Assistant Surgeon Gideon J. W. Griffith passed away on
26 August shortly after arrival. He was aged only twenty-six. A
name such as that is not difficult to track on genealogy sites, and
there he was: Gideon James William Griffith, baptised 22 November
1828 in Rathkeale, County Limerick, second son of the Rev. James
Griffith of Dublin and his wife Margaret Susan Griffith. M. S.: there
we have it. For once, Mary Seacole has not got the better of us.[11]

As soon as the worst of the epidemic was over, Mary was on the
move again – back to Panama, for she had unfinished business there
to attend to. Firstly she needed to *wind up the affairs of my late
hotel at Gorgona*', which it would seem Edward had not wanted to
continue managing. A friend from Jamaica, '*Mr H*' (perhaps one
of the Henriques family) met Mary at Navy Bay, from where she
went straight to Gorgona. There she met up again with Edward,
and together they took mules the 20 miles down to Panama City;
but she did not linger there long and was soon back at Navy Bay.[12]
Here the indefatigable Mary once more opened a provisions store,
but the city was as chaotic and lawless and uncivilised as ever and
after three months she gave it up. She had now set her sights on a
new and rather exciting venture: '*an opportunity offered itself to
do something at one of the stations of the New Granada Gold-
mining Company*,' based at Escribanos (today known as Boca de
Escribano), on the Atlantic coast of Panama.

   This was located about 50 miles west of the port of Chagres, but
there was no way of getting there overland, the rainforest was so
dense and impenetrable that it '*would have resisted the attempts
of an army to cut its way through*'.[13] Mary therefore had to travel
there along the coast, by small boat braving the notoriously rough
seas.[14] For the next few months at Escribanos she pursued a new
profession – that of gold miner, her own particular vested interest
being the Fort Bowen mine, one of several in the area.

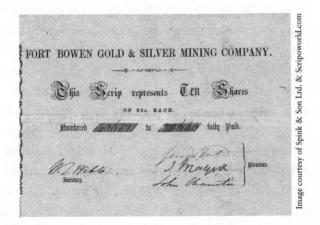

Escribanos lay on the border of the provinces of Colón and Veraguas on a tributary of the larger Belén River that flowed out into the Atlantic Ocean. The area had proved to be rich in seams of gold and silver, which the Spanish had discovered in Veraguas province in the 1800s. A prospectus for the New Granada Gold-Mining Company had been issued in London back in May 1835 after British survey-ors had scouted the area four years previously.[15] But the project seems to have gone into abeyance – for lack of investment and/or labour – until, in May 1850, the Veraguas mines, which had since been abandoned, were reopened on the back of the gold rush in California.

A new enterprise, of which the Fort Bowen mine was part, was set up under the title of the West Granada or Veraguas Gold and Silver Mining Company in 1852, offering 100,000 shares at £1 each.[16] This was contingent upon a report being made on the quality and via-bility of the ore, which would need to be extracted from the quartz in which it was embedded. Published in the *Daily News* in London on 8 December, the report confirmed the presence of four lodes of gold at the Fort Bowen site in Veraguas, with the principal lode lying about 50 feet above the Belén River. There was plenty of water power available, and an abundance of timber in order to build the mine shafts, and local native labour was 'cheap and plentiful'. The near-est settlement for the miners was at another mine at Howardsville

three quarters of a mile away, and from there the river was navigable
north to Escribanos 9 miles from the mine. From Escribanos the gold
would be transported to Chagres by boats in a couple of days. All
in all, the Fort Bowen mine seemed a good investment, as the report
suggested: the amount of gold there was 'much greater than the
measurement stated in the history of the Mine, on which the original
contract was based'. The company had, on this basis, bought the land
from the government of the Republic of New Granada for £80,000
and reported back to shareholders that 'the working of these mines
is a most promising undertaking.' In December 1852 arrangements
were made to send out machinery and staff to set up the enterprise;
there was accommodation at Howardsville for twelve mining officers
and forty workmen, enough for Mary to see an opportunity for
setting up a store.[17]

She did not embark on this new venture at Fort Bowen mine
without taking advice, and indeed Mary made the decision to travel
back to Panama on the invitation of the superintendent of the mine,
a certain Mr Day, whom Mary with her usual vagueness describes
as *a distant connection of my late husband*.[18] Thomas Day – we
don't ever learn his first name from Mary – became Mary's business
partner in Crimea, and is linked to an address in Gracechurch Street
where Edwin and Charles Witton Seacole may well have begun their
trading as West India Merchants. If we recall Mary's visits to the
City of London selling her West Indian pickles in 1824-5, it is also
where the Oil & Italian Warehouse of the Day family was located.[19]
But his name, like John Grant's without a middle name to help us,
or any identifying dates of birth, marriage or death, is the kind
of dead end genealogists so frequently come up against. So far it
has been impossible to prove this Thomas Day's connection to the
Gracechurch Street Days and the Seacole family. For now at least we
must assume that Mary had met Thomas Day on her earlier visit to
London through the Seacole brothers, and that she had since maintained some kind of business connection with him. The suggestion to
invest in the mine might perhaps also have come from her brother-in-
law Charles Witton Seacole, who now was living with his unmarried

sister Anne at St Luke's, Chelsea. Both were described on the 1851 census as 'fundholders' and might have been private investors in this project, for it was extensively advertised in the British press.

The mine promised speedy returns on investment and the company directors talked of expectations that the dividends 'will equal those of the richest gold and silver mines now known'. The shares were available on application to the directors of the company at Royal Exchange Buildings in the City of London.[20]

For a while Mary – as she honestly admits – succumbed to the lure of gold fever and fantasised about stumbling across a great find. But she also acknowledges her discomfort at discovering that many native women and children worked in the gold mine, which for them was '*hard and disagreeable*'.[21] In the end she stayed just a few months at Escribanos. The community was small – only two hundred people – and yet there were the same fights and troubles, all provoked by the transient population of gold-prospecting foreigners, that had dogged her time in Cruces and in Gorgona. The amenable Mr Day was called on to help the Escribanos *alcalde* repel a plot by deserters from an American ship to seize the mine and, inevitably, Mary's medical services were called on, for the same fevers plagued the miners there as elsewhere. She had to nurse Mr Day through a bout of sickness and also the surgeon of the West Granada Gold-Mining Company.[22]

Mary quickly became bored and restless at Escribanos; she was tired also of having to eat disgusting food – parrot, iguana, monkey even – and decided to embark on her own private prospecting trip, with one of the men from the mine – Mr Little – the *alcalde*'s daughter Juliana, and her maid Mary, down the Palmilla River that lay to the east of Escribanos. She had heard of a mine for sale there at a good price, and brought some quartz samples back with her, but tells us nothing more of the venture. For suddenly, without preamble, she announces that she upped and returned to Navy Bay and took a boat for England.[23]

After the best part of four years in Panama, Mary's parting shot was to record her admiration for the enterprising and hard-working

Black people she had met there and her dislike of the 'Spanish Indians', whom she found 'treacherous, passionate, and indolent, with no higher aim or object but simply to enjoy the present after their own torpid, useless fashion'. She was not sorry to leave; the mining adventure would, in the long run, prove a failure, a miscalculation. She does not shrink from the admission that she needed to travel to England to 'look after my share in the Palmilla mine speculation', but her impulse was far from being entirely pecuniary.[24] Mary now had a much stronger reason to head back to the mother country, for just before she had left Jamaica for Escribanos, Britain had declared war on Russia.

War in 1854 had come as a shock to a nation that had enjoyed almost forty years of peace since the defeat of Napoleon at Waterloo in 1815. It was the result of a long-running, centuries-old dispute known as the 'Eastern Question'. In essence it had originated with Russia's self-appointment as defender of the rights of Christians living under Turkish (Muslim) occupation in the Balkans ever since the old Ottoman Empire had begun seizing control of those territories in various incursions from the fourteenth century. In response, the Russians sought to protect not just the rights of Christians in the region but also their access to holy sites in Turkish-controlled Palestine. In support of their claim in 1853 they had invaded the Turkish-held Danubian Territories of Moldavia and Wallachia (both of which were absorbed into Romania in 1859). The Russians had expected their incursion to go unchallenged, but underestimated British concern about the threat of a further advance by Russia into the region, particularly any that would affect their sea and land access across the Black Sea to the Mediterranean and south to their most valuable colony – India. And so, with considerable reluctance, Britain allied itself with Turkey – the strategic bulwark against Russian expansion – and France and declared war on Russia on 28 March 1854 (although Turkey and Russia had been at war since the previous October).[25]

For the average Victorian, this was a distant war, entered into for obscure and little-understood reasons, a very long way from home. For loyal subjects of the empire in Jamaica, it was even more remote – 6,300 miles away as the crow flies. But the longing to witness war and be of service to the British Army was very strong in Mary, and the wish to make her way to the scene of the conflict became even stronger when she discovered that *'many of the regiments I had known so well in Jamaica had left England for the scene of action.'*[26]

In Britain, an expeditionary force had in fact begun departing for the East, in anticipation of conflict, from the end of February 1854 – initially to rendezvous with its Turkish and French allies at Constantinople and then at a base camp at Varna on the coast of today's Bulgaria. At the time, nobody had been certain where these armies would eventually engage with the Russians. Then, almost six months later, after some initial clashes in the Danubian Principalities, the order came for the British, French and Turkish forces – some 55,000 in all – to set sail for the Crimean Peninsula, which was then part of the Russian Empire. On 7 September a vast flotilla of allied ships left Varna. The objective was to launch an attack on the historic naval base – and pride of Russia – located at Sevastopol, 300 miles across the Black Sea on the northern coast of Crimea.

In Mary's hometown of Kingston, news of the war had been greeted with loyal enthusiasm. Several companies of Black Jamaicans in the West India regiments volunteered to serve and there may even have been other skilled Jamaican sick nurses like Mary who would have wished to offer themselves for the war effort. But in the absence of any evidence (bar a couple of West Indian volunteers who came forward in London), Mary occupies a unique place on that score. Having wound up her business interests in Panama, she sailed straight for England from Navy Bay at the end of August 1854, probably on the Royal Mail steam packet *La Plata*, which served Panama and the West Indies and docked at Southampton on 18 October. Having endured a heavy gale at sea on 11 October that had lasted thirty-six hours, Mary was no doubt enormously relieved to set foot in England again. But her arrival came not long after news of the first major engagement of the war – the Battle of the Alma on 20 September.[27]

In her narrative, Mary chides herself for still nursing misplaced ambitions of pursuing her mining speculation on arrival in London. It was a fool's errand; what had seemed *'so feasible'* on the ground, in Panama, was now, from the distance of England, a *'wild and unprofitable speculation'* and she felt ashamed. For a while she had prioritised it over her concern for *'my old friends of the 97th, 48th'*. Over in Crimea, these men were *'battling with worse foes than yellow fever and cholera'* and she now threw all her energies into making her way there to offer her support, both medical and practical.

But to get from England to Crimea, by sea and as a civilian, would involve a journey of 3,000 miles at a time when the majority of commercial ships had been commandeered by the government. How was Mary to *'persuade the public that an unknown Creole woman would be useful to the army before Sebastopol'*? More importantly, how was she to persuade the British military authorities and the team now interviewing and recruiting nurses for Crimea to take her on? Mary Seacole knew that in persisting with her plan she would be defying every prevailing Victorian social convention and all the constraints placed on her race and her sex, most notably, her lower status as a colonial subject. All in all it seemed *'too improbable an achievement to be thought of for an instant'*.[28] But here was one very determined, patriotic Jamaican who would not be put down or discouraged – as the army authorities and eventually the British public were about to discover.

CHAPTER 13

AN 'UNKNOWN CREOLE WOMAN' GOES TO WAR

It was almost thirty years since Mary Seacole had last been in London and a great deal had changed in that time. As a young woman, she had seen the capital during the reign of the unpopular profligate, George IV. Now approaching forty-nine, she returned at a time of burgeoning and vigorous British self-confidence; a period of colonial expansion, and of a country riding the crest of the wave after the triumph of the Great Exhibition of 1851. It was the height of the Industrial Revolution, in which British talent and inventiveness led the world and at the helm was a bright young queen – Victoria – with a cultured and serious-minded husband in Prince Albert, and a growing family. Together they represented the admirable solidity of British morality, family values and God-fearing respectability. This would be the audience for Mary's postwar memoir, and in many ways it sets the parameters of the constraints under which she would write it.

Initially, the announcement of war had roused unprecedented levels of anti-Russian xenophobia in the British public that fuelled what would prove to be the war's short-term popularity. From the first, Queen Victoria was extremely enthusiastic about Britain quickly teaching those nasty Russians a lesson, and she swooned at the sight of her favourite brave, scarlet-coated Scottish Fusiliers marching off to war. Frustrated that she could not go and fight, Victoria threw herself into mobilising the home front, exhorting the women of Britain – and even her own daughters – to knit and sew and put together parcels for the troops in Crimea. But news was spasmodic and the fastest a message by telegraph could reach England – after being taken across the Black Sea and then telegraphed from Bucharest* – was five days.[1] The wait was an anxious one and when news finally came from the front it was extremely grim and distressing.

After assembling with their French and Turkish allies at Varna on the coast of today's Bulgaria in the summer of 1854, 25,000 British troops had sailed for Crimea in September. Their commanders had promised that this would be a short and victorious war, and so the troops had been sent out under-equipped, without enough transport animals, proper tents or adequate supplies for a protracted campaign. Even before they sailed for Crimea, many of them had been felled by an outbreak of cholera in camp at Varna. They had had to struggle in the still fierce heat to cross the rocky Crimean terrain, only to encounter an enormous Russian force of 33,600 holding a 6-mile position blocking their route at the River Alma.[2] At the subsequent engagement, the Russians incurred heavy losses and although the Allies scored a victory and their dead were far fewer, there were around 4,500 wounded with only a few exhausted and hopelessly overstretched army surgeons to deal with them all. Many of these men, crowded on board ship with cholera victims, succumbed unnecessarily en route from Balaclava across the Black Sea to the Turkish Army barracks commandeered by the British as a hospital – at Scutari on the Bosporus.

After Alma, the British commander, Lord Raglan, made a fatal mistake that would put the campaign on the back foot before it had

---

* The British military authorities addressed this problem urgently and by April 1855 a telegraph cable had been laid for 340 miles underwater across the Black Sea. This linked Balaclava to Varna, and made telegraph messages transferrable between Crimea and the mainland and on to London and Paris within about five hours.

even got going. Rather than attack from the north, he decided to march his troops right round Sevastopol and lay siege to the naval base from the south and east, establishing a base at the port of Balaclava. It would cost the British Army dear, for it allowed the Russians time to dig in and throw up enormous defensive earthworks around the city.

Back home in Britain it was several days before the news of the Battle of the Alma arrived by telegraph. Church bells rang out to celebrate Britain's first victory; people crowded out the telegraph offices and newspaper sales rocketed, particularly those of *The Times*. Queen Victoria was enthralled by reports of the heroics of her soldiers; the British nation was 'entirely engrossed with one idea and one anxious thought, namely the Crimea', she told her uncle, Leopold, King of the Belgians.[3] Mary Seacole also was engrossed – and increasingly anxious – for, as she tried to plan how she might get to Crimea and how long her '*carefully husbanded*' funds might last when she got there, news came of two further big battles, at Balaclava and Inkerman.[4]

The second battle had occurred on 25 October, when the Russians tried to cut off the British base at Balaclava, during which a gallant line of 550 Sutherland Highlanders defending the head of the inlet leading into the port had repelled the Russians in what would later be immortalised as 'the thin red line'. This was closely followed by a rout by the 900 men of the Heavy Brigade of a much bigger force of Russians. But the heroics of the day – and the centrepiece of the subsequent mythology of the war – were focused on the Charge of the Light Brigade, when, due to an unfortunate misinterpretation of confused orders from Lord Raglan, British cavalry charged the wrong Russian gun emplacement at the end of a valley.

The historic charge, forever remembered thereafter by every Victorian schoolchild in the words of Alfred, Lord Tennyson's poem, sent 670 men on a suicidal frontal attack straight into the full firepower of the Russian guns – resulting in the deaths of 103 cavalrymen and the appalling loss of 340 fine cavalry horses and leaving 130 wounded.[5] A third and final engagement, at Inkerman, followed on 5 November, when the Russians launched a surprise attack on the exhausted, hungry and rain-soaked British infantry of the 2nd Division. At the end of an intense hand-to-hand battle lasting eight hours and fought in heavy mist and drizzle, the Russians were pushed back with almost 11,000 losses. The French and British lost 3,220 men. By November 1854, the British fighting force had been reduced to 16,000 men, but not so much by death and injury as by a great amount of sickness, malnutrition and neglect. With the cold setting in hard, frostbite and hypothermia were taking their toll as well.

People back home received the full horrifying details of the great battles thanks to the frontline reporting of the *Times* special correspondent in Crimea, William Howard Russell, who had sailed to Crimea with the troops in September. His long and graphic dispatches would effectively be the first of their kind from a correspondent embedded with troops in the front lines, and all the other papers then in existence depended on *The Times* for the most reliable news from Crimea. The realities of war were now being brought into the homes, hearts and minds of ordinary Victorians in an immediate and visceral way unlike any other war to date.

However, it was not until 12 October 1854 that the first news of the terrible suffering of the British wounded and their neglect for want of adequate medical facilities, doctors – and especially nurses – finally broke in *The Times* and galvanised the nation. It came in a dispatch not from Russell but from Constantinople-based correspondent Thomas Chenery, and it was not the kind of heroic account the government had wanted the British public to hear:

In the Turkish hospital at Scutari we are told of the 4,000 patients lying for hours and even days making desperate attempts to catch the surgeon on his flying visits from ward to ward. This deficiency, great as it is, can scarcely be called the greatest. There are no nurses at Scutari for the English, though there are Sisters of Mercy for the French. But what is almost incredible, but nevertheless true, there is not even linen or lint to bind wounds.[6]

Complacency, inefficiency, neglect, and a downright cold-blooded disregard for the rank and file were now exposed, and the British Secretary at War, Sidney Herbert, was in the direct firing line.[7] While the public immediately were mobilised to raise funds – with enormous generosity – to send comforts, bandages and medical supplies for the sick and wounded, Sidney Herbert was faced with finding a team of nurses to send to Crimea and enlisted his wife Elizabeth's help. But there were no trained nurses at that time, let alone any experienced in nursing war wounded. It would fall to a frantic recruitment drive among the few semi-skilled hospital nurses available, a handful of experienced cholera nurses, and nuns from Catholic and Anglican nursing orders. The woman Herbert selected to take a team of nurses out to Scutari was Florence Nightingale, and on 19 October an official announcement was published: 'We are authorized to state that Mrs [sic] Nightingale, who has for some time been acting as superintendent of the Ladies Hospital at No. 1 Upper Harley Street, has undertaken to organize a staff of female nurses who will at once proceed with her to Scutari at the cost of the Government ... Mrs Nightingale will herself select the persons who will accompany her.'[8]

On 23 October Nightingale entrained for the coast with the first party of thirty-eight specially recruited nurses: six Anglican nuns, eight Sellonites, ten Roman Catholic sisters and fourteen hospital nurses, leaving Elizabeth Herbert to interview and recruit more in England. In the meantime, with stalemate in the fighting and a long siege of Sevastopol now setting in, the British Army was facing a cruel winter, exposed in shallow trenches and with few tents, on the freezing and treeless Crimean plain.

Mary Seacole followed the news of the war with increasing alarm; she was distressed to hear of the *'mismanagement and suffering'* and to learn that

the hospitals were full to suffocation, that scarcity and exposure were the fate of all in the camp, and that the brave fellows for whom any of us at home would have split our last shilling, and shared our last meal, were dying thousands of miles away from

the active sympathy of their fellow countrymen ... Hundreds
were dying whom the Russian shot and sword had spared, and
that the hospitals of Scutari were utterly unable to shelter, or their
inadequate staff to attend to, the ship-loads of sick and wounded
which were sent to them across the stormy Black Sea.[9]

She knew that her years of nursing the sick through cholera and
yellow fever and other enteric disease, of extracting bullets and
binding up knife wounds in Panama had perfectly equipped her for
the task at hand: *'what delight should I not experience if I could be*
useful to my own "sons",' she wrote. Mary was resolute: *'I made*
up my mind that if the army wanted nurses, they would be glad of
me ... I decided that I would go to the Crimea.'[10]

In the meantime, Sidney Herbert had been swamped with a great
many eager, but largely unsuitable, female nursing applicants: 617
such letters survive today and can be found in the National Archives
at Kew.[11] But such was the hopeless unsuitability of the majority of
candidates that he had had to publish a letter warning that volunteers
would encounter horrors that 'would try the firmest nerves'. 'I fear
we should have not only many inefficient nurses, but many hysterical
patients, themselves requiring treatment instead of assisting others.'[12]
All the more reason, surely, for hiring a woman of Mary Seacole's
calibre and exceptional nursing experience, particularly when
William Fergusson MD, Inspector General of Military Hospitals,
as long ago as 1846 had observed that 'In the colonies, the coloured
women of every class, whether blacks, mulattoes, or mustees, make
the best sick nurses in the world. Nothing can exceed their vigilance
and tenderness. They also delight in the office far beyond European
women of any class, and *it is to be regretted they should not always*
succeed in obtaining the place they are so well calculated to fill.
[my italics]'

Fergusson was full of praise for Black and mixed-heritage nurses.
As early as 1815 he had advocated 'black creole nurses, instead of
white soldier orderlies or even soldiers' wives' being hired in military
hospitals. These women, he noted, 'have an aptitude for the office,

and seek it on all occasions', and he championed them based on first-hand experience. He himself had suffered 'a terrible attack of yellow fever' when with the army at Port au Prince in St Domingo. Two women of colour had been assigned to nurse him, and told him that nine British officers had already died of the disease. The 'English doctors had killed them all', they said, urging him 'not to take their physic', but that they would prepare drinks 'of sovereign virtue' for him. The nurses had been 'unwearied in kindness' in their care of Fergusson and he had been 'much beholden to their Creole kitchen for many comforts during a long and difficult convalescence.'[13] Dr Fergusson* might almost have been composing a testimonial for Mary Seacole herself; enteric diseases, *all of them more or less known in tropical climates*', as Mary asserts, were already decimating the army in Crimea. Those recruiting more nurses to follow Florence Nightingale to Scutari should have welcomed her with open arms as being absolutely *'the right woman in the right place'*.[14] But no.

With *'judicious decisiveness'*, as Mary describes it, she set out on a dispiriting round of all the official departments where she might offer her services, in resigned expectation of receiving at each stop *'a fresh set of rebuffs and disappointments'*. She makes no apology for describing the bitter sense of rejection and humiliation that she encountered in her resolute campaign to become *'a Crimean heroine!'* It seemed so blindingly obvious that her experience in Panama *'would not only render my services as a nurse more valuable, but would enable me to be of use to the overworked doctors'*.[15] She even took the precaution of collating a sheaf of testimonials to take with her to back up her application, including one from the former medical officer of the West Granada Gold-Mining Company – (sadly initials only and so far not identified) – who commended Mary's 'peculiar fitness, in a constitutional point of view, for the duties of a medical attendant'.[16]

Mary's first objective was to try to see the Secretary at War,

---

*   Fergusson, who died the year his book was published, made an important study of malaria, based on his observations in the West Indies and elsewhere, though he never quite made the connection with mosquitoes as the carriers of the disease.

Sidney Herbert, at the War Office on Horse Guards, Whitehall. In retrospect, her *'ridiculous endeavours'* to do so proved a complete waste of time, as she was fobbed off by a succession of civil-service minions without getting a foot in the door. She then strode off to the Quartermaster-General's Department, but he was essentially responsible for food supplies, forage and quartering of the troops and their animals. His clerks did at least allow Mary in and listened to her with *'polite enjoyment'* before gently advising that *'had I not better apply to the Medical Department'*. This would suggest that not only was Mary offering her services as a nurse, but also her long experience as a store keeper and provisioner. For clearly her ambitions in Crimea were twofold: to *'nurse her "sons"'* and also to set up some kind of accommodation and/or general store, offering food and drink to the soldiers, which would fund the cost of buying supplies and providing nursing care. But this offer by *'a motherly yellow woman'* was once more dismissed out of hand.

While doing the rounds Mary dropped in several times to the United Service Club, the elite club for senior army and navy officers, located on Pall Mall, *'seeking to gain the interest of officers whom I had known in Jamaica'*, again to no avail.[17] So she was left with one final option: to volunteer as a nurse to the Secretary at War's wife, Elizabeth Herbert, currently recruiting more nurses on behalf of Florence Nightingale from her home at 49 Belgrave Square. Mary *'laid the same pertinacious siege'* to the Nurses Enlistment Centre at Herbert's home as she had the War Office, stubbornly sitting for long hours in the great hall waiting to be seen and being rudely ignored. She was only too aware how much they all were irritated by her persistence. Mrs Herbert did not deign her with an interview but in the end sent a note informing Mary that *'the full complement of nurses had been secured.'* Her offer *'could not be entertained'*. It was, of course, a lie; and it was reiterated to Mary by one of Mrs Herbert's fellow recruiters. *'I read in her face that had there been a vacancy, I should not have been chosen to fill it,'* Mary regretfully concludes.[18]

The same rebuff was meted out to at least two other West Indian women of colour who applied to nurse in Crimea: a Miss Belgrave and a Mrs Elizabeth Purcell. Their letters of application survive in the National Archives and testify to similar lame and thinly veiled racist reasons for their rejection. Miss Belgrave had looked to be robust and perfectly well equipped for the task but was turned down for the nonsensical reason that a 'West Indian constitution is not the one best able to bear the fatigue of nursing', and besides, the patients might object 'to a nurse being so nearly a person of colour'. As for Mrs Purcell, the respectable wife of a British soldier who came on the recommendation of a surgeon apothecary, she was rejected outright for being too old and 'almost black'.[19]

After this succession of belittling rejections, Mary had nowhere else left to appeal other than to the Times Crimean Fund for the Relief of the Sick and Wounded that had been set up on the back of the Chenery dispatch of 12 October. She was after all earnestly seeking to do her bit to relieve the suffering out in Crimea, but that appeal for funding failed too. Mary's wholesale rejection by all official channels forced her to ask the question she had resisted till now: '*Was it possible that American prejudices against colour had some root here*' – in Britain. '*Did these ladies shrink from accepting my aid because my blood flowed beneath a somewhat duskier skin than theirs.*' This was the closest she would come to calling out overt British racism in her memoir.[20]

At the end of her tiring and fruitless traipse round the bastions of officialdom, Mary stood in the chill and mist of a winter evening '*in the fast thinning*' streets of London; the tears flowed and she did not care if people passing by saw them. But she was never one to be downcast for long: the following morning she recovered her equilibrium – and her resolve. She would go to Crimea '*upon my own responsibility and at my own cost*'. And if she could not go as a nurse, which she would have done willingly, '*should I not open an hotel for invalids in the Crimea in my own way?*' Mary knew she would see some friendly faces there who would support her venture – officers whom she had nursed from the regiments she had known in Jamaica; army surgeons who had lodged with her; even '*a general who had more than once helped me, and would do so still*'.[21]

Having booked her ticket, she had some business cards printed announcing her Crimean venture and sent them on ahead '*to my friends before Sebastopol*'.

> **"BRITISH HOTEL**
> Mrs. MARY SEACOLE
> (*Late of Kingston, Jamaica*),
> Respectfully announces to her former kind friends, and to the
> Officers of the Army and Navy generally,
> That she has taken her passage in the screw-steamer " Hollander,"
> to start from London on the 25th of January, intending on her arri-
> val at Balaclava to establish a mess-table and comfortable quarters for
> sick and convalescent officers."

Mary also met up again with Thomas Day, now returned from the Fort Bowen mine, which seems to have been abandoned. Coincidentally, it would seem, he too was on his way out to Crimea '*upon some shipping business*'.[22] By this we must assume Day intended to supply provisions of some kind to the army in Crimea; the two friends quickly resolved to enter into a partnership running a store, they hoped, '*in the neighbourhood of the camp*'. Mary's idea of establishing, in addition, an actual hotel in the war zone seems naïve, to say the least, and would come to naught. For the meantime she invested some of her capital in various '*home comforts*' to take to her friends in Crimea, and a supply of medicines, thanks to the '*kind aid of a medical friend*'.[23] This friend was undoubtedly her old Kingston acquaintance, Dr Amos Henriques, who now lived with his family in Upper Berkeley Street. It was a most useful connection, both professionally and socially, and one that Mary would exploit on her return from the war.[24]

Mary Seacole did not quite make it out of London on the date announced on her business card. It was virtually impossible, as a civilian, to get onto a navy ship and so she had had to find passage on a commercial vessel heading for Constantinople. It was actually 15 February before she finally left England, via Gravesend and Deal, having managed to secure a berth on a brand-new screw steamer – the *Hollander* – owned by the Dutch company of J. P. van Hoey Smith of Rotterdam and captained by M. J. Frantzen.[25] The newly built ship had been chartered in haste under the British flag prior to its official registration, in order to get urgent supplies out to the army. The Netherlands was neutral in the Crimean conflict, and so with a shortage of British vessels to do the job, the government hired it temporarily. But this meant that the *Hollander*'s January departure had been delayed for last-minute loading at the East India Docks. Intriguingly, Mary drops in one of her typically evasive details by telling us that '*I had scarcely set my foot on board the "Hollander" before I met a friend. The supercargo was the brother of Mr S––, whose death in Jamaica the reader will not have forgotten.*' He gave Mary a '*hearty welcome*', so she tells us. By '*Mr S*' Mary must surely be referring here to her own husband, the late Mr Seacole (though why she has to be so coy about it is infuriating). If so then there is only one possible candidate for the supercargo: Charles Witton Seacole, since the other Seacole brothers – Thomas, John and Wintringham – were all dead. We have no way of knowing why Charles Witton, who retired back to England on an annuity, should take up work supervising the loading of the *Hollander* on behalf of its owners. But there is perhaps a clue in the fact that when he first went out to Jamaica he was listed as Harbour Master at Black River and may well have had a merchant marine background. Perhaps he had taken up this role for the duration of the war?[26]

On 14 February the *Hollander* was finally cleared from the London Custom House and sailed the next day.[27] Thomas Day had already gone on ahead to Crimea to negotiate with the military authorities for permission to establish a store near the British Army camp. But Mary did not set off on the 3,000-mile sea journey to Crimea alone. Remember those allusions to the '*little girl*' and '*my little maid*' when Mary was in Panama?[28] There is good reason to believe that this in fact was her own daughter, who had been with her all through her Panamanian adventures. Sarah, like the luckless Mr Seacole, is not part of the story Mary constructs for public consumption, and there are understandable reasons why she chooses to omit her. But we are nevertheless the poorer for it. We shall return to her and the question of her putative father – a man as elusive as Mary's own – later in this story. But we can at least be confident this time that there were others in Crimea during 1855-6 who bore witness to Sarah's presence.

CHAPTER 14

'THE RIGHTNESS OF THE STEP I HAD TAKEN'

Travelling to Crimea, Mary was extremely fortunate not to have to share the terrible privations of the sea journey to the East experienced by the British Army wives who had been brave enough to venture there with the transport ships the previous year. These women had been crowded for the two- or three-week duration of the journey to Constantinople into the orlop of old wooden sailing ships rather than the better-equipped screw steamers that were carrying the troops. The orlop was the lowest deck of the ship just above the evil-smelling bilges. Here they had had to endure a total lack of sunlight and fresh air, for the orlop had no portholes and if the voyage was rough they had no escape from the sight and smell of others vomiting. Many women grew sick with disease such as fever and typhus. Some died; others even gave birth in these horrific conditions. After as many as ten days held virtually captive below decks, many of the women gave up their journey as soon as they reached Gibraltar and begged to go home.[1]

Mary counted herself a '*good sailor*' and she had no complaints about her own sea journey to Gibraltar, where the *Hollander* docked on 23 February for a brief stopover. The comfort of this part of the voyage depended on the long, heavy westward swell on the Atlantic, with the ship's stern plunging deeply into water often made turbulent by the winds around the Bay of Biscay, notorious for its terrifying gales. Mary was lucky: the weather was cold but fine and the *'sea good-humouredly calm'*.[2] She might well have caught sight of porpoises and even whales, but was long since inured to such sights, being as she was such a seasoned traveller. Though when the ship sailed down the coast of the Algarve, she did go up on deck to view the bare rocks and white walls of the ruined convent at the Cape of St Vincent, and to the east of it, beyond Cadiz, the *'long bay where the Trafalgar's fight was won'*. She took delight in the sight of so many vessels out on the high sea following the same route out to Crimea as they were. As the ship approached the Straits of Gibraltar, Mary's *'conviction of the rightness of the step I had taken'* grew ever stronger.[3]

On shore at Gibraltar she found herself a local guide and took a tour of the excavated fortifications, and admired the vista of the broad bay, beyond which lay Africa on one side and Europe on the other. It was, of course, full of Allied ships on their way to Crimea. Back in the market place Mary took note of the *'strange and motley population'* of the rock – which, as one traveller noted, was an exotic mix of nationalities: Barbary-coast Jews in their long black robes; Egyptians wearing fezzes; turbaned African Moors.[4] Then suddenly she had heard an English voice call out: *'Why, bless my soul, old fellow, if this is not our good old Mother Seacole,'* and saw two English officers, both sporting the bushy Crimean beards that the men had grown there over the winter. It was a moment or two before she was able to recognise them as men of the 48th Regiment, *'who had often been in my house at Kingston'* but who were now sadly being invalided home. Both men seemed to think it a capital idea that 'Mother Seacole' should be going out to Crimea to offer womanly care and comforts, but they were concerned that *'it's not the place, even for you, who know what hardship is.'* They were worried she would not find adequate shelter. Mary told them she would be happy to *'rig up a hut with the packing-cases, and sleep, if need be, on straw'*.[5] Nothing would deter her.

From Gibraltar, the *Hollander* sailed into the Alboran Sea heading for the Mediterranean. It skirted the soft conical hills of the coast of North Africa – past modern-day Morocco and Algeria and on to Cape Bon on the northeastern tip of Tunisia – before turning southeast past Sardinia to the next stop-off at Malta. Here we have our first and very rare sighting of Mary and her daughter Sarah. It comes in a somewhat garbled listing in the *Malta Times* of ships' passengers arriving at Valetta on 1 March: 'Per Hollander from London and Gibraltar – Mr C Keen, *Mrs Sencold*, and *Mrs Grant*. [my italics]'[6]

Such listings, often taken down and transcribed in haste, are notorious for typos, particularly in foreign papers unfamiliar with English names. In twenty years of Seacole research I have seen many misspellings of her name and have no doubt that this Mrs Sencold is Mary Seacole. More intriguing, however, is the listing of her daughter Sarah travelling under the surname Grant (and ignoring the misattribution of 'Mrs', a frequent error in many Victorian sources). Putting it another way: what other women might have been travelling by sea to Constantinople on a British-commandeered supply ship in the middle of a war?[7]

During the Crimean War, Malta's then population of 120,000 was at times overwhelmed by the influx of troops, either en route out to Crimea or being invalided home, and the island struggled to produce enough food to feed them all. The capital and major port Valetta was 'like a fair' with the constant hubbub of the arrival and departure of 'men-of-war, packets, transports, and troops and the innumerable preparations required by men about to undertake a campaign'. It kept the local townspeople 'in incessant activity'; and it also provided a wealth of victims for pickpockets, including Mary, who complains of being *'robbed by the lazy Maltese'*.[8] There was good money to be made during the war, and lots of it in circulation, which pushed up the prices of goods in the markets, especially comestibles. 'Every tradesman is busy, morning, noon, and night,' wrote *Times* correspondent William Howard Russell when he passed through, 'and the intense pressure of demand has raised the cost of supply enormously. Saddlers, tinmen, outfitters, tailors, shoemakers, cutlers, all the followers of the more useful and practical arts, are in

great request, and their charges have crept up till they have attained
the dimensions of the West-End scale.'[9]

Mary took herself and Sarah on a brief walkabout before the
Hollander sailed, struggling up the steep streets of Valetta – a daz-
zling but dusty, dry town surrounded by thin vegetation and rocky
outcrops, and beyond an expanse of intensely blue sea. Arabs, Romans
and Crusading Knights had all passed through and left their mark and
now it was the turn of the British military on their way to another
conflict.[10] But Mary took little or no interest in the tourist sights,
for her attention was once again quickly captured by the sound of
English voices, and she was thrilled to see yet more familiar faces from
Kingston – this time medical officers, including a 'Dr F––' on his way
back home from Scutari.[11] When Mary told him she was intending to
go there to pay her respects to Florence Nightingale as Superintendent
of the Female Nursing Establishment of the English General Hospitals
in Turkey, he gave her an all-important letter of introduction.

At this point, and true to then-prevailing Victorian literary nice-
ties, Mary tries to anonymise this medical man. But without success;
for there is a very strong candidate for the part: Dr John Forrest, a
long-serving and distinguished member of the Army Medical Staff,
who in his early career had served with the 8th West India Regiment
in Jamaica. In March 1854 Forrest had been promoted to Deputy-
Inspector of Army Hospitals and in December posted to Scutari.
However, in January 1855 he had fallen seriously ill with kidney
disease and had been forced to resign his post. He had left Scutari
by sea on 26 January, thus chiming with the encounter with Mary
Seacole in Malta.[12]

Malta rapidly receded into a faint haze as Mary's ship sailed
towards the Dardanelles, where she provides us with a lyrical aside:
'*So on, until the cable rattles over the windlass, as the good ship's
anchor plunges down fathoms deep into the blue waters of the
Bosphorus – her voyage ended.*'[13]

Its literary flair might perhaps be that of her editor interjecting
something of his own sentiments here, which plays into suggestions
that Mary's book was ghostwritten, or partially so; but without

any documentary evidence, such as Mary's original manuscript, we simply cannot be certain of this, as with so many other things.

Arriving in Constantinople on 8 March, Mary tells us she spent the next six days there (in fact it was probably about eight), wedging her *'well filled-out, portly form'* into Turkish caiques and crossing back and forth between the old city and the European section on the other side of the Golden Horn at Pera. Having walked round the narrow cobbled streets of the city, she spent the nights back on board the *Hollander*, while she awaited a British transport ship to take her across to Balaclava. She found the Turkish boatmen *'politely careful of my safety'*, although the *'cunning-eyed Greeks'* she encountered seemed surprised at the sight of an *'unprotected Creole woman who took Constantinople so coolly'*; likewise the English and French, who expressed puzzlement at her presence there. Mary remained unfazed; she was well used to being an object of curiosity wherever she travelled; indeed, she accepted their stares *'as a compliment'* and even tolerated the intrusive inspection of Turkish women.[14]

While she was in Constantinople Mary picked up letters from Thomas Day at the Poste Restante, but they were hardly encouraging. *'He gave a very dreary account of Balaclava and of camp life'* but nevertheless he sent a list of additional stores she should obtain while still in Constantinople.[15] But before the *Hollander* departed for Smyrna, Mary organised a caique to convey her across the Bosporus to Florence Nightingale's hospital, located in the old Selimiya Barracks at Scutari. These had been handed over to the British military for conversion into a hospital when the Crimean campaign began. But the sight – and overwhelming stink – that had greeted Florence Nightingale and her first group of thirty-eight nurses when they arrived there on 4 November had been horrifying. In the overcrowded, filthy hospital – though one could barely describe it as such – she discovered the most primitive, verminous conditions. Disease and infection were rife, for the wounded, who had been lying there in rags, largely untended since the battles of Alma and Balaclava, were languishing in a pitiable state of squalor. Their wounds were suppurating and maggot-ridden, with old dirty dressings, if any at all; as a result, many had become gangrenous. On top of this, once at Scutari many men had contracted cholera or dysentery from the insanitary conditions.[16] Within a few days of arriving, Nightingale's team was overwhelmed with an influx of new wounded from the Battle of Inkerman. Between 17 December 1854 and 3 January alone, the hospital took in another 4,000 sick and wounded and men were dying at the rate of 50-60 a day.[17] That winter, November to March, around 5,000 of the sick and wounded at Scutari had died largely as a result of bad sanitation, septicaemia and cross infection – as Nightingale herself concluded after the war.[18] She herself was worn ragged trying to stay on top of a myriad of pressing issues: 'I am really cook, housekeeper, scavenger ... washerwoman, general dealer, store keeper,' she complained as the desperately needed stores took an age to arrive, held up by unnecessary and byzantine army bureaucracy.[19]

It took weeks of exhausting cleaning, scrubbing and reorganisation by the overworked team of women and medical orderlies to render the wards clean, refill mattresses with fresh straw, wash and organise bed-linen and put the inefficient kitchens into some kind of order, providing wholesome invalid food. Through it all Nightingale, who rose heroically to the task and was indomitable in her determination to alleviate the acute levels of suffering, proved herself to be an able and tough administrator who fought long and hard to cut through bureaucratic delays and obstruction in getting the supplies she so badly needed. Many of these in the end came from the public funds set up to assist the war wounded; even Queen Victoria dipped into her own private purse to send out supplies of creature comforts for the troops, including hand-sewn and knitted goods made by herself and her daughters.[20]

Mary Seacole never saw Scutari at its worst, therefore, but only after four months of relentless toil during which Florence Nightingale and her nurses had worn themselves ragged imposing levels of cleanliness and order. Ahead of her, as she walked up the hill from the landing stage, loomed this 'great dull-looking hospital', and it exuded an uncanny atmosphere of suffering that Mary sensed the moment she entered. The eerie silence struck her immediately. The hospital was full with *'long wards of sufferers, lying there so quiet and still. A rush of tears came to my eyes,'* she writes, but soon she was cheered to see a Jamaica acquaintance – *'an old 97th man – a Sergeant T who I had known in Kingston'* – among the walking wounded, who took her on a tour of the hospital and pointed out men who had previously been based at Up Park Camp.[21] Once again Mary was greeted with calls of *'Mother Seacole!'*, many from Irish soldiers, for the 97th was the Earl of Ulster's Regiment of Foot. She was deeply moved by their *'patient unmurmuring resignation'* and even now the desire some had, once they recovered, to go back to the front and *'have another "shy at the Rooshians"'*.[22] Only when she sailed to Crimea, they told Mary, she must take the troops plenty of vegetables, for the men were suffering terribly from scurvy – and eggs were extremely hard to come by.

As she stopped by the beds and chatted to the wounded, Mary's caring instinct inevitably kicked in: she could not resist *'the temptation of lending a helping hand here and there – replacing a slipped bandage, or easing a stiff one'*. But there was no escaping one troubling thought: there was so much suffering and pain here at Scutari – *'what must it not be at the scene of war?'* She was sure it would be far, far worse. It reinforced Mary's certainty that her place was not here, at Scutari, but at the front: *'I felt happy in the conviction that I must be useful three or four days nearer to their pressing wants than this.'*[23] This is an important statement of intent that is often overlooked in subsequent interpretations of the meeting between Mary Seacole and Florence Nightingale at Scutari, for it is often suggested that Nightingale turned down Mary's offer to nurse there. In fact, Mary made no such offer; once she had been rejected, it had never been her plan to try once more to be taken on to Nightingale's team. She wanted to do things her own way and use her nursing skills where they were most needed, in Crimea itself, and in tandem with running a store and catering services that would provide the income to support her endeavours and buy the medical supplies she needed.

Eventually Mary found herself at the cold and draughty northwest tower of the barracks that had been converted into barely adequate quarters for the female nursing staff and where the nuns and nurses were still enduring considerable privation and infestations of fleas and vermin. Here she presented her letter of introduction from Dr Forrest to Nightingale's administrative assistant, Mrs Selina Bracebridge, apologising in advance for intruding on Miss Nightingale, '*whose every moment is valuable*' as she well knew. Dr Forrest had apparently been so persuasive in his letter that Mary's request could not be refused by Mrs Bracebridge, who appeared to assume that Mary wished to volunteer at Scutari. Her response was brisk but polite: Bracebridge did not think there was any vacancy, to which Mary responded that she had come east '*to be of use somewhere*' but that she was '*bound for the front in a few days*'.[24] After half an hour's wait she was finally admitted to the presence of the sainted Nightingale.

Unfortunately, we only have Mary's account of what must have been an extraordinary encounter between two opinionated, fiercely independent, strong-minded women. There could have been no greater contrast between them: Seacole, warm, open and solicitous in her uniquely Jamaican way; Nightingale, guarded, frosty and with a clinical detachment that did not invite friendship. Her small, slight frame belied her strength of character, for there was no missing the '*keen enquiring expression*' on her face as she stood there sizing Mary up. '*What do you want, Mrs Seacole*,' she asked, '*anything that we can do for you? If it lies in my power, I shall be very happy.*'[25]

As it was late and Mary did not want to travel back in the dark to the *Hollander*, she asked for a bed for the night and offered to help with the sick in the meantime. Unfortunately there was no bed to be had with the nurses and nuns, whose sparsely furnished rooms were already extremely overcrowded. Nightingale instead offered Mary accommodation over in the washerwomen's quarters that had been organised by volunteer Lady Alicia Blackwood as a means of giving useful employment to the army wives left behind at Scutari when their men embarked for Crimea. The women were kind and accommodating, but not so the other occupants of the premises – the fleas – which tormented Mary for most of the night.[26]

Throughout her stay in Constantinople Mary makes no mention

of Sarah, but she does tell us that, before leaving, she hired a young Jewish Greek boy who had acted as her guide in the city. '*Jew Johnny*', as she refers to him, '*turned out to be the best and faithfullest servant I had in the Crimea*', but he is only mentioned in passing on one more occasion.[27] In the event, and despite more discouraging news from Mr Day, Mary sailed for Crimea, in the company of Johnny and Sarah on a cold and windswept day – probably 17 March 1855 – on the *Albatross*, a screw-powered British transport ship No. 69 built in 1850 at the Clyde shipyards. It was, she recalls, '*laden with cattle and commissariat officers*'; records show that the *Albatross* and its 240 head of cattle arrived in the crowded Crimean port of Balaclava on 19 March.[28]

Mary Seacole was fortunate to arrive at the '*dark, rock-bound coast*' of Crimea after the worst of a sub-zero Crimean winter had passed. The *Albatross* negotiated the narrow entrance channel with caution, into a '*small land-locked basin, so filled with shipping that their masts bend in the breeze like a wintry forest*'.[29] The harbour was in fact still recovering from the after-effects of a terrible hurricane the previous November that had destroyed twenty-one British ships in port, including the brand-new steamship *The Prince* loaded with long-awaited and desperately needed food and hospital supplies from England. Most of these ships had not yet been unloaded, when at 5 a.m. on the morning of 14 November, a hurricane-force wind, followed by torrential rain that rapidly turned to sleet and snow, had turned the harbour into a seething, roiling mass of foam in which the anchored ships swung and crashed back and forth against each other.[30] This continuous battering in the high winds had pulled many from their moorings, including *The Prince*, which was smashed against the rocks like matchwood; other vessels were pounded to pieces, sending tons and tons of food and medical supplies – all the winter clothing for the army, blankets, boots, and hay for the cavalry horses and mules – to the bottom of the harbour. Further out to sea supply ships were also torn from their anchors and sunk and their helpless crews drowned. The devastation after the storm had passed was a heartbreaking sight for the beleaguered troops

so desperate for warm clothes and fresh food. Balaclava harbour
was choked with dismasted ships, drowned men and animals and
floating cases of water-soaked supplies. Morale after the storm had
sunk to an all-time low as the continuing desperate shortages of food
and winter clothing brought yet more suffering and death upon the
emaciated men of the British Army and their animals camped up on
the plateau outside Sevastopol.[31] Throughout the winter the rank
and file had been reduced to subsisting on mouldy biscuit, salt pork
and raw green coffee – which they had no firewood to roast. Scurvy,
dysentery, frostbite and hypothermia were rife.

Among the extraordinary collection of photographs taken in Crimea
by British photographer Roger Fenton, there is by a great stroke of
luck one of the *Albatross* moored at the Cattle Pier at Balaclava
shortly after its arrival in March 1855. Here it is marked No. 69;
Mary might even have still been on board when this was taken.[32]
Fenton, who famously captured scenes in the British camp and at the
Siege of Sevastopol in Crimea during the war, had arrived shortly
before her, on board the *Hecla*. Like Mary, he remained in port on
board ship for several days until accommodation could be found for
him, and one cannot help wondering whether the two civilians might

have encountered each other on the wharf. Fenton's correspondence is, inevitably, silent on the subject of Mary Seacole, despite his noting that everyone in Crimea wanted him to take their photograph (something one would imagine Mary would have enjoyed). Disappointingly, during his photographic forays on the Crimean Peninsula Fenton never ventured to Mrs Seacole's establishment but concentrated, in the main, on photographing the officers in camp and only a very few army wives.[33]

For now, Mary found herself at Balaclava with a pile of stores that Thomas Day had accompanied to Balaclava separately on a fruit clipper, the *Nonpareil*, and which needed urgently to be offloaded.[34] The *Nonpareil* had been ordered out of the harbour to make way for other incoming ships, but there were no warehouses on the wharf where she and Day could safely store their goods; Mary was therefore obliged, with considerable trepidation, to approach Admiral Edward Boxer, who was in charge of the port, for permission for the ship to remain a little longer while they unloaded their supplies. Boxer had a fearful reputation for a blustering bad temper and so Mary took Captain Cospatrick Hamilton of the Naval Brigade along for moral support.

Boxer had worked hard since January to re-establish order after the devastation of the hurricane and to impose a system on the entirely haphazard way in which ships were moored. He created a continuous line of wharf frontage with rocks and rubble from the hills behind the port, in order that thousands of troops and horses could be embarked and disembarked daily. Cranes had been brought in by the railway company to transfer heavy guns and mortars from lighters to the railway trucks to take them up to the front lines. Ships were moored in tiers 'with as much regularity as if in the London docks', allowing a working channel in the centre to ensure the smooth transition of ships in and out twenty-four hours a day amid 'nearly two hundred vessels of all nations, with a floating population of several thousand souls'.[35] When Boxer proceeded to growl at Mary in response to her request, she reminded him that she had known his son in the West Indies.[36] Boxer relented and the supplies were offloaded*, but all Mary and Thomas Day could do was stack them under a suspended tarpaulin on the quayside and hope they would not be spoiled – or worse, pilfered by the light-fingered boat-men working in the port – Greeks, Maltese and Turks – whom they were obliged to hire to help ferry the stores ashore from the *Albatross* and the *Nonpareil* and of whom Mary was very wary. Young Johnny was given the somewhat futile task of watching over the stores at night and intercepting attempts at pilfering. It was a losing battle; the *'thievery in this little out-of-the-way port was something mar-vellous.'*[37] And the thieves themselves were at constant war among each other, as Mary observes with wry humour; without the army authorities to keep control of the situation, *'no life would have been safe in Balaclava, with its population of villains of every nation.'*[38]

Meanwhile, the *Albatross* was about to sail back to England and Mary had to find alternative accommodation for herself, Johnny and Sarah. She did so on board ship No. 45, the *Medora*, which was one of four transports damaged in the November gale that had been dismasted on Boxer's orders to be used for storing ammunition.† The sooner Mary's army friends up in camp knew of her arrival, the sooner she knew she might be able to enlist their help and their custom. She had already set up an improvised shop under the awning where her goods had been offloaded, where the navvies of the Land Transport Corps were soon visiting her, not just for supplies, but also for her medicines.[39] She meanwhile wasted no time in paying a local man to take a letter to her friends of the 97th Regiment based up in the Light Division camp just off the Vorontsov Road approaching Sevastopol. She also sent word to other acquaintances: Captain Sir William Peel of the Naval Brigade, who was commanding officer of Hamilton's ship, HMS *Diamond*‡ and Major General Sir John Campbell in command of the 1st Brigade of the 4th Division – both

---

*   By June, however, the indefatigable admiral was dead, a victim of the cholera.
†   The gunpowder in the *Medora* was subsequently removed to another ship and it was then used as a coal depot.
‡   Peel (1824-58) was the third son of former Prime Minister Sir Robert Peel. He was wounded during the Assault on the Redan on 18 June 1855, after which Cospatrick Hamilton took over command of HMS *Diamond*.

of whom she had known in Jamaica. She was particularly touched when her favourite young officer of the 97th, Hedley Vicars, *'whose kind face had so often lighted up my old house in Kingston'* and who had arrived in Crimea the previous November, immediately responded to her note. He rode down to Balaclava from the Light Division camp and *'came to take me by the hand in this out-of-the-way corner of the world'*. Mary was delighted to discover that, since his riotous younger days in Jamaica, Vicars had recently experienced a Damascene conversion and had embraced a rampant Evangelism. It would be all too brief a reunion, for only a few days later he was killed during a night-time engagement with a Russian sortie on the siege lines outside Sevastopol.[40] Copies of a posthumously published tract by Vicars, 'Walking with God Before Sebastopol', would soon be made available by the Soldiers' Mission and happily thrust into people's hands by Mary at her establishment up at Spring Hill, which, slowly but surely, was finally now under construction.[41] A posthumous hagiography, *Memorials of Captain Hedley Vicars,* depicting him as the archetype of the Good Christian Soldier, was the biggest bestseller in Crimean War literature for many years afterwards.

*

When she left Panama to volunteer for the war effort, Mary had planned to invest her *'carefully husbanded funds'* of some £800 made during her time in Central America in setting up a 'British Hotel' in Crimea – as per the advertisement she had proudly placed in the British press before leaving England.[42] Arriving in Crimea ahead of her, Thomas Day had already begun negotiations with the British authorities – in the person of Major General Richard Airey, Quartermaster General at Balaclava, for permission to construct 'a store, a hotel and a dwelling house'. Thanks to the discovery of a letter 'hidden away in a large box of unindexed letters and reports in the National Archives'* by Dr Mike Hinton of the Crimean War Research Society, we have a crucial original source describing the Day & Seacole collaboration. It was Day who had recced a site for their joint enterprise, at a spot Mary later named Spring Hill (after the freshwater spring nearby). But its location would not be, as Mary had originally hoped, 'at the end of the Light Cavalry's camp', which was about a mile further to the northeast of where she finally set up shop.[43] Such an advantageous position would no doubt have catered to Mary's preferred officer clientele of the Dragoons and Hussars of the Light Brigade. It was, however, refused; perhaps because the army authorities deemed the availability of alcohol so close to camp as being undesirable.[44]

In his letter of 23 March, Day described how 'I have recently arrived from England with a cargo of goods adapted for the supply of necessaries and comforts to Her Majesty's forces now before Sebastopol, and there being no accommodation at this port for warehousing goods, I have no alternative but to land and convey them some distance inland.'[45] He went on to explain how he had inspected the line of communication between Balaclava and the main army encampment and had rejected the idea of setting up shop at the busy sutler's settlement located at a place called Kadikoi about a mile north of Balaclava, anticipating that the hot Crimean summer might

---

*   It is precisely in places such as this where we can still hope that documents referring to Mary Seacole during the Crimean War may yet turn up.

bring water shortages there, not to mention other 'inconveniences'. Cannily, Day had chosen a spot further up the route of the newly constructed railway line (which was completed as far as the depot at the Col de Balaclava by 26 March) 'to what appears to me a more salubrious locality'. Not only was it a healthier spot, away from the dirt, overcrowding and already notorious licentiousness at Kadikoi, where drinking and whoring were rife, it also had 'the advantage of greater proximity to the troops whose wants my establishment is intended to supply, namely a site near the stationary engine, about a mile beyond Kadikoi in the vicinity of a rill of clear water, which is my principal inducement for selecting the spot.'[46]

Another unspoken inducement was the presence of the civilian Land Transport Corps based near the stationary engine, who were better paid than the army rank and file and thus more likely to spend money at the Seacole establishment. This was, after all, a business venture.

Mary Seacole's storehouse has, till now, been variously described as an amalgam of sheet-iron, wood, and flotsam and jetsam salvaged from hurricane-damaged ships in the harbour. But Thomas Day makes clear that he had arranged with Lieutenant Colonel West, commander of the 21st Regiment, to purchase 'an iron house' – i.e. one of the prefabricated buildings sent out by sea from England – and that he was 'in treaty for two more with the supercargo of the *Ann Mclean*' – pending approval by the commandant at Balaclava, Lieutenant Colonel Harding. Day then went on to describe in detail the complex of buildings that he and Mary envisaged erecting at Spring Hill: 'Three iron houses, one to be occupied as a store, one as an hotel, and the other as a dwelling house with such wooden outhouses, stabling, etc. as may be required as appurtenances to the main building.'

There would also be a vegetable garden of about half an acre to the rear of the buildings. He concluded by enclosing a list of the goods he had brought with him on the *Nonpareil* for sale, and a circular detailing the hotel that 'my friend Mrs Seacole wishes to establish'.[47] Word was in fact already circulating about Mary's intention to 'set up a hotel in the heights [above Balaclava] ... fitted up for the accommodation of such invalid officers as have not sufficient leave to enable them to quit this port'. If this had been Mary's original intention – to set up a hotel at Balaclava and a store further up near the front lines – the hotel certainly did not materialise. Other contemporaries noted that Mary had rather counted on being able to do this, in anticipation of 'a liberal share of patronage when excursion visitors come out to the siege in the summer'. This was indeed the case: battleground tours became a feature in the summer of 1855, with even intrepid ladies in crinolines signing up for visits to the Crimean battle sites.[48]*

Thomas Day's letter was circulated among the top brass and various responses were written on it, beginning with Major General Airey, who was brutal: 'This man will probably be ruined,' he wrote. Lord Raglan was consulted and suggested, 'I think he had better come higher up' – i.e. nearer the British camp. But Airey worried that if the establishment were any closer to the infantry camps 'he may attract fire.' And then Airey added a comment that proved to be a concern shared by other officers in Crimea, and even Florence Nightingale herself over at Scutari: 'Altogether I am opposed to his application. I see no advantage in a house of call [i.e. public house]. Men get drunk.'[49] Major General Jones countered by having no objection to a 'sutler under proper regulations establishing himself within the lines', especially as a component part of a division. Airey was advised to give Day permission for his project, 'but without consenting to all he asks for with respect to such houses' – a proviso that no doubt put paid to Mary's ambitions for a hotel. And Day must understand that he would of course undertake this project fully aware of the 'risks of being dispossessed on military grounds at any moment'. He must thus ensure that his site did not in any way interfere with the railway lines or transports to and from the front lines.[50] Further correspondence in the file confirms that Mr

---

* Both male and female tourists – nicknamed Travelling Gents and Lady Amateurs – ventured to Crimea even while the siege was still on. There was a considerable influx in the spring of 1856, taking advantage of the £5 tours by boat from Constantinople.

James Beatty, the chief engineer of the Crimea Railway, had been approached to assist in the transportation of the two iron houses, made by a Glasgow firm named Robertson & Lister, from the *Ann Mclean* in Balaclava harbour to the site at Spring Hill. Presumably the purchase of the third iron house – perhaps intended for Mary's British Hotel – fell through. The name is, as can be seen, a misnomer; for the sake of accuracy Mary's premises will be referred to throughout this narrative by the far more popular sobriquet used by the troops in Crimea of 'Mrs Seacole's'.*

But we run ahead of ourselves; it is March 1855, it is cold and wet and Mary is making do in primitive circumstances on the wharf at Balaclava. She is going to have to sit it out here for at least another six weeks before Spring Hill is ready for occupation, struggling back up the side of the *Medora* each night in her heavy skirts to go to bed. She took it all with good humour: her berth on board, she writes, *'would not altogether have suited a delicate female with weak nerves'*, for she, Johnny and Sarah *'slept over barrels of gunpowder and tons of cartridges, with the by no means impossible contingency of their prematurely igniting and giving us no time to say our prayers before launching us into eternity.'*[51]

---

* It was also referred to as 'Mother Seacole's', 'The Half-Way House' (halfway to the nearest infantry camps), 'The Iron House' or even 'The Iron House near the Col', but rarely as the British Hotel. It was only really Mary herself who used that rather grandiose name and some later postwar memoirs by officers.

CHAPTER 15

A 'TEA-SHED' AT BALACLAVA

When Mary Seacole embarked on her voyage to Crimea, she was in her fiftieth year. Up until her arrival at Balaclava in March 1855, we have effectively had only her version of the events that shaped her life and have been feeling our way tentatively down a long, dark corridor of factual uncertainty. And then, after a long period of semi-darkness, once we are in Crimea the door opens and the light floods in, for we are blessed with a wealth of contemporaneous material about her exploits during the war and just after. For the next three years Mary's indomitable, idiosyncratic, unforgettable personality takes centre stage – not just in her own words, but in those of others who knew her at first hand, as well as in the accounts of her to be found in the contemporary press.

The primary source material at our disposal does, however, dent a popular myth: that Mary arrived in Crimea and immediately strode off to rescue the wounded, single-handed, from the battlefield. It is also a myth – and one that has gained a lot of unsubstantiated currency in recent years – that she constructed and ran a hospital there. She did not. However, forced to kick her heels at Balaclava while Thomas Day oversaw the construction of their premises at Spring Hill, Mary Seacole, being the determined and active woman she was, made herself useful. Indeed, as she readily admits, she *waited for no permission* to do so.[1] With her warm Jamaican generosity, she started serving up refreshments and much-needed care and sympathy to the wounded waiting on the sick wharf at the head of Balaclava harbour that had been set aside for embarking them on ships for Florence Nightingale's hospital at Scutari.

It is likely that in so doing Mary responded to the efforts already being made by Captain Derriman of HMS *Caradoc*. He had received a specific request in late January from the British commander Lord Raglan, to 'establish at Balaclava a place where the sick and wounded brought down from the front would be under cover, and where they could be supplied with hot tea and coffee.' Derriman had set up a framework of spars, covered over with awning from the *Caradoc* as an improvised 'tea shed'. Mary followed his example, as Douglas Arthur Reid in his Crimean memoirs many years later confirmed: 'Mrs Seacole … out of the goodness of her heart and at her own expense supplied hot tea to the poor sufferers while they were waiting to be lifted into the boats.' He adds that she 'did not spare herself if she could do any good to the suffering soldiers. In rain and snow, in storm and tempest, day after day she was at her self-chosen post, with her stove and kettle, in any shelter she could find, brewing tea for all who wanted it, and they were many. Sometimes more than 200 sick would be embarked on one day, but Mrs Seacole was always equal to the occasion.'[2]

Mary makes no mention of Captain Derriman, perhaps wishing to appear to be the sole ministering angel on the wharf. Certainly she was able to go one better than his offering of a 'bowl of hot coffee or tea and a biscuit' with slices of her home-made sponge cakes, baked on board the *Medora* with eggs, so hard to find at Balaclava, that they were specially '*brought from Constantinople*'. The wounded '*liked the cake, poor fellows, better than anything else*', she recalled; '*perhaps because it tasted of "home"*'.[3] She also naturally enough '*eased the stiff dressings*' of those wounded groaning in pain on their pallets on the quayside. They were grateful for the unexpected touch of a woman's hand; some in their delirium imagined she was their wife or their mother. Mary made a point of not entirely neglecting her feminine appearance either, wearing what would be her signature colours in Crimea: '*a favourite yellow dress, and blue bonnet,*

with the red ribbons'.[4] No doubt Mary was assisted in her efforts
by Sarah, for we have an extremely rare sighting of them together,
in a dispatch from Balaclava. It was published in the *New York
Tribune*, one of the largest and oldest American dailies at the time.
Interestingly, it predates any mention of Mary in the British press,
which, bar one or two rare exceptions, did not begin mentioning her
until September that year.

Entitled 'Excursion to Sebastopol: British Camp Before Sevastopol
Thursday April 26', the writer describes how 'We fell in with a black
woman and her daughter all the way from Panama' – this in itself
being helpful confirmation that Mary and Sarah had indeed travelled
straight from Panama to England and not from Jamaica:

> Mrs Seacole came to Balaclava to put up a tavern for travellers or
> the officers. She had just arrived and was landing her goods and
> chattels on the shore over the spring of the port and opposite a
> sad display of mud – the only appearance of the article which we
> any where saw during our visit. Mrs Seacole, (perhaps I should
> spell her name more correctly with two a's for she was quite black
> enough*) disdained the name of Aunt Sally, and daughter that of
> Cousin Lucy, and with offended dignity told me that she knew
> Governor this and Colonel that, and a whole host of Majors and
> Captains, in ordinary, all from the States, and that she liked the
> Americans hugely.[5]

This account confirms how Mary is never shy in drawing on the
names of former clients and acquaintances in promoting her own
status as a Black woman in the company of whites; although she
carefully leaves out any mention of the racism she had suffered at
the hands of the 'Yankees' in Panama.

Another valuable eyewitness account of Mary at this time,

---

* A crude pun on sea kale – a dark-green plant of the cabbage family that grows wild on
seashores. 'Aunt Sally' was a disparaging American term for an elderly Black woman;
it was later the title of an American anti-slavery tract. 'Cousin Lucy' is presumably
another Americanism used to refer to Black women at the time.

published in the *Argus* in Melbourne, Australia in 1857, confirms that having provided herself with 'a large supply of bandages, lint, styptic and other curative appliances', she spent 'the first six or eight weeks after her arrival in the Crimea devoting herself to the men on the sick wharf, at the head of Balaclava Harbour'. The article, clearly written by someone with personal knowledge of Mary in Crimea, goes on to say that she

> made it her business, with the sanction and approval of the Admiral of the Port and the Military Commandant, to receive the disabled men, wearied and bruised by their seven miles' journey over the worst roads and by the worst conveyances – to shift and renew the bandages, which were frequently displaced by the accidents of travel – to chafe and warm their half-frozen limbs – to administer warm tea or refreshing diluent drinks to the fasting and fainting and to cheer the desponding with kind and hopeful words.[6]

Further on the article states that its author was one of Mary's 'nearest neighbours for upwards of a year', thus enabling a possible, and rare, identification (the vast majority of newspaper reports on Mary being anonymous). At Spring Hill, mustered with the Land Transport Corps from June 1855 to July 1856, which was based nearby, was one Major John William Cox, who is probably this eyewitness of Mary's many acts of kindness during that period.[7]

Of particular significance is the fact that Cox notes that Mary offered medical assistance with the full approval of 'the medical officers, who fully appreciated the value of so efficient a coadjutor'.[8] Mary would not have been able to operate in the war zone without official army approval and this fact alone suggests a degree of respect for her nursing skills, not to mention her usefulness as an unofficial army sutler, able to offer a ready supply of goods and catering services at a time when the Commissariat was notorious for its inefficiency. What is more – and it is a fact that intensely irritated Florence Nightingale – Mary had the support in her endeavours of none other than Sir John Hall, Principal Medical Officer in Crimea, 'to whom she applied when her own stores were getting low, [and who] gave a general order that Mrs Seacole should be supplied with everything she might require from his department – an order that was acted on until the end of the war.'[9] Hall was a thorn in Nightingale's side for most of the war, during which they had frequent clashes over control of the nurses. Nightingale's sister Parthenope later noted that, according to Florence, 'Dr Hall looked over her [Mary's] medicine chest & gave her his sanction to prescribe to mark the difference with F, i.e. that he extended his protection to Seacole & opposed F to his utmost.'[10]

It is important to acknowledge the significance of this endorsement by Sir John. For it not only explains why Mary Seacole appeared to have carte blanche to operate in Crimea as a freelancer, but it also confirms Nightingale's resentment of what she perceived as Seacole's meddling in her own medical domain of nursing. Indeed, so implacably hostile was the highly controlling Nightingale to Mary Seacole operating outside her official jurisdiction as Lady Superintendent of Nurses, that when she later set up two hospitals in Crimea, she 'had the greatest difficulty in repelling Mrs Seacole's advances and in preventing association between her and my nurses'. For Nightingale, such fraternisation was 'absolutely out of the question'.[11]

From the outset, therefore, Florence Nightingale resisted all and any 'rivalry' between her own nursing establishment in Crimea – which comprised the General Hospital at Balaclava and the Castle Hospital on the heights above it – over which she had jurisdiction, and the ad hoc drop-in clinic operated by Mary Seacole at Spring Hill.[12] So much so, that when Nightingale collapsed during a visit to the peninsula in mid-May 1855 (possibly suffering from brucellosis), she refused an offer of nursing care from Mary, despite being ill with fever at Balaclava for ten days. 'She wanted to quack me', Nightingale told Parthenope after the war, the bluntness of this rejection implying her antipathy towards Mary's holistic Jamaican remedies.[13]

Although there is no official army confirmation of Sir John Hall's approval of Mary Seacole's methods, we can imply a degree of approval tangentially. In 1817 Sir John (born 1795) had been sent to the West Indies as an army hospital assistant. During his time there he 'served through the whole of two dreadful epidemic visitations of yellow fever, which occurred in Jamaica in 1819 and 1825'. He himself nearly died of an attack of yellow fever and his health was 'so impaired during the latter epidemic that he was compelled to return to England in 1827 to recover'. By that time he had been pro-moted to Assistant Surgeon to the Forces in the West Indies. After recuperating, Hall returned to Jamaica in December 1828, and went back again in 1832 as Surgeon to the 33rd Regiment. In all he served twelve years at the Port Royal station on the outskirts of Kingston. During that time it is more than likely that he encountered the herbal remedies of the Jamaican doctresses – and may even have encoun-tered Mary's mother – during which time he developed a degree of respect for their nursing skills in the treatment of the enteric disease that was currently so prevalent in Crimea.[14]

By the time Mary left the wharf at Balaclava, even the gruff Admiral Boxer had come to pay her a visit and thank her: '*I am glad to see you here, old lady, among these poor fellows*,' he told her.[15]* Mary had not yet got close to the front lines but already had witnessed scenes of heartbreaking suffering that prompted even '*rough bearded men*' to '*stand by and cry like the softest-hearted women*'. But all was not entirely grim sadness; one day she heard a voice shout, '*Why as I live, if this ain't Aunty Seacole, of Jamaica!*' The wounded man, who had lost a leg, was one of the crew of HMS *Alarm* that had been stationed in Kingston '*a few years back*'.[16] Such enthusiastic welcomes from soldiers she had known in Jamaica must have been more than enough to reassure Mary of her decision to travel out to Crimea.

By mid-May of 1855 Mary was finally established up at Spring Hill, although building work would go on until September, by when

---

* Quite why virtually all the officers of the British Army persisted in referring to the vigorous 49-year-old Mary as 'old' is puzzling.

The Times would report that the iron store house was now complemented 'with wooden sheds and outlying tributaries'.[17] (Mary in
fact states that her premises were never completed; when they left
a year later, the storehouse still had no shutters.)[18] Until then Mary
repeatedly went down to Balaclava begging for materials and help
in the construction, eventually hiring two English sailors and two
Turkish carpenters – the latter thanks to the help of General Omar
Pasha, commander of the Turkish forces camped near her at Spring
Hill. Regrettably, Mary complains that his men turned out to be
*deliberate, slow and indolent, breaking off into endless interrup-
tions for the sacred duties of eating and praying*. Omar Pasha later
moved camp to Kamara but his kindnesses towards Mary continued,
with regular gifts of food, and frequent visits to practise his English
and drink Mary's champagne (in so doing turning a blind eye to his
religion).[19]

When he had time, Thomas Day – described as 'a big Englishman
like a navvy' but also so 'mild' and 'unassuming' that he gets barely
a mention from anyone – assisted in the running of the storehouse.[20]
He seems to have spent much of his time, however, travelling back
and forth to Balaclava, troubleshooting over the transportation of
supplies into the port, and rarely returning to Spring Hill before
nightfall. He was also busy importing horses – of which there was
a shortage in Crimea – to sell to the army. This left Mary having to
depend, for the running of the store, on *'two black servants, Jew
Johnny, and my own reputation for determination and courage'*.
Sarah, alas, does not get a mention.[21]

Spring Hill was a lonely, even desolate spot, without tree cover and
exposed to the elements. Standing out as it did in the wilderness of
the Crimean plain, it was roughly two and a quarter miles north of
Balaclava, with the front lines four and a half miles further up. The
storehouse was about a mile to the west of the stationary engines
that were the terminus of the cables that winched the railway wagons
up the tracks from Kadikoi. An all-weather road to serve the army
camps, built by the civil engineer William Doyne, had replaced the
earlier French road and went out from Kadikoi to the east, right past

Mrs Seacole's and north towards the siege lines at Sevastopol. The commander Lord Raglan's HQ was located at the Col de Balaclava a mile and a half further up the road.[22] So the site was well positioned and accessible for troops coming down from the camps higher up. War artist William Simpson made a very rough sketch of 'Mrs Seacoal's' in 1855.[23] It also appeared on a couple of army wartime maps and was even quoted in General Orders as a point of reference, ensuring it would become a well-known landmark on the peninsula – a welcome refuge to many a tired and hungry man, as well as to the walking sick and wounded who went there in droves to solicit Mary's medical help.[24]

Lady Alicia Blackwood, who in the spring of 1856 came to Crimea on a one month leave of absence from Scutari with her husband, the Rev. James Stevenson Blackwood, who had been appointed army chaplain for the hospitals of Constantinople and Scutari, drew the only other image we have, though it is a very distant one. But it does at least locate Mary's premises – just discernible on the far extreme left – in relation to her nearest neighbours, the Rev. Charles Josiah Hort (chaplain to the Land Transport Corps*) at Zebra Vicarage and the hut of Major William Cox, supervisor of the LTC, where he lived with his wife.[25]

Lady Alicia described Mary's storehouse as 'a perfect Omnibus shop'; and indeed Mary prided herself on the range of goods on offer on 'its counters, closets and shelves – you might get everything at

---

* Hereafter referred to as the LTC. This drawing was made April/May 1856. Hort was appointed chaplain to the LTC on 24 February 1856 so was not in occupation when Mary first arrived.

Mother Seacole's, from an anchor down to a needle' – not to mention 'all sorts of eatables'. In their diaries and letters home soldiers talk variously of stopping off to buy a kettle, cigars, tins of soup, bottled fruit, butter, onions and potatoes; the quality of Mary's goods was better than at Kadikoi, they said.[26]*

Close to the storehouse Thomas Day had two small wooden houses erected as sleeping accommodation for himself, and for Mary and Sarah. There were also *'outhouses for the servants'* – 'Jew Johnny', and two Black West Indian cooks, the latter suddenly appear out of nowhere in the Crimean section of Mary's narrative without any explanation of how they got there. We must assume they travelled out from Jamaica specially, or had been with Mary in Panama and had followed her there. We sadly have no way of knowing; but it is good to acknowledge the presence of Francis, who is at least named, and the other may have been Mac, who was with Mary in Panama. In any event, they were consigned along with 'Jew Johnny' to an outhouse where they *'slept among the flour barrels'* and were plagued by rats. The Crimean rats were a prodigious breed: *'they had the appetites of London aldermen and were as little dainty as hungry schoolboys'*. Poor Francis was attacked and bitten by them on several occasions and threatened to quit. Colonel Drummond of the Coldstream Guards sent down his cat Pinkie from the 1st Division camp to try to deal with the problem, but Pinkie thought otherwise and kept running away.[27]

Across the yard was a separate canteen for the *'soldiery'* – the rank and file, who, in line with military convention, were segregated from the officers. A stables, a pigsty and a yard for the livestock added to the menagerie of horses and mules – though protecting these from endless thievery was a losing battle and Mary was forced to hire two local boys to keep an eye on the cavalry officers' horses when they tied them up outside the store, or they would be stolen.[28] She paid

---

* An article published in the Jamaican *Gleaner* on 17 August 1910 suspected that Mary might also have been 'a smuggler on a small scale, getting for the soldiers the things that were forbidden by the officers' – thus accounting in part for the huge popularity of her store in Crimea.

a man five shillings to watch their livestock overnight but still *'our losses were very great'*: twenty horses, four mules, eighty goats and too many sheep, pigs and chickens to number. The army, too, were suffering theft of livestock on an industrial scale. What the locals did not steal, the harsh winter weather killed.[29] The greatest loss to Mary was that of her black mare Angelina, *'for which Mr Day had given thirty guineas, and which carried me beautifully'*. The stolen horse later turned up at Mary's store ridden by a naval officer who had bought it in good faith. She only had Angelina back for a fortnight before she was stolen again. Mary battled with constant pilfering inside her store too – especially by the French Zouaves, whose baggy trousers *'could accommodate a well-grown baby or a pound of sausages equally well'*, not to mention pounds of tea and coffee. All in all, the *'Crimean thievery reduced us to woeful straits'*; even the washing they sent away – clothing and table linen – was stolen.[30]

Nevertheless, such would be the *'comfort and order'* that Mary worked hard to install at her storehouse-cum-restaurant that it would rapidly become the preserve of the officer class, as well as gentlemen tourists who arrived later – all of whom would pay high prices for Mary's brandy, champagne and cigars, and refreshing glasses of sangria in summer.[31] Until then, with the weather turning warm, the culinary delights of Mrs Seacole's had already been discovered by several British war correspondents. As William Howard Russell – already highly critical of the unprofessionalism of his colleagues – noted in a letter to his editor John Delane: 'The *Morning Advertiser* is represented, I understand, by a Mr Keane, who chiefly passes his time in preparing cooling drinks at Mrs. Seacole's.' It was an ominous sign; for Mr Keane and his associates, along with many officers, as was the common practice of their class, would soon be running up large bills on the tab that would ultimately contribute to the ruination of the warm-hearted and trusting Mrs Seacole.[32]

CHAPTER 16

'A GOOD MOTHER, DOCTOR AND NURSE TO ALL'

In the Crimean section of her *Wonderful Adventures*, Mary Seacole vividly conveys the warmth and affection accorded her by the soldiers to whom she became a very welcome source of hot dinners, womanly compassion and medical care. This is not to mention the many with whom she became friends – friendships that continued after the war.

But how was she, as a Black woman, perceived by the white British military who encountered her in the war zone? Black people were certainly in evidence in Britain by the mid-nineteenth century, especially in urban areas, but the average soldier had probably never encountered such an extraordinary individual as Mary Seacole, for she broke all the conventional expectations of the colonial subject as submissive and self-effacing. Simply being there, as a self-starting, independent woman rather than one of the on-the-strength army wives, was a shock to the Victorian psyche, but Mary's presence as a Black woman was a unique first. Contemporary newspapers and other accounts of her indicate that within about a couple of months of her arrival up at Spring Hill, word had circulated throughout the Crimean Peninsula that a Jamaican woman operating as a sutler, a pharmacist and doctor-cum-nurse had installed herself not far from the Col de Balaclava. Beyond the inevitable expressions of surprise, there was an extraordinary degree of acceptance offered towards

Mary compared to then prevailing British attitudes to race and colour, due no doubt to the fact that some of the troops had already encountered her in Jamaica.

Descriptions of Mary and references to her skin colour by soldiers in Crimea that were subsequently published were often openly warm, if euphemistic, speaking of her 'dark features quite radiant with delight', or her 'flat face full of good sound common sense and knowledge of the world'. There were references too to her size: the motherly Mrs Seacole was a 'dear fat bundle of clothes with a smiling dark countenance'.[1] Others identified her by her West Indian ethnicity: 'the active Creole'; 'a kind-hearted Jamaican Mulatto'.[2] Sometimes the darkness of Mary's skin tone was emphasised: she was as 'black as the ace of spades' or 'black as any coal'.[3] Occasionally she was referred to as a 'negress', though Staff Surgeon Calder who did so was quick to qualify that she was 'not of African type'.[4]

Several drew attention to the bright primary colours Mary always wore and how on great occasions in camp she 'appeared in the brightest of ribbons' on her bonnet. She loved vivid colours, for they reminded her of her Jamaican roots and the costumes of the music and dance festival known as Junkanoo, held at Christmas and New Year, when rival factions paraded in the blue of Scotland and the red of England. Her variegated ribbons were a proud emblem of Jamaica, Britain, Empire and Queen. Some of the soldiers shared a degree of amusement at her quirky appearance: one army medic talked of her 'hair gathered up in a kind of queue' that 'came out below a broad hat, like a seaman's, and gave her a peculiar appearance'. 'Who, in the name of Crimean incredibilities, is that?' exclaimed Chaplain John Boudier in disbelief when he first caught sight of her.[5] There are, inevitably and regrettably, some remarks that play to the Victorian mindset of racial inferiority: 'I do not feel sure she is any thing more than a monkey or chimpanzee,' wrote Colonel Edward Goulburn of the Grenadier Guards. 'Is she anything like a woman in her conversation and manners? Is she not a sort of giraffe?' asked another officer. One news report, adhering to then-current thinking on 'the Negro' as a distinctly inferior species, alluded to Mary as 'an amusing specimen of the adaptability to circumstances of the darker species of the genus *homo*'.[6]

Most of these views of Mary came from war correspondents or officers writing home; but in referring to Mary's broader skills many were generous in acknowledging her usefulness to the army. Mrs Seacole was, wrote Rev. Boudier, 'Quite a Caleb Quotem [jack of all trades] in her way' – a 'grand purveyor to the army, doctor of medicine, cook, confectioner, and nurse'. But it was undoubtedly the common man who appreciated Mary for what she really was – a caregiver and Good Samaritan: 'While the soldier looks to Miss Nightingale – the navvy swears by Mrs. Seacole, of Spring-hill,' wrote special correspondent Nicholas Woods of the *Morning Herald*, drawing attention to the one group above all others who had much to thank Mary for and who did so, loud and clear.[7]

There is no doubt that during Mary Seacole's sixteen months in Crimea, it was the men of the LTC and their replacement the Army Works Corps who formed the backbone of her clientele and who never forgot what she did for them. True, officers came down from camp to buy her good wine and cigars and enjoy her cooking, and Mary certainly offered medical help and advice if they solicited it. But unlike the more glamorous fighting men of the army, the two corps of navvies were based much closer to Spring Hill and seemed to have an inherent distrust of the army hospitals. At Mary's store they could get all the *'sick-comforts and nourishing food'* that they needed.[8]

The LTC, under the command of officers who had served in India, had arrived in February 1855 to take charge of the transportation requirements of the British Army in Crimea, including the construction of the railway from Balaclava docks to the camp before Sevastopol. Until this was done the task of transporting food, supplies and ammunition up to the front lines was a slow and grinding one using pack animals. The men of the LTC were recruited in England in December 1854, while agents for the government were sent on ahead across Asia Minor to purchase pack animals for their use. (It may well be that Thomas Day saw the LTC as a ready market for the horses he was importing.) More popularly referred to as navvies, these men were as famous for their hard labour as their hard drinking, and notorious also for their lack of discipline. 'Earn it like donkeys and spend it like asses' was a popular metaphor attributed to them, for they were paid five shillings a day in addition to soldiers' rations and, being so much better off than them, aroused resentment among the regular troops.[9]

But they earned it. Working day, and night, on inhospitable open terrain in all weathers, the men of the LTC built the railway up to Kadikoi in record time, immediately greatly ameliorating the supply of the front lines. By the time Mary arrived at Spring Hill in mid-May, the navvies, having completed most of their main work on the railway, were becoming increasingly truculent and difficult to manage. By August they had been largely sent home, and replaced by a newly created, 1,000-strong civilian battalion, the Army Works Corps. The AWC, split into gangs of twenty-five, carried out various engineering and building projects, such as constructing a new road alongside the railway line from Kadikoi to the British infantry camps, digging sanitation drains and trenches, erecting temporary storage sheds and huts for the troops and generally supporting the siege lines outside Sevastopol.

Mary Seacole could not have arrived in Crimea at a more opportune time, for in March 1855 enteric disease was taking a terrible toll on the navvies. They seemed to be more susceptible to falling sick due to the exhausting work they had to perform in all weathers, often underfed and in wet clothes, and their camp was also in an extremely unsanitary state. Cholera in particular wreaked havoc among the LTC during May-August 1855; the death rate running at 34 per cent, a considerably greater ratio – two and a half times – than in the army generally. Ninety-eight men died of cholera during that time; although it had receded by the winter of 1855, other fevers took its place to continue inflicting many deaths on the LTC and the AWC.[10] A Sanitary Commission sent out to Crimea to inspect the army's medical facilities noted that many of the men 'were puny, ill nourished, and badly developed', and that a large proportion 'would not have been accepted as recruits'. Significantly, 'many bore the marks of intemperance and bad habits'.[11]

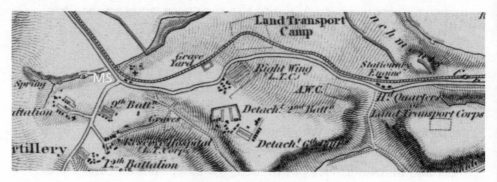

Courtesy of Dr David Jones

In this campaign map, Mrs Seacole's (MS) can be seen in relation to the Right Wing of the LTC camp and the AWC camp. Both appear to be due east of her along the road past Spring Hill but in fact the direction was due north and the map should be viewed on the vertical (a confusion that occurs in other maps showing this area). The freshwater spring Thomas Day spoke of can be seen on the far left.

In the summer of 1855 hospital marquees (the small black rectangles below the graveyard in the map above) were pitched in the LTC camp near the railway in front of Mrs Seacole's for the nursing of the sick LTC men, and Mary would make it a habit to visit them there.[12] Those of the walking sick who could do so made their way up to her store for medicines when word got out that the Jamaican lady had great skills in dealing with enteric disease, for Mary's store was said to be a veritable 'apothecary's shop'.[13] By September William Howard Russell was noting in a dispatch to *The Times* that '[Mary's] hut was surrounded every morning by the rough navvies and Land Transport men, who had faith in her proficiency in the healing art, which she justified by many cures and by removing obstinate cases of diarrhoea, and similar camp maladies'.[14] Staff Surgeon William Menzies Calder came across her one day administering good advice to a navvy on a preventive for cholera, 'laugh[in]g him out of his fears ... and giving him sound advice as regards regimen, drinking etc.' As a medical man he was deeply impressed: 'Her powders for diarrhea and cholera ...

seem to have worked miracles; she used them with great benefit in Panama – I gained her favour by telling her her fame was known in England, and she promised me some of the powders; they certainly cannot be *less efficacious* than all our drugs &c for cholera, from all the varieties of which I have as yet seen little benefit here.'[15]

It was indeed true that as early as July 1855, an article in the *Morning Advertiser* had related how Mary had, as a result of her travels, 'acquired great experience in the treatment of cases of cholera and diarrhoea. Her powders for the latter epidemic are now so renowned that she is constantly beset with applications, and it must be stated, to her honour, that she makes no charges for her powders.'[16]

The Rev. Kelson Stothert, a chaplain of the Naval Brigade, reiterated this last fact: Mary's medicinal cures were 'bestowed with an amount of personal kindness which, though not an item of the original prescription[,] she evidently deemed essential to the cure'. 'Innumerable sufferers had cause', he wrote, 'to be grateful for her "sovereign'st thing on earth" for their ills, as well as for her "gentle deeds of mercy".'[17]

So rapidly did Mary's 'fame as a doctress for Cholera and Diarrhoea' spread 'all over camp' – not to mention word of the good cheer and 'warm refreshment' she offered to convoys of wounded as they passed by on their way down to Balaclava to be evacuated to Scutari – that an officer writing home in March 1856 described Mary as by now enjoying a self-appointed honorary role as 'principal medical officer to the army works corps or ci-devant navvies'. When the cholera had taken hold among them the previous summer, she had 'used to prescribe pomegranate juice', for she believed it to be a 'never-failing specific' for gastro-intestinal disorders. (Pomegranate bark was also used successfully to treat tapeworms.) Decoctions from the juice, rind and root bark of pomegranate contain tannins and ursolic acid, ideal for astringent remedies, and the juice of the fruit also contains antibacterial elements that were highly effective against the cholera pathogen in its milder diarrhoeic forms.[18] It is clear that Mary had readily adapted the Jamaican pharmacopoeia of logwood and mahogany in preparing astringent remedies to what she could obtain in Asia Minor. Pomegranates grew in profusion all around the Black Sea and could have been imported to Balaclava by Thomas Day. He would also have been able to obtain cinnamon bark, another of Mary's major ingredients, as well as ginger from the spice markets of Constantinople. Mary's drinks made of cinnamon* with pomegranate juice for diarrhoea were made of *boiled* water too, thus reducing the infection risk.[19]

Many of Mary's grateful patients wrote her thank-you notes after they recovered. In *Wonderful Adventures* she includes a selection from them, though often consigning their authors to initials only. Mr M [possibly Macquarie], paymaster of the LTC, wrote to say that her medicine had twice cured him of dysentery, as well as his clerk and other men in his corps. Sergeant Knollys of the LTC confirmed that he had taken 'a great deal of medicine' for a severe attack of diarrhoea, but that 'nothing served me until I called on Mrs Seacole'; her remedies had soon cured him. Mary had also devised a '*capital prescription*' for jaundice: so great was the demand for it from the navvies that '*I kept it mixed in a large pan, ready to ladle it out to the scores of applicants who came for it.*' 'FM' of the LTC attested that it had certainly done him 'a deal of good'.[20] All in all, as a letter published in the *Aberdeen Journal* under the heading 'The "Good Samaritan" of the Crimea' confirmed the following spring: 'The number of navvies and Land Transport Corps men who have been cured by her of the head-aches, stomach-aches, fevers, and other maladies, rendered the doctors almost jealous of her.'[21]

Final confirmation of the efficacy of Mary's medicines and skills came from the top medical man himself – Sir John Hall – who provided a glowing testimonial in which he acknowledged the unique experience she had gleaned in the West Indies in nursing enteric disease and in administering not just 'appropriate remedies', but also in offering the 'proper nourishment' that was essential in the recovery of men from such sickness.[22]

---

* A correspondent to *The Times* in 1954 acknowledged that Mary's 'treatment of cholera with copious draughts of water in which cinnamon had been boiled, though empirical, was certainly as good as the medical profession could devise at the time'.

When dealing with patients with cholera, Mary applied the same methods she had used in Jamaica and in Panama; ensuring that they were kept warm, and when recovering that they received proper nourishment. She would even ride up to the camps with offerings for sick officers of '*some cooling drink, a little broth, some homely cake or a dish of jelly or blanc-mange*' – the kind of '*little delicacies with which a weak stomach must be humoured into retaining nourishment*'.[23] No doubt these officers paid well for Mary's invalid food. In fact, many of those who wrote of her kindness and nursing skills did not hold back in commenting also on the high prices she charged; William Menzies Calder noted in his diary that Mary had 'an immense business in her store and must be coining money'. Woods of the *Morning Herald* wondered the same: while commending Mrs Seacole's famous 'sangaree' (sangria) and remarking that nobody could make it '*comme il faut*, save Mrs Seacole herself', he added that she was 'a good Samaritan as well as a just speculator'. Commander Richard Ramsay Armstrong was of the opinion that since Mary had a monopoly on trade at Spring Hill, she 'would have established a big fortune'. True 'her charges were high', but 'her good old heart was larger still'. Mrs Seacole, he insisted, 'gave very liberally to the sick and wounded'; she was 'a good Mother, Doctor and Nurse to all'.[24]

Armstrong and many others in Crimea at the time, as well as Mary herself, all made clear that she never charged those who could not afford her help. It was the income derived from officers with extravagant tastes that subsidised the care of others gratis. For, in between all her other tasks up at Spring Hill, Mary would hold a 'levee every morning after breakfast' – effectively a walk-in clinic-cum-dispensary for the sick and wounded. (It is important to be clear that she did not run a *hospital* with resident patients at Spring Hill.) Here she offered medicines and medical advice, changed dressings, bandaged wounds and dealt with all kinds of injuries and even cases of frostbite.[25]*

Mary's near neighbour – Major Cox of the LTC – 'frequently witnessed', during the year he was based up at Spring Hill, 'a levee of fifty or sixty [men] around her of a morning' – consisting of soldiers of the line, men of the naval brigade (who were based in the 3rd Division camp), in addition to her usual clients from the LTC and AWC, stressing that all these patients went to Mrs Seacole's 'with the sanction of their officers, regimental as well as medical' because they *'preferred treatment at her hands, to seeking relief of their ailments at their own hospitals'* [my italics].[26]

Indeed, according to army chaplain John Boudier, up at Spring Hill you 'were sure to meet with sick men of every nation, belonging to the Land Transport ... waiting for a preventative against cholera, fever or the other incidental illnesses of the place'.[27]

But Mary's care of the sick did not stop there. Somehow she found time in her very busy day to regularly visit the nearby hospital huts of the LTC and AWC, 'her arms laden with papers' and other gifts sent out by the generous British public – as she later reminisced in *Punch*. Mary's motherly presence was an enormous comfort to the troops – indeed some of those who had known her in Jamaica referred to her affectionately with the patois word 'mami' ('mammy'), harking back to old colonial connotations of the faithful Black domestic servant of pre-Abolition days.[28] Not content with waiting for patients to come to her, Mary even took her motherly presence, her first-aid kit and supplies of food and drink up to the observation point at Cathcart's Hill. She was often seen riding out 'loaded with baskets of food and medicines of her own preparation, particularly after an engagement with the enemy'.[29] None of the army wives in camp or any civilian observers were allowed to venture beyond this point, but they could stand here with the

---

*   It has been asserted by detractors that Mary's 'catering service' was exclusively for officers – in effect an ad hoc Crimean 'officers' club', and that she did not run a clinic. At Spring Hill, while certainly the main storehouse was a restaurant for officers – for it was how Mary made her living – there was also a canteen for the rank and file, and when it came to the sick and wounded and those who needed her help, Mary Seacole *never ever* discriminated according to rank.

journalists, military commanders and other visitors watching the action during the year-long siege of Sevastopol that had begun the previous October. As the wounded men were brought up from the siege lines Mary offered what help she could to them. One newspaper correspondent talked of how she 'took in hand whoever came up wounded' to Cathcart's Hill and appeared to fully understand what was needed, for he himself had watched her 'dress a wounded man's head in masterly style'.[30]

Despite Mary's many obvious virtues and her generosity of spirit, there was, however, one niggling problem – as far as the authorities were concerned – with regard to her business up at Spring Hill, and that was alcohol. Riding back to camp one night Captain Scott of the 9th Regiment noted how he and a friend stopped off late at Mrs Seacole's to buy cigars, to find 'a number of French Officers having a wine party, and very uproarious', for alongside her legendary sangaree, Mary's mulled claret was rated as 'first class'.[31] It was one thing that private drinking parties among officers were held after hours at Mrs Seacole's; for the army turned a blind eye to them. But it was quite another when the men of the rank and file laid their hands on too much alcohol. Mary herself fought a constant battle against the navvies' 'propensity for ardent spirits' and tried to 'keep them from excessive drinking', as she clearly states:

> *Drunkenness or excess were discouraged at Spring Hill in every way; indeed, my few unpleasant scenes arose chiefly from my refusing to sell liquor where I saw it was wanted to be abused. I could appeal with a clear conscience to all who knew me there, to back my assertion that I neither permitted drunkenness among the men nor gambling among the officers. Whatever happened elsewhere, intoxication, cards, and dice were never to be seen within the precincts of the British Hotel. My regulations were well known.*[32]

Unfortunately, although Mary could lay down the law at her establishment, and in the most stentorian tones at that – for she was renowned across Crimea for her 'pretty homely and unmistakable language' – she clearly found it hard to control the hard-drinking men of the LTC and AWC.[33] During their time in Crimea they accumulated a lot of unspent pay. Up at their base near Spring Hill, the only available place to spend it – aside from a trip down the road to the sutler's camp at Kadikoi – was at Mrs Seacole's. Such was their unruly behaviour and heavy drinking, and the inability of their commanders to maintain discipline over them, that by September 1855 a formal letter of protest was lodged with Sir George Augustus Wetherall, Adjutant General to the Forces, by Captain Shervinton of the 46th regiment. In it he passed on a report from Deputy Provost Sergeant McNeil of the LTC, as follows:

> During the past week the drunkenness of the navvies on the premises belonging to Mrs Seacole has been most disgraceful ... her house is the most disorderly and conducive to crime of all the shops between Balaclava and the camp. I should state in consideration of the above that upon going my usual rounds on Sunday last, the neighbourhood of Mrs Seacole's establishment was most disreputable, several navvies lying on the centre of the road in a most unparalleled state of intoxication using the most disgusting language to all passers by.[34]

One should note here that some of the bad behaviour clearly took place once the men had left the premises, but nevertheless such a complaint contributed to later negative comments by Florence Nightingale that Mary ran a 'bad house' – or drinking den – in Crimea. Alcohol was Nightingale's bête noire: she abhorred the men having access to drink, for alcoholism was rife in the army. She also took a strong line with any of her nurses if they indulged and several were dismissed and sent home for intoxication. The reputation of nursing in Crimea was something that Florence Nightingale very rightly defended, and fiercely. But alas, Mrs Seacole was a loose cannon, outside her control, a fact that infuriated her. If Nightingale could have had her way she would have had the sale of alcohol to the army banned altogether, for she considered it to be 'the real pestilence with which ... we have to struggle in an army idle and sick'.[35] After the war, in a private note in reference to Mrs Seacole's, Nightingale stated: 'I will not call it a "bad house" but something not very unlike it.' The allusion here is to the traditional sense of the bad house as a beer house or tavern where prostitution was also on offer, and which was a feature of most English garrison towns or places where the army was based on campaign. It seems unlikely that Nightingale was insinuating the latter, for she added that Mary Seacole 'was very kind to the men, and what is more to the Officers, and did some good'. Her problem was that Mrs Seacole 'made many drunk' by selling them alcohol.[36] However, in a speech given after the war, Lord Panmure, a former minister at war, when referring to 'grog huts' being closed down in Crimea, made a point of insisting that Mrs Seacole's was the exception and that throughout the war she had 'conducted her business with respectability'.[37]

In an attempt to spy on Spring Hill, Nightingale installed a favourite nurse and ally Jane Shaw Stewart as matron at the Land Transport hospital to report back on the men getting access to 'the raki' – the cheap Turkish aniseed-flavoured spirit – which she assumed was sold at Mrs Seacole's.[38] But she was wrong there: in her book Mary makes a point of expressing her strong disapproval of this spirit: '*the raki sold in too many of the stores in Balaclava and Kadikoi was most pernicious*'; the army authorities had banned its sale and it was sold illicitly.[39]

There is perhaps an underlying motive to this unfair accusation: personal jealousy. The uncomfortable fact for Nightingale was that here in Crimea Mary Seacole had very quickly, if not unwittingly, usurped the Lady Superintendent's own self-awarded sobriquet of 'Mother of the Army'. For Mary makes a point of emphasising her own motherliness in the Crimean chapters of her memoir, and has no compunction in boasting of her usefulness to the overworked doctors as an archetypal Victorian ministering angel. She takes great pride in '*the position I held in camp as doctress, nurse and "mother"*'. Unsurprisingly, Nightingale deeply resented Mary

Seacole's challenge to her own elevated status in this regard and it was a fact that appears to have unduly influenced her attitude to Mary after the war.[40] No Victorian could have missed this allusion to Victoria made by Mary in her narrative, for Lord Tennyson the poet laureate had, in 1851, celebrated the Queen as 'Mother, Wife and Queen'. Mary's is a bold assertion of her unique talents, her position and the respect that she very rightly felt she had garnered. *'Their calling me "mother" was not, I think, altogether unmeaning,'* she proudly declares, in so doing becoming the first woman of colour in the British Empire to assert herself in print in such a self-confident way. As far as she is concerned, in making her own independent way to Crimea, she was fulfilling an almost God-given mission, and she is determined to make her readers aware of *'how hard the right woman had to struggle to convey herself to the right place'.*[41]

CHAPTER 17

'THE DARK MAID OF THE EASTERN WAR'

In May of 1855 a larger-than-life, charismatic figure to equal Mary Seacole arrived in Crimea. Like her, he was a civilian also intent on doing good and improving the quality of the food served to the rank and file of the Allied armies. The celebrated French chef and gastronome Alexis Soyer, or as Mary would proudly proclaim – '*the great high priest of the mysteries of cookery*' – had been doyen of London's Reform Club from 1837 to 1850. When he heard the stories of the terrible food and inadequate supply and preparation of it at Scutari and on the Crimean Peninsula, he offered his services to the authorities gratis. He had had experience in Dublin of running a soup kitchen during the 1847 Irish Potato Famine, was known for his charitable work for the poor and had promoted simple home cooking for them in his bestselling *Soyer's Shilling Cookery for the People*, which rapidly sold a quarter of a million copies after publication in 1855.[1]

That March, at around the same time Mary was on her way to Crimea, Soyer set off on what he called his 'Culinary Campaign' and arrived at Scutari at a time when 100 or more wounded were dying every day.[2] He set to work immediately in overhauling the inefficiency of the hospital kitchens and quickly revamped the

ALEXIS SOYER.—(SKETCHED AT BALACLAVA, BY H. VIZETELLY.)

ways in which the food was cooked and prepared to a far higher
standard. He threw out all the old tainted kitchenware and utensils
and retrained the soldier cooks in preparing satisfying and nutritious meals based on his own soups and stews.[3] Content that he
had done his best for the sick and wounded at Scutari, on 2 May
Soyer swept into Crimea to reform the management of the army
kitchens in the war zone, particularly those of the General Hospital
at Balaclava, which took the first convoys of wounded before they
could be evacuated across to Scutari. Soyer began by making the
hospital bakeries more efficient, devising a far more palatable kind
of bread-biscuit to replace the inedible hardtack on which the army
had largely subsisted during the previous winter and introducing
the use of dried vegetables.[4] By mid-May he was setting up efficient kitchens in the army camps that would make use of his own
specially designed portable field stove – a combination of steam

boiler and 'baking stew-pan' – and showing the troops how to make better, more nutritious, use of their rations.[5]

Later that month, Soyer was riding up from Balaclava to his base at the 4th Division camp when he lost his way and found himself at Spring Hill. Catching sight there of a group of officers, he stopped to chat with them at what seemed to be a 'road-side gipsy tent'. It was, in fact, the embryonic 'British Hotel'. 'An old dame of jovial appearance' soon emerged from the tent, recalled Soyer, asking 'Who is my new son?' The flamboyant monsieur, dressed in his signature gold-braided waistcoat, white dust coat and red and white cap, introduced himself with a flourish of his *jewelled hands*.[6] Mary was delighted to meet him, responding with her usual Jamaican expansiveness, and telling Soyer that she had bought *'many a score of your Relish and other sauces'*. Indeed, she had sold a gross of them in the last ten days alone. She invited Soyer into her tent for a glass of champagne with Sir John Campbell – and other officers whom she referred to as *'my Jamaica sons'*. Soyer now realised that he was in the presence of a Crimean legend – 'the celebrated Mrs Seacole'. Not only that, but Soyer later confided to Mary that 'she knew as much about cooking as himself.'[7]

Knowing Soyer was a businessman, Mary asked his advice on how best to manage her own enterprise, in which she had sunk all her money. Indicating the 'two iron houses in course of construction on the other side of the road', she told Soyer she hoped to provide accommodation for visitors there. But he immediately disabused her of the idea, informing her that most of the civilian visitors stayed on board ship in Balaclava harbour. During their conversation Mary spoke wistfully of Florence Nightingale and how she had hoped that she might have *'called to see me'* during her visit to Crimea, but that she had fallen sick. Mary still hoped to go and visit *'the dear lady'* and *'present my best respects'*. Was she comforting herself that despite the slight, Nightingale thought well of her, or was she being ironic? Mary wanted so much to garner her approval, yet Nightingale – if the truth be told – was even then doing her utmost to avoid seeing Mary and wanted no truck with her offers of medical assistance during her illness.[8]

Soyer, in contrast, could not praise Mary enough; she swelled with pride as he complimented her for her '*soups and dainties*'. Not that Mary did not already have a strong sense of her own culinary skills: '*I always flattered myself that I was his match, and with our West Indian dishes could of course beat him hollow, and more than once I challenged him to a trial of skill.*' During their encounter they enjoyed a lively good-humoured badinage, joking about how after the war they would combine their talents '*to open the first restaurant in Europe*'.[9]

On leaving Mrs Seacole's, Soyer discovered to his horror that his horse had been stolen from outside. Thomas Day lent him a pony to get back to camp. A week later Soyer again visited Mary to thank her for the loan of the pony, and heard that his own missing horse had been found. This second time, he had the most welcome surprise: 'On reaching her place, I found several mounted officers taking refreshment; when Miss Sally Seacole (her daughter), whose name I have not yet introduced, called out – "Mother, mother!" here is Monsieur Soyer.'[10]

Over the course of several subsequent visits to Spring Hill Soyer struck up an affectionate, fatherly relationship with young Sarah, whom he referred to by the pet name of Sally. He loved to tease her with references to 'Sally ... in our alley', alluding to a popular song.* 'Go along with you,' she would respond, 'you are always making fun of me.' Not at all; Soyer was in fact rather smitten with Sally, 'the Egyptian beauty ... with her blue eyes and black hair' and her sweet modesty; as too are we – albeit fleetingly.[11] Now that Sarah has entered the stage as Sally, and is at last an acknowledged player in Mary Seacole's story, let us stay with that pet name, for we need to make an important digression ...

It was Alexis Soyer who unwittingly gave the carefully concealed game away about Mary's illegitimate daughter Sally in his Crimean memoir, *A Culinary Campaign*. Published in September 1857, it

---

* Henry Carey's 'Ballad of Sally in Our Alley', 1725: 'Of all the girls that are so smart / there's none like pretty Sally / She is the darling of my heart / and she lives in our alley.'

appeared three months after *Wonderful Adventures*, from which Mary deliberately excludes all overt mention of Sally. Contemporary biographies of Soyer failed to mention either Mary Seacole or Sally, but in *A Culinary Campaign* Soyer was fulsome in his admiration for the pretty girl whom he nominated 'the dark maid of the Eastern War'.*

Modern commentators are divided as to whether Sally really was Mary's daughter and argue that her addressing Mary as 'Mother' was simply a case of her using an attribution popular with everyone else in Crimea – i.e. that it was not indicative of a blood relationship.[12] However, we have at least three other eyewitnesses who refer to Sally as Mary's daughter, beginning with the *New York Tribune* correspondent who met them on the wharf at Balaclava when they first arrived.[13] On 16 June, William Douglas of the 10th Royal Hussars recorded in his diary how he and a friend had 'called at the "Iron Hut", Mrs Seacole's, where we had some refreshment, and a long chat with the old dame and her daughter about the West Indies'.[14] A couple of months later, Staff Surgeon William Menzies Calder wrote of a visit to Mrs Seacole's and that she 'has a daughter about 16, called Sarah, a great character too'.[15] Then, just to confuse us, Richard Ramsay Armstrong of the Naval Brigade, when describing Mrs Seacole's in his journal, mentioned the presence of her 'pretty half caste niece'.[16] Had Armstrong assumed this, or had Mary introduced Sally as such in order to conceal the truth? Clearly she had obvious and pressing reasons not to acknowledge her as anything other than her daughter by her now dead but legal husband Edwin Seacole. For an admission of her illegitimacy would have prompted the obvious follow-up question: 'Who's the daddy?' Soyer referred to her as 'Sally Seacole' in his memoir, but was that merely his assumption? When she travelled out to Crimea with Mary on the *Hollander*, the newspaper note of the ship's arrival at Malta suggests she had been travelling under her mother's maiden name, as 'Sarah Grant', which in itself confirms that she was not Edwin's daughter.[17]

---

* Perhaps an allusion to the 1631 play by Thomas Heywood, *The Fair Maid of the West*.

After the war, Florence Nightingale also privately confirmed to her sister Parthenope that Mary had had a 'daughter about 14 with her' in Crimea. This allegation was not discovered and published till 2004.[18] More importantly, it was Nightingale who named Sally as being the 'child of Colonel Bunbury'. But which Colonel Bunbury? One would assume Nightingale's reference to Sally refers to the year 1855, when she first arrived in Crimea. If Sally was between fourteen and fifteen years old at that time, this would give us a birth date of c.1840 to 1841 – a time when Edwin Seacole was still very much alive and he and Mary, as far as we know, were still living at Black River in St Elizabeth's. Biographer Jane Robinson plumped for Sir Henry William St Pierre Bunbury (1812-75) as the possible culprit. But although he later fought in the Crimean War, in the 1830s he was on active service in Western Australia and from 1837 in South Africa and later the North-West Frontier.[19]

If Nightingale has the correct name – and alas we only have her word for it – then the most likely candidate is Colonel Thomas Bunbury of the 60th Foot. The fact that Nightingale was aware of Sally's illegitimacy and the identity of her father suggests that either she had been privy to gossip among the officer class to this effect, or that it was already common knowledge in Crimea. There is certainly a proven link between Bunbury and Mary Seacole, but that comes in Jamaica in the late 1840s, as we shall see. Did Nightingale assume that their relationship went back further? Even though Thomas Bunbury's candidacy is not without pitfalls let us take a closer look at him.

Thomas Bunbury was from a well-known Irish family of landed gentry, born in 1787 in Cranavonane in County Carlow, son of a captain in the British Army, whom he followed into service when he was seventeen.[20] His first tours were in various regiments, in the West Indies (1804-11), on the Continent and in America. By 1822 he had achieved the rank of Lieutenant Colonel and in 1824 he transferred to the 60th Rifles, as Colonel in Chief.[21] After fighting in the Peninsular War in Portugal 1827-8, Bunbury transferred regiments in 1838, as colonel of the 67th Foot. He had married in London in

1812, and by his wife Jane had three sons – Thomas, Stonehouse and Harry – all of whom followed him into the army. Although Stonehouse joined his father in the 67th in 1840, neither he nor his brothers were in Jamaica in the crucial time period.[22]

Bunbury certainly had solid Caribbean connections; his older brother Hugh Mill Bunbury was one of the wealthiest sugar plantation owners in Demerara and master of 478 enslaved people.[23] But if Bunbury and Mary had had an extramarital relationship that resulted in the birth of Sally in around 1840, it would have required Mary to travel beyond Jamaica – and away from her husband at Black River. For in 1839 Thomas Bunbury was based over 1,475 miles away as acting governor of Demerara, and prior to that had fulfilled a similar role for a year in St Lucia. If Mary did not make the journey to Demerara, which seems unlikely, then the only possibility is that at some point Bunbury was in Jamaica. But by September 1839 he had returned to London, involved in a court case over a debt of honour. The only logical possibility is that he travelled home via a stop-off in Jamaica; for if Sally was indeed his child, she would have had to be conceived before he left the Caribbean in the late summer of 1839.[24] Bunbury's next few years in the army were spent between London and Dublin, in command of the 67th. In 1835 King William IV had appointed him a knight of the Royal Guelphic Order. In 1846 he was promoted to Major General of the 67th Foot and in 1855 he was given the vacant colonelcy of the 60th.

Two pieces of evidence confirm a definite link between Bunbury and Mary Seacole: first, the account by an officer of the 60th, Maurice O'Connor Morris, entitled *Memini or Reminiscences of Irish Life*. Here, Morris paints an amusing portrait of the grossly fat and ebullient Colonel Bunbury – a Rabelasian figure with a prodigious greed for food and gambling in equal measure – and states that he was 'faithfully nursed in an illness by "Mother Seacole"'.[25]* Further confirmation of this comes in an 1856 newspaper article,

---

* Bunbury's well-documented obesity and the fact that he was in his late fifties in the likely conception period 1839-40 of course begs the question of whether he was in fact physically capable of fathering a child at this time.

which mentions that Mary Seacole 'was at one time in General Bunbury's employ'.[26] But both clearly refer to their later association, when, in October 1848, Bunbury was appointed lieutenant governor in command of the troops in Jamaica. He arrived with his son Stonehouse as his assistant military secretary.[27] But, according to newspaper reports, Bunbury and Stonehouse fell ill during the cholera epidemic of 1849-50 and Mary may well have nursed them both at that time.[28] By July 1851, Bunbury had returned to London, where he made his will. There is, unsurprisingly, no mention of Sally, or of Mary for that matter. In May 1852, he was forced to give up his post in Jamaica due to persistent ill health.

All of the foregoing begs the question: if Bunbury was indeed Sally's father, did Mary Seacole hide her pregnancy from her husband Edwin, give birth to her in secret and leave her in the care of others until after his death in 1844? Or is it possible she passed Sally off to Edwin as his own child? This seems unlikely. The evidence in Mary's memoir indicates that she certainly had Sally with her by the time she went to Panama in 1851, where she hid her in plain sight as her *'little maid Mary'*. But if she had been Edwin Seacole's legitimate child there would have been no reason for Mary to conceal Sally's presence with her there, or in Crimea, or even the fact of her birth for that matter. We can only really draw one conclusion from all of this and that is that Sally must have been the product of an extramarital affair. It does rather dent the respectable public image Mary projected and seems to run counter to everything we know about her – or rather, *think* we know. But we must bear in mind the very different sexual mores of colonial Jamaica at that time, as discussed earlier. White British planters and military men were well known for their predatory behaviour and for taking sexual advantage of Black women in their service, both before and after emancipation. Was Mary preyed upon or was she willingly seduced?

This is not quite the end of Sally's story, for we are left with a final very tenuous alternative possibility, thanks to a tantalising discovery made by Dr Douglas Austin. He has made a close examination

An 1820 view of Kingston from James Hakewill's *Picturesque Tour of the Island of Jamaica* conveys the lushness and beauty of old colonial Jamaica but none of the iniquities of slavery that had made the fortunes of British planters.

Up-Park Camp established by the British Army in the late eighteenth century housed 500 troops but was a breeding ground for disease. Mary nursed the sick here during outbreaks of yellow fever.

Lady Maria Nugent's Jamaican midwife and nurse, Flora, would have offered the same holistic skills as Mary Seacole.

The pomegranate, which grew in profusion in Jamaica, was a staple in holistic medicine practised by the doctresses, who boiled its bitter skins to make astringent drinks for treating cholera and dysentery.

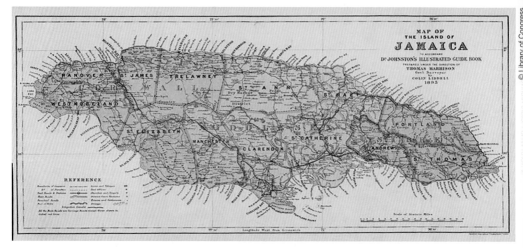

This map of Jamaica shows Kingston Harbour in the south of St Andrew parish (right) and the parish of St Elizabeth (left) where Mary was born, near Lacovia. She went back there with her husband, Edwin, in the 1830s and ran a business at Black River.

The junction of Harbour Street and King Street in downtown Kingston in the 1820s, illustrating the strong British military and mercantile presence, many of whom patronised the lodging houses located in this area.

Date Tree Hall on East Street was probably the grandest and best known of the lodging houses, but was destroyed, along with Blundell Hall next door, in the 1907 earthquake. It is unlikely that Mary Seacole's establishment was as grand as this.

Black River was an important port for the Jamaican trade in mahogany and other hard woods, brought down to the coast for export. It was also notorious as an arrival point for enslaved people transported on the Middle Passage from West Africa.

This Royal Mail Steam Packet served the West Indies from Southampton and typifies the kind of paddle steamer on which Mary Seacole would have sailed back and forth to England and Panama.

In August 1843 the Great Fire of Kingston destroyed large sections of the city, including Mary Seacole's home. It also burnt down the Roman Catholic Trinity church nearby, as seen in this dramatic lithograph, one of a series made of the fire by Jamaican artist Isaac Belisario.

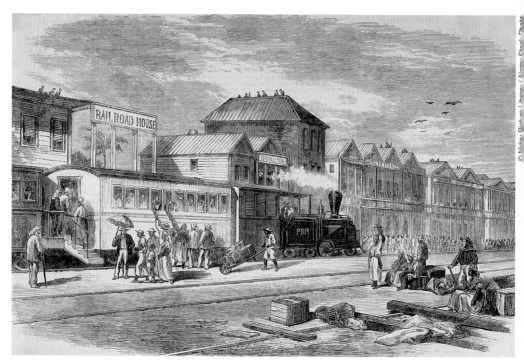

The Panama Railroad terminus at Aspinwall on the northern coast of the Isthmus. Later renamed Colon, it was here that Mary arrived from Jamaica late in 1851 and took the train, for the first few miles that had been completed, to Gatun.

At Gatun Mary was obliged to swap to river transport and hire a bongo boat to take her down the Chagres River to the town of Cruces, which would be her base for the next couple of years.

By the time Mary arrived at the British military hospital at Scutari in March 1855, Florence Nightingale had transformed the filthy, vermin-ridden former army barracks into an efficient hospital. Mary was impressed but she wanted to be with 'her sons' at the front – over on the Crimean peninsula itself.

Once established up at Spring Hill, Mary Seacole became a familiar sight riding around the army camps with her satchel over her shoulder containing bandages and other medical supplies, ready and willing always to help those in need.

When her ship docked at Balaclava Harbour in March, Mary was obliged wait for six weeks before her storehouse at Spring Hill would be ready. In the meantime, she set up a refreshment stall for the wounded being brought down from the front lines for transportation to Scutari.

William Howard Russell's *Plan of the British Camp before Sebastopol 1855* here superimposed over a Google Earth aerial image of today's Crimea. Far left: Mrs Seacole's near the railway (solid line) and the new French road (dotted line); centre: the navvies' huts on the Col; far right: the British Army headquarters where Mary visited Lord Raglan.

The artist Julian Portch was sent to Crimea by the *Illustrated Times* and made the only known image of the interior of Mary Seacole's storehouse, where she is seen entertaining Alexis Soyer. Published in September 1855, it provided the by now curious British public with the very first image of Mary Seacole.

Sir John Campbell (seated), commander of the 38th, elevated to commander of the 4th Division in Crimea, seen here photographed by Roger Fenton. He had known Mary in Jamaica and was one of her regular customers at Spring Hill. Mary lamented his loss when he was killed during the attack on the Redan on 18 June 1855.

The Royal Surrey Gardens music hall in Newington south London, venue for the rousing four-day Grand Military Festival held in July 1857 in aid of the Seacole Fund. Attended by up to 80,000 people, it nevertheless proved a disaster when the company managing the venue went bankrupt and Mary received very little money.

William Howard Russell, special correspondent of *The Times*, photographed by Roger Fenton in Crimea. His extensive reporting from the front brought the war home to ordinary Victorians in a way not previously achieved, thanks to the advent of the telegraph.

Henry Robinson-Montagu, 4th Baron Rokeby, one of Mary's most high-profile army patrons. On his return to London from Crimea, he was a leader of the fundraising to release Mary from debt in 1857.

Prince Victor of Hohenlohe-Langenburg, nephew of Queen Victoria, and from 1861 Count Gleichen. He knew Mary in Jamaica, where he witnessed her nursing skills, as well as in Crimea. After he left the navy, he turned to sculpting and produced a terracotta bust of Mary that was exhibited at the Royal Academy in 1872.

Alexandra, Princess of Wales, photographed in 1867, precisely the time when Mary Seacole was treating her painful knee condition with massage and visiting her regularly at Marlborough House.

The Mary Seacole statue by Martin Jennings was unveiled in August 2016 outside St Thomas' Hospital in London. It took eleven years of concerted fundraising to achieve this and the statue is now a focal point for admirers of Mary and her work.

of Crimean War photographs over many years and in 2017 in the *War Correspondent* – the journal of the Crimean War Research Society – he posited a fascinating theory surrounding a photograph that is held in the Royal Collection at Windsor. It was probably taken in May 1856, not by Roger Fenton but by the assistant to another Crimean War photographer, James Robertson (who operated out of Constantinople). The photographer's name was Felice Beato; he and Robertson were known to have been in Crimea between March and May 1856 when this was taken.[29]

The photograph, seen below, is labelled 'Group outside hut, including two ladies, a Minister and horse' and appears to show some kind of religious ceremony – perhaps the taking of communion.[30]

What is so immediately striking about this photograph is the pretty young girl in the centre. She looks to be dark-skinned, of mixed heritage perhaps – and her age? Well, she could be fourteen or fifteen in my estimation. Is this the face of Alexis Soyer's Sally? What makes it such a strong possibility is that the place where the photograph was taken is Zebra Vicarage, very close to Mrs Seacole's at Spring Hill. The only drawing of the collection of huts at Spring Hill, including the vicarage and Mrs Seacole's, was made by Lady Alicia Blackwood when she visited from Scutari in April-May 1856 (see page 159 of this book).

Over the course of several emails Dr Austin and I discussed the identity of the personalities in this photograph. I suggested that the lady and the priest in the centre might well be Lady Alicia and her husband Dr James Stevenson Blackwood. The Blackwoods had travelled to Crimea with two young Swedish sisters, Ebba and Emma Almroth, who were Christian volunteers at Scutari.[31] As accommodation for civilians was at a premium, Rev. Josiah Hort offered the Blackwoods the use of Zebra Vicarage. During their month at Spring Hill, Lady Alicia and the Almroth sisters made the acquaintance of Mrs Seacole and no doubt her charming daughter too.[32] But the young woman in this photograph is not Nordic-looking. Surely she is not one of the Swedish sisters?

Dr Austin has identified the splendid officer in the cocked hat on the left (the young man on the right may well be his equerry). He is Brevet Colonel John Studholme Brownrigg (1814-89) of the Grenadier Guards, who served in Crimea from September 1854 to October 1855, but returned for the repatriation of his regiment at the end of the war.[33] What would have taken Brownrigg up to Spring Hill? The Grenadier Guards were based up the road in the 1st Division camp, but maybe Brownrigg had other reasons to wish to visit Mrs Seacole's beyond savouring her good cooking?

What is tantalising is that Brownrigg *does* have a Jamaica connection, for, as a newly promoted Captain, he spent eighteen months with the 2nd West India Regiment, from December 1840 to May 1842, at Spanish Town, and later Up Park Camp. Did he meet Mary Seacole during that time, or hire her as a nurse?[34] Mary appears to have still been living with her husband at Black River until early 1842, although it is possible she travelled back and forth to Kingston in response to requests for nursing care. She certainly is known to have delivered the babies of army wives in Jamaica, and on 27 June 1841 Brownrigg's first child, a son, was born to his wife Katherine at Spanish Town. His Jamaican service does chime rather neatly with the most likely period of Sally's conception. Edwin Seacole seems to have been sickly for a long time and was possibly infertile as a result. Did Mary, then thirty-six and childless, take advantage of an opportunity to be a mother before it was too late? Dr Austin has speculated – with no proof as yet – that Brownrigg might have been Sally's father. If so, perhaps on this final return visit to Crimea he had gone up to Spring Hill to see her and had commissioned this photograph as a souvenir?[35]

There is one final possible sighting of Sally, in the crowd watching the evacuation ceremony for British troops on the Ordnance Wharf at Balaclava, in this engraving published in the *Illustrated London News* on 30 August 1856.

© Look and Learn / Illustrated Papers Collection / Bridgeman Images

On the right dressed in plaid is Mary Seacole, and next to her is the familiar tall figure in white kepi and long boots of *Times* correspondent William Howard Russell.* The civilian standing next to him may well be Thomas Day, and between him and the equally striking and

---

* Russell had gone back to England in December 1855, but returned to Crimea to witness the farewell of the Allied troops in July. Not long after getting home he was sent back to Russia – to Moscow for the coronation of the new tsar, Alexander II, on 7 September.

portly Alexis Soyer is a demure young woman. Why would she be standing with this group and so close to Soyer, with whom she had struck up a friendship, if she were not Mary's daughter?

In the end all hope of finding out anything more about the elusive Sally rests on whether Florence Nightingale was correct in naming her father as 'Colonel Bunbury'. Maybe she was right about the initial letter 'B' but wrong about the rest of it. So let us return to the Colonel with one final thought: Thomas Bunbury was an Irish Catholic. When he died at his home at 4 Lower James Street in Soho on 13 April 1857 he was buried – at his specific request – 'without ostentation in a plain stone grave' in what the following year would be designated St Mary's Catholic Cemetery at Kensal Green.[36] Early that same year Mary had moved to lodgings at No. 14 Soho Square, opposite St Patrick's Roman Catholic chapel, which was only a ten-minute walk from Lower James Street. Had she nursed Bunbury in his final illness? When Mary herself died in 1881, she too was buried, only a few hundred yards away from Thomas Bunbury, in the same Catholic section, where he lies forgotten under a flat and unostentatious gravestone (centre below).

As for Soyer's lovely Sally, after 1856 she vanishes from sight. But let us not forget her 'Egyptian' beauty, for the word in its then sense often meant 'gypsy', and Sally, as Alexis Soyer noted, had that very distinctive Irish colouring of blue eyes and black hair.

CHAPTER 18

'Nothing in the World I Would Not Do for Them'

As the cold blast of winter across the barren and muddy Chersonese plateau receded and gave way to the spring of 1856, Mary Seacole tried hard to find the positives amid the suffering that she witnessed, day in, day out. She looked for the *'transient gleams of sunshine'* and began to *'smile at the fun and good nature that varied its long and weary monotony'*.[1] Everyone in the British camp was cheered by the change in the weather: 'the influence of a few hours sunshine here is remarkable,' wrote William Howard Russell of *The Times*, noting the incredible explosion of spring flowers, especially snowdrops and crocuses: 'We have a few warm days only, and yet the soil, wherever a flower has a chance to spring up, pours forth multitudes', even 'thro the crevices of piles of shot, and peering out from under shells and heavy ordnance'. The birds too revived in the sunshine; you could hear them 'piping and twittering about the bushes in the intervals of the booming of cannon'. At long last spring was spreading its 'genial influences' across Crimea.[2]

Till then, recalls Mary, it had been all too easy to be dragged down by *'the pathos and woe of those dreadful months'*. Ironically enough, business in the war zone boomed, as news of her presence circulated. Hungry officers – *'the dandies of Rotten Row'* – would come on their half-starved *'sorry nags'* from the camps higher up to raid Mary's store of food and provisions. She admits that keeping up with demand was exhausting, and before too long, maintaining '*a capital table at the British Hotel*' was beyond her strength.[3] Suffering from overwork, Mary hardly slept, getting up by daybreak and rarely having even the time to eat. There was so much to do – joints to cut, chickens to pluck and gut, pastry to mix, cakes to bake, coffee to brew – and customers would begin arriving by seven. For Mrs Seacole's was well positioned near the road from Balaclava up to Lord Raglan's HQ and the camps, and there was a constant rattle and clatter of army traffic passing by.

But even with the help of '*a few boys, two black cooks, some Turks ... and as many runaway sailors or good-for-noughts in search of employment as we could from time to time lay our hands upon*', it was a constant battle to keep on top of the demands of her many customers. Mary nevertheless prides herself that there were always chickens, mutton and beef on the spit, curries on the hob, '*a good Irish stew, nice and hot, with plenty of onions and potatoes*', not to mention her trademark '*capital meat pies*'.[4] For she well understood that old adage: 'an army marches on its stomach'. In this sense, in newspaper accounts and memoirs she was often referred to as a sutler, or even the French equivalent – a *vivandière*, the historical term for women provisioners who had once followed in the baggage train of armies on campaign. The '*firm of Seacole & Day*', Mary was proud to say, offered an extraordinarily comprehensive range of goods for a war zone. There is a nod to Mary's skin colour in the fact that soldiers nicknamed it Day & Martin, in reference to the shoe-blacking firm for whom young Charles Dickens had skivvied when his father went bankrupt. Indeed, as Russell of *The Times* more graciously put it, many in camp nicknamed Mary's business enterprise 'Night and Day', 'in an allusion to the fine mahogany hue of the warm-hearted West Indian'.[5]

Certainly, Mary provided all the usual goods demanded of an enterprising sutler on campaign: aside from '*linen and hosiery, saddlery, caps, boots and shoes ... cigars, tobacco, snuff*', there was every kind of tinned food, especially '*salmon, lobsters, oysters*' – so much that they all became sick of eating them. When Thomas Day brought in fresh vegetables from Constantinople, Mary's custom- ers – many suffering from scurvy – fell upon them: '*Ah! What a rush there used to be for the greens*.'[6] But, quite apart from her solicitous nursing care and invaluable dispensing of medicines, Mary's ministrations went far beyond those of the average army sutler. Rice-pudding day became legendary at Spring Hill, provid- ing that unmistakable, comforting '*taste of home*'; when she made jam tarts, Mary would fight off eager clients jostling to grab them straight out of the oven. All the while her '*good-for-nothing black cooks, instead of lending me their aid, would stand by and laugh with all their teeth*'.[7]

Mary frequently became infuriated with her staff at Spring Hill and was often heard berating them in the loudest and most fulsome Jamaican patois, for she could not abide idleness. As gentleman tourist Edwin Galt noted during his visit, her English was 'not the purest description, although there is a lurking desire to introduce fine words, and thus the reproofs she is constantly administering to her servants in her Negro-Anglo dialect becomes amusing and at times positively ludicrous.' But Mary's bark was worse than her bite, insisted Rev. John Boudier: 'her voice is harsh, but her heart is soft,' for she had 'a good deal of the milk of human kindness in her bosom'.[8]

On any given day Mary would be forever interrupted in her cook- ing by requests to bandage wounds and mix medicines; from around 9.30 a.m. patients '*with every variety of suffering and disease*' (frost- bite being the worst she had to deal with) would begin arriving at her dispensary, taking up at least two hours of every morning. But men of the LTC or AWC were often involved in accidents and brought to her at any time to be patched up. And when she heard of an injured officer being brought back to camp from the siege lines she would often go and visit him – uninvited – to offer comfort, certain in her conviction that he would be glad to see a surrogate mother at such a time. Mary's working day never finished before 8 p.m., when trading ceased, though she draws a discreet veil across any quiet partying after hours among officer friends. Eventually, with many other traders setting up in business down the road at Kadikoi, she began shutting up shop on Sundays and having the day off.

After the long hunkering down over the winter had brought a lull in the fighting, sooner or later the war would awaken and gather pace again. On Easter Monday, 8 April, with the army now well supplied and the railway bringing in the heavy munitions, a second bombardment of Sevastopol was opened up. 'It was something grand, but awful,' recalled Royal Fusilier Timothy Gowing; with 570 Allied guns opening up against some 600 heavy guns and mortars being fired by the Russians, 'the ground seemed to tremble beneath the terrible fire'; but all to no avail: the Russians in Sevastopol held firm.[9] And so it continued with intermittent fighting throughout the summer, followed by third and fourth bombardments on 6 and 17 June.

Often, when officers knew that they were going into action the following day they would ride down to Mrs Seacole's for a good meal to cheer them beforehand, in anticipation of their possible death, and to say goodbye to Mary in lieu of doing so to *the dear ones at home*. Mary would console them with words *'about God's providence'*, mindful of the fact that she was the only motherly presence in whom they could take comfort at that time. *'There was nothing in the world I would not do for them,'* she tells us, and she spent many an anxious night worrying for their safety: *'I used to think it was like having a large family of children ill with fever, and dreading to hear which one had passed away in the night.'*[10]

There is not a moment throughout her Crimean narrative where Mary doubts her essential function in Crimea as provider of creature comfort, love and succour. But it was so hard when she became overly attached to any of her wounded 'sons'. Many a time, when they died in her presence, she was the one to close their eyes and lay them out and follow them to their burial in a simple grave on the Crimean plain. So much grief to contend with, day in, day out, and, as Mary admits, *'a day was a long time to give to sorrow in the Crimea.'*[11] Although Spring Hill did not come under direct fire, on one occasion 'a piece of shell was hurled … against her store' when 250,000 pounds of gunpowder blew up at the French Artillery Park 3 miles away, sending debris in many directions.[12] Mary was, however, always at a degree of risk from long-range shot and shell from the Russian artillery when she rode up nearer to the front lines. Booming and tremors from the guns were a constant all over Crimea, but the biggest trial, even for those like her observing the action from a distance, came on 18 June 1855, when the French and British staged a major assault on two Russian fortified strongholds: the Malakhov Tower and the Great Redan. Word was out the previous evening about an imminent attack: '*I never remember feeling more excited or more restless than upon that day,*' Mary writes. She got up very early and with her helpers prepared piles of sandwiches, bread, cheese, slices of chicken and ham, plus bottles of wine and spirits and loaded them onto two mules. Then, filling the large satchel of medical supplies that she always carried across her shoulder (and which can be seen in the cover illustration of her book), she packed up plenty of '*lint, bandages, needles, thread, and medicines*'.

Before the sun was even up on the 18th, Mary headed off on horseback with her '*steadiest lad*' leading the two loaded mules.[13] She covered several miles that day in her efforts to help the wounded. No one had asked her to do this; no army official had come and hired her to act as a one-woman first-aid station, providing food, drink and medical help. Out of the goodness of her heart and wishing only to be useful, she took it upon herself to be there, as a witness, as a helper. Army pickets tried to stop her getting near to the scene of the action, but once they knew who they were dealing with, they let the indomitable Jamaican pass. She rode the three and a quarter miles up to Cathcart's Hill, where she left the loaded mules with her lad and proceeded another mile or so further ahead up the Vorontsov Road, and now under fire, to where a temporary field hospital had been erected. She took it all in her stride: '*more frequently than was agreeable, a shot would come ploughing up the ground and raising clouds of dust, or a shell whizz above us.*' People called out anxiously, '*Lie down, mother, lie down!*' and she would be forced to dive for cover;

in so doing she fell badly on one occasion and dislocated her thumb.

The whole tumultuous day passed in a blur, during which Mary bandaged and comforted many wounded men: *'the grateful words and smile which rewarded me for binding up a wound or giving a cooling drink was a pleasure worth risking life for at any time.'*[14] She then rode back to Major General Eyre's 3rd Division at the Picket House observation point, on the extreme left of the attacking forces, and crept forward to help injured men where they had been moved back from the front line.

Mary returned exhausted to Spring Hill very late that day, only to hear the bad news the following morning of much-loved soldiers killed and injured in the engagement, among them two of her favourites. One of the commanders of the Light Division, Colonel Lacy Walter Yea, and Sir John Campbell, in command of the 4th Division, had both been killed in the same assault – Sir John who had *'been my kind patron for some years'* and for whose wife Mary had acted as midwife in Jamaica.[15] Among the wounded was Captain William Peel of the Naval Brigade, who had come to Mary's assistance in Balaclava harbour. When a live shell with a burning fuse had fallen into his battery, he had picked it up and flung it over the parapet just as it burst in mid-air. Later, leading a ladder party in the assault on the Redan, he was severely wounded. For this action he would be awarded one of the first Victoria Crosses.[16] Mary anxiously went to find out what had happened to other favourite officers, only to be greeted by a *'fearful sight'*. But she cannot bring herself to wish never to see such things again, for war had given her a purpose, and a role, that transcended the conventional limitations placed on her colour and ethnicity. It was in war, in *'scenes of horror and distress'*, that she, as a compassionate woman, feels she *'can do so much … because I wish to be useful all my life'*.[17] This, perhaps, is the intrinsic message of her story.

Barely a week after the losses of the Redan, death returned to camp in the guise of cholera. General Estcourt, another of Mary's regular customers, succumbed and died of the disease, although he had at least the comfort of his wife and daughter visiting him at the time.[18] But a greater calamity was the loss of the British commander Lord Raglan, who succumbed on 28 June, his health worn down by the failures of the campaign. During his illness Mary rode up to Army HQ on several occasions to enquire after him; she was even accorded the privilege of seeing him laid out in his coffin prior to his funeral, such was the respect in which she was held by the British Army.[19] Mary was well remembered on this occasion, as well as at the burials of other soldiers in Crimea that she attended, for relieving the gloom by wearing gaily coloured ribbons on her bonnet – 'no matter what the colour of her costume'. 'The more exalted the dead, the brighter was her headgear,' recalled one journalist many years later. 'She excelled herself at Lord Raglan's funeral, at which the ribbons in her bonnet would have shamed the rainbow.'[20]

Not long after Raglan's death, Mary was enlisted to nurse a distinguished patron, whom she had known when he was serving as a young midshipman in Jamaica: Prince Victor of Hohenlohe-Langenburg (better known later as Count Gleichen). Son of Queen Victoria's half-sister Feodora, during the heat of summer Prince Victor had come from the Naval Brigade camp to see his '*mami*' – as he called Mary fondly – begging her assistance in warding off the flies that plagued him. She had straight away ridden down to Thomas Booker's store in Kadikoi specially to purchase a piece of muslin to sew him a fly net.[21] Not long after, Prince Victor fell dangerously ill with cholera and Mary was sent for. Many years later, his son Edward recalled how Prince Victor was 'brought round by the devoted nursing of the well-known Mother Seacole, the West Indian black woman, who had become much attached to him'. Gleichen never fully recovered his health, but his fond relationship with Mary would continue long after the war.[22]

Although Mary had missed the three great set-piece battles of the previous autumn, there was one final battle on 16 August 1855 that she was able to witness at first hand. This was an engagement with the Russians by allied French, Turkish and Sardinian forces (with British cavalry in reserve) at the Traktir Bridge by the River Chernaya on the outskirts of Sevastopol. Early that morning Mary heard the firing and rode off to the battleground – '*prepared and loaded as usual*' with her satchel crammed full of bandages and supplies, and 'utterly unmindful of the shot and shell flying about her in all directions,' as Rev. Boudier noted.[23] She was impressed by the courage of the Russians, who, although they vastly outnumbered the Allied forces, were '*shot down by scores*'. She has to admit that the sight of the '*dark-plumed Sardinians and red-pantalooned French*' who repulsed them was '*so excitingly beautiful that we forgot the suffering and death they left behind*'. After it was all over and oblivious to the risk from stray fire, Mary went down among the scattered bodies with kegs of brandy and water, 'which she kindly distributed to friend or foe', to see what she could do for the wounded. Her friend William Howard Russell was there, making notes on the battle for his next dispatch; after the war he would testify, from first-hand observation, to seeing Mary 'go down, under fire, with her little store of creature comforts for our men', a testimonial that Mary proudly singles out and quotes mid-narrative.[24]

The aftermath of the fighting was, she admitted, '*a fearful scene. The ground was thickly cumbered with the wounded ... all wanting water, and grateful to those who administered it.*' Mary was horrified to see how quickly groups of scavengers descended to rob the wounded and desecrate the dead, stripping them of their boots, valuables and even clothes. Mary did not just assist the wounded French and Sardinian troops; she also '*derived no little gratification from being able to dress the wounds of several Russians*'.[25] They were clearly mystified, if not taken aback at the presence of a Black woman on the battlefield, but the press reported that Mary 'was received by the Russians with great politeness'. She tried to help one poor dying Russian who had been shot in the mouth, only for him to bite so hard on her fingers that she was left with a permanent scar. Another whom she helped '*took a ring off his finger and gave it to me ... kissed my hand and smiled far more thanks than I had earned*'.

Many others thanked her in Russian that she could not understand; but the depth of their gratitude was all too apparent. A couple of the newspapers back home reported with amusement on the Russian reaction, they never having 'seen a negress before'. During fraternisation that took place after the battle, the Russians 'lifted their hats to her' as Mary rode up: 'One gallant Russian took one of the medals [religious medallions] that they wear as relics round their necks and threw it across to her, and she, not to be outdone in generosity, threw back a bag full of tobacco'. Mary said she would have the medallion – which had *the Virgin Mary painted on one side, and Christ on the reverse* – set into a bracelet at Malta, on her way home. Before leaving the battlefield – depicted as 'The Lady with the Gamp' in this fanciful engraving below – she picked up a Russian metal cross as a memento and pulled a few buttons from greatcoats.[26]*

" . . . 'Come back, Mother Seacole!' "

* These may be the buttons donated to the Jamaican Nurses Association by Mrs Ansell Hart some time in the 1960s, thought at the time to have come from a dress Mary wore in Crimea.

The interminable roar of the guns continued to echo across Crimea until the first chilly days of September set in. Day after day Mary rode up to Cathcart's Hill to watch the action and help the wounded as they trickled back from the siege lines. Then, on 8 September, came the final big push to seize Sevastopol and end the stalemate, with another assault on the Malakhov. It felt like the end of the world, Mary recalls, for '*every battery opened and poured a perfect hail of shot and shell upon the beautiful city*'. She spent the whole day up at Cathcart's in the piercing cold wind, on hand with her supplies as she had been on 18 June; she 'had quite an apothecary's shop in a little basket', noted one observer. From Cathcart's, Mary saw '*fire after fire break out in Sebastopol, and watched all night the beautiful yet terrible effect of a great ship blazing in the harbour, and lighting up the adjoining country for miles*'. And then she watched as the French '*roll[ed] into the Malakhoff like a human flood*'.[27] But the Redan, for which the British were fiercely fighting, had still not fallen, resulting in a flood of wounded being brought up to Cathcart's Hill – far more of them than on 18 June.

Writing of that fateful assault many years later, a correspondent of *The Lancet* well remembered that 'amongst the motley crowd which assembled in a storm of wind and dust', Mary awaited the arrival of 'that long string of wounded which trailed up for hours from the trenches' and 'braved the shell which were bursting over her head, and busied herself in helping the poor blackened and wounded soldiers'.[28] Another anonymous correspondent of the *Irish Metropolitan Magazine* – recalling the assault on the Malakhov after the war – offered a rather more colourful account of Mary's extraordinary, idiosyncratic presence at Cathcart's Hill:

A very different representation of the fairer sex, was present on the hill that day, lacking not her own train of admirers. On a shaggy pony, bearing a family resemblance to a Newfoundland dog, her pleasant mulatto visage encased in a brown beaver bonnet, with a cloak doing duty for a riding-skirt, and in hand an umbrella of supernatural proportions, sat Mrs. Seacole of world-wide fame; if not a ministering angel, at least entitled to the more lowly praise of being the kindest and most charitable of women. From her side depended a small keg – in her front was strapped a bundle of necessaries for the wounded soldier. She had come up from her store on this, as on all similar occasions when danger was present, and when her succours might be needed – and for her, the 'Figlie del Reggimento' [Daughter of the Regiment], every officer had his kindly word and greeting.[29]

Out among the wounded, Mary did not disguise her preference for prioritising the wounded officers of *'my old regiment, known so well in my native land'* – the 97th, for they had played a major role in the attack and had suffered terrible losses by murderous Russian fire from the Redan.[30] As she helped dress their wounds, the shells continued to fly overhead, one of them landing very close to her. Such testimony in addition to that of other eyewitnesses, including *Times* correspondent Russell, gives the lie to disparaging claims that Mary was never under fire and not at risk during her time in Crimea. 'She often marched under fire,' noted *Punch* in 1857, describing Mary as 'The Mother [rather than Daughter] of the Regiment'. Her neighbour at Spring Hill, Major Cox, also confirmed that she 'took her place with the medical officers and orderlies in dressing the wounded on the field of battle, in the fulfillment of which duty she came more than once under the enemy's fire'.[31]

It was Russell who, in a dispatch on 'The Fall of Sebastopol', finally drew British readers' attention to Mary Seacole being 'always in attendance near the battle-field to aid the wounded'. She had, he asserted, 'earned many a poor fellow's blessing'.[32] That he should single out a solitary civilian – and a Black woman to boot – in the closing words of this extensive, four-page dispatch speaks volumes. The only other civilian woman accorded such press attention was Florence Nightingale. But she was across the Black Sea in the relative safety of Scutari; Mary Seacole was here, in the thick of it.

By the end of that day, the whole of Sevastopol was ablaze and the air thick with a pall of black smoke. After the capture of the

Malakhov by the French, the Russian commander had decided to abandon the southern side of Sevastopol and with it bring to an end the 349-day siege. Thousands of Russians now retreated across the pontoon bridge to the northern side of the inlet; as they left, the remnants of the Russian fleet were sunk and the bridge destroyed. The Russian wounded and dying were, however, abandoned to their fate in the ruined city hospital amid the putrefying bodies of the numberless unburied dead. The scene was, for Mary, *'enough to unnerve the strongest and sicken the most experienced. I would give much if I had never seen that harrowing sight.'*[33]

It is no surprise that somehow or other the persuasive Mrs Seacole managed to talk her way past the pickets and be the first woman to ride into Sevastopol after the city fell. Indeed, she had 'demanded and obtained admittance into Sebastopol, when even general officers were refused', according to one newspaper account.[34] She tells us that she had long had it in mind to be the first woman *'to carry refreshments into the fallen city'*.[35] But little was left of this once splendid naval base; the jewel of the Russian Imperial Navy was now a hideous smoking ruin. Mary rode in with Thomas Day and some other friends, leading a couple of mules packed with food and drink for the now occupying troops; but only thanks to her talking General Garrett – who had been placed in charge of the city – into allowing her in. The men were very glad of her offers of food and drink. Some had raided the wine cellars of abandoned houses; others (the French Zouaves in particular) were busy looting. Mary was offered a whole range of souvenirs, but in the end accepted only a few token objects – a teapot, an altar candle, a cracked bell and, bizarrely, a parasol *'given me by a drunken soldier'*. The most precious souvenir she brought home with her was a painting of *'the Madonna'* (of course it would have been a Russian Orthodox icon of 'The Mother of God') that had been cut from an iconostasis by a French soldier who had begged her to buy from him.[36]

Back at Spring Hill, the sense of relief that Sevastopol had finally fallen was palpable. Life assumed a more mundane pattern, with Mary often assisting men of the AWC with their *'money matters ...*

remittances, and change of coin be it Russian, Turkish, French, English, or Spanish, all but his own being understood by him', for she wished to protect them from being duped on exchange rates by wily traders. The *Morning Herald* noted that Mary had now without doubt won the navvy's undying loyalty: 'Mrs Seacole stands as his friend, and the curious letters of thanks she has received are countless.' Mary must have shown these letters to the *Herald*'s correspondent, for she also informed him that when the men returned home, they passed on recommendations to any coming out to Crimea to be sure to patronise her business.[37]

The worst of the fighting might be over, but the sick were still lining up daily at Mary's door: 'the lady administered to all their wants, while giving them physic,' wrote an unidentified war tourist in late November 1855, who observed that 'she never lost an opportunity of giving them a short lecture, in pretty homely and unmistakable language.' He noted that so grateful were the soldiers for her many kindnesses that they were 'now subscribing to give her a handsome testimonial'. This is the first and only mention of such a venture prior to the official one set up in June 1857.[38] None of this is surprising given Mary's warmth and generosity in the happier days that followed. As the horror receded, an extraordinary transformation spread across the peninsula: the barren Crimean plain mutated into a microcosm of home – a Little England on the Black Sea – complete with its own familiar customs and social circuit. Earlier in the summer there had been occasional shooting parties, picnics and cricket matches; now, in the approach to Christmas, there were parties, balls, theatricals and even race meetings – and, to crown it all, the joy of English plum puddings, courtesy of Mrs Mary Seacole of Spring Hill.

CHAPTER 19

'THE "GOOD SAMARITAN" IN THE CRIMEA'

In the run-up to Christmas 1855, there is no doubt that Mary Seacole was now revelling in being 'a great celebrity in the camp'.[1] With the military vantage points of the Picket House and Cathcart's Hill now being deserted for the cafés of the French sutlers' village at Kamiesch, the stores of Kadikoi and Mrs Seacole's at Spring Hill, the Allied armies were in an increasingly self-indulgent, even celebratory, mood. *'My restaurant was always full, and once more merry laughter was heard,'* writes Mary, delighted that the discerning French, including celebrities such as the Duc de Rochefoucauld and Viscount Talon, were now *'test[ing] my powers of cooking'.*[2]

Race meetings became a regular occurrence after the fall of Sevastopol. In a dispatch from Crimea on 3 November, the *Morning Herald* correspondent talked of how on race days – complete with the 'Screw Stakes', the 'Alma Stakes', the 'Crimean Sweepstakes' and even a race for mules – Mary was a regular fixture, coming among the spectators 'with all her good things and good intentions': 'Dismounting from her side saddle, she takes her stand at a table, with a well-filled cart behind her, and during the intervals between the heats dispenses with untiring urbanity, sandwiches, cakes, champagne, ginger beer, porter, ale, and cider to all comers.'

The weather was still surprisingly warm and everyone greatly appreciated the sight of 'Mother Seacole', and 'all the races this week brought her a long line of customers.'[3] Writing of the 2nd Division races held on 31 October, the *Liverpool Standard* described the considerable gathering of 200 mounted officers and a few ladies and how 'Mrs Sekole [*sic*] of Jamaica, and Crimea notoriety, came on the ground attended by her spirit bearer, *a coloured boy with drinkables, about two [in the afternoon]* [my italics]* and was received with all honours by his Royal Highness Prince Victor-Hugo, lieutenant of the Leander.'

Mary's prices were steep: 'beer was obtained at 2s. per bottle, sandwiches, two for 6d; cakes and tarts 1s. each; mince pies 9d.; champagne 7s. a bottle', but she was catering for officers who could afford it.[4] It would help pay for all the free food, drink and medicines she had been handing out to the sick and wounded since arriving at Spring Hill six months previously. As *The Times* noted on 4 December, at a race meeting attended only by the military elite of 'divisional generals, brigadiers, colonels and staff officers' – so many that they were 'as plentiful as blackberries' – Mrs Seacole was 'the only representative of the fair sex' and 'presided over a sorely-invested tent full of creature comforts'. None of the top brass seemed to have any complaints; indeed, Mary's catering was 'very acceptable after a hard ride' to those taking part.[5] She was also, inevitably, called on to administer first aid, should contestants fall and injure themselves, which they did, frequently.[6]

But it wasn't always the officers who were treated to Mary's food and hospitality. On one occasion men of the 33rd regiment, who had just been marched down from camp to Balaclava to be issued with new Minié rifles, were halted by their commander at Spring Hill on their way back to camp, upon which Colonel Mundy paid for bread and cheese and three casks of Sicilian wine to be shared

---

* This statement comes as something of a surprise, if not a shock. A mixed-heritage boy with Mary in Crimea? One can only assume he was a local Tatar boy hired for the purpose. Unfortunately, we cannot travel further down this road, for this is the one and only mention of him. 'Prince Victor-Hugo' here is Mary's friend, the Prince of Hohenlohe-Langenburg, aka Count Gleichen.

among some 500 of these 'hungry and grateful men'. It was more than Mary and her staff could cope with and Mundy joined in helping to cut the bread and cheese. The fact that Mary was able, at short notice, to cater to such large demand is a testimony to how well stocked her stores were.[7] But even these were strained to the limit when Christmas came.

With the arrival of violent rainstorms and heavy winds across Crimea, everyone began hunkering down under canvas or in pre-fabricated huts in the run-up to the festive season. The soldiers took great pleasure in decorating their billets with any spruce and fir branches they could find, and with artificial flowers bought at Kadikoi displayed in vases improvised from empty meat tins. Some rode out in search of mistletoe that grew in abundance on wild pear and apple trees. Across the tented camps of the peninsula there were parties and even balls, at which the few army wives in the Crimea were the centre of attraction. Mary and Sally refused to go, for the dances were attended by French *cantinières* in their trousered uniforms: 'Do you think mother or myself would go to such a place, where the women wear soldiers' clothes? Not likely,' Sally told Alexis Soyer in disgust.[8]

In stark contrast to the previous winter, warm clothing was now arriving by the bale-load; food parcels were pouring in – even Christmas cakes miraculously arrived unscathed all the way from doting families back home. Officers with money could buy food hampers from familiar English provisioners such as Oppenheim's, Crockford's and Fortnum's, who had all set up shop in the sutler camp at Kadikoi.[9] British officers were busy throwing dinner parties for their French allies, and raiding Mary's store in the process. As for Christmas dinner, although wild turkeys were found in Crimea, there was also an indigenous bird: the bustard (apparently a tasty cross between woodcock and wild duck). Huge flights of them had been spotted towards the end of the year and hunting parties were out with their new Minié rifles, bagging as many as possible. Mary herself had one for sale – so the British press reported – weighing nineteen and a half pounds.[10]

In the weeks before Christmas she was besieged with orders for her puddings and mince pies: '*I can fancy that if returns could be got at of the flour, plums, currants, and eggs consumed on Christmas-day in the out-of-the-way Crimean peninsula, they would astonish us.*'[11] Chaplain John Boudier found Mary one morning 'deep in the mysteries of baking and boiling'. She 'had made eighty plum-puddings to order, so she told me'.[12] In a dispatch from the front, Chief of Staff Major General Charles Windham confirmed that the 'celebrated old lady, Mrs Seacole' was keeping a 'pudding book' 'in which page after page is written, Major– pudding for 30, Captain– pudding for 20, Ensign– pudding for 20 and Colonel Somebody, pudding for 5, and so on.'[13] Even the French commanders were initiated into this culinary delight; Queen Victoria had sent out a plum pudding for the delectation of French commander Marshal Pélissier, but he had been so perplexed as to how best to prepare this traditional English dish that he 'specially sent an aide-de-camp to Mrs Seacole, at Spring Hill stores, to be initiated into the art and mystery of properly warming it up for table.'[14]*

On Christmas Day Mrs Seacole reigned supreme, as 'the tutelar goddess of plum-pudding and mince pies, with many blessings ... showered upon her head'.[15] Crimea was transformed for the festival, as the entire army took time off to celebrate: '*I think there was something purely and essentially English in the determination of the camp to spend the Christmas-day of 1855 after the good old "home" fashion,*' Mary tells us.[16] Such had been the rapid descent of press reporting, from the heroics of war to the mundane enjoyment of food and other creature comforts, that some found it all rather trivial: 'Mrs Seacole's hut lives in an imperishable immortality of

---

* Despite a concerted search, and the fact that numerous French officers patronised her establishment at Spring Hill, the only French source that refers to Mary seems to be that of the Comte de Castellane: *Madgy: Souvenirs de L'Armée Anglaise en Crimée* (Paris 1878, 294-5), in which the author describes how British officers referred to Mary as 'la mère Jamaïque' [the Jamaican mother] and claimed that 'every country in the world knew her' and that she had been 'in the Indies, the Cape of Good Hope, China, Australia and elsewhere'. According to Castellane, 'Mistress Seacole was The Jamaican, in the same way that the grand Scipio was referred to as The African [Scipio Africanus] – by right of conquest'.

piquancy and small pies', wrote the *Saturday Review* in sneeringly Dickensian tones.[17] The correspondent clearly had no concept of how welcome those pies and puddings were to men who had lived through the hell of war for over a year and had had no Christmas at all during the terrible privations of the previous winter.

Mary achieved all this prodigious output not without the help of her two West Indian cooks, and no doubt Sally too. For days they worked from dawn to dusk to fulfill her many orders. And it didn't stop there; on New Year's Day she baked another large batch of puddings and mince pies and took them to the sick and wounded in the LTC hospital. It was just one of many acts of kindness freely made by Mary Seacole that Christmas *'to remind the patients of the home comforts they longed so much for'*.[18] No wonder the men in the Crimea all loved her and spread the fame of her legendary good works when they returned home to England. At Christmas, of all times, Mary Seacole's humanity and Christian charity shone through. As the *Standard* reported, on New Year's Day 1856, 'about 120 men of the left wing of the Land Transport Corps were regaled by Mrs Seacole of Spring Hill Stores, with wine and mince-pies and plum pudding' – at her expense – and for which she was 'received with immense cheering'.[19]

In the New Year, with Allied troops uncertain whether the fighting would be renewed on the northern side of Sevastopol, news broke that the Russians were suing for peace, and in fact had been doing so for several weeks. A Peace Congress was called in Paris and an armistice was signed on 29 February; the news arrived in Crimea the following day by telegraph. Under the terms of the Treaty of Paris that formally ended the war on 30 March 1856, the Allies were given six months to pack up and evacuate their forces from Crimea. Mary greeted the peace with mixed feelings: she was glad to hear of it but knew full well that *'it would cause our ruin'*: *'We had lately made extensive additions to our store and out-houses – our shelves were filled with articles laid in at great cost, and which were now unsaleable, and which it would be equally impossible to carry home. Everything ... must be sold for any price.'*[20]

The fighting might be over, but Mary's first-aid skills were still much needed, even as she began winding up business at Spring Hill. In April 1856 Florence Nightingale arrived on a visit to the LTC hospital nearby. En route there, the mule-drawn vehicle she and her party were travelling in overturned and 'one of the ladies [was] rather hurt'. She was removed to Spring Hill, where 'the ever-ready Samaritan Mrs Seacole immediately made her appearance to tender assistance'. On another occasion, a French soldier fell off his mule 'about 200 yards from Mrs Seacole's hospitable home' and was concussed. They picked him up and brought him straight to Mary. 'There was[,] in fact, considerable difficulty in warming him into life at Spring-hill Store,' the *Standard* reported, but on recovering with Mary's assistance, 'he was fed and liberally treated and forwarded in due time to his destination.'[21] First aid was one thing, but Mary's compassionate care of the dying was also apparent, even now. One day in early February a man of the AWC employed in blasting rocks by the road to the front was caught in a shower of stone after a blast misfired.

> On his comrades reaching him they found he had lost a thumb and both eyes, and that his cheeks were hanging down, expos-ing the superior maxillary bones, while in his forehead there appeared a hole through which the brain was visible. A stream of blood poured from the man's mouth. Carried into Mrs. Seacole's[,] that 'good Samaritan', unscared by the ghastly sight before her, washed the wounds of the sufferer, and, those who were present, speak of the scene as the most heart-rending. 'Save me, save me' were the words the choking man faintly but perse-veringly pronounced; for he remembered well that, when sinking from diarrhoea, Mrs Seacole had, like a good angel, stepped in and cured him.

His name was James Bailey; sadly, there was nothing even the sur-geons could do to save him, and he died in hospital a day later.[22]

*

Early in 1856 Mary was called on to help with a new form of entertainment in Crimea – amateur theatricals. Army officers eager to fill their time began rehearsals – some of course having to take the ladies' parts. They were faced with the problem of having no suitable clothing in which to perform and soon were beating a path to Mary's door, being that of one of the few women in the area, to obtain bonnets, petticoats 'and other unmentionables' which would 'enable them to create quite a sensation among their audience'.[23] 'The wardrobe of an old black woman – [there it is again – why must they all describe Mary as old?!] – who keeps what she calls an "hotel", is the only stock of stage "properties" that can be depended upon for the costume of heroines of all descriptions,' wrote Colonel William Pakenham in a letter home to his family.[24] Mary had been most obliging about lending some of her *gay-coloured muslins* to the 'lady' actors of the 1st Royals and even helped them with the *little difficulties about the Toilette* by lacing them into their corsets, so tight that they turned *blue in the face*. She also taught them how to *manage their petticoats with becoming grace, and neither to show their awkward booted ankles, nor trip themselves up over their trains*. Lieutenant Lacy of the 63rd was one of her greatest successes, transforming into a most attractive feminine figure in tableaux entitled 'The Mustache Movement', 'To Paris and Back for Five Pounds' and 'Betsy Baker'.[25]

So ubiquitous, so indispensable had Mary Seacole become to daily life as 'the Good Samaritan in the Crimea', that a joke began circulating 'as to whether the Czar will not think it necessary to preserve in the Crimea so useful a person as Mrs Seacole'.[26] She was by now regularly seen at parades and presentations, such as a review by Marshal Pélissier at the end of February, when Staff Surgeon Calder noted that she 'was out in grand array and attracted universal attention'.[27] Sooner or later, with so many accolades to her generosity, her compassion and her devoted care of the sick and wounded, the inevitable question of Mary being given some kind of award or medal for her services was raised. The Crimean campaign medal had been approved in December 1854 and first distributed to those who had returned to England in May 1855; in Crimea, the army had begun handing them out in September 1855.

The 'occasional correspondent' of the *Daily News* had been the first to broach the subject, when in a dispatch from camp on 15 April 1856 he noted that 'this Jamaica lady ... has been of more service to both officers and men, and has cured more sickness amongst the French and English troops than would, perhaps, be possibly supposed.' She had, he said, already been given 'a medal for her services to the Turkish troops when they were encamped last winter near her iron house':* 'Without doubt a Crimean medal with the Sebastopol clasp would be well bestowed upon her. The Russians have decorated those women who helped to build the Little Redan – why should not we decorate those few women, who have, out here, been of use to the army.'

This assertion, published on 3 May and repeated in the *Illustrated London News*, was confirmed in *The Times* on the 15th by William Howard Russell, who reported that 'the Sultan has sent [Mary] a medal, but she is anxiously expecting the English Government to decorate her with the Crimean riband and its metallic appendage, to which she lays claim, for "services rendered in the field".'[28]

On 6 June Mary attended Army HQ for the Investiture of the Order of Bath upon Marshal Pélissier, as one of only four English† women – the others being officers' wives – invited to be present. Here she was personally introduced to Field Marshal Sir Hugh Gough, former commander-in-chief of the army in India, who had travelled out from England specially to perform the ceremony and 'who appeared greatly pleased with her'.[29] Not long afterwards, Gough's personal advocacy of 'Decorations for the Crimean Ladies' was published in *The Guardian*: 'It is said that Lord Gough is of opinion that English women who were in the Crimea previous to the armistice at

---

* Mary helped any wounded men who solicited her medical care, even enemy Russians. It is greatly regretted that no evidence has yet come to light in either French or Turkish or Russian language sources in support of this. However, as with so much in Mary's story, absence of evidence is not evidence of absence.

† This contemporary usage seems odd but both Lord Gough and Mary herself – as well as other Victorians – tended to use the word 'English' where we today would of course say 'British'.

the end of February, ought to be decorated with the Crimean ribbon solely. On Mrs Seacole it might well be bestowed, but I fear that to decorate any more, although they may richly deserve it, would be to induce more women to follow their husbands in any future war.'[30]

The *Morning Chronicle* seconded Lord Gough's sentiments, pointing out that Mary 'and other labourers [i.e. the LTC and AWC] who were out here previous to the armistice deserve to have the Crimean ribbon, and the army would be more glad to see them wearing it than to be obliged to see, as they do now, commissariat officers and ordnance clerks wearing four clasps [one for each of the battles Alma, Inkerman, Balaclava and the siege of Sevastopol].' It seemed outrageous that 'post office clerks [were] strutting about with the Balaclava clasp, simply because they happened to be in Balaclava on 25 October 1854' – the day of the battle.[31] This issue was subsequently taken up by others, who argued that some men were awarded the medal without doing anything at all to deserve it, while none of the nurses, not even Florence Nightingale, were decorated in this way. The exception, of course, was Mary Seacole. How she came to be awarded the medals she proudly wore back in England after the war is highly contested, and a subject that we must return to in the next chapter.

In the meantime, with evacuation from Crimea imminent, Mary was busy trying to sell off her excess stock at Simferopol and Bakchiserai (where her companions *'tried hard to persuade the Russians that I was Queen Victoria'*) as well as Balaclava. Down at Kadikoi, many of the sutlers were also shutting up shop and leaving. Thomas Day bought the contents of Mr Golborn's store at a knockdown price, in hopes of a quick bit of speculation in reselling it at Spring Hill.[32]

It must have been a sad sight for them both to see the army – with Mary's beloved sons – leaving. As the press reported on 9 June, when men of the 30th and 55th of the 2nd Division marched down from camp to the sound of the drums and fifes of the Guards, they stopped at Mrs Seacole's to say goodbye. Here 'this old lady's hospitality was dispensed in the shape of curaçao and other liquors, from the officers down to the drummers.' As they left, the men 'gave the good old woman a round of hearty cheers'. *'Mutual suffering and endurance had made us all friends'*, writes Mary; she was sure it was her war work that had kept her going, and she was deeply apprehensive of where life would now take her: *'how like was it that my present occupation gone, I might long in vain for another so stirring and so useful.'*[33]

In July, Alexis Soyer had returned to Crimea to see the troops leave. He took a final ride round the now deserted camps and went to bid 'the illustrious Mrs Seacole' adieu. He found her, true to form, 'in the act of dressing the wound of an Army Works Corps man, who was cut severely in the forehead'.[34] There was something touchingly sad about her request that Soyer say goodbye to Miss Nightingale for her when he stopped off at Scutari on the way home: 'you must know, Monsieur Soyer,' she insisted, 'that Miss Nightingale is very fond of me'; and she repeated for 'about the twentieth time' how kind Nightingale had been to give her board and lodging when Mary visited her en route to Crimea. For all her wishful thinking, Mary never won a word of public acknowledgement or praise from the Lady Superintendent. Soyer did, however, note that when he subsequently passed on the message, no doubt betraying his great affection for Mary in the process, Nightingale conceded that 'I am sure she has done a deal of good for the poor soldiers.'[35]

On 21 June, the *Daily News* reported that Mrs Seacole had 'pulled down the iron portion of her house', which was packed up for transportation back to England. *'But the Russians got all of the out-houses and sheds which was not used as fuel,'* Mary explains. They had to give away most of their horses too. She became so upset at having to sell off fine wine at knockdown prices that *'I snatched up a hammer and broke up case after case.'*[*][36] Soyer passed by not

---

* When sculptor Martin Jennings, who created the Mary Seacole statue that stands outside St Thomas Hospital, visited the site of Spring Hill, using location details provided by Dr David Jones of the CWRS, he and members of the Sevastopol Museum found a collection of old broken bottles buried there. These almost certainly were the unsold bottles of wine and spirits that Mary had been forced to smash when she finally abandoned Spring Hill in July 1856.

long after to survey the 'ruins of the Seacole Tavern'; the *London Evening Standard* correspondent also walked up to Mrs Seacole's to find Mary standing there, 'gazing on the wreck of Spring Hill Store, this week to be abandoned forever'. The sale of all the excellent comestibles that Mary had had there, he reported – 'tongues, tins of salmon, pickles, wines, and preserved vegetables' – had ceased, and the 'casks and boxes containing the residue were now being carted off for Balaklava'. From there, he said, any remaining unsold goods were to be 'shipped for and bonded in London, *en route* for Australia, to which gold region Mrs Seacole is now bound.'[37]

Whether the Australian plan was a serious one or not, Mary's first port of call had, however, to be London. Three weeks before the final evacuation of Crimea, she and Sally moved into Balaclava, where Mary was to be seen still trying to sell off her excess of port wine at one shilling a bottle from a temporary store on the Commissariat Wharf.[38] She continued to tell everyone who would listen that 'Lord Gough ha[d] promised to do his best to get her our Crimean medal.'[39]

A medal would have been some consolation; for the brutal reality was that the firm of Seacole & Day was now facing ruin. With the unexpected end to the war, Mary and Thomas Day had gone bankrupt and were obliged to face their debtors back in England.[40] Still undaunted, Mary began informing her army contacts that she intended to continue her business enterprise there: a news item was syndicated across more than forty British newspapers – and especially in the Scottish and Irish press – as follows:

> Mrs Seacole.—Mrs Seacole, the celebrated proprietress of the provision store in the Crimea, intends setting up a similar establishment at Aldershot. Her fame in this particular department of business is so well known among all military men that success in her new speculation is almost certain.

So well known was Mrs Seacole – 'the famed sutleress' – at home and abroad by July of 1856 that she was now accorded her own rubric in the press.[41] Mary consoled herself, that along with all the many verbal expressions of thanks, the hugs and kisses, the presents she had received from men as they left, there had been many *'kind letters full of grateful acknowledgements for services so small that I had forgotten them long, long ago'*. They touched her deeply, particularly those from *'the working men'* of the LTC and AWC – not officers, but men with no social cachet that she could exploit to her own advantage. She knew she was leaving Crimea with many friends; but was haunted by thoughts of those whose lonely graves she would leave behind. Mary visited the army cemeteries to take one last, fond look and to plant shrubs and flowers, even *'little lilac trees ... and flowering evergreens'*. Thoughtful to the last, she also *'picked up pebbles, and plucked simple wild-flowers, or tufts of grass, as memorials for relatives at home'*.[42]

The British Army was the last of the Allies to leave Crimea. On 9 July the remaining civilians and army wives gathered on the Ordinance Wharf in Balaclava to watch the evacuation of the final regiment to go – the 56th West Essex Regiment of Foot. It was a fine and sunny day, and the occasion was memorably engraved by Robert Thomas Landells for the *Illustrated London News*, in which Mary, Mr Day – and possibly Sally – are in the middle of the picture.[43] Standing alongside Mary were her two great Crimean friends – William Howard Russell of *The Times* and Alexis Soyer. The Frenchman was deeply moved by the occasion, and also by what a wrench it was for 'this excellent mother' to have to part with 'all her sons, thus ending her benevolent exertions in the Crimea'. He saluted Mary – 'la mère noire' (the black mother) – one last time, as he headed off for the other Mer Noire – the Black Sea – while she prepared, with Sally, to take a ship to Constantinople.[44]

CHAPTER 20

'AM I NOT A
FIRST-CLASS WOMAN?'

In the second week of July Mary Seacole set sail from Balaclava to Constantinople where, on the 14th, she transferred to a French Messageries Impériales steamer, the *Indus*. She does not tell us whether Francis and Mac, her two loyal but much-berated cooks, sailed with her, but Sally surely must have done, as she was still only a teenager. We know this much thanks to a letter to the editor of the Melbourne newspaper *The Argus* from Samuel A. Patterson, an army surgeon who clearly had first-hand knowledge of Mary in Crimea and who moreover had already been told of her gifts as a 'humane and skilful nurse' in Jamaica by medical colleagues who had served there. Patterson had also travelled on the *Indus* but disembarked when it reached Marseilles on 21 July. Back at his home in the Melbourne suburb of St Kilda, he praised Mary's dedication and self-sacrifice during the war, urging that a fund be set up for her.[1]

It is unclear whether Mary transferred immediately to another ship to England. She tells us she '*did not return by the most direct route, but took the opportunity of seeing more of men and manners in yet other lands*'. But she could not have gone that far as we next have sight of her inside a month in London. There is also the puzzling statement that on her return she and Thomas Day '*set to work bravely at Aldershott to retrieve our fallen fortunes*', but there is no record to be found of them getting as far as actually opening a store at the camp, which had recently been established in this garrison town 35 miles from London. It is more likely that negotiations to do so never got off the ground.[2] Mary might have been a household name in Britain, but she was now facing the grim reality of the collapse of her business enterprise. During her journey on the *Indus*, she had 'expressed a dread' to Samuel Patterson 'that in consequence of losses inevitable in the disposal of her remaining stock, her affairs would end up badly'. She returned '*shaken in health*', she tells us; no doubt suffering the effects of months of grinding overwork, not to mention a bout of illness while in Crimea and exposure to the bitter winters there.

Who did Mary have to turn to in terms of family when she came back to England? The Seacole home in Mansion House Street in Kennington had gone with the death of Thomas Fowler Seacole in 1848. Mary's unmarried sister-in-law Ann, who had lived on an annuity in the same boarding house as her brother Charles – off Thurloe Square in South Kensington – had died of stomach cancer on 7 June, just before Mary's return.[3] Charles Witton was the only Seacole left, but there is no sign of any contact between them. Mary did, however, have a nephew, William James Kent, son of her other dead sister-in-law Maria, who was living in Addington Road, Bow, and worked as a commission agent in the City. In the years to come Mary would develop a close relationship with him and his wife Sarah.[4] But for now, on arriving in London, she opted to stay centrally and took up temporary lodgings in Tavistock Street, in Covent Garden, announcing that any friends who wished to call on her there would be most welcome.[5] For in her declining years, it would be the friends from Crimean days, whom she encountered '*in omnibuses, in river steamboats, in places of public amusement, in quiet streets and courts*', who would keep her going and remind Mary that she was not forgotten.[6] Nothing could be more cheering than '*a smile of recognition*' from a soldier on sentry duty in Whitehall. '*Would all this have happened if I had returned to England a rich woman?*' Mary asks, as she comes to the end of her story.

Just as she arrived back, the first account of Crimea by a civilian battlefield tourist was published. In his *The Camp and the Cutter*, Edwin Galt gave a lively portrait of Mrs Seacole as the 'celebrated mulatto woman' who had been 'a sort of mother to the officers of the army' and 'a good, kind nurse', but the first public confirmation of the extraordinary interest that her exploits in Crimea had aroused came in August, when Mary was feted with 'rapturous enthusiasm' as the 'illustrious' guest of honour at a Dinner to the Guards.[7] This was held at the Royal Surrey Gardens music hall (coincidentally just a stone's throw from the old Seacole home in Mansion House Street). Constructed of cast-iron girders and plate glass, much along the lines of Prince Albert's Crystal Palace built for the 1851 Great Exhibition, it was a popular venue for large celebrations, meetings and concerts. On 25 August, the dinner was attended by several thousand, the numbers clearly augmented by so many wanting to take a look at this much-talked-about Jamaican lady, and, indeed, 'few amongst them attracted more notice' than Mary.[8] As the men dined below, she regally viewed the scene from the gallery above, her 'dark features . . . quite radiant with delight and good humour'. Her pleasure was equalled by that of the men; on seeing her perambulating in the gardens after the dinner, they cried out 'Mother Seacole!' and burst into rapturous applause. Very soon Mary was picked up and 'chaired around the gardens'. She might well have 'suffered from the oppressive attentions of her admirers were it not that two sergeants of extraordinary stature gallantly undertook to protect her from the pressure of the crowd.' The *Examiner* was pleased to report that 'the excellent lady did not appear in the least alarmed, but, on the contrary, smiled most graciously, and seemed highly gratified.'[9] Indeed, Mary attracted more attention, according to the *Globe*, 'than even Gen. Beatson,* with his waving white plumes'. The correspondent provided his readers with a lively snapshot of the good lady, 'who has dark blood in her veins, and whose eyes lack none

---

* In Crimea Major General William Beatson had commanded the Osmanli Light Cavalry – nicknamed Beatson's Horse – in which Samuel Patterson had served as surgeon.

of the vivacity of the tropical races'. Mrs Seacole was in her element and 'held quite a court of her old acquaintances, and received with affable dignity the new acquaintances who were presented to her. She is a good-humoured and jovial person, whilst her features bear the stamp of energy, vigour, and decision, quite sufficient to account for her extraordinary success in her mercantile venture in the camp.'[10]

This news item was widely circulated – across about fifty national newspapers. On 8 September, Mrs Seacole's 'sheer pluck and love of the species' were celebrated in toasts at a dinner to Crimean Officers held in Ledbury in Herefordshire and she was invited to another celebratory dinner in Portsmouth on 23 September.[11] By October, the first of many racehorses named after her made an appearance when Captain Brabazon's filly Mrs Seacole won her event by half a length at the annual garrison races at Woolwich Common.[12] However, while the British Army was celebrating Mrs Seacole's contribution to the war effort loud and clear, and the British press was widely reporting on it, one person who one might have expected to voice her approval was decidedly silent. The Queen.

One of many who had written to Mary in Crimea thanking her for all she had done for him had said: 'I am sure that when her most gracious Majesty the Queen shall have become acquainted with the service you have gratuitously rendered to so many of her brave soldiers, her generous heart will thank you.'[13] It goes against the grain of everything we know about Victoria that she would not have sent her a note, if not been consumed by curiosity to meet the celebrated Mrs Seacole. Queen Victoria had long had a concerned interest in her Black and Asian subjects and did not share the views on race and colour held by most of her peers, for she took pride always in judging people on their merits alone. In 1833, as a fourteen-year-old, she had wholeheartedly welcomed the emancipation of enslaved people across the British Empire and, later, with her husband Prince Albert, had been a staunch supporter of Abolition in the United States. At the Great Exhibition of 1851 she expressed great interest in the sole Black exhibitor, Josiah Henson, who had been the inspiration for Harriet Beecher Stowe's eponymous hero in *Uncle*

Tom's Cabin, a book over which Victoria had wept. So moved had she been, in fact, that Victoria had contrived a private meeting with Mrs Beecher Stowe when she visited England.* Most notably, in November 1850, she had taken under her wing an Egbado princess, Omo'ba Aina (who was given the name Sarah Forbes Bonetta), who had been rescued from captivity in Dahomey by Captain Frederick Forbes; she paid for her education and on numerous occasions invited Sarah to Windsor.[14] We know that the Queen later donated privately to the second Seacole Fund of 1867 set up for Mary, so why did she not invite her to tea on her return from Crimea? After all, she had the personal recommendation of members of Victoria's own family who had served in Crimea, such as Prince Victor of Hohenlohe-Langenburg, Prince Edward of Saxe-Weimar (a colonel in the Grenadier Guards) and the Duke of Cambridge (who had commanded a division).

There can be only one rational explanation: Florence Nightingale. It's clear how greatly she disapproved of Mary, despite grudgingly acknowledging her obvious good works; and this was for the simple reason of Mary's perceived lack of propriety. She sold alcohol, and some of her customers at Spring Hill drank more than they should. But worse, of course, was the private knowledge Nightingale had of Mary's illegitimate daughter Sally by a white British officer. For Queen Victoria, that would be *too schocking* – as the monarch might well have said with her unmistakable German intonation.

For her part, Victoria regarded the Lady of the Lamp as a paragon of feminine virtue, whose opinions she took as gospel. So much so that she was extremely anxious to meet her the minute she set foot back in England – or rather Scotland, for Victoria commanded Nightingale's presence at Balmoral in September 1856 as soon as

---

* When Beecher Stowe visited England in 1853, on the back of publication of her best-selling *Uncle Tom's Cabin* the previous year, Victoria, who was a passionate fan of her book, wanted to meet her, but the American embassy in London objected, arguing that a formal meeting would be seen as a royal endorsement of the Abolitionist cause in the US and be diplomatically compromising. In defiance, Victoria contrived an 'accidental' meeting when they both passed through Paddington station, Stowe en route for Scotland and Victoria arriving from Windsor.

she heard she was making a visit to the royal physician Sir James Clark at nearby Birkhall. Over the course of several subsequent private meetings in Scotland there is no doubt the Queen interrogated Nightingale on all things Crimean, and this must have included the much-lauded Jamaican heroine.[15] Predictably, there is no mention of Mrs Seacole in this regard in either Nightingale's letters or the Queen's, nor for that matter in Victoria's journals. Was Mary deliberately redacted out of them?

Some kind of public acknowledgement from Queen Victoria, at this difficult juncture, might have been a great morale-booster for Mary, for at the end of October, she and Thomas Day were hauled before the bankruptcy court in London. The previous day, 26 October, Mary had been involved in a nasty accident. The horse-drawn omnibus in which she had been travelling suddenly tilted over, flinging her and several other passengers to one side. Mary's face was cut and her arm injured, but as she clambered out 'Madame Seacole' – as a press report grandly referred to her – was 'instantly recognized by an officer and some of the Crimean heroes, who at once offered their services, and abused the driver for what they considered his carelessness.'[16] Mary was down, hurt, but not defeated; though she now had a fight on her hands to clear her good name.

The following day, Mary Seacole and Thomas Day junior, of 1 Tavistock Street, Covent Garden and 17 Ratcliffe Terrace, Goswell Road,* 'late of Spring Hill and Balaklava ... provision merchants and traders', appeared in court for the adjudication of the petition of George Ponsonby, Master Mariner of No. 47 Mark Lane, who was named as the Petitioning Creditor, being owed £56 'for goods sold and delivered'. He was in fact one of several suppliers to whom Day & Seacole were indebted, to the tune of around £2,029 (which today is the equivalent of £224,146).[17] But they were not the only Crimean provisioners to have suffered in this way. In September,

---

* Tavistock Street is located just below the Covent Garden piazza, though No. 1 has since disappeared through redevelopment. Ratcliffe Terrace was demolished to make way for a new housing scheme when the area was heavily damaged by bombing during the Second World War.

the owners of St George's Stores, based at the Crimean sutlers' site of 'Donnybrook', had gone bankrupt with equally large debts and losses of £1,635. They too had gone to Crimea on the 'rumours of large profits' but asserted that they had never 'enjoyed a single hour's quiet repose' there due to the 'depredations of thieves' who stole whole cases of wine and brandy and were 'caught rolling away a hogshead of ale'.[18]

Seacole & Day's hearing was set for 6 November before Mr Commissioner Evans at the Bankruptcy Court in Basinghall Street. Here details emerged that Mr Golborn of Kadikoi, the contents of whose store Thomas Day had bought as a speculative venture on behalf of Seacole & Day, was owed £462 on 'goods sold and cash advanced on bills of exchange drawn at the camp'. Mary had 'sold part of the goods he supplied to different regiments, and sent part back to England in her own name'. When examined, she explained how when news of the peace had come, 'the goods at her store ... did not go off so well' and she had only a fortnight to sell all the unsold stock at Balaclava before leaving Crimea. She and Thomas Day admitted liability for £441 in this regard, but there was also the debt incurred by Thomas over horses he had bought in for £353 but had only been able to sell for £120; after the armistice, 'the price of horses so decreased,' he insisted, 'that those which fetched as much as £20 were given away on the troops leaving the Crimea'. At the end of the hearing Mary and Thomas's solicitor asked that the bankrupts be each allowed three guineas a week to live on while the case was adjudicated; the amount was challenged by one of the creditors and reduced to two. Mary was outraged: 'I have got my washing to pay,' she loudly declared, provoking much laughter in court.[19]

We must pause here for an important digression, because Mary Seacole's appearance in court for her bankruptcy hearing attracted considerable attention and press comment, due to the fact that she was seen proudly displaying medals, 'the gaily coloured decorations on her breast being in perfect harmony with the rest of her attire'. According to the *London Evening Standard*, she had been 'honoured

with four Government medals for her kindness to the British soldiery'. The *Illustrated London News* qualified this by saying that
Mary had 'received four medals from *government agencies of various countries*' [my italics]. Unfortunately, none of the contemporary
sources that reported Mary's penchant for wearing her medals wherever she went – and she did so for many years after the war – seems
to have queried how and when she came by them. Nor did any of
the press specify which medals they were. Because of this, confusion
and controversy have reigned ever since, making this one of the most
hotly contested aspects of Mary's Crimean career.[20]

It probably seemed perfectly logical immediately after the war that
the 'Crimean Heroine' had more than earned her medals, and thus
there was no reason to challenge their legitimacy. But at the time
women simply were not singled out for medals; just as they were
excluded from so many other things, such as attending university,
or training as doctors, or even, if married, having control of their
own money. Whether or not Mary's sex was the major obstacle, she
appears nevertheless to have been *given* – perhaps more accurately
than *awarded*, as they did not come through official channels –
the Turkish Medidjie, the French Legion of Honour,* the British
Crimean, and possibly the Sardinian Al Valore Militare. Jamaican
sources speak of a possible fifth medal – a Russian one awarded
posthumously.† The earliest image we have is a pen-and-ink drawing of Mary by William Simpson, probably executed in Crimea or
soon after,[21] in which she is wearing what appear to be two ribbon
bars (lower right-hand side), and possibly the Turkish Medidjie
around her neck.

---

* Both the Medidjie and the Legion of Honour had five classes, but it is not known which
  class Mary's medals were. Mary's surviving Legion of Honour has an imperial crown at
  the top, indicating that it was issued before the fall of the Second Empire in November
  1870. Medals issued after that date had a laurel and oak wreath replacing the crown.
† It is possible that the Russian medal, if she had it, was the special silver medal 'For
  the Sisters of Charity in the Crimea', created for women by Empress Alexandra
  Feodorovna, rather than the military medal 'For the Defence of Sevastopol'. Mary was
  also awarded the Jamaican Order of Merit posthumously in 1999. It may be that this
  Russian item was in fact a religious medallion, given to Mary by a wounded Russian
  after the battle of the Chernaya and not a medal.

MRS. SEACOLE.

Mary can be seen wearing three medals in her 1869 portrait, and four in the terracotta bust made of her by Count Gleichen in 1871; she is also wearing three ribbon bars without medals in a pastel drawing of the 1850s and a later photograph. Occasionally she wore the smaller, dress miniatures of three of them, as in another photograph probably taken for the 1867 Seacole Fund.[22]

In the 1850s it is likely that few people were aware of the protocols involved in the award of the British Crimean medal, which was strictly given to male participants who had been in Crimea prior to the fall of Sevastopol in September 1855. Even in 1856 there was already controversy over the handing out of the campaign medal willy nilly to those who had just happened to be in Crimea at the relevant time but who in fact had never set foot on the battlefield. In addition, Foreign Office files in the National Archives at Kew attest to the strictness of the rules on the acceptance of foreign medals by non-military personnel, with the specification for eligibility being for 'services performed by the Command or with the sanction of Her Majesty'. The only exception to acceptance of a foreign medal was 'as a mark of consideration which might appear to be merited, provided it were not a decoration *intended to be worn*' [my italics]. It was, however, conceded that as the Sultan was omnipotent, any failure to pass on such an award from him might well offend.* It was a delicate matter of diplomacy to say the least.[23]

As we have seen, in a dispatch from Crimea William Howard Russell confirmed in early May 1856 that 'the Sultan has sent Mary a medal'. This probably came about as the result of a personal recommendation by Mary's regular customer the Turkish commander Omar Pasha; or possibly even her friend Dr Amos Henriques in London, who himself had been awarded the Medidjie for his work organising the medical services of the Turkish Army in the 1830s.[24] An interesting and heated debate on the subject of the Sultan sending unsolicited medals to non-combatants can be found in Foreign Office papers at the National Archives, where several FO officials got very hot under the collar about this perceived breach of their sacred protocols. For several British officers and male civilians were sent the Medidjie by the Sultan for their services to the Turks in Crimea, but officials insisted that 'the civilians could not in the opinion of this government be brought in any way within the spirit of the rule'. It would appear from all this that Abdulmecid I had sent Mary the medal on his own initiative and she naturally enough had gratefully accepted, without knowing that she needed permission from the Foreign Office.[25]

There is sadly no mention anywhere to be found of when Mary received her other foreign decorations, but she certainly possessed the French Legion of Honour, for that and the Medidjie were passed on to her sister Louisa after Mary's death and are now in the Institute of Jamaica in Kingston.[26] At one time the Institute had a third medal, but this was sadly lost when an earthquake in 1908 badly damaged the building. Dutch Seacole researchers Corry Staring-Derks and Jeroen Staring inspected the two surviving medals in Jamaica in July 2006, although the ribbons to which they were originally attached had by then been sadly misplaced.[27]

---

* Three other women are known to have been awarded the Medidjie: Queen Victoria, Lady Layard, and – the most well documented – Baroness Burdett-Coutts, who was awarded the Diamond Star and the Medidjie 1st Class by Sultan Abdul Hamid II for her philanthropic work for Muslim women and children during the Russo-Turkish War of 1877-8. Lady Layard was the wife of the British ambassador to Constantinople, who did similar humanitarian work during that war.

While it is possible that the French made some special concession to award their national medal to a female civilian for her humanitarian and nursing care, the award of the British Crimean medal, which was governed by very strict protocols, is more difficult to explain. In his 'Reminiscences of the War in the East', published in 1856, chaplain John Boudier noted that Mary had applied for the British Crimean medal while still out in Crimea. Writing his memoirs in 1911, surgeon Douglas Arthur Reid noted that 'the Authorities, in recognition of her benevolent services, awarded [Mary] a Crimean Medal' and that when he bumped into her after the war parading down Charing Cross, it was the medal that 'first attracted my eye'.[28] Indeed, she continued to wear them long after the war was over, as a way of keeping the memory of her finest hour alive and sending out a signal to all those she might encounter of who she was.[29] A Belgian newspaper in 1858 also noted a sighting of Mary wearing three of her medals (see page 250).

Mary Seacole detractors have, over the years, repeatedly attempted to discredit her wearing of the Crimean medal in particular, claiming that as a female civilian she simply was not eligible and that absence of documentary evidence is sufficient to label her a fraud. They seem unable, however, to support this claim by showing that Mary obtained her medals by devious means; nor are they willing to entertain the perfectly logical possibility that so anxious were the powers-that-be to acknowledge Mary's much-appreciated contribution that they circumvented the established protocols and gifted the medal to her, 'by the back door' as it were. True, this would not have made it official, for on paper there were no exceptions with regard to the medal being given to a female civilian, and many hours of searching the medal records at Kew confirmed that to me. But just because there were rules, does not mean they could not be overlooked in exceptional cases such as Mary's and, given how greatly she was loved and admired by the military, we should give her the benefit of the doubt.

The most likely explanation is that Mary's high-profile patrons in the army and the royal family used their influence for an exception to be made in Mrs Seacole's case.[30] Indeed, they might even have taken the matter to the ultimate arbiter, Victoria herself, who had the prerogative powers to do what *she* saw fit and instruct the Duke of Cambridge as commander-in-chief of the army, or even Lord Panmure at the War Office, to waive the rules.* (Interestingly, Lord Panmure just happened to be well acquainted with Mary's friend and champion, Alexis Soyer.)[31] Surely it would be an acceptable indulgence, not just of Mrs Seacole's burning desire to be rewarded for her work in Crimea, but of those who had benefitted from or witnessed it, including the Queen's own nephew? Propriety might not have allowed the Queen to meet Mary formally, but she could support her privately by making this gift possible. In conclusion, we must ask ourselves this important question: would Mary Seacole have paraded around among Crimean War veterans – many of them high-ranking – wearing medals that she had not been rightfully given, and in so doing risk being reprimanded as a fraud? An anonymous article in the *Journal for the Society for Army Historical Research* in 1956 perhaps is the closest we shall ever come to the truth: 'I know of no award of the medal to those who were not on the roll of the Expeditionary Force except Mrs Seacole ... *who was granted the Crimean Medal without clasp, after much trouble.* [my italics] But she was, as far as I know, the only one who got the medal.'[32]

Whether or not Mary flouted official rules in the wearing of her medals, everyone seems to have turned a blind eye. We have no way of knowing how exactly she came by them, bar the Medidjie sent to her by the Sultan when she was still in Crimea, for, like so many aspects of her story, there is no paper trail. But it is puzzling that she makes no specific mention among her 'jewellery, ornaments and trinkets' in her will written in 1876 of those precious medals of which she was so inordinately proud.[33]

*

---

* The Duke was one of the most distinguished patrons of both the 1857 and 1867 Seacole Funds, to which he donated £10 and £15 respectively. Might he have put in a word for Mary getting the Crimean medal? Fox Maule-Ramsay, 2nd Baron Panmure from 1852, had been appointed Secretary for War in Lord Palmerston's new government in February 1855.

In the final hearing of the Seacole & Day bankruptcy in January 1857, a full audit of their debts revealed that the partners had losses of £2,342 (over a quarter of a million pounds today), with £997 alone on property that they had been forced to leave behind at Balaclava. Many of their debtors, inevitably, were 'chiefly military and naval officers', the worst being a £35. 5s. forged draft on Cox's bank by a Captain St Clair, who had promptly done a bunk from Crimea. Thomas Day had additional liabilities carried over from his mining speculation in Panama, for he had 'drawn bills on the West Granada and Veraguas Gold and Silver Mining Company which the chairman, since bankrupt, refused to accept'.[34]

The news of the serious debt Mary was in was widely circulated in the British press; it came as a shock to her many supporters and 'elicited many expressions of regret from those who were witnesses of her exertions and acts of benevolence' in Crimea, for 'it was thought that the old lady had returned home in good circumstances.'[35] On 22 November it prompted one of Mary's many supporters to write a 'spirited' letter to *The Times* suggesting Mary's friends 'rally round' to help her:

> That good old soul whose generous hospitality has warmed up many a gallant spirit on the chilly heights of Balaklava has now in her turn been caught in the worst storm of all – the gale of adversity.
>
> Where are the Crimeans? Have a few months erased from their memories those many acts of comforting kindness which made the name of the old mother venerated throughout the camp? While the benevolent deeds of Florence Nightingale are being handed down to posterity with blessings and imperishable renown, are the humbler actions of Mrs Seacole to be entirely forgotten, and will none now substantially testify to the worth of those services of the late mistress of Spring Hill?[36]

The writer, who signed himself 'Da Meritis', concluded by saying he was 'happy to forward a check for £20' to any fund for Mary's benefit.

The letter was sent from the Reform Club – not by Alexis Soyer, who had left his employment there and was now suffering chronic ill health – but probably by one of Mary's high-ranking military friends.

Lord Rokeby, who had commanded the 1st Division in Crimea, was soon to lead the charge to rescue her. Three days later he put his name to a more formal appeal in *The Times* describing how Mary had paid him a visit recently 'requesting advice and assistance'. How typical of Mary to go to the top to seek help! She could not have had a more distinguished patron to kickstart her campaign, for Major General Lord Rokeby KCB, who had been honoured with the Order of the Bath at the ceremony attended by Mary at Army HQ, confirmed that the idea of a subscription had first been mooted when Mary was still out in Crimea. This clearly had not got off the ground and Rokeby had now assured her that he would promote a fundraiser to help her set herself up in business again, once she was released from bankruptcy. He had already approached the bankers Cox & Co. to handle any funds raised.[37] On the 27th, another supporter, signing himself 'A Friend to Merit', wrote to the *Evening Mail* describing how he had recently visited Mary at Tavistock Street. He had known her 'for some months in the Crimea' and could testify 'to her self-sacrificing and bountiful kindness to all sick and wounded who came under her notice'. Like many others, this witness confirmed the 'numerous diseases that she had to contend with' there and that 'she has been several times under fire.'[38]

Mary was touched by the efforts being made to assist her and from Tavistock Street wrote to Lord Rokeby, in duly humble terms, thanking him for his *'past kindness'*. That and the generous concern of others was helping to *'sustain me in my present difficulties'*, she said. Indeed, she *'would much rather suffer my present poverty, with the knowledge that the Almighty permitted me to be useful in my sphere,'* she went on, *'than have returned wealthy without the esteem and regard of the brave defenders of our country'.*[39] Mary's letter was published in the *Evening Mail* on 1 December and five days later the popular weekly magazine *Punch* finally set the ball rolling with a spirited 'Stir For Seacole', extolling Mary's care and compassion at her iron house near the Col, set to the tune of the popular song 'Old King Coal':

[DECEMBER 6. 1856.]　PUNCH, OR THE LONDON CHARIVARI.　221

EASIER SAID THAN DONE.

Hair-Dresser. "*M'sieu wish ze barbe shave?*"

Resident Parisian. "*Oui, je fay—a—that is, I do.—And—a—I say, just trimmay le moostarsh à l' Omperoor, sivvooplay—like—a—that is—com le vôtre—I mean, you know, like yours!*"

SCOTLAND SNUBBED

THERE can be no doubt in the breast of any impartial Scotchman that a conspiracy has a long time existed among Englishmen, in fact, the plot has become an English affair—to Snub Scotland. Otherwise, it has been and is forcibly put—otherwise, why the exclusive use of the word English, which simply implies things of England, to the contemptuous disuse of British, that comprehends both countries? In our thriving contemporary, the *Caledonian Mercury*, the case is admirably put. Indeed, the columns of the *Mercury* seem especially chosen by all patriotic Scotchmen with a grievance. Thus, when in his recent lectures, our tender and judicious THACKERAY, with gentlest breath that would have scarcely stirred a white rose-leaf, ventured to say something of the living and vivacious dust of MARY QUEEN of SCOTS, there was great indignation. The *perfervidum genium Scotorum* glowed at white heat; and sundry patriots in the *Mercury* did battle for MARY, proving her every bit as nice and as judicious as our virgin ELIZABETH, whose chastity, like a *chevaux-de-frise* defied even cavalry. However, THACKERAY has made his peace; and MARY rests, like a folded lily, every bit as pure as when THACKERAY entered Edinburgh.

And now in the *Mercury* a Scottish patriot draws his claymore steel-pen for his country. He writes, and what is more cruel, brings in ALISON:—

"Even historians, ALISON, for instance, constantly use the word English, a mere translation from the French, who have no word for Britain except that of their own old Province. Some years ago a letter was published under the heading of 'LORD PALMERSTON and the QUEEN's English,' according to which his Lordship gave assurance that, in using on some occasion which caused remark in Scotland, the word English and England, he meant no disparagement to Scotland, Ireland, or Wales."

And the potato slept quietly under the slight; so did the leek—but not so the thistle. *Nemo me impune!* Nevertheless, it is a part of a system to annihilate Scotland.

"I cannot help thinking that there is *a systematical design* in some petty-minded quarter *to consign the word Scotland to oblivion*, and that the custom above mentioned has been introduced surreptitiously *by underlings in public departments* without the knowledge of persons in authority."

And when we consider the number of Scotch clerks in public department's in England—clerks who originally swam the Tweed, carrying their clothes in a bundle in their teeth—the neglect, the ingratitude on their part is the more atrocious. Scotchmen, it is known, generally bring with them to England a very beautiful account; and yet it is painful to witness the designs, yes, the "systematical designs" on the part of English wives to take the very words out of their Scotch husbands' mouths, and so to deprive them of their own

lovely Doric. We have known the design so far succeed that after only one year's residence in England a Scotchman has wholly forgotten the Scotch hawbee in favour of the English shilling.

We think, with the *Mercury's* correspondent, the whole matter in its length, breadth, and depth worthy of gravest consideration. Why should there be anything exclusively English, and why not everything comprehensively British? Let the word English henceforth cease and determine; and let us enter into a national bond to use only the word British.

For instance, let an English fog be a British Mist:
Let the English Constitution be a British Pact:
Let an English Mastiff be a British Tyke:—
And, above all, and as a great sustaining hope, and comfort, and consolation unto all men, henceforth let the Bank of England be—*A British Bank!*

A STIR FOR SEACOLE.

DAME SEACOLE was a kindly old soul,
　And a kindly old soul was she;
You might call for your pot, you might call for your pipe,
　In her tent on "the Col" so free.

Her tent on "the Col," where a welcome toll
　She took of the passing throng,
That from Balaklava to the front
　Toiled wearily along.

That berry-brown face, with a kind heart's trace
　Impressed in each wrinkle sly,
Was a sight to behold, through the snow-clouds rolled
　Across that iron sky.

The cold without gave a zest, no doubt,
　To the welcome warmth within:
But her smile, good old soul, lent heat to the coal,
　And power to the pannikin.

No store she set by the epaulette,
　Be it worsted or gold-lace;
For K.C.B., or plain private SMITH,
　She had still one pleasant face.

But not alone was her kindness shown
　To the hale and hungry lot,
Who drank her grog and eat her prog,
　And paid their honest shot.

The sick and sorry can tell the story
　Of her nursing and dosing deeds,
Regimental M.D. never worked as she
　In helping sick men's needs.

Of such work, God knows, was as much as she chose,
　That dreary winter-tide,
When Death hung o'er the damp and pestilent camp,
　And his scythe swung far and wide.

And when winter past, and spring at last
　Made the mud-sea a sea of flowers,
Doating, race and review her brown face knew,
　Still pleasant, in sunshine or showers.

Still she'd take her stand, as blithe and bland,
　With her stores, the jolly old soul—
And—be the right man in the right place who can—
　The right woman was Dame SEACOLE

She gave her aid to all who prayed,
　To hungry, and sick, and cold:
Open hand and heart, alike ready to part
　Kind words, and acts, and gold.

And now the good soul is 'in the hole,'
　What red-coat in all the land,
But to set her upon her legs again
　Will not lend a willing hand?

Humanity in the Slave Market.

THE *New Orleans Delta* insists that "the African *slave trade* and African slavery conducted on humane principles, and regulated by law, must have the preference over every other form of compulsory labour." When Humanity has quite settled itself as a slave-dealer, of course we shall have Philanthropy beginning business as a housebreaker, and Rectitude making its way through a crowd as a pickpocket.

No monies, however, could be collected on Mary's behalf until she was freed from her bankruptcy. The final hearing came on 8 January 1857, when Commissioner Evans audited the accounts.

The Times reported the following day on the collective shame of Mary's debtors, who 'included about 100 generals, colonels, majors, captains, lieutenants, and other officers', who it was hoped, as 'good' debtors owing smallish sums, would yet pay her back. The worst of them was William Knight, who had replaced Nicholas Woods as special correspondent of the *Morning Herald*, and who owed her £260 on his account at Spring Hill; even William Howard Russell had prevailed on the lady's goodwill, owing her five shillings and ninepence.[40] Mr Evans concluded that Mary and Thomas Day should be issued with Class I certificates, indicating that they were not personally at fault in becoming bankrupts.[41]

Mary finally got her ticket of leave, which would allow her to set up in business again, at the certificate meeting on 29 January. As bankruptcy cases went, this was a very speedy dispatch, no doubt precipitated by her celebrity. As she left the court, Mary was asked what class certificate she had been granted. To which she responded in 'a voice sufficiently audible to be heard by everybody': '*What class! A first to be sure. Am I not a first-class woman?*'[42]

Mass circulation of this characteristic Seacole witticism in the British press confirmed that Mary had no intention of being forgotten. She was confident, she told the court, that '*though bankrupt, she had a numerous family – the British Army – who would not forget her*'. What is more, she was '*quite ready to go out to India if she could be of any service to the army*' – an offer of service that anticipated the later one she made after the outbreak of the Indian Rebellion in May.[43] In the meantime, Mary was still trying to claw back some money from her remaining unsold stock. A small ad in the *Morning Advertiser* announced the 'Important Sale of Crimean Stores, without the slightest reserve, being a large portion of the Stock of Mrs Seacole, supplied by first-class houses, and re-packed and removed for convenience of sale' at Old Swan Wharf, Upper Thames Street.[44]

It wasn't until April 1857 that William Howard Russell launched the long-promised Seacole Fund. In a letter to *The Times*, he extolled Mary's virtues and courage, emphasising that 'if this poor woman had been paid what she was owed [presumably he had now paid off his own debt?] ... she would need no subscription', and adding cryptically that 'she has been deceived and robbed by one in whom she placed trust and confidence'.[45] This appears to be a veiled dig at Thomas Day.

A few days later 'Mrs Seacole's late partner in the Crimea' – aka Day – wrote to *The Times* explaining the reason for the bankruptcy, clearly concerned that this would cast doubt on Mary's good character and also that the bad debts from officers might prejudice the amount of money donated to her fund. Most of these debts had now been paid, he stated, adding that 'The principal causes of the bankruptcy, as proved to the satisfaction of the official and trade assignees, were losses by the elements and by robbery, and the depreciation of stock-in-trade and buildings consequent on the unexpectedly rapid evacuation of the Crimea on the conclusion of the war.' Russell, however, would have none of it; the following day he responded in *The Times*: 'I beg to say it was from Mrs. Seacole's lips I heard the story that she had lost much money, and was likely to lose more, by the injudicious manner in which "her partner" cashed bills – I did not say the bills of officers of the army – in the Crimea.'[46]

The implication here is that Day had badly mismanaged the financial side of things, control of which had been put into his hands by the too-trusting Mary. Russell also clearly sought to defend the relatively small debt of the military. One wonders, going on his comments, whether Thomas Day had also perhaps been equally inefficient or reckless with the money Mary invested in his Panamanian mining enterprises. Either way, this is the last we hear of Thomas Day; indeed, Mary tells us at the end of her memoir, written at around this time, that '*one of us started only the other day for the Antipodes.*' Did Day set off in search of better prospects, perhaps in the Australian goldfields or some other speculation?[47] With such a common name and no other concrete details to go on, finding him is impossible. He leaves the stage as unobtrusively as he entered it.

As for Sally, and whether she was there in London to share in her mother's postwar celebrity, we have no word at all.

CHAPTER 21

WONDERFUL ADVENTURES OF MRS SEACOLE IN MANY LANDS

The spring of 1857 was a trying time for Mary, as she waited for fundraising on her behalf to gather momentum. The initial response to the Seacole Fund had not been very good. To put it bluntly, 'Poor old Mrs Seacole is hard up now', *Punch* told its readers on 2 May; with its wide reach and appeal it clearly hoped to get the word out where smaller news items had so far failed.[1] Mary had, of course, been in financial difficulty before and was never one to idly sit back and wait for others to dig her out of trouble. So, in the meantime, she used her initiative and set about exploiting the one remaining resource she could draw on – her memoirs.

She would not be the first Black woman to publish a book in England – that honour goes to the Boston poet Phillis Wheatley, a former enslaved woman who was provided with an exceptionally good education by her master and rapidly showed promise as a talented poet. Unable to publish her work in America, she had sailed to England in 1773 to bring out her *Poems on Various Subjects, Religious and Moral* with a publisher in Aldgate.* Much to the

---

* Wheatley was America's first published Black author – male or female. Her book provoked considerable controversy and curiosity, but she died tragically young of TB, before her second collection could be published. Mary Prince's 1831 *History of Mary Prince* predates Mary Seacole's, but she was unknown prior to publication.

surprise of a London literary establishment predisposed to look down on the 'Negroes of Africa ... as a dull, ignorant, and ignoble race of men', Phillis Wheatley's volume of poetry was as a whole deemed to be 'indeed extraordinary, considered as the production of a young Negro, who was, but a few years since, an illiterate barbarian.' What is more, the female author had showed herself to be 'of a ferocious, and religious turn of mind'.[2]

Mary's book would, however, be the first Black celebrity memoir and certainly the first account of war by a Black woman. We do not know whether the publisher James Blackwood of Paternoster Row invited Mary to write it; but with a successful line in adventurous, anecdotal travelogues, in cheap cardboard yellowbacks, he clearly sensed the potential of such a book. It would have been ideal for his circulating library market, if Mary's then widespread fame was anything to go by. Either that, or Mary enlisted friends such as William Howard Russell to help her find a publisher and put in a word for her; Russell was certainly more than happy to write a glowing introduction to it. Either way, *Wonderful Adventures* was written at speed; but with regard to the timeframe of its conception, writing and editing, there is not a shred of evidence in the surviving documents in the James Blackwood archive at Oxford University.[3]

When Mary sat down to write, she had moved to new lodgings at 14 Soho Square. Although she had the comfort of the Roman Catholic chapel of St Patrick across the Square, this was another temporary address at which she did not linger long. We know this much because she wrote a grateful letter of thanks from there to her champions at *Punch*. It came in response to a piece the magazine had published on 2 May, headlined 'The Mother of the Regiment', lauding Mary's talents not just as a sutler but as 'a mother and nurse to the wounded soldier'. Mary's letter was published, with an illustration under the heading 'Our Own Vivandière', on 30 May. 'Mother Seacole loves to acknowledge the kindness shown her by her sons, whether in black or red coats, of a suffering army, and hastens to assure *Punch* that she has long felt a mother's affection for him,' she wrote, describing how vividly she recalled how she had 'walked through the wards of the [LTC] hospital at Spring Hill, her arms laden with papers' and how 'the sufferers would plead for a glimpse of *Punch*, which seldom failed to have a heart-stirring piece of poetry or a noble sketch in appreciation of their struggles'. She drew strength from remembering those sad old times, for '*it stirs the heart of MOTHER SEACOLE like the sound of the old war-cry she may never hear again, to find her poor name noticed in the columns which cheered on England to a noble contest.*' Mary could not resist laying on the faux humility at this juncture, by alluding to the now very straitened circumstances in which she found herself:

> *And more than this. MOTHER SEACOLE in this, her season of want – for the Peace which brought blessings to so many ruined her – feels that the notice of her good son* Punch *brings sunshine into the poor little room – not quite a garret yet, thank God, she has one more weary story to climb before her pallet rests so near the sky – to which she is reduced.*

OUR OWN VIVANDIÈRE.

Nothing was more guaranteed to move her supporters than the image of good old Mother Seacole shivering in a draughty garret, and without a blush Mary exploited this opportunity of galvanising sympathy with her closing words:

> *Not that the army's mother murmurs at her lot. She knows that she is not flung aside – like some of the brave men for whose blood there is no further need; and she believes there will yet be work for her to do somewhere. Perhaps in China, perhaps on some other distant shore to which Englishmen go to serve their country, there may be woman's work to do – and for that work if her good son* Punch *will cheer her on old MOTHER SEACOLE has a heart and hands left yet.*[4]

Punch had a circulation of around 165,000 in the 1850s, especially among London's middle classes, and the publication of Mary's letter certainly elicited the desired response. On 13 June, a Seacole Fund Committee under the chairmanship of Major General Lord Rokeby, KCB was announced in *The Times*. The names were impressive and included Prince Edward of Saxe-Weimar, the Duke of Newcastle, the Duke of Wellington, General Burgoyne, Major General Airey, Rear Admiral Lushington and William Howard Russell. The treasurer, William T. Doyne, late Superintendent General of the AWC in Crimea, set up bank accounts and was pleased to accept subscriptions at his home at 2 Derby Street, Westminster. The following day, a major validation of Mary Seacole as 'A Real Crimean Heroine' – one for the working classes, not just the toffs – was published in the extremely popular and radical *Reynolds's Weekly Newspaper*. Published weekly at a price of one penny, *Reynolds's* had a reach of around 350,000 copies among the working classes, thanks to its vigorous championing of the rights of the common man.[5]

The article is important in that it addresses an issue ignored by the majority of the press, that being the preoccupation with awarding attention and medals to 'a lot of titled popinjays' who went around 'flaunting it in all the pride of military promotion' with their breasts 'blazoned with ribbons, crosses, and medals', while the real heroes of the Crimean War – the rank and file of the army – had, during the campaign, been 'perishing, like rotten sheep, from famine, exposure and disease'. While these 'miserable impostors' had had an easy war or had managed to get themselves sent home early on some excuse or other, 'one brave-hearted and noble-spirited woman remained at her post – firm, undaunted, and undismayed – giving food to the hungry soldier, and tending him like a mother in the hour of sickness. We allude to that gallant old lady, Mrs Seacole, whose humanity, fortitude, and genuine Christian benevolence were often alluded to in terms of the highest praise in the admirable letters written by Mr Russell and other newspaper correspondents, from the Crimea.'

The paper did not flinch from mentioning that Mrs Seacole had set up her business in Crimea, 'of course, with a view to making it a profitable concern', but such had been the level of suffering in the army encamped in Crimea that her store at Spring Hill had become far more than that. It had been a refuge, where Mary had acted as a 'ministering angel' to 'many a gallant fellow who would, without her aid, have probably perished, either by disease or by famine'. For indeed, 'many a half-starved soldier, who came away empty-handed from the commissariat, obtained "a bit and a sup" gratuitously at "Mother Seacole's".' The article went on to berate the government for looking after the aristocrats in the army, 'the Cardigans, Cambridges, Lucans etc.', and urged that Mary be granted a pension.[6]

When we come to the writing of Mary's memoir, we run up against questions that have been asked about its authorship that once more require us to pause. At the end of *Wonderful Adventures* Mary tells us: '*I kept no written diary*' and apologises for the fact that '*I have jumbled up events strangely*', adding that '*Unless I am allowed to tell the story of my life in my own way, I cannot tell it at all.*'[7] She clearly wrote her highly idiosyncratic account straight from memory and without much preparation – as a stream of consciousness, which would have needed help in getting it all down on paper so quickly. The memoir would be an important asset to the fundraising campaign on her behalf, thus perhaps explaining why it was written at short notice.

It is possible that Mary sat down with her editor and dictated it to him and they discussed it as they went along; or she drafted it first and he then went over the text correcting the grammar and spelling and ironing out any lacunae. At the time, the *Literary Gazette* noted in its review that 'a clever editor has put her recollections into a readable shape.'[8] But unfortunately, Mary's critics – often the same ones who insist that she wore her medals fraudulently – are eager to make the leap from 'editor' to 'ghostwriter' and dismiss the book as not being Mary's own work at all. To do so is to deny what a highly articulate and witty woman Mary Seacole was. Everything we know about her from contemporary accounts suggests she had a gift of repartee and a spontaneous and vivid turn of phrase. She never shrank from expressing her opinions, or lecturing others on subjects that preoccupied her, such as slavery. She was a natural raconteur, who loved to talk and laugh and share memories of her travels with anyone who would listen.

No doubt there is an implicit racism lurking behind the rejection of a Black woman's ability – or that of any other Black author, male or female at that time – to write such an engrossing, amusing and frequently moving text. How could a Black woman have written for a genre that was then dominated by male writers? On the other hand: could a white, middle-class, male, Victorian editor, with probably no experience of Jamaica, have produced this highly idiosyncratic narrative, with its distinctively feminine West Indian lilt?

Doubts about Mary's authorship – then and now – in themselves say more about the prejudices of the deniers than the presumed dishonesty of the author. Nevertheless, they certainly surfaced at the time. For example, *The Critic* asserted that 'it may, indeed be said that Mrs. Seacole has not written a line' of her book; the *Leader* thought that *Wonderful Adventures* was 'probably composed for the valiant widow', though it conceded that to all appearances it was 'substantially truthful'. The critic of the *Examiner* thought that 'Mrs Seacole tells, through the pen of a ready writer, the authentic story of her life', at least conceding that Mary had a natural talent for telling a story.[9] But would the respected war correspondent William Howard Russell have put his name to the introduction if he had known that the memoir was not Mary's own work? Suggestions that Russell was the ghostwriter simply do not hold water. Having returned from the tsar's coronation in Moscow at the end of 1856, on Charles Dickens's advice he set about preparing a lecture tour on the Crimean War, as well as writing his own account of it, before heading off to cover the Indian Rebellion. What a shame that the two-volume biography of Russell published in 1911 makes no mention whatsoever of his preface, or Mary Seacole, or Russell's role in her fundraising campaign.[10]

So who then *was* Mary Seacole's elusive editor, named on the title page, in initials only as 'W.J.S.'? For the Seacole biographer that tedious Victorian reticence of initials is utterly infuriating when one already has to battle against so many gaps in her story. In her 2005 biography Jane Robinson plumped for the most logical candidate: William James Stewart, a writer and novelist who in 1857 edited Gustav Freytag's *Speculation; or Debtor and Creditor: A Romance from the German*, that was also published by Blackwood, in November.[11] But we have nothing at all to link Stewart to Mary Seacole other than him having the right initials. Rather than capitulate, let us consider for a moment an intriguing comment in *Wonderful Adventures* that could suggest another possible option.

Just like Sally, might Mary's editor have been hiding in plain sight? For in chapter 2 on page 7 she drops a significant clue when she says the following:

> It may be *as my editor says* – [my italics]
> 'That gently comes the world to those
> That are cast in gentle mould.'

The quotation is from a poem by Alfred, Lord Tennyson; written in 1833, it is entitled 'To J.S.' The dedicatee is his very dear friend James Spedding, and the poem was written to console Spedding for

the death of his brother, Edward. At university, Spedding was in
Tennyson's circle of 'Cambridge Apostles' along with their mutual
friend Arthur Henry Hallam, who died tragically young and was
famously celebrated in Tennyson's *In Memoriam*. Spedding is best
known as the editor of the works of the philosopher Francis Bacon,
but until about 1841 he had served in the Colonial Office with
another Cambridge friend, Henry Taylor, a powerful advocate of
Abolition. At the Colonial Office, where he was 'considered one of
the bright lights', Spedding published several government papers
on colonial problems such as 'The Condition of the Labouring
Population in the West Indies', 'The Jamaica Bill' and 'Negro
Apprenticeship'.[12] Could it be that, with an understanding of the
West Indies and the issue of Black emancipation, he was enlisted
to cast a sympathetic eye over Mary's text? Spedding's work at the
CO was strongly abolitionist and Mary held very outspoken views
with regard to slavery in America. They would have had much in
common. It would make sense, for Spedding lived in chambers at
60 Lincoln's Inn Fields, only a mile or so from Mary's garret in
Soho Square. But no, I cannot for the life of me explain the 'W'
of W.J.S. – unless it is '*with* James Spedding'; and that, alas, is the
problem.[*13]

Wonderful Adventures of Mrs Seacole in Many Lands was published
in the third week of June 1857 in a print run of 10,000 copies. It
featured a splendid front cover engraving of Mary, satchel over her
shoulder and bandages in hand, executed by the promising young
wood-engraver Thomas Dewell Scott. He would have worked from
an original drawing, possibly that of Mary by war artist William
Simpson on page 220. He might well have been acquainted with
Simpson thanks to his work for *Illustrated London News*, to which

---

*   On page 119 Mary relates how 'my editor' told her the story of the Hydra of Greek
     and Roman mythology. Spedding had been a tripos classical scholar at Cambridge,
     graduating in 1831. Francis Bacon, whose life and letters he edited between 1857 and
     1859, wrote about the myth of Hercules and the many-headed Hydra in his *The Great
     Instauration* of 1620, with which Spedding would have been well acquainted.

they both contributed.[14] To tie in with publication and satisfy a growing demand for images of this famous personality, a fortnight later
the Royal Polytechnic Institute in Regent Street offered for sale 'an
admirable likeness of the MOTHER of the British ARMY'.[15] It is too
early for this 'likeness' to have been a mass-produced *carte de visite*
photograph, but it might have been a print of Dewell's engraving,
although copies of it were very expensive at 5s., 10s. and £2. 2s.

When the book was published, many newspapers, even if they did
not review it, carried advertisements in their columns, often with
puffs, such as this one in the *Morning Post* for 20 August:

Tenth Thousand, 1s. 6d., with Portrait, post free,

MRS. SEACOLE'S WONDERFUL
ADVENTURES in MANY LANDS.

" We can safely recommend this little work."—Illustrated News.
" A sketch of her life was wanted to render complete the literature of the Crimean struggle."—Athenæum.
" Mrs. Seacole tells, through the pen of a ready writer, the
authentic story of her life."—Examiner.
" Quite unique in literature."—W. H. Russell ("Times" Correspondent).

London : James Blackwood, Paternoster-row.

The first review came in the *London Evening Standard* on 2 July. It
was warm in its commendation of the book's 'humble and spirited
pages' that reflected 'the humanity and heroism of Mrs Seacole'
and her 'extraordinary qualities'. The *Standard* did not feature
an extract, but many papers, rather than review the book, instead
offered lengthy extracts prefaced by only brief introductory comments. *Reynolds's Weekly Newspaper* did so, drawing its readers'
attention to the narrative as being 'given in a plain, homely, unassuming style'. Some of the more high-minded journals, however,
could not resist a condescending tone, such as the *Examiner*, which
noted that Mary tells the 'authentic story of her life ... with an
agreeable complacency'.[16] It also pointed out that the profession of
sutler 'was raised to the dignity of a Fine Art by Mrs Seacole'. On
this topic, the literary journal *The Athenaeum* was at pains to contrast Mary Seacole's virtues with the sutler-cum-camp follower of
eighteenth-century military campaigns, such as the pipe-smoking,
gin-swigging Moll Flagon, immortalised in a 1780 comic opera

The Lord of the Manor by John Burgoyne.* The *Kentish Gazette* was much more positive in the way in which it focused on Mary as 'the stout, brown, middle-aged, kind-hearted woman, the queen of "sutters" and *cantinieres*, who went about among the wounded in the Crimea, administering healing and comfort from her capacious store'. It noted too that her business 'was not conducted on commercial principles, for she contrived to do more good and lose more money at the seat of war than any other person of her class.' The *Lady's Own Paper* drew particular attention to the fact that 'the medical knowledge she had acquired in the West Indies proved of eminent service,' as did the *Illustrated London News* – in one of the most important, major reviews – which spoke of her as a 'Creole doctress, skilled in the qualities of herbs etc., and familiar with diseases, the very names of which sound terrible to our ears', and also lauded her 'powers of energy and endurance' that are rarely found in women.[17]

It was the snobby literary journal *The Critic* that over a dense, two-page review indulged its own withering sense of literary superiority. Its elitist bias is unmistakable, not to mention its misogyny with regard to female authors, when it opens by saying, 'Our uniform desire to do justice to the productions of the ladies would prevent us from being too critical with this book.' It was dismissive too of Russell's introduction, which was 'not very remarkable' and conceded that the narrative was adequate enough 'to take up a couple of hours' amusement'. Mrs Seacole was 'a jolly old soul', but her holistic medical skills were little more than 'leechcraft'. *The Critic* did at least note Mary's 'especial detestation' of slavery; but her experience of racism at the hands of the 'Yankees' was seen as mere 'annoyances'. In contradiction of this narrow view, it is interesting to note that many press extracts singled out this precise episode in her story, specifically titled 'Mrs Seacole and the Americans'.[18] Was

---

* Several papers drew attention to Mary's profession as 'sutler' in somewhat condescending tones, and without giving equal acknowledgement to her numberless generous acts of kindness and the medical and pharmaceutical skills that she freely gave to those who needed them. It is an attitude that has persisted even with critics today.

Mary's book perhaps a secret weapon in the continuing campaign for the abolition of slavery in the USA?

Only a few papers expressed a degree of negative bias towards Mary, not on racial grounds but rather on the strength of her sometimes self-aggrandising personality and perhaps too her lack of dutiful humility, as might be expected from a colonial subject. Such self-confident expressions from a Black Jamaican woman were, after all, something of a surprise to many. Either way, *Wonderful Adventures* was a runaway success and the fact that Mary had triumphed in the male world of war did not go unnoticed. Her 'sense of discharging her duty, in a sphere which few women have the courage or the animal spirits to approach', was admirable, wrote the *Weekly Star & Bell's News-letter*. The *Bristol Mercury* agreed; it was 'a stirring tale of real life such as few females have encountered', that was 'calculated to evoke a greatly expanded appreciation of [Mary's] character and services'. It had the added advantage that 'its cheapness places it within the reach of all classes of readers.' And now, in the wake of her book's publication, a spectacular four-day fundraiser was being held at the Royal Surrey Gardens music hall, which it was hoped would ensure 'a comfortable independence ... to smooth the latter days of the energetic, untiring, humane and faithful, Mary Seacole'.[19]

At the end of July 1857, Mary Seacole was at the zenith of her postwar fame. As the guest of honour at the Royal Surrey Gardens, she unashamedly revelled in the acclaim and adoration of her many fans, both military and civilian. It was the kind of reception that would have been accorded Florence Nightingale, 'had she not studiously avoided it'.[20] A great deal of energy had gone into what was an enormous and ambitious 'Grand Military Festival', under the musical directorship of the impresario and conductor Louis-Antoine Jullien. Jullien, like his compatriot Alexis Soyer, was a natural showman and rose to the occasion with a flamboyant and thrilling musical programme, conducted with a diamond-studded baton. It featured an immense ensemble comprising Jullien's own orchestra and the combined talents of eleven bands drawn from the regiments of the Life Guards, Horse Guards, Grenadier Guards, Scots Fusilier Guards, Royal Engineers, Royal Artillery, Royal Marines and the 11th Hussars. It was claimed that 1,000 performers, drawn from an assortment of opera houses and choral societies, took part, with solos provided by leading vocalists of the era: Madame Hermine Rudersdorff, Monsieur Edouard Gassier and Madame Josefa Gassier, and Mr Sims Reeves. Mrs Seacole, not one to miss a gift horse, would of course be there, only too willing, so the *Era* announced, to 'provide her friends with copies of the "History of her Adventures" [*sic*].'[21]

The programme for the festival was extensively advertised on the front pages of the *Sun, Morning Advertiser, Morning Chronicle, Morning Post*, and other leading dailies, detailing a selection of Jullien's own specially composed military quadrilles, such as the 'British Army' and the 'English'; rousing tunes guaranteed to please: 'God Save the Queen' accompanied by a 'discharge of cannon, fired by an electric battery', 'Rule Britannia', 'See the Conquering Hero Comes'; and classical favourites from Handel's 'Hallelujah Chorus', songs by Purcell, arias from Mozart's *Don Giovanni*, and a Beethoven symphony.[22] Tickets for the exclusive opening night – Monday 27 July – were a pricey five shillings, no doubt designed to keep out the hoi polloi; the price was halved for the three remaining evenings, but even 2s. 6d.* at that time was way beyond the reach of the average working man. This was a festival to draw in the moneyed middle classes; and rightly so if it was to raise money for Mary's comfortable retirement.

Reviews of the opening night appeared on 28 July, congratulating the 'genius' of Jullien in producing an occasion that was 'equal to the moment and the cause'. For he had considered 'not only the claim of Mrs Seacole on the English nation, but the manner in which, with all the world looking on, the English nation should display its sense

---

* Five shillings in 1857 had the equivalent purchasing power of almost £68 today; 2/6, almost £34.

of the sacrifices Mrs Seacole had made'.[23] But the steep entrance fee
was a major miscalculation; in seeking to restrict the opening to the
London elite, and despite the fact that around 2,000 had attended,
Reynolds's Weekly Newspaper reported that 'the Hall looked bare
and the galleries were nearly empty'. The '"select" system was a total
failure,' it concluded, 'and the first night could have added little or
nothing to the exchequer.'[24]

Mary had, nevertheless, greatly enjoyed the concert, seated next
to Lord Rokeby in the lower gallery opposite the orchestra, and she
revelled in all the attention. 'As soon as she was recognized, [she] was
greeted with loud cheers and every demonstration of enthusiasm';
'the concert-room echoed gloriously with the volleys of plaudits that
ascended in her honour'. Mary 'bowed and curtseyed her thanks
to the brilliant assemblage', looking 'extremely hale and hopeful,
and smiled with great complacency on her applauders from under
her brand new bonnet'.[25] Even her friend William Howard Russell
had noticed her outfit, for on 27th he noted in his diary that he had
attended the first night and that they had 'made nearly £160 for Mrs
Seacole, who is great in her fine dress.'[26]

A tourist from New York, George Smith Fisher, had had the
good fortune to attend the benefit night for 'this colored lady who
performed real prodigies of labor and self-sacrifice', and who,
he was surprised to discover, was 'almost as popular ... as Miss
Nightingale'. He was greatly impressed: 'The enthusiasm was
unbounded, real Anglo-Saxon, of an unexampled character to us,
and the good-natured and good-looking middle-aged lady received
a bumper. The whole affair was a feast of reason and a genuine
flow of soul! The music was grand, and its voluptuous sounds rolled
out over that assembled multitude, with great effect. Every part
was perfect.'

Fisher and his wife could not help sharing in this British 'glow
of pride ... in acknowledgment of true merit' – even though 'the
subject of it was a colored woman'.[27] No such reservations were
expressed in Britain, even if privately felt. Rather the opposite; on
the third and fourth nights the Royal Surrey Gardens was 'thronged

by a greater multitude' than the previous evenings: 'the music-hall was literally crammed', reported *Reynolds's Weekly Newspaper*, 'many hundreds of persons being compelled to remain in the grounds, unable to penetrate into the interior of the building'. It is estimated that up to 80,000 people attended over the course of the four nights.[28]

On the final evening Mary had responded to the applause and cheers by addressing the audience, telling them that 'She would make the best return in her power' on this enormous show of support, 'by proceeding to India at once, and tending their closest friends and relations'. Not only that but she 'begged they would join in three cheers for her who had done so much for the British army – Florence Nightingale'.[29] It was a warm and generous gesture, particularly when one considers, that in stark contrast to the fanfare of drums and trumpets and fireworks for Mrs Seacole, Florence Nightingale had crept back into England quietly and unobtrusively under the alias 'Miss Smith'. Suffering from nervous exhaustion, she had locked herself away at Harley Street, sought no paeans of praise from anyone and attended not a single celebratory function. Consumed by an overwhelming sense of responsibility for the high infection and death rate at Scutari, she spent the next years scrupulously analysing the mortality rate there and coming to painful terms with her own perceived failures in controlling it.[30]

Mary Seacole in contrast was going from strength to strength; when she spoke to those gathered at the Surrey Gardens in July she announced that she had recently had an interview with the Secretary for War, Lord Panmure, about going to India to nurse. The British Army was currently fighting the rebellion that had broken out in May in the northwestern provinces. Sensationalist accounts in the press of the massacre of British women and children by rebels at the garrison town of Cawnpore, and the continuing siege at the British Residency at Lucknow and attempts to relieve it, had provoked unprecedented public concern. Mary very rightly wanted to help; she hungered for a purpose and to be needed; and wished only to continue doing what she did best – nursing her sons of the British Army:

'Give me my needle and thread, my medicine chest, my bandages, my probe, and scissors, and I'm off.'*[31]

Such instincts were laudable, and certainly it would be a high point on which to leave England, once more on a mission to serve the nation. But India was not Crimea; these were two very different wars, as Mary was soon to discover.

Takings for the Seacole Festival meanwhile had clearly been very good, if Russell's £160 for the first night are anything to go by. Everyone involved rejoiced at the thought that Mary would now 'have the means of following the bent of her benevolent inclinations' and set off for India. Indeed, it was expected that the festival would make 'a substantial provision for [Mary] and her family'.[32]† But within three weeks, those hopes all came crashing down. On 20 August the London Evening Standard announced to its readers that a calamity had befallen Mrs Seacole: 'We are sorry to learn that this kind-hearted old lady (who is about to proceed to India, and has lately been several times seen in high spirits, and gaudily attired, in the neighbourhood of Basinghall-Street) has, for the time at least, been deprived from deriving any benefit from the entertainment got up for her at the Surrey Gardens, the proceeds not having been handed over to her.'[33]

The Royal Surrey Gardens had gone bankrupt; in fact, its directors had known it was in considerable financial difficulty even before the Seacole Festival took place. Monsieur Jullien immediately served a writ for non-payment of his considerable share of the proceeds and once again Mary was obliged to 'dance attendance in Basinghall-Street'. At the winding-up hearing on 24 August it was revealed that

---

*   As has been seen in Chapter 20, Mary had announced her desire to go out to India earlier in the year, but there appears to have been some confusion over this, with the Australian and New Zealand press reporting that she was 'quite ready to go out to India for the Persian War'. The intention here was perhaps that she wished to go to India via Persia to first nurse the wounded of the recent Anglo-Persian War that was over by April 1857.

†   The eagle-eyed reader here will notice this allusion to Mary's 'family'. Which family? The only family Mary had in England was her brother-in-law Charles and nephew William Kent and his wife Sarah. Might this be a nod to more immediate family – her daughter Sally – implying that she was still with her mother in England in 1857?

the Royal Surrey Gardens Company had debts of £26,000; Jullien alone was owed £6,000. Mary's solicitor explained that she had been guaranteed 'a clear third of the proceeds of the entertainment', but that as yet 'no account [had] been rendered to her by the company.' He put in an urgent application for her to be permitted to 'inspect the books under peculiar circumstances', for 'she wanted to go to India, but was prevented by the position of her affairs with the company.'[34] On 28 August James Copock, one of the directors of the Surrey Gardens, wrote to *The Times* claiming that 'the full amount due to the Seacole Fund has been paid to Cox and Co, the bankers.' The net profit to the fund, he stated, was £228. 9s. 8d.In the end the RSG creditors received five shillings in the pound of what was owed them; so whether Mary actually received the whole £228 or merely around £57, as has been suggested, is not certain.[35]

The popular press was outraged by the Surrey Gardens debacle: 'Mother Seacole attacked by Wolves' announced the *Marylebone Mercury*; 'the whole affair was a "catch" by which both the worthy *vivandière* and the people were duped', declared the *Inverness Courier*. Her case should be taken to the highest level, insisted the *Evening Mail*: 'The claim of Mrs Seacole … is of a character not to be postponed'; Prime Minister Lord Palmerston should himself intervene.[36] The social justice warrior, *Reynolds's Weekly Newspaper*, ready as always to champion the underdog, alleged that the Surrey Gardens bankruptcy was 'as famous or infamous as the Royal British Bank scandal' (referring to the recent collapse of the joint-stock bank). 'Who got the money?' it demanded. 'Poor old warm-hearted and ready-handed Mrs Seacole' was once again a victim; 'she had suffered greatly in the Crimea from the bad memories of the "gentlemen and the officers", who neglected to pay her for the delicacies with which she supplied them' and now once more she had been defrauded of what was rightfully hers. The *Cork Examiner* chimed in with its own condemnation of 'the wretched plundering of poor Mother Seacole by a parcel of people in London.'[37] But while everyone rose vigorously to Mary's defence, she could only think of one thing: India.

CHAPTER 22

'MY SISTER WANTED
TO GO TO INDIA'

On 21 September 1857 a letter appeared in the *Daily News* that
runs rather counter to Mary's insistence on embarking on a
one-woman mission to India. For it appeared that many other like-
minded women, inspired by stories of the heroic nurses at Scutari
during the Crimean War – and even some of those who had themselves served there – also had the same thought in mind. A letter
was published that day by 'A Nurse in the Late War', in response
to the paper's recent call that 'women should go out to India to
nurse the sick and wounded.' The lady in question explained that
she and others had already applied to the East India Company, the
British government's agent in India – on 18 July in fact – 'requesting to be permitted to proceed without delay to superintend and
direct the wives of soldiers in nursing the sick and wounded'. She
herself had had five months' experience at Scutari during the war
and had 'heard that 40 ladies (myself among the rest) have offered
their services to Mrs Seacole.'[1] Once again the women of England
were rallying round; and who better to lead the vanguard than
the renowned Mrs Seacole. It is a testament to Mary's reputation
in 1857 that nurses such as this looked upon her as a source of
inspiration, just as others, equally, were investing their admiration
in Florence Nightingale. Lack of evidence is, however, the recur-
ring problem; it prevents us from quantifying any transformative

influence on the public perception of women as nurses that Mary might well have had at that time. While she undoubtedly wanted to lead from the front in person, and go out to the seat of war, Nightingale in contrast remained in retreat from public view. Nevertheless, in the postwar years it was Nightingale who got the lion's share of the accolades, thanks to her establishment of her Training School for Nurses in 1860. As a woman of colour, Mary never had the power and influence to do such things; but she *could* for a while trade on her celebrity and use it to set an example for other nurses. It is impossible to claim more than this without substantiation, although a lone source in 1871 noted at the tail end of a paean to Nightingale that Mary's 'honest and humble efforts' in nursing during the Crimean War 'are still remembered'.[2]

In the late summer of 1857, James Cosmo Melvill, secretary of the East India Company, had already firmly put the dampeners on the ardour of those women volunteers. On 22 August he wrote to the nurse in question thanking her and the other volunteers for their 'benevolence' but explaining that 'in India every station has its regimental hospital, and every moveable force in the field its regimental and general hospital', and that, in any event, 'no European women would be allowed to follow the camp'. He therefore regretted that 'the military service in India affords no opening' to these gallant lady volunteers.[3]

This was not a truthful response, by any stretch of the imagination. It may well be that the presence of female nurses in the predominantly Muslim areas where the rebellion was taking place would have been taboo – on religious grounds. But in fact, as a correspondent out in India reported to the *Morning Advertiser* in November, the East India Company's assertion that all the sick and wounded were well catered for was a lie: 'The sufferings our soldiers, when disabled by wounds, or prostrate by fever, will have to endure, are hardly estimated at home. In the first instance, all or most permanent station hospitals have been burnt down, or so far damaged by the rebels, that they can hardly be made available before the setting in of the next hot season.'

The native male attendants then being employed were churlish and ungracious; 'if ever there was a call for British nurses for our troops,' the correspondent went on, 'it is now in India.'[4] One can only imagine Mary Seacole's anguish at reading this, for she was still badgering the authorities in October that year to be sent to India; all to no avail. The 2013 discovery of a brief manuscript letter written by her, on 1 October 1857, addressed to Sir Henry Storks, Secretary for Military Correspondence at the War Office, confirms this. For it shows that she asked his approval of the draft of a letter she wished to send to Lord Panmure on the subject. It was typical of Mary to lean on a friend in high places – ('*My kind Sir Henry*' is a surprising degree of familiarity for a letter to the War Office) – to put in a word with another known patron of hers, Lord Panmure. The accompanying draft letter sadly is lost, but one can imagine that it would have contained an appeal for Lord Panmure to make an exception in Mary's case and overrule the decision of the East India Company.[5]

Mary had by now moved again, to lodgings at 11 Rathbone Place, off Oxford Street, from where she continued to pursue her India mission into the following year. The fact of this house's survival has till now been missed, but this Grade II Georgian terraced house is still to be found at the Tottenham Court Road end of Oxford Street. Along with Mary's equally brief lodgings in Soho Square (which have a blue plaque commemorating the fact), Rathbone Place is her only other surviving London address.

In early February 1858 other would-be nurses for India were still writing to the press urging to be allowed to go there – at a time when, much like the Crimean campaign, more casualties were dying in hospital of neglect and disease than killed in action. A nurse signing herself 'A Soldier's Friend' no doubt spoke for Mary when she said, 'neither the severest privation, nor fear of death, would deter us from going forth to India to assist our suffering countrymen.'[6] Mary clearly was refusing to take no for an answer, for a letter to the *Morning Advertiser* on 16 February 1858 confirmed that 'In five weeks from this time the devoted Mrs Seacole will sail for India to commence again her work as mother, nurse, and friend of the British soldier. May He who watches over all protect this woman in her Samaritan labours, and restore her in safety to these shores.'

In the meantime, Mary was out gathering support, on 10 February attending a meeting at Willis's Rooms in aid of soldiers' wives and families, where many greeted her and shook her hand, remembering 'how nobly the woman of colour had done her part'. The press was still reproducing stories headed, 'Mother Seacole on her Travels to India' at the end of February, but by then officialdom had clearly put paid to Mary's aspirations. Who and precisely when, we do not know.[7] Over in Jamaica, a few years later, Mary's sister Louisa put a romantic spin on the Indian endeavour, when she entertained the writer Anthony Trollope at Blundell Hall. 'My sister wanted to go to India ... with the army you know,' she told him. 'But Queen Victoria would not let her; her life was too precious.' Ah, if only this were so; if only we knew what the Queen had really thought of Mrs Seacole.

The disappointment of Mary's failed mission to India must have been great; nevertheless, on 20 March 1858 she attended a public meeting at the Theatre Royal Drury Lane on the setting-up of a Havelock Memorial Fund, honouring Sir Henry Havelock, who had died of dysentery the previous November after his heroic relief of Lucknow.[8] Mary's Crimean exploits had received a further boost with the publication of her friend Alexis Soyer's *A Culinary Campaign* in September 1857, with many newspapers choosing to extract the section on his encounter with Mary at Spring Hill.[9] She must have been gratified too by the continued fundraising on her behalf. A fancy-dress ball in Brighton under the patronage of the Duke of Beaufort, held at Christmas 1857, had brought in receipts of £253. 4s., of which £104. 1s. 8d. had made its way to Mary; but the £10 proceeds of a benefit held in Rochester, Kent by an amateur group of Royal Engineers had vanished with the organiser, who had bolted soon after.[10]

Mary had also been honoured in the pantomime season in a production of *Queen Mab: or, Harlequin Romeo and Juliet* at the Surrey Theatre, during which Mrs Richard Barnett had appeared 'in the form of a quasi Mrs Seacole' dressed as a *vivandière* and 'and sang a patriotic song'.[11] More importantly, there was heartening news on sales of *Wonderful Adventures*, which, at the end of 1857, had appeared in Rotterdam in a Dutch translation by Rev. Jacob Jongeneel, as *Mary Seacole's Avonturen, in de West en in de Krim*; it reprinted the following year. The French translation came out at the beginning of 1858 in both Lausanne and Paris, as *Aventures et Voyages d'une Créole, Mme Seacole, à Panama et en Crimée*, translated by Mlle Victorine Rilliet de Constant Massé. In March 1858 the English edition was reprinted, with a few typographical changes; 12,000 copies were now in circulation; a third printing was mooted but appears not to have gone ahead.[12]

Mary may have been delighted enough with the success of her

book in the Netherlands to take the boat to Antwerp in Belgium in June, from there travelling 62 miles north to Rotterdam to visit her Dutch publisher. Interestingly, she applied for a passport just before doing so, at a time when they were not mandatory. Perhaps Mary was still planning to travel further afield, to somewhere where she might have wished to have proof of her nationality as a form of protection?[13] Amusingly, though in itself an indicator of the level of Mary's international celebrity at the time, a brief item in the Brussels newspaper the *Nord* on 14 June had reported that 'The Belgian steamer *Baron Osy* arrived yesterday in Antwerp from London, having on board Lady Seacole, who has been decorated with the order of the Legion of Honour, the English Crimean medal and the Medidjie ... On the arrival of the vessel, Lady Seacole was adorned with all her decorations.'[14]

It is a further, useful sighting of Mary wearing three of her medals. Shortly before travelling to Antwerp she had helped run a stall at a two-day Fancy Bazaar organised at Wellington Barracks by Alexis Soyer to raise funds for the wives and families of soldiers and sailors, but by 5 August he was dead, at the age of only forty-nine, after much suffering, and having never recovered his health since falling sick with typhoid fever in Crimea.[15]

One would like to think that Mary attended Soyer's funeral in what was then the General Cemetery of All Souls, Kensal Green on 11 August, when he was buried with his artist wife Emma (who had died in childbirth in 1842) beneath a splendid monument that Soyer himself had designed, in St Mary's Catholic Cemetery at Kensal Green. Newspaper reports make no mention of Mary, but the funeral was attended by a great number of Soyer's friends. In a poignant reminder of their Crimean friendship, the *Morning Chronicle* for the day of the funeral chose to run Soyer's account of meeting Mary and Sally in Crimea.[16] Two years on from the end of the war, she was still making the most of her Crimean celebrity, doing the rounds of her friends and admirers in the army and navy. In February 1859 several papers reported on Mary's visit to 'the military and naval heroes doing duty at Sheerness' in Kent, after having first stopped off at Chatham Barracks and the Melville Hospital.[17]* The hospital had received many of the Crimean wounded during 1855-6 and Mary was 'received with the best feelings by the officers and men. Many of the heroes of the Crimea surrounded her and cheered her most enthusiastically'.[18]

In late July Mary was in Dublin, staying at the European Hotel, and once again visiting the military. She had a great many Irish admirers, for Irish troops made up around 35 per cent of the army, with over 30,000 of them serving in Crimea. By the autumn, however, this endless processional had clearly begun to pall, and Mary grew restless, seeking new challenges. She decided to head back to Jamaica, or rather stop off there en route back to Panama. Several British papers noted that on 18 October 1859 Mrs Seacole had set sail in the Royal Mail Company Steamer the *Shannon*, captained by George Abbott in the company of 215 passengers that included 'seven sisters of charity'.

> THE OUTWARD MAILS.—SOUTHAMPTON, Monday.—The steamship Sultan, Captain Vincent, left this day with the usual Peninsular mails, for Oporto, Vigo, and Lisbon, 29 passengers, and a full cargo. The steamship Shannon, Captain Abbott, left this day with the usual West India and Pacific mails, specie, value £1,521; jewellery, value £8,000; and 215 passengers, among whom were Captains Darling, Dunlop, and Wyott; Ensigns Mitchell and Miller; Mrs. Seacole, and seven sisters of charity.

A fellow passenger on board the *Shannon*, who was sailing on to Belize, recalled the charismatic personality of 'Mrs Seacole of Crimean fame' making her inimitable presence felt during the crossing, by indulging in her usual vigorous networking. By the time the ship arrived at St Thomas, 'the good old soul [had] asked every body on board, about 200 people, to drop in at her little house in Jamaica.'[19]

*

---

* It is possible Mary encountered a fellow Black celebrity of the time during her visit to the Melville at Chatham – young Sarah Forbes Bonetta, the captive African princess rescued from Dahomey in 1850? After Sarah was brought to England by Captain Frederick Forbes, she lived for several years with the family of a former missionary, Rev. James Friedrich Schön, at Palm Cottage in Gillingham. Schön was the chaplain for the Melville Hospital at that time; it is hard to imagine that, had Sarah known the celebrated Mrs Seacole was visiting, she would not have wanted to meet her.

When Mary arrived back in Kingston, it was five years since she had last been there. In the meantime, her celebrity had preceded her, as the English novelist Anthony Trollope discovered when he visited a few months earlier in the year. At the time employed by the Post Office as a surveyor responsible for postal routes, Trollope travelled a great deal and in 1858 had been asked to go to the West Indies to shake up the existing system there. He travelled out from Southampton on a Royal Mail steam packet arriving in Jamaica in December 1858. He gives us a good sense of the Kingston Mary Seacole would have returned to in his memoir *The West Indies and the Spanish Main*. It was not an attractive one. He found the town unalluring: the streets had a 'rugged, disreputable, and bankrupt appearance'; many of its wooden houses were 'unpainted, disjointed, and going to ruin'. The streets were unpaved and flooded in wet weather; but worst of all for this Englishman unused to the heat, it was 'hotter than almost any other [town] in the West Indies'.[20]

Kingston, with a then population of around 40,000, was displaying all the signs of a remorseless downturn in the economy. It had lost much of its importance as a Caribbean centre of trade with the advent of direct steamship services to Latin and South America. An atmosphere of 'poverty and industrial prostration', as one traveller described it, had descended since the abolition of slavery and the abandonment of the old plantation system. Jamaica had such wealth in its land and abundant natural landscape, yet all the 'productive power of the soil' seemed to be 'running to waste'; land lay unworked; workers were indolent; apathy and idleness were rife. The value of real estate had plummeted since 1833: 150 sugar estates had been abandoned and 500 coffee plantations. Exports of sugar, rum and coffee were drastically reduced – down to a third of what Jamaica had exported during the heyday of its prosperity.[21]

'Can nothing be done for Jamaica, where Nature does so much and man so little?' asked the Scottish poet James Linen when he visited in 1854. 'Its past history proves what its deserted plantations are capable of producing. It is one of the most productive islands in the world, and certainly one of the most beautiful.' Yet, notwithstanding all its charming beauty, Jamaica had been 'abandoned by England, her natural protector. England broke the chains of slavery which despotism had forged, it is true; but she left her wrapped in darkness and in ignorance.' A handful of devoted sectarian preachers and 'a few Sisters of Charity' could do but little he added.[22] (This explains the presence of those ladies on Mary's ship – presumably Catholic nuns going out to Jamaica to undertake relief work among the poor.)

Trollope could not help noticing that 'hardly any Europeans, or even white Creoles, live in the town. They all have country seats, pens as they call them, at some little distance'. He felt that Kingston, although not without wealth, was urgently in need of being redeemed from years of neglect and 'from its utter disgrace'.[23] Some of the negatives were made up for by the warm and generous hospitality he received there. He was at least relieved to find comfortable accommodation at one of the grandly named 'Halls' – the lodging houses down near the harbour in and around East Street. And it just so happened that he plumped for Blundell Hall [he spells it Blundle], where much to his delight he found that 'the landlady in whose custody I had placed myself was a sister of good Mrs Seacole.' He was amused and touched by the fervour with which she insisted on serving him English traditional fare such as beefsteak and onion, bread and cheese, and 'bad English potatoes', when he would much rather have sampled the local food.[24] But his encounter with Louisa Grant is fortuitous, for it gives us an opportunity to reacquaint ourselves with Mary's equally indomitable sibling.

In August 1855, when Mary Seacole was away in Crimea, the owner of Blundell Hall, Grace Blundell, had died. In her will Grace mentioned her 'Lodging House', though not by name, and said that she would like it to be 'conducted and carried on as at present in order to afford some benefits by way of employment to my old friend Miss McLelland', who presumably had helped her run it.[25] Grace's nephew, a Kingston solicitor named Henry Franklin, wound up her estate and rented the property to Louisa Grant, for she was clearly in residence as proprietress by the time Anthony Trollope arrived in January 1859. In an 1878 advertisement she placed in the Kingston

Gleaner, Louisa later described herself as 'proprietress for more than 20 years' of Blundell Hall, thus confirming that at no point was it Mary Seacole's business after Grace Blundell's death, and certainly not before. An item in the *Colonial Standard* in early 1859 further substantiates this, reporting the theft of some silver spoons from 'Mrs [sic] Louisa Grant' that had been laid out on a breakfast table 'in the front portico of her lodgings (Blundle's)'.[26]

When Mary returned to Kingston in 1859 she did not stay with Louisa at Blundell Hall, at No. 8 East Street; but rather in a house across the road at No. 7, for a young resident named Marie Glanville later recalled visiting her there and listening to her reminisce about the Crimean War.[27] What is unclear is what had happened to the lodging house that Mary had left in the care of a 'cousin' when she had sailed for Panama in 1851. Mary would appear to have given it up by now, otherwise surely she would have stayed there. She is last listed in the Poll Tax Relief list in 1853 – for No. 2 Stanton Street; her mother Rebecca's last address at 27 Duke Street was by now recorded as 'shut up'. Either way, she did not dwell long in Jamaica, presumably having concluded that the depressed economic state of the island was not conducive to business; instead, she began planning to return to Panama.

Mary stayed long enough, however, to stand as sponsor to two Roman Catholic baptisms at Holy Trinity, Kingston's Catholic church on Duke Street: of thirteen-year-old Christopher Hendricks on 16 May 1860 and Edward Ambleton on 1 July. Ten-year-old Edward is thought to have been her now dead brother Edward's illegitimate son (he had died in Panama), born *c*.1850. Christopher is rather more interesting, for in November 1860 he entered the Royal Navy at Port Royal in the 'Boys' list – as Christopher Seacole Henriques, born Spanish Town 1846, residence Kingston. Earlier that year, Mary had tried to use her powers of persuasion to get young Christopher taken on to the screw steam frigate HMS *Emerald* when it was at Port Royal. Admiral Sir Alexander Milne, who had arrived on the *Emerald* to inspect the ships of the West India Station, was collared by Mary when, on 21 April, she grandly swept on board 'in high

Crinoline', her dress perhaps a tad inappropriate for the occasion. She had come with a special request. 'She wants me to Enter a Boy,' Milne noted in his journal, 'but he is all head and no body.'[28] Shortly afterwards Christopher appears to have been taken on anyway, assigned to HMS *Imaum*, at Port Royal. It was an ill-fated ship, for twenty-one of its crew were wiped out in a yellow fever epidemic that struck in October, although Christopher survived and lived on till 1894. But what was his relationship to Mary? We are left with yet another puzzle.[29] Hot on its trail comes another discovery that is equally hard to resolve, but which involved a major scandal that broke in Kingston in August 1860.

It came with publication of a pamphlet entitled 'Seven Months in the Kingston Lunatic Asylum and What I Saw There', in which a woman named Ann Pratt, who for that time had been an 'unwilling prisoner' in the asylum, provided a devastating exposé of systematic cruelty – including torture by 'tanking' in filthy water – that was regularly inflicted on patients perceived as difficult.[30] This was carried out by various members of staff, most notably the psychopathic matron, Mrs Judith Ryan. Pratt's account was truly shocking in its graphic detail of how 'inmates are made sick or well, strong or weak, to perform all kinds of servile labour, they are made every morning to carry water to wash out their cells, and if they do not do it, they are tanked and beaten, locked up and stained.'[31]

The Kingston Lunatic Asylum when Ann Pratt was taken there in January 1860 was then still part of the public hospital on North Street. She had suffered a mental breakdown after being attacked and raped but the asylum at that time would have done nothing to assist in her recovery. It was overcrowded, little more than 'stables for animals', as one medical officer described it, and the treatments offered were cruel and primitive, with the only 'medication' being alcohol – brandy, wine, rum or gin.[32] It is during the course of her description of the treatment of inmates, their hair cut off close to the skull on admission, their only clothing an unbleached calico shift stamped in large letters PUBLIC HOSPITAL, and their shoes taken from them, that Ann Pratt suddenly drops an unexpected detail, that

'Mrs Branigan, as the sister of Mrs Seacole, was allowed a mattrass [*sic*] on her admission, they took away her shoes and stockings also her flannel, but she soon got them back.'

Ann concluded that this was because '*It was too evident that the Crimean heroine influence was dreaded in this place*' [my italics].[33] She went on to state that because of Mrs Seacole's celebrity, and the attention and respect she commanded now in Jamaica, the medical staff would 'sometimes condescend to go and visit this inmate and will sit down and converse with her; seldom are the other patients honored with like favors'. What is more, Mrs Seacole's mere presence on a visit to the asylum to see her sister clearly put the fear of God into even the sadistic Mrs Ryan, who Pratt tells us was 'vastly polite and courteous' in her presence. Indeed, the staff were instructed not to say anything 'about the treatment of the people before Mrs Branigan' in case she repeated it to her sister, and Branigan herself was granted special perks to keep her compliant.

Ann Pratt was released from the Asylum in July and the minute her pamphlet was printed Mrs Ryan and two of her nurses were sent packing and an urgent inquiry instituted, during which Mrs Branigan and other residents were interviewed.[34] The authorities refused to accept that Ann Pratt, a 'mulatto', was literate enough to have written her own pamphlet. A note in the British medical journal *The Lancet* reported on this 'most extraordinary and frightful case of abuse', and although the conclusions of the inquiry tried to discredit Pratt and exonerated most of the other staff involved, there was widespread acknowledgement of the need for 'immediate alteration' of the system at Kingston. In 1863 this led to a wider investigation by the Colonial Office into asylums across the empire.[35]

Fortuitously, thanks to my discovery of that Wesleyan Methodist wedding in Kingston in 1843, we know that the Mrs Branigan here was Mary's half-sister, Amelia. But it comes as a shock to have never heard tell of her till now. Like so much else in Mary Seacole's story, there is a chasm between the small amount we know of her public, Crimean life, and her quite separate complex and relaxed (by Victorian moral standards) family interrelationships in Jamaica. All

there is to find of this elusive half-sister is the death of her husband
Arthur James, at the age of twenty-eight in 1849, and her own,
aged forty-six in 1862. Mary had probably used her influence on
her return to Jamaica at this time to get Amelia out of the asylum –
indeed, it might well have been the reason for her return – for Amelia
died not long afterwards, at Stanton Street, presumably Mary's
lodging house at No. 2 that Amelia had run for her when Mary went
off to Panama.[36]

CHAPTER 23

'THAT BRAVE AND CHARITABLE
OLD WOMAN'

At the end of August 1860 Mary Seacole once more took a ship back across the Caribbean Sea to Panama. When she arrived at the port of Aspinwall she did not this time dwell long on that side of the Isthmus. She decided to try her fortune on the southern side, at Panama City itself. The rail link from north to south had been completed in 1855, and what had been an exhausting and perilous 47-mile crossing on her first visit was now a leisurely train ride of four hours, costing around $25. At Panama City we have an extremely valuable sighting of her, which confirms Mary's intention of once more setting up in business on the Isthmus. For on 1 September 1860, the *Panama Star and Herald* was reminding its readers of 'the name of Mrs Seacole, formerly a resident of Chagres, where her kind offices were invaluable to many a sick wayfarer, but who has been more recently and more prominently brought before the public by the services she rendered the wounded soldiers during the Crimean war'. The paper was pleased to announce that 'Mrs Seacole appears to have a predilection for our Isthmus where she has recently returned to, and she is now, although known to but few, a resident of Panama. We understand she has brought some merchandise with her, and intends opening a store on Main-street for a short time, for the disposal of her goods.'

This once splendid Spanish city – the oldest European one in the Americas – was founded in 1518 and built on gold and silver stolen from its indigenous people by the Conquistadores, only then to be sacked by pirates in the seventeenth century. Now deprived of its former splendour and wealth, the city was squalid. The narrow, badly maintained streets and uneven pavements gave a general idea of 'ruin, poverty, dirt, and pigs', not to mention the many 'lean and languid' mongrel dogs that roamed the streets. It took a strong constitution to tolerate the blistering heat; the temperature often was above 96 degrees and as high as 110 in the shade. Aspinwall and the northern shore were positively balmy in contrast, and certainly cleaner according to many travellers.[1] Nevertheless, Panama City was still the centre of sea traffic along the west coast of North and South America, mainly in the form of the steamers of the Pacific Mail Company from California and the British Pacific Steam Navigation Company.

The name of the city's principal thoroughfare where Mary set up shop was the Calle de la Merced, an avenue with a cobblestone pavement and stone-built houses either side. Around the market plaza were a range of stores and restaurants, run-down churches and amid them a fine, spacious cathedral. Visitors would take a stroll through the ramparts of the old city and admire the beauteous blue Bay of Panama, but there were few other attractions; life in Panama City seemed stagnant and languishing. It is fortuitous that the famous British traveller and writer Richard Burton passed through here with his wife Isabel at the end of 1860 and confirmed Mary's presence. In his travelogue *The City of the Saints*, Burton recalled landing at Panama on 15 December from Mexico. During his visit he met officers of the US Squadron, the editors of the *Panama Star and Herald* and various other local dignitaries. And there, hobnobbing among them: 'Last, but not least, I must mention the venerable name of Mrs Seacole, of Jamaica and Balaclava.' In her own later biography of her husband, Lady Isabel noted the 'lively pleasure' with which they met Mary again, for in fact the couple had encountered her when they made a tour of Crimea during the war.[2]

Mary was still in Panama City in March of 1862, for the *Panama Star and Herald* mentioned her again, in an article largely taken from the London *Daily Telegraph* on camp followers and sutlers, in which it agreed with the author of the article that 'Mrs. Seacole is a bright exception' to that profession's usually dubious reputation. 'She has lived many years on the Isthmus and is now a resident of Panama and has always been ready to aid the sick and afflicted whether rich or poor, more we believe through real sympathy than from any other cause.' The paper also confirmed that Mary had far from faded in the public consciousness: 'that brave and charitable old woman is still remembered with enthusiastic affection by the survivors of the Crimean struggle.'[3] It wasn't till a month later that the British press finally caught up with the fact that 'Mrs Seacole, the famous Crimean camp follower, is now living at Panama.'[4]

Panama might be a long way from England, but it was not too far for Mary to mourn the sudden and premature death of Prince Albert in December 1861 and to send a donation of ten shillings to the Scottish National Memorial to him. In her absence, a new variety of lilac-and-maroon-striped dahlia had been named 'Mrs Seacole' in her honour at the Chelmsford Horticultural Show.[5] The Rev. J. Haldane Stewart was also keeping her memory alive, doing the rounds with his lecture on 'A Week in the Crimea at the Close of the War', in which he 'gave a humorous sketch of "Mother Seacole"' and 'alluded to the extraordinary respect which was entertained for this kind-hearted mulatto woman by the soldiers in the Crimea.' Published accounts of the Crimean War were also acknowledging her contribution, with William Cooke Stafford writing in *England's Battles by Sea and Land* of how, by the summer of 1855, the 'condition of the men was ... from various causes, very much improved', thanks to the advent of Alexis Soyer's stoves and the 'dinners, wines and refreshments' made available at Spring Hill by 'Mrs Seacole and Mr Day', which had 'caused a feeling of content and satisfaction to pervade the British troops'.[6]

We know nothing of Mary's business dealings in Panama City, but as far as socialising was concerned there was really only one place to meet visiting British and American naval men, or travellers such as the Burtons, and that was at the city's best hotel, Aspinwall House. 'The Aspinwall hotel is the exchange where the foreign merchants or traders – chiefly American, German and French – most do congregate, discuss politics and imbibe "long" and "short" drinks,' recalled a naval cadet of his own journey to Panama in July 1863. 'In this delightful locality we saw the sunny face of Mrs Seacole, of Crimean renown, gadding about with naval officers, on leave from the frigate Orlando.'[7] Another Panamanian resident, Tracy Robinson, recalled a similar occasion when Mrs Seacole appeared at a ball 'given by Captain Kennedy and his officers on board her majesty's ship *Reindeer* in the bay of Panama'. The quarter-deck was crowded with people including 'the then widely known Madame Seacole, an Afro-English woman'. As usual the gregarious Mary was in the thick of it, dressed in full flamboyant rig, wearing 'a number of decorations' and busy patronising 'those whom she knew'. She struck Robinson as 'a queer, quaint, jolly, vain, self-important old brown woman' and had apparently made a point of impressing on one lady that 'If you could see me, madam, under my dress, you would be surprised how white I am. It is exposure to the air that makes my face and hands so brown.' In white social settings Mary clearly was highly sensitive to her colour and racial difference and anxious to ingratiate herself and cross that exclusive boundary into acceptance by the colonial establishment. It is perhaps this aspiration that many of her admirers today find an unsettling negative in Mary's personality, and it has, over the years, been cause for criticism.[8]

It would appear that on this new trip to Panama, Mary had decided to try her luck beyond grubby, run-down Panama City, on the island of Taboga 10 miles off the coast, although she probably came and went on the mainland regularly. At a glance, Taboga was a seemingly delightful location, with its blue hills, babbling streams and lush tropical vegetation. The romantic South Seas beckoned beyond, but once on land, the heat of Taboga was at times intolerable, for its little wooden houses afforded scant shelter, unlike the shuttered stone houses of the mainland. The overall air of dejection was worse even than Panama City: 'many more pigs, lean and hungry dogs and cats, and goats', and enormous crabs crawling around underfoot.[9] As one traveller recalled, the locals lived 'in contented idle isolation', but as far as business was concerned, however,

Mary had made a canny decision: Taboga had now become the
port of choice for Panama City because its surrounding waters were
deeper and could take larger ships. The Pacific Steam Navigation
Company of Liverpool used the island as a base for repairing ships,
and storing coal and supplies for them; a great many other ships
sailing in and out of Panama docked at Taboga to take on supplies;
for which reasons the harbour was always crammed with vessels.
There was plenty of trade to be made with a transient population
who preferred to pick up their connecting ships here than in Panama
City. For Mary, it was a captive market and she installed herself here
among the small colony of English and American settlers some time
in the early 1860s. The island offered a hospital, a theatre, three
hotels, billiard rooms, and several wholesale and retail stores, but
not much else – except the ever-ubiquitous tropical disease.[10] Yellow
fever was rife on Taboga, in 1859 alone it had carried off half the
workforce – thirty men – of the Pacific Steam Navigation Company
depot and in 1863 there was an epidemic of smallpox.[11]

At Taboga we have a valuable sighting of Mary by a naval
officer, Henry Woods, who, on a voyage from Valparaiso on HMS
Charybdis, was anchored off the island from 24 May to 29 August
1863. While there, he got into an altercation with the locals but tells
us that 'I subsequently made my peace with the inhabitants, largely
owing to the good influence of an old coloured lady called Mother
Seacole. If there be any still living who were in the Crimean War and
saw anything of Balaclava, they will doubtless remember having met
or heard of Mother Seacole. She was a West Indian negress, and had
a sutler's store out there during the whole War.'[12]

It is in another account from the same period, however, that we
are taken aback by a startling revelation that provides a sobering
pause for thought. It comes in the account of a young Scottish
sailor from Dundee named William, of a Pacific voyage he made
on a merchant ship – the *Benjamin Bangs** – travelling out to the

---

* William does not fully identify himself, sadly, or the ship he sailed on, but research
suggests that this is the only ship that fits his narrative.

Chincha Islands off Peru to take up a valuable cargo of guano. After two months at sea out from Liverpool, he and his companions went ashore at Taboga, where 'we saw Mrs Seacole, of Crimean Fame'. The good lady now kept a store on the island, he confirms, 'but has been unfortunate in a matrimonial relationship with some scamp of a native, who led her to the altar and then bolted with a portion of her pecuniary means. Still her heart appears to be whole, full of life as ever, and she has a short sword hanging ready at hand, which she can handle expertly in play, as well as boldly if any troublesome customer attempt to annoy or rob her.'[13]

Mary Seacole talked into remarrying! Then robbed of her hard-earned money! What terrible, bitter misfortune. Who was the dastardly con artist who tricked her? Was their marriage held at Taboga's little Catholic church of San Pedro? There is no sign of it in those Panama marriages digitised so far for the period. As the author of 'Panama as a Home' – an article guaranteed to discourage anyone with that thought in mind – concluded in his article for Dickens's *All the Year Round*, 'Panama is, to the world in general, a part only of the road leading to better, more genial places ... Few can lead a happy or a profitable life there.'[14] The ever-trusting Mary Seacole, now approaching sixty, had once more been robbed, at a time when she most needed something put by for her old age. There was nothing for it but to cut her losses and head back to Jamaica, clinging steadfastly, now more than ever, to the former married name that had secured her fame and that still had some currency in calling in favours among her erstwhile friends. She would need them.

By February 1865 Mary was back in Kingston and staying with her sister Louisa at Blundell Hall, for her presence there was noted by the visiting Bishop of Columbia, George Hills. On arriving in Jamaica he and his wife had taken lodgings at Blundell Hall, 'to which we had been recommended'. It was kept, he noted, 'by a respectable mulatto lady, Miss Louisa Grant'.[15] Like everyone else, even ten years after the war, the Bishop referred to Mary as 'Mrs Seacole of Crimean fame': 'The book of her life and adventures was open on the table, edited [sic] by Mr Russell, the correspondent of the *Times*, who in the preface speaks of the high estimation in which Mrs Seacole was held, and of her philanthropic and Christian labours for the sick, the wounded, and the hungry. A picture of the heroine is presented on the cover, with face and bonnet bespattered with blood, in the act of preparing a bandage on the battlefield.'

Hills also confirms one important fact when he tells us that Mary's 'mother held a *similar establishment to this*, [my italics] and was famous as a doctress.' No doubt a proud Louisa had informed him of this fact. Hills and his wife were delighted to have the chance to meet 'the illustrious lady herself', as he recalled: 'Mrs Seacole is an intelligent person, and on Monday came to greet us, dressed in green silk; and decorated with the Turkish and other Crimean medals.'[16]

While she was back in Kingston, Mary made the most of acquainting herself with old friends in the Kingston elite, such as Captain William Salmon Cooper. Like her he had been born in St Elizabeth parish and served in the Royal Navy and was now Kingston agent for the Royal Mail Steam Packet Company, as well as serving as harbour master and a sitting magistrate. Cooper was well connected socially, right up to the English governor, Edward Eyre. One day, as Kingston resident Mrs K. Stewart recalled many years later, Mary was visiting Captain Cooper, when 'a carriage drove up with a "Big Gun" resplendent in gold lace and a string of medals', who had come to see his old friend Cooper. Mary was delighted. As the visitor (probably a government official or military man from England) entered the drawing room, 'the old lady sprang up, "Oh my dear!", holding out her hands. In a moment the big man's arms were round her and he was hugging and kissing her like his long lost mother. When their excitement quieted down a little he told us: "But for this little woman I would not be here today. Her nursing saved my life in the Crimea."'[17]*

It is clear that Mary was still very much enjoying her celebrity, for at home in Jamaica she seems to have been treated almost as royalty.

---

* Could this possibly have been her friend Prince Victor of Hohenlohe-Langenburg, now Count Gleichen, who was still serving in the Royal Navy, as a captain on the *Racoon*, that was on the West Indies station *c*. January 1863-April 1864?

It was she who was chosen to greet Queen Emma of Hawaii when she stopped off in Kingston from the Royal Mail steamer the *Tyne* en route to London. All the local dignitaries turned out to greet the young queen, who was honoured with a royal gun salute and met by a guard of honour of the 1st West India Regiment. The *Colonial Standard* reported on this remarkable meeting: 'A carriage was in attendance at the wharf to receive Her Majesty and as soon as she entered the carriage Mrs Seacole requested the honour of placing around Her Majesty a magnificent cloak that had been presented to her [Mary] by the Sultan, which she accepted, thanked Mrs Seacole and shook hands with her.'[18]

There was, however, one notable absence at this ceremony, and that was Edward Eyre, the British governor of the island. The fact that Mary Seacole stood in for him speaks volumes in terms of her status at the time. Eyre had good reason to be absent, for there was serious trouble brewing in Jamaica: in October a rebellion broke out at Morant Bay that would mark the final death knell of the old plantation economy and once more bring financial ruin down on our beleaguered heroine.

So far in our journey through Mary Seacole's life, we have encountered little or nothing on her reaction to the abolition of slavery and the revolt of enslaved people in Jamaica in 1831, although her abhorrence of slavery itself and her awareness of the continuing oppression of her people is abundantly clear in the *Wonderful Adventures*. But with the Morant Bay Rebellion we at last get a sense of where Mary's allegiances lay through her response to it, as well as that of her sister Louisa, her old friend from Black River, John Salmon, and Captain William Cooper.

In October 1865 a revivalist Baptist deacon from St Thomas, Paul Bogle, organised a protest about the hardship being suffered by local Black farmers in St Thomas's parish as a result of high food prices (resulting from the American Civil War), crop failures, increasing poverty and strained labour relations with the repressive local government. Abolition had compensated their former masters financially to the tune of millions; but not they, the victims. The price of land was too high for most of them to buy any; they were heavily taxed and still very much at the bidding of the white planters, having no political rights. With the support of George William Gordon, a mixed-heritage landowner and minister in Kingston, Bogle challenged the traditional plantocracy over several longstanding grievances. He was a loyal subject to the Queen but the situation rapidly escalated when Governor Eyre threatened the protesters with serious consequences, upon which Bogle led a large crowd of villagers from his farm at Stony Gut to Morant Bay, where on 11 October they converged on the courthouse. A riot ensued; the *custos* (chief magistrate) was murdered and the courthouse was set on fire; during the fighting between rebels and troops, a further twenty-two people were killed and thirty-four wounded.

Although the rebellion was essentially small-scale, confined within mainly the southeastern parish of St Thomas's, Eyre greatly feared an island-wide insurrection like that in Haiti at the end of the eighteenth century. Bogle, now with a price on his head, turned to the Maroons in their mountain enclave for help, but they sided with Eyre, who also held George William Gordon responsible. In the subsequent roundup of the rebels over the next two weeks there was an orgy of killing; 1,500 died as the result of mass hangings and shootings, with many more viciously flogged and their homes set on fire. Bogle and Gordon were both executed, to be thereafter venerated as martyrs by the Black population. Initially, Eyre was hailed as a hero back in London, but his heavy-handed suppression of the rebels and the severity of the trial by court martial and subsequent hanging of Gordon from the yardarm of HMS *Wolverine* was heavily criticised. The official British response to the rebellion was harsh: the Jamaica Assembly was dissolved and the island reverted to a Crown Colony, with Eyre recalled to London where attempts were made to put him on trial. Although many public figures such as Dickens and Tennyson defended him, public attitudes towards race after the rebellion shifted dramatically, with Black people now being denigrated as a different and inferior species, leading to the acceleration of scientific racism and debates about the 'dangers' of genetic weakening through miscegenation.

In response to the attacks on Eyre, Mary's old friend John Salmon, who had been *custos* and president of the legislative and privy councils at her former parish at Black River, composed an 'Address to His Excellency Edward John Eyre', thanking him on behalf of his community – who were still anxiously dreading further trouble – for his 'wise and immediate action' in 'checking and putting down the rebellion' and for saving their families 'from worse than death'.[19]*

Mary's sister Louisa was one of many mixed-heritage Jamaicans who added their signature. Secretary of State Sir Henry Storks – the acquaintance to whom Mary had written in 1857 about going to India – was appointed to oversee the subsequent public inquiry and arrived in Jamaica the following January. Not surprisingly, he took up residence for the first few days with Louisa Grant at Blundell Hall.[20]

Things were looking up for Louisa Grant; such was her success and the preeminence now of Blundell Hall that she made no bones about exercising her own racial preferences in terms of the visitors she entertained there. As Trollope had noted in his *West Indies and the Spanish Main*, Louisa refused point blank to take 'Black' – i.e. African – guests and would only entertain those like her who were mixed heritage. This strict rule meant that even the exiled Faustin Soulouque, former Emperor of Haiti, was denied the comforts of her lodging house when he was looking for accommodation in Kingston: 'Him king indeed, the black nigger!', Louisa grumbled to Trollope, 'I won't keep a house for black men. ... Queen Victoria is my King.'[21] No exceptions were made, even when a white visitor to Kingston staying at Blundell Hall wished to invite Robert Gordon, Kingston's first Black headmaster – of the Wolmer Boys Grammar School – to dinner at Blundell Hall. Louisa declined to admit a 'black', prompting an outraged letter by Gordon to the *Daily Gleaner*.[22] His protest

---

*   Mary's friend Captain William Salmon Cooper was one of many Kingston grandees who signed Governor Eyre's Farewell Address; he personally saw him off with his family at the Royal Mail Steam Company's wharf on 24 July 1866.

did nothing, however, to halt the onward march of the indomitable Miss Louisa Grant, who in 1870 opened another lodging house named Belle Vue up near the army camp at Newcastle.[23]

Mary, in contrast, was once more in the doldrums; a story published by the London correspondent of the *Belfast Newsletter* – who appears to have had personal knowledge of Mary – tells the sorry tale of yet another failed business venture and money lost. After her return to Jamaica in 1864 Mary had apparently 'invested her savings in a farm and shop in the parish of Vere'*; but her 'British proclivities made shipwreck of the whole during the recent insurrection.' It was the last straw for Mary and she decided to return to England, where, as the *Belfast Newsletter* related, 'it is proposed to establish her in a lodging-house in St James's, where many of her Crimean friends will be able to serve her. Mrs Seacole's lodging-house will, I have no doubt, soon become a British institution; at all events, her patrons may depend upon being comfortable under her roof, as she is a famous cook, and boasts that she has the faculty of making things about her "cosy-like", as she says.'

After the financial disasters of Taboga and Vere, Mary was once more 'in a condition of almost destitution'.[24] But she remained unbowed. She returned to London in time to give her erstwhile friend George William Gordon, whom she had known for many years at Black River and in Kingston,† a roasting at a large public meeting about the Morant Bay Rebellion held at London's Exeter Hall in December.

At first Mary had sat and 'listened to the reading of articles in the English papers, censuring her "Sons" [i.e. the British army] for shooting a large number of black men and women'. After several

---

* Vere was one of the smallest of the original Jamaican parishes located at the southern-most point of the island in Middlesex County. In 1866 it was absorbed into Clarendon parish to the immediate north of it.

† Gordon, born 1820 the son of a wealthy white Scottish planter, was given his freedom at the age of ten and sent out to Black River to be educated, in 1836 opening a large store in Kingston as a dealer in produce and becoming involved in politics. He grew wealthy on this enterprise; perhaps Mary had business dealings with him that prompted this jaundiced assessment.

speeches had been given, someone in the audience noticed her and called out: 'here is a coloured lady who is a native of Jamaica, and she will be able to afford some information to the meeting.' Upon which Mary was conducted to the platform:

> On being seated, the question was put to her whether she was personally acquainted with Mr George William Gordon. Without any hesitation she rose from her seat, advanced to the front of the platform, and said, 'Yes, I knew George William Gordon, from his childhood, and he was as great a hypocrite, and as big a villain as ever lived.' This information was followed by groans and hisses, but, nothing daunted, the old Lady of Crimean notoriety, on leaving the platform exclaimed, 'you may groan and hiss as much as you like, but I have told you the truth, and I am not ashamed at telling it.' She then resumed her seat from which she had been taken, and was frequently heard saying, 'these people here know nothing of Jamaica.'[25]

It is perhaps telling that this report did not appear anywhere in the British press – only in Jamaica. Mary also made a point of publicly offering her solidarity with the white colonial administration and former Governor Eyre by attending his court hearing in February 1867, when she was conspicuous 'occupying a seat behind the witness box'.[26] As unbowed, uncompromising and opinionated as ever, Mary Seacole was not going to risk prejudicing the white London elite to whom she knew she must now turn for support in her hour of need. So be it; as the *Era* noted, in reporting the return of 'this energetic and benevolent lady' to England: 'It is understood that several noblemen and influential personages, who took part in the war with Russia, are concerting the means of retaining Mrs Seacole in London.'[27]

CHAPTER 24

'MRS SEACOLE'S SPECIFIC'

It was during one of my regular random searches for new material on Mary Seacole that I fortunately discovered that there was, in fact, another far more pressing personal reason behind her return to London in October of 1865; and that was her health. Mary was suffering from pterygia, which was affecting her eyesight, and urgently needed to see an eye specialist. On arrival she visited Dr Henry Haynes Walton,* an expert on the condition, which was a diseased growth of fleshy tissue across the conjunctiva of the eye, which, if left untreated, could have seriously impaired her eyesight. Dr Walton was a resident surgeon at St Mary's Hospital in Paddington, as well as having a private practice in Brook Street, and recalled the consultation with 'Mrs. Seacole, of Crimean notoriety' vividly in his *Practical Treatise on the Diseases of the Eye*. Mary's condition was, he wrote, one of the most 'marked instances of pterygia as ever I met with'. It turns out that this was not the first time that she had consulted him for the condition, for Dr Walton added that 'This heroine was brought to me, about ten years ago, by Mr Ambler, formerly

---

* Walton (1816-89) is a fascinating personality. He was born in Barbados, the last and twenty-third child of John Walton, provost marshal of the island. He came to England to study medicine and proved a brilliant student. He studied at St Bartholomew's Hospital, passing MRCS in 1839, was House Surgeon at the Royal Ophthalmic Hospital at Moorfields, FRCS in 1848, and became Ophthalmic Surgeon to St Mary's Hospital in 1851. He became a well-known and wealthy society doctor based at his home on Mayfair's Brook Street.

one of my pupils at St. Mary's Hospital.' At that time, which must have been on Mary's return from Crimea in 1856, both eyes were affected, with one in particular more advanced than the other. But now Walton noted that the pterygium in the second eye was 'as much developed as the former'. There was an obvious cause for this acceleration in her condition: Mary 'had been travelling about since then, and has been a long time in the tropics' in and around the equator. Exposure to direct, strong sunlight over many years and probably also the dry, dusty terrain in Crimea had greatly worsened the condition. Dr Walton operated on the second eye, noting that the first operation he had done ten years previously had been 'quite successful'.[1]

No longer now in the best of health, Mary had no Seacole relatives left to turn to in London. The last of them, Charles Witton, had died in 1861 and joined his sister at Brompton Cemetery. But Mary's nephew, William James Kent, and his wife, Sarah, still lived out at Bow in the East End and now had five children; the youngest, born in May 1861, had been named Florence Seacole Kent in honour of two Crimean heroines.[2] Mary chose her new London lodgings carefully, no doubt opting to be centrally placed and near to where the 'several noblemen and influential personages' who were 'concerting the means of retaining her in London' lived. Indeed she fortuitously found lodgings in the very same street as her good Jamaican friend Amos Henriques, his wife Julia and their children, who lived at No. 67 Upper Berkeley Street in Marylebone and who may well have helped her find her accommodation. Amos's place of worship was the West London Synagogue – the first Reform synagogue in London – of which other Jamaican Henriques cousins in London had been founders. The synagogue was completed at 35 Upper Berkeley Street near the junction with Edgware Road in 1870.

Mary took rooms only a few doors away from here at No. 40, which like the rest of the street was an early 1800s four-storied ter-raced house that was part of the Portman Estate development. This estate was owned by a group of twelve West Indies proprietors, one of whom was Mary's patron Lord Rokeby. He just happened to live at the posher end of Upper Berkeley Street, in Montagu House on the corner of Portman Square.* At the time, Marylebone had the highest number of Black residents of all the London boroughs and perhaps there was a greater air of tolerance here. The borough was also the home of several women social reformers such as Octavia Hill, the pioneer of social housing for the poor, at Garbutt Place, and the Langham Place Group of women, who were campaigning for suffrage and women's rights. Another champion of women's medicine, Elizabeth Garrett Anderson, also just happened to be living on Upper Berkeley Street at precisely the same time as Mary – at No. 20 – from where she undertook the planning for her New Hospital for Women opened on the Marylebone Road in 1874. One has to wonder whether she and Mary Seacole ever passed on the street.

All of this brings us to a new and fascinating narrative opening up in Mary Seacole's life that we must now explore. Here she was, a single, unprotected but independently minded woman in need of making a living, but there were few options open to a respectable widow at that time, particularly one who was already socially hamstrung by the colour of her skin. Although she was more than capable of once again going into business running a boarding house or opening a restaurant or store even, other less stressful options might have been more dignified and have had greater appeal as Mary turned sixty.

She could not, of course, practise as a doctor, despite having equivalent skills, and at a time when medicine was not yet quite a profession but rather still an amalgam of the practise of apothecary, physician and surgeon. It was, however, a closed shop that was strictly based on status and class and which still excluded women. Mary would not have wished to knuckle down to drudgery as an overworked and underappreciated hospital nurse, but she did have

---

* Bombing in 1941 unfortunately destroyed Montagu House. No. 40, where Mary lived, and the 200-year-old Brunswick Chapel nearby were demolished in 1977 to make way for a new office and housing development. Fortunately, Elizabeth Garrett Anderson's home at No. 20 has survived and has a blue plaque commemorating her as the first British woman to qualify as a doctor.

years of experience as a carer, a practitioner of holistic medicine and a pharmacist. She was not a homeopath as such, but like them abhorred the allopathic reliance on opiates, bleeding and purging. Fortuitously, she had arrived in London at a time when homeopathy was attracting a lot of interest, among precisely the moneyed, military and upper classes to whom Mary gravitated, despite it being sneered at as 'quackery' by a rampantly antipathetic medical establishment.

Considerable interest in homeopathy had in fact been gathering at the time of the Crimean War, in publications such as the *British Journal of Homeopathy*.[3] In 1855, as the journal indicates, the homeopathic community in London and some of its illustrious patrons had made efforts to get the Minister at War, Lord Panmure, 'to allow one of the civic hospitals about to be established near the seat of war, to be under the superintendence of homeopathic practitioners.'[4] The medical authorities had of course blocked this, but by now London already had its first homeopathic hospital. Established in 1849, thanks to the support of numerous royal and aristocratic patrons, the hospital had opened at 32 Golden Square in Soho with twenty-five beds. It was named for Dr Samuel Hahnemann (1755-1843), the German founding father of homeopathy.

One of the hospital's first staff members in 1849 had been Dr Amos Henriques, who was appointed a surgeon and physician-accoucheur for the hospital. After returning to London from Jamaica in 1847 he had embraced homeopathy and by 1850 had built a large private practice, publishing a *Homeopathic Medical Dictionary and Home Guide* providing useful home remedies for medical self-help, and in 1859 *Art versus Nature in Disease: A Refutation of Naturalism*. Amos was a regular contributor to the *British Journal of Homeopathy* on a wide range of topics, especially cholera and yellow fever, and the treatment of gonorrhoea – drawn from his years in service to the Ottoman Army at Constantinople and treating British troops in Jamaica.* Like Mary, he advocated the use

---

* Henriques had noted that in cases of severe yellow fever in the West Indies, patients had recovered after drinking copious amounts of champagne, for which they seemed to have a craving. Mary ensured she had plenty of bottles in stock in Crimea.

of bark (in his case, cinchona – Peruvian bark) in the treatment of intermittent fever. A great deal of the homeopathic literature of the time was devoted to alternative treatments for cholera, which was rife, with London suffering major epidemics in 1848-50 and again in 1854 and 1866.

The 1854 epidemic devastated the working-class areas of Soho. Five hundred people died inside a week and the nearby Hahnemann Hospital had taken in a great number of the victims. It was Dr John Snow, who made a close study of the epidemic in and around Broad Street during 1854, who came to the breakthrough conclusion that the cholera germ was carried in water – in this case from the Broad Street public pump – and was not an airborne 'miasma', as had been traditionally thought. The cholera patients at the Hahnemann had enjoyed a surprisingly successful rate of recovery in comparison with those taken to the Middlesex Hospital. But such was medical establishment opposition to homeopathy that the Hahnemann's results were suppressed and practitioners given a hostile reception when they tried to set up practice, for fear that they threatened the livelihoods of allopathic doctors.[5]

By the time Mary returned to London at the end of 1865, the Hahnemann Hospital had been so successful that in 1859 it had transferred to three houses in Great Ormond Street that now accommodated fifty patients. When we look at the names of the hospital's patrons, many of Mary's social and medical connections going back to the Crimean War fall into place, beginning with the fact that Amos Henriques dedicated his book *Art versus Nature* (just as Mary had her *Wonderful Adventures*) to none other than Lord Rokeby, 'to show how highly I, in common with the whole of that profession of which I am a humble member, appreciate the services your lordship has rendered to that great cause [homeopathy] which concerns the interests of the world.' Lord Rokeby, according to an article in the *British Medical Journal*, professed to have 'experienced benefits of homeopathy personally during his service in Crimea', most likely a reference to medical help he received there from Mary Seacole.[6]

© Wellcome Collection

THE LONDON HOMŒOPATHIC HOSPITAL, GREAT ORMOND-STREET.

The guiding light of British homeopathy and the impetus behind setting up the Hahnemann Hospital was Dr Frederic Quin, who had adopted Hahnemann's principles with enthusiasm in the 1820s and had founded the British Homeopathic Society. Quin was extremely well connected at court and highly favoured by members of the royal family, several of whom supported homeopathy, especially Bertie, Prince of Wales, and his wife Alexandra.[*7] Like Amos Henriques, whom he knew well, Quin published treatises on the homeopathic treatment of cholera. In 1824 he had been

---

* Queen Adelaide, wife of William IV, favoured homeopathy and had had remedies sent from Germany. She also consulted a German homeopath, Dr Johann Ernst Stapf. Although Queen Victoria expressed no obvious support for homeopathy, Prince Albert had given the movement his tacit support. When he died in December 1861, the homeopathic press argued that his four eminent doctors had mismanaged his treatment and that the prince would not have died if placed under the 'mild and efficacious medication' of homeopathy.

appointed physician to Prince Leopold of Saxe-Coburg, uncle to the then Princess Victoria; by 1866 Victoria's son Prince Alfred, the newly created Duke of Edinburgh, was a devoted patient and begged Quin to take up residence at his home, Clarence House. Other aristocratic fans were Lord George Augustus Paget, a Crimean veteran and one of the influential Paget family who held key positions at court; the Queen's uncle the Duke of Cambridge – who had also served in Crimea – as well as his mother the Dowager Duchess of Cambridge, who had embraced homeopathy in the 1820s; and his daughter Mary, Princess of Teck. The Duke of Newcastle was another leading Seacole patron, whose wife was a patient at the Hahnemann.

Any essentially irregular medical practise that Mary entered into at this time would have had to be discreet, and reliant on personal recommendation by her friends and patrons in the homeopathic world. Despite Mary's colour and class, her skills as a healer and herbalist were so considerable and so highly regarded that this appears to have rendered her socially acceptable, where other women practitioners – particularly Black ones – would have been rejected outright. She was, in every way, a unique exception to the social rules of the day and favoured as a practitioner regardless of her medical marginality, her Blackness and her femaleness. This in itself is a testament to Mary's unique position in Victorian society as a Black woman.[8] It is perhaps no coincidence either that homeopaths were, in general, ardent antislavery campaigners (some had even been active in the underground railway in the USA and had trained Black male and female lay homeopaths). They would have thus been more receptive to a woman of colour such as Mary in their midst.[9]

Within months of her arrival back in London, Mary Seacole's nursing and pharmaceutical skills were called on when another serious outbreak of cholera came, in June-August of 1866, during which 5,600 died in London alone. The outbreak was concentrated in and around the Port of London, from the Tower of London eastwards to the Isle of Dogs. Eventually the source of infection was traced to water that had seeped in from the River Lea to the East London Water Company reservoir supply in Bow. Mary was one of many who responded generously to the Cholera Relief Fund. The *London City Press* noted under the 'Donations of Stores': 'Mrs Seacole Crimea, 100 Bottles of Anti-Cholera Medicine and 100 Boxes of Pills' – a considerable gift; but was Mary making them herself at home?[10]

This is certainly suggested by a small ad in the short-lived satirical newspaper *The Owl* on 18 July, which reminded people of Mary's success in curing the cholera in Crimea and announced that her medicines were to be obtained at 40 Upper Berkeley Street.[11] The audience for this advertisement would have been small, but not that of the *Morning Advertiser*, where Mary soon also took out an ad:

> **MRS. SEACOLE'S SPECIFIC** for DIARRHŒA, DYSENTERY, and CHOLERA.—This preventive and curative Medicine has been highly successful in the Crimea, Panama, and in London during the present epidemic. Its efficacy has been proved by numerous testimonials from medical officers. May be had at her residence, 40, Upper Berkeley-street, Portman-square.

A variant advertisement in the military press under the banner headline 'Mrs Seacole's Preventive and Curative Medicines' deliberately used Mary's wartime calling card to target Crimean veterans, by adding that 'These medicines were highly approved of by Medical Army and Naval Officers during the Crimean War. Numerous testimonials.' What better recommendation could any practitioner have?[12] It is, however, hard to visualise Mary manufacturing vast amounts of pills and potions in her rooms at Upper Berkeley Street, so perhaps she had them made up to her own specification by a homeopathic pharmacist, such as Leath & Ross, who supplied the London Homeopathic Hospital and were located not far away in Vere Street.

The advertisement in the military press was well timed, for at the end of September Mary was a distinguished guest at a 'Grand Divisional Field Day' held at Aldershot army camp. All the top brass were there, and Mary was in her element hobnobbing with

her old Crimean friends, most notably the Crimean commander
Lieutenant General Sir William Codrington KCB.[13] As the
Aldershot Military Gazette reported (once again confirming that
Mary had three medals certainly by 1866):

> Mrs Seacole of Crimean celebrity, decorated with her three
> war medals, the Crimean medal, with three clasps, the Legion
> of Honour, and the Turkish medal that had been presented
> to her by the different governments for the valuable services
> rendered by this extraordinary lady to the allied army during
> this memorable campaign, was also present with her nephew
> and attendant ... as the troops were formed up to march past,
> she was recognized by the generals, and Sir James [Simpson]
> rode up to her, and shook her warmly by the hand, and, as well
> as the other generals inquired where she had been since the
> Crimean War.

The day after the review, at the special request of Crimean veteran
Major General Hodge, Mary had visited the female hospital at
Aldershot camp, 'which she found in excellent order, with every
improved arrangement for the comfort of the mothers and the little
ones, as well as other patients'. Once more this strikes one as an
extraordinary mark of military respect for Mary and her medical
reputation. Perhaps even more interesting is an almost throwaway
remark at the end of the article that 'For some few weeks past [Mrs
Seacole] had been making herself useful in the east end of London
distributing her cholera mixture amongst the patients, and which
had been found of great service.' This ethos of providing medicines
to the poor for free and only charging the rich, as Mary had done
in Crimea, was very much in the spirit of Samuel Hahnemann's
'homeopathic way'.[14] For the biographer, it is particularly deflating
then to come upon such a valuable piece of evidence only to find
that all attempts at following through on it draw a blank. For I
found no other mention of Mary's humanitarian work in the East
End other than a passing mention in *The Lancet* on 9 February,

informing its readers that 'during the recent epidemic of cholera [Mrs Seacole] renewed these kindly exertions for the helpless for which she was formerly famous.'[15]

Even curioser in this Aldershot report, however, is one tiny telling clue that we might quite easily miss. Mary attended the Grand Review according to the report, 'with her nephew and an attendant'. The former must be William James Kent; but who was the 'attendant'? Might this just possibly be Sally, and had she been with her mother all this time without us knowing? If so, it would perhaps have been easier and safer for Sally to stay under her mother's protective wing than to try to make her own way in the world with so much stacked against her as a woman of colour. But nothing has emerged to date to confirm her continuing presence with Mary.

The Lancet was one of several publications that in February 1867 announced the setting-up of another subscription for 'Old Mother Seacole' of Crimean fame to help provide some financial security for her old age. It came in a letter to the editor of the *Morning Post* by a Mr Hamilton Hume* of 9 Waterloo Place, as 'one who had met with many little kindnesses at [Mary's] hands' and who regretted to inform readers that she was now 'sadly in want':

> It is impossible that any of those who knew Mrs Seacole in her days of prosperity can read the appeal made in your columns today on her behalf without feeling the deepest commiseration that such an appeal should be necessary ... The fact that her Majesty takes a kind interest in her future welfare, and that the Prince of Wales, the Duke of Edinburgh, and the Duke of Cambridge are patrons of the fund, and that the committee is

---

* Hume (1797-1873) was an early explorer of Australia and a Fellow of the Royal Geographic Society. He was also Honorary Secretary of the Eyre Defence and Aid Fund, and it may well be that he knew Mary through this Jamaican connection. The Eyre case was currently in court and Mary had been attending. See 'Jamaica Prosecutions' in e.g. *Reynolds's Weekly Newspaper*, 17 February.

composed of several leading and influential men in both services, will, I trust, induce many unconnected with the army
and navy to assist in securing a trifling independence for the
old lady.[16]

The *Army and Navy Gazette* chimed in, exhorting its military
readers that Mary 'ought not to remain unbefriended. It would be
a disgrace to this country if this humble woman, who, out of the
sympathy of her large heart, volunteered generous service during
a time which was as disastrous as it was glorious, were allowed
to feel the want of succour she so unsparingly supplied to others'.

The support of the Queen and three top-drawer royals was no
mean feat for this second appeal; Victoria allowed it to be stated
that she was 'graciously pleased to express her approbation of Mrs
Seacole's services' in the official promotional leaflet.[17] In terms of
what she *could* have done to acknowledge Mary's work in Crimea,
it is better than nothing. It is thought that Queen Victoria made
a private donation of £50, but, as a strict rule of thumb, she
adamantly refused to put her name publicly to any such subscriptions.[18] Bertie Prince of Wales made a large anonymous donation
of £25 and his brother Alfred Duke of Edinburgh £15; Count
Gleichen gave £2; Lord Paulet £2; Prince Edward of Saxe-Weimar
£1; and the Prince of Leiningen 2 guineas. Several of the names on
the list of donors published in *The Times* on 2 and 11 March are
familiar from the fund of ten years previously – a whole plethora
of lords, ladies, honourables, graces and military officers.*[19] The
amount of money raised within a few short weeks was £137. 18s.,
equivalent to more than £16,000 today. There is no indication of
what the final total was, but it would have been a most welcome
nest egg for Mary.

---

*   Neatly tucked in among them, interestingly, is a certain Colonel Brownrigg CB, who
      gave £2. 10s., a generous £260 in today's money. Readers may recall him as a putative
      father of Mary's daughter, Sally.

MAULL & C? 187ᴬ PICCADILLY
AND
62 CHEAPSIDE

It is around the time of this second Seacole Fund that a photograph of Mary appears to have been produced for public consumption, when photography was capitalising on *carte de visite* mania. The popularity of these small affordable images of popular public personalities – royalty, politicians, actors and even criminals – mounted on a durable backing of stiff card, had taken off with the unprecedented demand for photographs of Prince Albert after his death in December 1861. Back in the early 2000s, a *carte de visite* of Mary Seacole surfaced which at the time was dated to the early 1870s, but research has shown that the photographer Henry Maull was in business from the mid-1850s and this may well have been a reissue of an earlier photograph taken by him, probably for the 1867 Seacole Fund. It is a clever exercise in PR; Mary is not looking straight to camera, but modestly gazing down at the pestle and mortar in her lap in acknowledgement of her dedication, first and foremost, to her medicinal art. This and the array of pharmacy bottles on the table at her side would have sent out a strong signal that she was very much still in business as a purveyor of her herbal cures. Perhaps she even used the photograph as a form of business card.[20] Also of interest at this time is a tiny announcement buried in the Classified Ads column of the *Daily News* in late February and March 1867, which listed under 'Saturday's Sales' at the Great Rooms on 211 High Holborn, among various goods up for auction, an 'original portrait of Mrs. Seacole'. This cannot be a reference to the Challen painting that I discovered in 2003, which is clearly dated 1869; so might there have been *another* portrait of Mary in circulation at the time, that is now lost? We shall return to this later.[21]

Overall, the response to and the press coverage of the second Seacole Fund were low-key in comparison to the fanfare for the first one in 1857. On 19 July, the Wandering Thespians gave a benefit performance of the 'romantic drama' *The Marble Heart: or, The Sculptor's Dream* by Charles Selby along with 'other entertainments' at the Bijou Theatre, Haymarket. But, as the press regretfully noted in Kingston, Jamaica, this particular fundraiser had been 'pecuniarily a failure' due to 'the concurrent counter-attractions of the Concert at the Agricultural Hall and the Ball at the India House'.[22] People were out of town, or on holiday, or simply had better things to do; the Crimean Heroine was no longer the crowd-puller she had been ten years previously. In New Zealand, however, Mary was not forgotten, for far away in Wellington a 'Grand Dramatic Entertainment' was staged by officers and men of HMS *Charybdis* which raised 'more than £50' for her.[23]

It is around this time – 1867 – that we encounter a most intriguing aspect of Mary's post-Crimean War medical activities. Details of it are confirmed by the account by British temperance campaigner Sarah Robinson, founder of the Portsmouth Soldiers' Institute, who met Mary on a visit she made to the navy there in 1867. Robinson recalled in her 1892 memoirs that Mary told her that 'she made a good living as a "rubber" (we were not cultured enough to say *masseuse*), and had "rubbed" the Princess of Wales at that time of her lameness.'[24] This suggests that Mary was also offering massage as one of her therapies – 'rubbing' being a technique she had long employed with her cholera and yellow fever patients.

Princess Alexandra had certainly been suffering terribly at the time. Just prior to giving birth to her daughter Princess Louise on 20 February 1867, she had been very unwell with severe inflammation of her right knee that had left her with considerable pain and stiffness in the joint and a permanent limp.[25] This came at precisely the time members of the royal family were promoting the second Seacole Fund, so it is not difficult to figure out how Mary had got her introduction. Dr Frederic Quin of the Homeopathic Hospital was a very close friend of the Prince and Princess of Wales, so much so that he had accepted an offer to live in apartments at their home – Marlborough House, off the Mall. Perhaps it is he who recommended Mary Seacole or one of the princess's other royal relatives such as Count Gleichen.

During this patronage by Princess Alexandra we learn that Mary made a special request to her friend Captain William Cooper, superintendent of the Royal Mail Steam Company, when he was about to return to Jamaica on furlough, to bring back to England with him 'a basket of mangoes "on the ice"' as she wanted them for her 'dear Princess' who 'wished to taste Jamaica mangoes'. Captain Cooper was only too happy to oblige; when she received them, Mary took the mangoes straight to Marlborough House and delivered them personally to Princess Alexandra, who had 'at once eaten one and said she enjoyed it'. The Jamaican resident Mrs K. Stewart, who relayed this story to the *Daily Gleaner* in 1938, continued: 'I impertinently enquired of Mrs Seacole if she had made a nice curtsy when she entered the reception room. "Oh, me dear child. I don't go there. When I go to see the Princess, I go up to her private sitting room and we sit and talk like the old friends we are."'[26]

This suggests an extraordinary – if not unprecedented – level of informality that Mary, as a Black woman, enjoyed in her relationship with the princess. Confident in her usefulness, Mary did not stand on ceremony: typescript notes in the National Library of Jamaica speak of how 'Once she just walked over to Buckingham Palace [Marlborough House is probably intended] and rang the bell. Rebuked by the guard for having come without an appointment, she said: "Cho, me son, the Riyal Family is glad any time to ask me up to tea."' Mary claimed that Queen Victoria addressed her personally as 'Mother Seacole'; another unsubstantiated report of an extremely informal relationship with the royals stated that she 'invariably called on the Duke of Cambridge, whom she called "George".' She also made personal medical recommendations suggesting warm baths during the Prince of Wales's recovery from a near fatal bout of typhoid fever in November-December 1871.[27]

These are vivid anecdotes that give us a wonderful sense of Mary Seacole in all her unconventional, uncompromising glory, but if we turn to the Royal Archives and also to published sources on Queen Victoria, the Prince and Princess of Wales, or any of their immediate family at that time, bar a couple of businesslike letters from Count Gleichen about the Seacole Fund in the Royal Archives, there is not a single, solitary word to be found.[28] Even more surprising is that there is nothing in Queen Victoria's diaries; nor in her letters, and, worst of all, no hope of finding anything relating to Princess Alexandra. For along with her husband King Edward VII, she left instructions for all her personal papers and letters to be destroyed on her death (in 1925). If any manuscript evidence of Mary Seacole's friendship with her various royal patrons once existed, it would appear that it has been most efficiently redacted out of British royal history and consigned to the flames.[29]*

---

*   The press did, however, note that when the Prince and Princess of Wales visited Crimea in the spring of 1869 in the company of William Howard Russell, he took them to the Col de Balaclava and past the site of 'Mother Seacole's'. In royal terms, that is as good as the evidence gets.

CHAPTER 25

'A NICHE IN THE TEMPLE OF FAME'

During the next few years, while she still had the energy, Mary continued to maintain her public profile on visits to old friends and Crimean veterans in and around Britain. In June 1868 she ran a stall at a bazaar in aid of the building fund for a new school and lecture room at the Gospel Oak Chapel in Kentish Town, and a couple of months later made a trip to Cork in Ireland, where she appears to have had eminent connections.[1] For on her arrival there in September she was the guest of William Wrixon Leycester, the Sheriff of Cork, who lived in a big house, East View, on the estuary of the Lee River. The link came through his sister Barbara, who was married to Lieutenant Colonel William McCall, who had acted as honorary secretary of the 1867 Seacole Fund and was a gentleman at arms in the royal household.[2] The *Cork Constitution* was delighted to report the presence in the city of 'the Crimean celebrity', who had been 'most assiduous in her attentions to our wounded soldiers on the field of battle, dispensing comforts on all sides without any remuneration', and how Lieutenant Colonel McCall of the 79th had himself been an eyewitness to 'Mrs Seacole's heroic devotion to our wounded soldiers'. The news report also confirmed sight of Mary once again wearing 'the Crimean medal, the Turkish medal and the medal of the Legion of Honour'.[3]

Back in London, there were still plenty of people intrigued to meet Mary even now, and none more so than a promising young artist named Albert Charles Challen. Some time in early 1869 – we assume – he painted a portrait of Mary which today hangs in London's National Portrait Gallery. Born 8 October 1847, Albert grew up in Islington where his father was a warehouse manager, but by the 1871 census the family had moved to West Kensington Gardens, Hammersmith.[4] They may have moved there so Albert could attend an art college in the area, for on the census he was listed as an 'art student (painting)'.[5] The portrait, dated 1869 on the back, was therefore executed before he even became a professional artist and there is perhaps a good reason that he wanted to paint Mary at that time. Challen may have been looking for a suitable subject to submit to the summer exhibition at the Royal Academy. Or is it remotely possible that at the age of only twenty he had produced the portrait two years earlier, in 1867? Going on Mary's celebrity at the time of the second Seacole Fund, this might have been a more logical date for the portrait's execution. If so, could this then be the 'original portrait of Mrs Seacole' that was put up for auction in High Holborn (see page 281), and Challen added the 1869 date later?

There certainly seems to have been a personal connection between Mary and the Challens, for thanks to the survival of the only other known manuscript letter written by Mary, she knew Albert's eldest unmarried sister Matilda Challen, and perhaps it was she who had introduced Mary to her artist brother. For the letter, written just after Easter 1869, opens with the more informal words '*My dear Miss Challen*'.[6] After a few mundane pleasantries about Mary's recovery from a cold and the unseasonably bad weather that had prevented her from visiting the family, Mary said she hoped to do so in a few days' time. But then she says something very important: '*I hope Albert will be successful in getting the Painting into the Academy*' – thus confirming that Albert had indeed submitted it to that summer's exhibition at the Royal Academy. The letter concludes by once more affirming what seems to be an informal and friendly relationship: '*with best love to your mama and papa also to your brother.*'[7] To date I have regretfully found nothing to explain the friendship and there is no indication of a Crimean War connection in the family.

The Royal Academy Annual Exhibition was held that July of 1869 at a new and specially created space at Burlington House on Piccadilly. But Albert Charles Challen's extraordinarily modern, impressionistic portrait was not chosen.*[8] Perhaps it was too bold, too unconventional; perhaps its Black subject, despite being a Crimean War heroine, was not deemed suitably attractive or racially acceptable. For it was, after all, the first stand-alone portrait of a Black woman to be submitted. Prior to that date British colonial subjects had generally been depicted as submissive servants and inferiors. In contrast, Mary Seacole's bold, proud – almost defiant – portrait in profile, wearing a red neckerchief, a symbol of her Jamaican Creole identity, went very much against the grain of conventional Black portraiture, such as it was at the time.[9] In any event, the competition had been fierce that year and only 1,320 paintings out of 4,500 submitted were chosen for the exhibition.[10] We know this much entirely retrospectively, for there is no specific mention of Albert Challen's portrait of Mary Seacole in any contemporary Victorian sources.

In July of 1870 and although she was now in her mid-sixties, Mary was once more looking for a mission, and when the Franco-Prussian War broke out had considered volunteering as a nurse. A public appeal for medicines, as well as practical and financial support, soon appeared in the press, with calls for the recruiting of first-aid volunteers to offer their services on a non-partisan basis. Even *The Lancet* mentioned Mary's name in this connection – albeit from the point of view of sutler/supplier. In a discussion of medical help for the French wounded, it suggested that 'The establishment of various depots for the supply of useful articles, such as Mrs Seacole's establishment afforded in the Crimea, would also be very expedient.'[11] It would appear that Mary did indeed make a prompt approach – to

---

* Art historian Jan Marsh suggests that the rough brushwork indicates the painting may have been 'an oil sketch rather than an unfinished painting'; perhaps Challen intended to do a more finished version of it.

the liberal MP Sir Harry Verney, who in response to the appeal had helped set up the British National Society for the Relief of the Sick and Wounded in War.* Unfortunately, Verney also just happened to be married to Florence Nightingale's sister Parthenope, and he immediately solicited Florence's opinion on the matter. In her response, in a letter dated 5 August and marked 'Burn', Nightingale made, what has become a notorious put-down of Mary Seacole that successfully blocked her application. The first comments Nightingale made, relating to Mary's establishment in Crimea and alluding to the drunkenness of her customers at Spring Hill during the war, have already been discussed (see page 172), but what is more concerning is this swipe at Mary's honesty that Nightingale fails to explain: 'A shameful or ignorant imposture was practised on the Queen who subscribed to the "Seacole Testimonial".'

Was Nightingale insinuating that the Seacole Fund of 1867 had been unnecessary; that Mary had hoodwinked people and had not needed the money? Or was it simply a reflection of Nightingale's own still-consuming jealousy that Mary had achieved an importance in the Queen's eyes that she felt did not merit the monarch's generous donation of £50? Nightingale's remark in this regard is quite pointed: 'I conclude (& believe) that respectable Officers were entirely ignorant of what I ... could not help knowing, as a Matron and Chaperone and Mother of the Army.'[12] 'Mother of the Army' is the key here; Nightingale resented Mary's use of that attribution; yet it was one that the troops in Crimea had freely given her. Her censoriousness may well be an allusion to the drunkenness of some of Mary's LTC and AWC customers at Spring Hill to which she was privy and of which she so greatly disapproved; or could she have been insinuating her private knowledge of Mary's illegitimate daughter? – a fact which would have horrified the Queen. As for Mary perhaps not needing the money; as the *Morning Advertiser* noted in a comment on widows' pensions for military wives at this time: 'Poor Mrs

---

* The society was the precursor of what, in 1905, would become the British Red Cross Society.

Seacole, of Crimean fame, was not pensioned.' We need only remind ourselves that her joint losses with Thomas Day at the end of the war were approaching a quarter of a million pounds in today's money.[13]

Undaunted by what appears to have been yet another rejection of her nursing services freely offered, at the end of August 1870 Mary took herself off to Southsea, to visit the nearby naval base at Portsmouth and join in fundraising events for the French war wounded. Once again she reconnected with an old Crimean friend, army chaplain Charles Josiah Hort, who had been based at nearby Zebra Vicarage up at Spring Hill.[14] Her presence at No. 6 Jubilee Terrace was noted for several weeks, during which time even the *Court Journal* reported on Mary's humanitarian work 'gathering for the wounded in the war now raging',* but adding that thanks to 'the gallantry of our allies at Inkerman, the "mother's" proclivities are entirely for the French soldiers.' The royals certainly were still standing by her, as the report went on: 'With the ever kind conde-scension of our Royal Family, the Commander in Chief [the Duke of Cambridge] on a recent visit to Portsmouth delighted the old lady by reviving his acquaintance with her by a very friendly notice. She has obtained a good store of medical necessities for the wounded; and with her hard experience of the horrors of war, few can be more prac-tical judges than one whose hand was ever ready to soothe the fearful sufferings of our soldiers of all ranks at the siege of Sebastopol.'[15]

One of the joys of the advent of the digitisation of newspapers and magazines from the Victorian era over the past twenty years is that historians can now make significant research breakthroughs where this had not been possible before. You never know what you may find simply by concerted keyword searching, and I was making such searches right down to the wire. The more persistent and creative you are sometimes can bring unexpected results – results that oblige you to reconsider what you thought you knew. This is the case with another

---

* On 31 October the *Morning Post* published a list of donations for the French wounded. Most of them were sums of money, but Mrs Seacole, it was noted, presented 'a Crimean case', presumably a travelling case of her holistic remedies and/or medical supplies.

intriguing discovery I made as I completed this book, which once more raises the unsolved puzzle of Mary Seacole's missing daughter. For, quite by chance, during one of my regular lucky dips, I stumbled upon this, from what was then known as *The Bazaar, Exchange & Mart & Journal of the Household*, for 22 February 1871:

> CRIMEA. Wanted, by a young lady, age 21, a situation as companion to a lady, or to an invalid. The highest references given. – Address Mrs Seacole, 40 Upper Berkeley-street, Portman-square.

'Crimea' as the heading, in capitals, would immediately have attracted the attention of readers in the know, especially given the tiny typeface of the listings. But what follows is a mystery: could this be a discreet advertisement for a job for Mary's daughter Sally? True it says 'age 21', but it was often the convention to say this when drawing a veil over a lady's precise age, implying merely that she was *over* the age of twenty-one (as often stated on marriage certificates).[16]

Sally was in fact around thirty by now but, as already suggested, may well have stayed with her mother, unmarried and living in utter obscurity, all these years. What other options had she had, other than to return to Jamaica, a place from which she no doubt felt very detached after a 17-year absence? Better perhaps to at least bask in the reflected light of her mother's now dwindling fame. But by 1871 Sally may have tired of constantly living in Mary's shadow and wanted to make her own living, in whatever modest way she could.

The position of lady's companion, like that of governess or teacher, was still about the only respectable 'profession' genteel young women could pursue, aside from the new one of nursing. We should not assume, however, that Mary had disguised her daughter's true relationship when she was among friends; maybe it was an open secret. Nevertheless, there is a terrible poignancy to Sally's hidden life. A part of me hopes that telling what I know of her story might trigger a connection being made somewhere, somehow, for I so want to know what happened to her.

*

It was June 1872 before Mary once more reappeared in the British press, with the inclusion in the sculpture section of the Royal Academy summer exhibition of a terracotta bust of her sculpted by her old Crimean friend, Count Gleichen, who since retiring from the navy due to ill health in 1866 had turned to sculpture. During the years since the war, he and Mary had stayed in touch; his son Edward later recalled that Mary had 'become much attached to him', and until her death 'the warm-hearted old lady used to come and see [Gleichen] and bring little presents for his children.'[17] The bust, which is half life-size, is dated 1871, and Mary would have sat for it at the studio that Queen Victoria had allowed Gleichen to build in the gardens of St James's Palace. It might have been a maquette for a bigger work that never got made, for most of Gleichen's busts of other people were executed in marble.*

At the exhibition the bust was put on display as exhibit No. 1457, alongside other royal and military busts. The *Illustrated London News* noted it as 'very clever and spirited' and 'deserving attention'; *The Times* thought it 'full of individuality'. Sadly, however, the bust was soon forgotten, as too the name of its subject. When I accessed the original album of photographs of Count Gleichen's work held at the National Portrait Gallery's Heinz Archive, I was dismayed to see that the photo of the terracotta bust of Mary was labelled as 'old Jamaican lady – nursed in the Crimea', 1871.[18]

The record is silent on the next five years of Mary's life; in Crimea, the last vestiges of her presence there were disappearing too. Travellers making the battlefields tour noted that 'extensive cultivation' had now 'obliterated' the remains of the British Hotel and all that was left was 'an immense heap of broken bottles by the roadside, glittering in the sunlight like thousands of black diamonds'.[19] The Crimean veterans

---

* There were apparently three copies of the bust; one of these, owned by Mary, was inherited by her sister Louisa in Jamaica and given to Dr Arthur Saunders in Kingston. His widow donated it to the Institute of Jamaica in Kingston in 1916. The other copies, possibly made for two trustees of the 1867 Seacole Fund – Lord Rokeby and Major Hussey Fane Keane – were in the 1970s acquired by Sergeant J. V. Webb, a collector of militaria in London. One of these two copies resurfaced in July 2020 and was auctioned for £101,000.

who had known Mary were also growing old and their memories
beginning to fade. As they began to die, the oral history that they had
shared of Mary's good deeds in Crimea diminished. All we know for
certain is that some time after the April 1871 census, Mary moved a
short distance to a lodging house at 26 Upper George Street, the next
road parallel to and immediately north of Upper Berkeley Street.* On
2 September 1876, and obviously now feeling her age, she drafted
her will with Horace W. Smith, a solicitor in the Strand. Or, rather,
Mary seems to have dictated it, for it states at the end of the document
that the text had been 'carefully and audibly read over to her' before
Mary signed it. This suggests that her pterygia was getting worse and
her sight was failing. It may have prompted her decision to return to
Jamaica – perhaps to put her affairs there in order or even with the
intention of retiring there. On 7 December 1876, the *Daily Gleaner*
was proud to announce Mrs Seacole's return:

Not long before Mary set off, a sad reminder of the English
Seacole family's past connection with the island had resurfaced
in an announcement in the *Daily Gleaner* in Kingston and the
London Gazette relating to arrears in Quit Rent and Land Tax for
plantations long since abandoned by their original white owners in
the wake of the abolition of slavery. Among those listed were 600
acres at Look Behind in south Trelawny parish, originally patented
by Charles Witter [Witton] Seacole, and another 300 acres of Look
Behind located in north St Elizabeth parish. If no one laid claim
to the land – which was in a dense and fairly inaccessible part of
Jamaica that by now would have been in a sorry state of neglect and
ruin – and no heirs came forward, it would be repossessed by the
Crown and sold. There is no indication that Mary made any claim
on it as the only living Seacole relative.[20]†

---

* By 1880 Mary's former home at 40 Upper Berkeley Street is listed as a 'coffee house'.
  No. 26 Upper George Street, which in 1985 had been renumbered as 147 George Street,
  was awarded a blue plaque commemorating Mary's residence there. But it sadly fell
  victim to redevelopment – despite its link to her – and was demolished in 1998. A few
  years later, and there would no doubt have been a campaign to save it.

† The 300-acre Seacole estate in St Elizabeth – 'abounding in timber and cedar' – went
  up for sale again in January 1911.

The Gleaner

AND

DE CORDOVA'S ADVERTISING SHEET,

CITY EDITION.

PUBLISHED DAILY.

TRI-WEEKLY

PUBLISHED

Tuesdays, Thursdays and Saturdays.

PACKET EDITION,

Published on the 9th and 24th of each Month.

THURSDAY. DECEMBER 7, 1876,

Arrival of the Packet,

The Royal Mail Company's steamer *Don*, Captain Woolward, arrived here early yesterday morning, with 98 passengers, 42 of whom are for this port. Among the ladies is Mrs. Seacole, who rendered herself conspicuous in Europe by her services to the sick and wounded, during the Crimean war. She seems to be in perfect health. Through the courtesy of the purser of the *Don* we have been placed in pos-

Back in Kingston, Mary's sister Louisa was still in business running what had long been acknowledged as one of the best lodging houses there, and still trading on the celebrity of being the sister of the 'Eminent Mother Seacoal' [sic]. There is a wealth of good sightings of her at Blundell Hall in the 1860s and early 1870s that indicate business had been flourishing.[21] Travellers' accounts also confirm that Louisa was very much her sister's Jamaican mirror image – in word and deed and dress:

Gayest of all the gay French bonnets, lightest and most volumi-
nous of all the gauzy and silken *modes* assembled and met together
in Kingston Parish Church ... were the bonnet and the dress of
Miss Grant, sister of the excellent Mrs Seacole, of Crimean popularity. To speak of Blundle Hall, and not to speak of Miss Grant,
proprietress and tutelary genius thereof, is a piece of glaring reticence akin to mentioning Brighton Pavilion and at the same time
ignoring George the Fourth. It would be like writing a treatise and
leaving out the subject.[22]

But by the time Mary arrived, however, Louisa appears to have run
into difficulties – perhaps through financial mismanagement, overwork or failing health, or a combination of factors. The previous
August Blundell Hall had been put up for rent, the property having
changed ownership. It was now 'part of the estate of Charles Hall
of Marlborough and New Buildings', based at Black River. Louisa's
rent appears to have been increased to £12. 10s. a month and it
seems likely that this change in circumstances had prompted Mary's
return visit.[23] On 17 March 1877 Louisa gave up Blundell Hall and
in October transferred her business across the road to No. 7 East
Street on the corner of Water Lane, naming her new lodging house –
just to confuse everyone and probably annoy the new owners – 'New
Blundell Hall'. She clearly did not wish to relinquish twenty or more
years of association with that name, but her new premises appear to
have been modest in comparison to the twenty-four rooms boasted
by the original Blundell Hall.[24*]

How long Mary remained in Kingston and whether or not she
stayed with Louisa or in one of the two freehold properties she
had acquired on Duke Street, we do not know.[25] It is more likely
that she rented these out. The larger of the two, located at No.
111, which she had had built on land that she bought after the

---

*   Blundell Hall, which by the end of the century had become the Control, Money Order
     and Telegraph Office, was already in a very serious state of decline when unfortunately
     it was destroyed in the 1907 Kingston earthquake. Its site is now occupied by the
     Institute of Jamaica.

Morant Bay Rebellion, would soon become known as 'Seacole Cottage'.*

It was still standing in Kingston in 2010, when it was up for sale for $30,000 (around £21,000). It would have been ideal, with funding, for conversion into a small Mary Seacole museum, but to my considerable regret, I discovered when completing this book that it has since been demolished.

Courtesy of Keith Atkinson

Mary probably returned to England no later than the early autumn of 1878, for an unsubstantiated article in the *Irish Times* on 21 September talked of rumours that she was in ill health, if not dying.[26] She returned to the Marylebone area, this time to rooms at No. 3 Cambridge Street, the other side of the Edgware Road from Upper Berkeley and Upper George streets. In June 1880 her dear friend Amos Henriques died, having suffered ill health for several years, but the press for the last three years of her life was totally silent on Mary until 12 January 1881, when the *Eastbourne Gazette* featured an article – the last in Mary's lifetime as it turned out – on 'Mrs Seacole the Soldier's Friend'. This came as part of a series on 'Noted Men and Women', and much of it was a résumé of the *Wonderful Adventures*

---

*   This is according to a letter to the *Gleaner*, 29 August 1939, from Mrs K. Stewart, who described it as a 'charming little bungalow' – so hardly big enough to be a lodging house.

and Russell's preface to it. But the article also commented: 'It is not often that persons born with every disadvantage of birth and education can rise so high as to obtain a niche in the Temple of Fame. But Mary Seacole is really one of those whose life has been devoted to alleviating the sufferings of others and whose services in the Crimean War are regarded by the poor soldiers who survive with even more gratitude than those of Florence Nightingale.' [27]

It was also noted that Mary's 'name has not been so much paraded on platforms as those who were well-born', but that she 'rejoices that she has lived long enough in the world to see her own race acknowledged amongst European peoples; and even the Yankees, who once taunted her have gladly accepted Mary Seacole as a guest.' More importantly, from Mary's point of view, it emphasised how important her white Scottish ancestry had been to her. This, Mary felt, had endowed her with an honorary 'Englishness' to which she had steadfastly clung throughout her life, rather more tenaciously perhaps than her Jamaican heritage.

It was an optimistic final word on the Crimean Heroine and her unique status in Victorian Britain, for the next would be the relatively modest announcement of Mary's death, on 14 May 1881. She had undergone a rapid decline during the spring of 1881 and died, according to her death certificate, of 'apoplexy' – probably a stroke, which she had suffered sixteen days previously. During the final three days of her life, she had sunk into a coma.

On census night six weeks previously, Mary had had staying with her a visitor from Jamaica named Rose Boyden.* Whether Rose had still been with Mary when she died, we do not know, but her nephew's wife Sarah Kent had come up from Lambeth, where the couple now lived, to be with Mary at the end. Sarah also registered her death (though she wrongly named Mary as the widow of 'Horace Seacole') and gave her age as seventy-six. It would be three months before

---

* Rose Boyden, aged forty-six, from Kingston, Jamaica, may well have been related to the late Grace Blundell, née Boyden, the original owner of Blundell Hall – possibly her niece. This suggests there may have been some kind of family or personal link with Mary Seacole, but so far I have been unable to establish precisely what it was.

Mary's substantial and surprisingly detailed will would be proved. Meanwhile, William and Sarah Kent arranged Mary's funeral according to her wishes to be buried 'in the Catholic portion of the Cemetery at Kensal Green and in a respectable manner'.[28] It was they who also would have commissioned the headstone that acknowledged Mary as 'a notable nurse who cared for the sick and wounded in the West Indies, Panama and on the battlefield of the Crimea 1854-1856'.

There were no press reports of the actual funeral but some of Mary's old Crimean War friends must have made their way to Kensal Green to bid her goodbye. *The Times* published an obituary on 17 May which was syndicated across more than thirty regional and colonial papers, announcing that 'The trustees of the fund established some time since in behalf of Mrs. Mary Seacole wish it to be known that she died on the 14th inst. The deceased, it will be remembered, greatly distinguished herself as a nurse on the battlefield and in hospitals during the Crimean War.'

Most papers dropped the announcement in among other news items. Even a few American papers ran the death notice, while in Jamaica the obituary on 9 June was, surprisingly, the briefest of all.[29] In Britain the banner headline 'Death of Mrs Seacole' was inserted on several accounts, on the assumption that there were many still alive who would remember Mary, even twenty-five years after the end of the war.[30] But an interesting regional variant on 26 May contradicted this: 'There has just died in a retirement so complete that it amounted to oblivion a lady whose name was often enough in men's mouths during the course of the Crimean War.'[31]

The Times obituary had, however, raised a note of disquiet; after stating how the money raised for Mary by the Seacole Funds had 'enabled her to end her days in comfortable ease', it had added: 'Strange to say, she has bequeathed all her property to persons of title.' This is of course untrue, based on poor information, but it nevertheless provoked a response in *The Times* only a few days later, from a Spencer H. Curtis, who from the content of his complaint must have had personal knowledge of Louisa Grant in Kingston:

It may not be inopportune to mention that her sister is now living in Jamaica – Miss Grant, late of Blundell Hall Hotel, Kingston, and is in very straitened circumstances. Perhaps the 'persons of title' to whom she has bequeathed all her property may be willing to help Miss Grant. She is well known and respected by all naval officers on the North American Stations and others who have visited Jamaica and she has been reduced almost to beggary by no fault of her own, excepting, perhaps, her own excessive liberality.[32]*

Probate had not yet been announced, but maybe Curtis had an inkling of the value of Mary Seacole's estate, which came in at £2,615. 11s. 7d. – the equivalent purchasing power today of over £320,000. Was Florence Nightingale right? Had Mary been squirrelling money away quietly and carefully all this time while pleading poverty? Her numerous legatees certainly benefitted from the very wise investment of the 'monies, stocks, funds and securities' held by the trustees of the Seacole Fund.[33] Louisa Grant was in fact the major beneficiary, and was very well provided for, being left £300 (nearly £38,000 today). Mary also willed that the smaller of her two freehold properties in Kingston should go to her in the event of the death of their nephew Edward Ambleton, to whom it was bequeathed.[34]†

Lord Rokeby, who had been a loyal and unstinting friend, was the first of her Crimean patrons to be named, with the gift of £50 'to purchase a ring if he so pleases' as 'a slight mark of gratitude for his many kindnesses to me'; likewise the Hon. Hussey Fane Keane, Deputy Adjutant General of the Royal Engineers, who had served on the committee of the 1867 Seacole Fund, who was also entreated to use his £50 'in the purchase of some ornament or jewel'. Count

---

*   Curtis was a director of several companies, including a West India merchants and the Royal Mail Steam Packet Company, and spent time in Jamaica. He had probably stayed with Louisa at Blundell Hall, hence his personal acquaintance.

†   A year later, Louisa used her inheritance to take out a mortgage on a property at No. 54 East Street. But by July 1886 she had defaulted and it was repossessed. She then appears to have lived at Seacole Cottage at 111 Duke Street along with other lodgers – Mary's executors having rented the property out. She died there on 21 July 1905. No. 54 Duke Street, like Mary's other property on that same street, has now been demolished.

Gleichen was bequeathed £50 too, and the special bequest of the diamond ring 'given to my late husband by his Godfather Viscount Nelson';* his eldest daughter Feodora was left Mary's 'best set of pearl ornaments'.³⁵ The Duke of Cambridge was acknowledged by a generous bequest of £100 to the Cambridge Asylum for Soldiers' Widows that had been established in memory of his father in 1851.

It was only natural that having spent most of her life since 1856 in England, Mary should remember the friends who had stood by her all these years in London, most particularly Amos Henriques (who of course predeceased her), his wife Julia and their children – for whom a trust fund was to be established by Mary's executors. The considerable list of bequests, including one to Thomas Day (c/o solicitors' chambers in the City; he clearly was still living abroad), the children of William and Sarah Kent, and three Jamaican cousins – Amelia Kennedy, and her sister Matilda Siminett [Symonette] and Louisa Cochran³⁶ – were of the uniform sum of £19. 19s., the amount being just below the £20 ceiling above which monetary legacies were then taxed.

The same amounts were left to other Jamaican friends and relatives: Edward Ambleton, her dead brother's son, was left £100 'to buy a house', and a David Henriques in Dundrum, Ireland, whom Mary described as a 'cousin', received £19. 19s.³⁷ But there is no mention at all, of course, of Sally – if she was still alive.† After all the numerous financial bequests, Mary passed on more practical items to Sarah Kent (in addition to ten guineas): 'my best bedstead and bedding and also two pairs of linen sheets and one pair of calico sheets and one counterpane'; all her other household effects, of furniture, plus 'pictures prints and engravings, plate linen and china' were to be sold as part of her estate. Louisa in Jamaica was to receive 'all the rest and residue of my household linen and

---

* An item in the *Morning Post* on 6 August detailing bequests in Mary's will contradicts this by stating that 'to Count Gleichen the diamond ring presented to her husband by his godfather, Viscount Hood.' Was this an error, or in fact the truth?

† A Jamaican historian, the late Professor Alan Eyre, insisted to me that no self-respecting Jamaican would ever mention an illegitimate child in a will. If Sally was still alive in 1876 when she made her will, then Mary must have made private arrangements for her.

also my watch and all my jewellery trinkets and ornaments of the person', as well as remaining monies after all bequests had been paid by her surviving executor William Neilson Farquharson (Amos Henriques was the other). Farquharson, who was from the Black River Farquharson family with whom Mary had long been acquainted, was now operating as a West India merchant in London, and administered the bequests.

It is striking that Mary makes no specific mention of her medals, but three – or even four – of them, as we have seen, were passed on to Louisa in Jamaica. Nor does she specify a particular piece of jewellery that in a last twist to this story may be the missing proof of Mary's connection to Princess Alexandra. As mentioned earlier, Sarah and William James Kent had five children, one of whom was named Florence Seacole. When her elder sister Ellen Augusta died in 1886, she specially stated in her brief will that 'I give my Dagmar brooch (presented to the late Mrs Seacole) ... to my sister Florence Seacole Tilt' (Florence had married in 1883).[38] This brooch must have come down to Ellen from their mother Sarah Kent. But what does it signify?

At the time of her wedding to Bertie Prince of Wales in 1863, Princess Alexandra of Denmark had been presented with many gifts, among them a replica of a thirteenth-century Dagmar Reliquary Cross in pendant form, from her father King Frederick VII. The Dagmar Cross was a well-known symbol in Denmark and commercial replicas of it, made of silver, were often given as gifts. Alexandra had adopted this idea when she became Princess of Wales, presenting replicas of the cross to selected friends; and she was doing so in the period when Mary was visiting her at Marlborough House.[39]

Florence Seacole Tilt had only one child – a daughter, Beatrice, born in 1884. Beatrice was an aspiring 'variety artiste' living in a boarding house in Kennington Park Road, Lambeth in 1911 when she met and fell in love with a fellow boarder.[40] He was an ambitious young 'musical composer', a Viennese Jew, whom she married the following year in Vienna. In October 1914 they sailed to New York to seek their theatrical fortune in the USA. The widowed Florence Seacole joined them in Manhattan in 1920 and became a US citizen; she died in the Bronx in 1930. Unfortunately Beatrice's marriage failed and she was divorced by 1925. But her former husband went on to greater things. His name was Max Steiner. In Hollywood during the 1930s he became one of the first great movie composers, his most famous score being for *Gone with the Wind*, set during the struggle for the abolition of slavery in America. What a delicious irony.

CHAPTER 26

'THE IDENTITY OF MRS SEACOLE: A LITTLE YELLOW WOMAN'

When we look at the best-documented aspects of Mary Seacole's life in Britain during and after the Crimean War, we can see a woman assiduously networking and cultivating prestigious friends and patrons, yet, despite the support she enjoyed in high places, the speed with which she vanished from the record after her death is startling. In contrast, the name of Florence Nightingale – immortalised as the Lady of the Lamp (a sobriquet she hated) – was everywhere. And rightly so, for Nightingale had established a nurses training school at St Thomas Hospital after the war and championed nursing as a respectable profession for women. She also became a major social reformer, campaigned on public health issues, reform of army medical services and was a gifted statistician.

For Mary Seacole there would always be insurmountable barriers preventing her from progressing to any semblance of a medical career – had she so wished, which seems unlikely. In white British society, much as she aspired to gain its acceptance, her colour prevented her from ever being considered a 'lady' in the then sense of the word. But racism is not the only reason that Mary was marginalised and forgotten. What happened seems in greater part to do with the fact that she had no immediate family to carry on her legacy (we have no idea what happened to Sally); but also, and most crucially, she left no archive. Unlike Florence Nightingale, Mary had no body of published work beyond her memoir; no institutes or pubs or streets or monuments were named after her to remind people of her contribution; she left no letters bar two in manuscript that have survived and sadly the album she crammed full of the many testimonials to her nursing and herbalist skills is also lost. Nor did Mary pass on the recipes for her medicines and treatments in written form either. Hers had been a tradition handed down from mother to daughter, learned not through books but through practical experience. For all these reasons Mary's name does not appear in any literature on women in medicine or nursing in the Victorian period. A Black woman from the West Indies who practised herbalism simply did not fit the narrative, even for enlightened women campaigners of the day. Sadly, even they had not a word to say about her either; although the feminist periodical the *Englishwoman's Review* did at least run her obituary in 1881.[1]

For the first few years after her death Mary's name did, however, remain on the lips and in the hearts of those who knew her and there would have been many who still cherished the fondest memories of her loving care, her warmth and generosity of spirit. But as the old Crimean veterans themselves aged, sickened and died, so the memory of Mother Seacole was lost and with it the oral record of her life. The published edition of her *Wonderful Adventures* had not been durable either: in its flimsy cardboard covers copies of the book would not have survived for long before falling apart, which is why so few survive today. The only thing that helped retain a memory of Mary for a while, and which has greatly assisted in the rediscovery of her story more than a century later, was her unusual surname. For many years, the name 'Seacole' was enough to trigger the memory for those who had heard of Mary's Crimean exploits. Had she been plain 'Mary Grant', this might not have been the case. It has certainly been the one enormous plus in trying to chase down her lost story: keyword-searching for 'Seacole' has brought many rewards where Grant would have been a lost cause.

*

It was in her homeland of Jamaica that Mary's memory was first recovered, but it did not come until 1892, and tangentially, when a long obituary for Count Gleichen, after the initial pleasantries, turned into a paean of praise to the 'sincere affection' shown him in Crimea by 'the celebrated Mother Seacole', his good Jamaican friend, whom the writer felt compelled to tell his readers was 'black as the ace of spades'.[*2] It was another thirteen years before Kingston magistrate and local dignitary Richard Walcott's 'Story of the Life of Mrs Seacole' appeared in the *Daily Gleaner*. He may well have known Mary, for he had been prompted to write his piece by the announcement of the death of her sister Louisa Grant in Kingston that July.

In his article Walcott asked the question I have asked myself many times during the research for this book: 'I wonder who can tell of where to find any of the highly complimentary letters that Mrs Seacole received from heroes, whose names are blazoned on the pages of history.'[3] Mary quotes a few of them in the *Wonderful Adventures* but there must have been so many more. Had they survived they might have put paid to the insistence by Seacole detractors that she never, effectively, did any real nursing. It is dispiriting to see that in his letter Walcott reported that no one in Jamaica even knew where Mary was buried: 'Who can point out the resting place of the honoured bones of Mrs Seacole? . . . In her own country, however, Mrs Seacole is "only the sister of Mrs Louisa M Grant". We Jamaicans should cherish the memories of our past more than we do, for if we trample out the footprints on our own sands of time, we deprive forlorn and weary brothers of seeing those foot-prints and taking heart again, and blot out the memories that remind us, we can make our lives sublime.'

As Walcott pointed out in a subsequent letter to the *Gleaner*, Mary had been very much representative of a vanished class of Jamaican women of colour, who had been lodging-house keepers, and who had now 'almost wholly passed away'.[4] The death of

---

[*] The obituary unfortunately wrongly stated that Mary had 'bequeathed all her worldly possessions to Count Gleichen'.

Florence Nightingale in 1910 prompted another reminder of the island's own nursing heroine as 'A Jamaican Veteraness'; and in 1916 a discussion of the heroism of women nurses in war drew attention once more to Mary's noble work.[5] Interest briefly revived in 1933, but the major rediscovery of Mary in Jamaica did not come until 1938-9 with a flurry of letters to the *Daily Gleaner*, which, in providing first-hand detail on Mary by people who knew her or of her, have proved absolutely crucial in the research for this book. This revival of interest in Jamaica had, however, been sparked by a letter to the editor of the *Sunday Times* in England. On 9 January 1938 'J. G. W.' of Moseley in Birmingham had written that he was 'desirous of identifying a hand-coloured print or photograph of a lady with some military decorations on the left side, signed "Mrs. Seacole 1859"' (this may be the Seacole photograph on page 280). The letter brought a reply from a Major A. C. Whitehorne, who gave some fascinating detail on Mary after the war in London, suggesting knowledge of her gleaned from his former regiment, the Welsh, which had served in Crimea. The correspondence was reprinted in the *Daily Gleaner* under the heading 'The Identity of Mrs Seacole, A Little Yellow Woman' and encouraged further recall of Mary and her life. The following summer the *Gleaner* proudly reclaimed Mary as 'Jamaica's Florence Nightingale' in a front-cover feature in its magazine.[6]

The *Times* correspondence had marked the first mention of Mary Seacole in the British press since her death forty-three years previously, bar a favourable mention of Mary's accomplishments in nursing care in the *British Journal of Nursing* in 1937.[7] More significant was the Black rediscovery of Mary, which began with a small pamphlet, 'Jamaicans Who Made Good', published by *Jamaica Times* journalist Thomas Service Phillips in 1932, and a profile of Mary as the 'Forerunner of the Red Cross Nurse' in volume two of *The World's Great Men of Color*, a landmark work published in the USA in 1946. But Mary was still virtually unknown in the USA, and it was not till 1955 that one of the leading African American newspapers, the *Indianapolis Recorder*, pointed out to its readers how she had been 'slighted by US historians'.[8]

THINGS YOU SHOULD KNOW

MRS. *Mary* SEACOLE
—— D.1881

A MULATTO, NATIVE OF KINGSTON, JAMAICA, THE FLORENCE NIGHTINGALE OF HER RACE, SLIGHTED BY U.S. HISTORIANS, SHE WAS KNOWN AT HOME AS THE "YELLOW DOCTRESS"! IN 1853 SHE VOLUNTEERED AS NURSE TO HELP ON THE CRIMEAN WAR BATTLEFIELD — WAS REFUSED MANY TIMES OUT OF PREJUDICE! SHE FINALLY PROVED HERSELF AND WON THE RESPECT AND LOVE OF THE BRITISH PEOPLE!

CONTINENTAL FEATURES

In Britain, sporadic mentions of Mary surfaced in Crimean War memoirs and letters published up to and just after the end of the nineteenth century. Two edifying Victorian collections – *Everyday Heroes: Stories of Bravery during the Queen's Reign* (1900) and *Noble Deeds of the World's Heroines* (1903), both published by the Society for Promoting Christian Knowledge – included Mary, albeit in a résumé of the narrative of her book. 'Mrs Seacole's' even appeared in some boys'-own-paper-style fiction, such as Hawley Smart's *Beatrice and Benedick: A Romance of the Crimea* in 1891.

The 100th anniversary of the outbreak of the Crimean War in 1954 at last brought an opportunity for people to be reminded of Mary Seacole, and a feature in *The Times* headed 'A West Indian Nurse in the Crimea' set out to counter negative views on immigration from the West Indies by the *Windrush* generation. What better example of the dutiful Commonwealth subject could there be than Mrs Mary Seacole, to reassure white Britons alarmed at what they perceived as a growing invasion of people of colour? The unnamed author of the piece thought it 'a pity that the work of this good and skilful nurse should be forgotten'. Mary Seacole's humanitarian work in Crimea 'might serve as a great example to the many West Indian nurses who now receive a better training than Mrs Seacole gathered from her mother and from her own well-tried experience, but who will need much to equal her determination and humanity.' In 1961, as the arguments for limiting immigration numbers increased in the run-up to the passing of the Commonwealth Immigrants Act of 1962, another letter, this time in defence of West Indian immigration to Notting Hill, reminded readers of the story of the 'Coloured Lady Nurse' that had been published in the *Morning Advertiser* during the Crimean War in 1855.[9]

The 1954 *Times* correspondent was right to mention West Indian nurses taking their example from Mary Seacole, for it was precisely a group of dedicated Jamaican nurses who had come to Britain during the *Windrush* years, who set the fuse for Mary Seacole's rediscovery. Some time in the early 1970s Elise Gordon, then secretary of the British Commonwealth Nurses War Memorial Fund and editor of *Nursing Mirror*, was given a copy of the *Wonderful Adventures* that had been 'bought for a few pence at a second-hand bookshop'. Someone had noted the details of Mary's death on a slip of paper in the back of the book, giving her place of burial. Elise Gordon found the grave's location and her organisation collaborated with the Lignum Vitae Club – established by Jamaican women in London, many of them nurses – in clearing Mary's long-forgotten grave of overgrown vegetation. It was, as Elise recalled, 'in a complete state of disrepair, stones cracked and crumbling', its white marble headstone 'dimmed with mildew and dirt'.[10] The group had an exact replica made, with the lettering in blue and gold. Carved into the stone was a Jamaican scene of palm trees on the right and, on the left, a flag to signify the Crimean War. After the restoration was complete the grave was reconsecrated in 1973 in a Roman Catholic ceremony and in the presence of the Jamaican high commissioner and members of the Jamaican Nurses Association.[11]

HERE LIES
MARY
SEACOLE
1805 – 1881

OF KINGSTON, JAMAICA
A NOTABLE NURSE WHO CARED
FOR THE SICK AND WOUNDED IN
THE WEST INDIES, PANAMA
AND ON THE BATTLEFIELDS
OF THE CRIMEA
1854 – 1856

'S GRAVE HAS BEEN RESTORED BY THE LIGNUM VITAE CLUB
JAMAICAN WOMEN'S ORGANISATION IN LONDON AND THE
RITISH COMMONWEALTH NURSES WAR MEMORIAL FUND

But the honours for facilitating the inexorable rise and rediscovery of Mary Seacole must go to Ziggi Alexander and Audrey Dewjee, who in 1980 mooted the idea of an exhibition on Black history to Brent Library Service. This opened in October that year at Harlesden Library in London, entitled 'Roots in Britain: Black and Asian Citizens from Elizabeth I to Elizabeth II'. During its run, Ziggi and Audrey were struck by how the exhibition's comments book was full of questions about Mary's life, which led Brent Library Service to organise the first memorial service for her on 14 May 1981, the centenary of her death. It also prompted Falling Wall Press, a small feminist imprint in Bristol, to contact Ziggi and Audrey about writing a book on the exhibition.

In response, they suggested a reprint of the long-forgotten *Wonderful Adventures of Mrs Seacole in Many Lands*, of which only a handful of copies had survived, and sought one out in the British Library. Its pages were uncut. The reprint – with an extended introduction and valuable notes provided by Ziggi and Audrey that was the first detailed discussion of Mary's life to date – was published in 1984.

In Jamaica, too, from the 1950s Mary Seacole began to be granted the national honours she deserved: in 1954 the Jamaican Nurses Association named their Kingston HQ Mary Seacole House and a ward at Kingston Public Hospital was named after her in 1956, shortly followed by another Seacole House – a women's hall of residence at the University of the West Indies.[12] In 1990 the Jamaican government posthumously awarded Mary the Order of Merit and issued a commemorative stamp. In 2020, in conjunction with the Mary Seacole Trust in the UK, the Mary Seacole Foundation was relaunched in Kingston to promote Mary's legacy in Jamaica.

The 1984 republication of *Wonderful Adventures* did much to ignite discussion and study of Mary Seacole; what began as a cottage industry has become, nearly forty years later, a major subject for academic discourse and commentary as well as discussion in nursing journals. Since the Falling Wall Press reissue there have been a succession of other English editions of her book, as well as new editions of the French and Dutch translations. But the intensifying of interest in Mary only exposed how little we really know of her life beyond what she tells us in the *Wonderful Adventures*, leading to a tendency to impose contemporary attitudes and interpretations on a text that is best evaluated on its own terms, within the time frame and social attitudes in which it was written. Today the story of Mary Seacole is being disseminated far and wide, particularly in the young adult market, with titles such as *101 Awesome Women, The Great Book of Badass Women, Fantastically Great Women Who Changed the World* all putting their own spin on her story, and in the process often misrepresenting or distorting the facts.

Mary Seacole's inexorable march towards immortality became unstoppable in the noughties after she was acknowledged as 'The

Greatest Black Briton' in an online poll organised by the Black heritage website Every Generation in 2004.[13] The poll attracted over 100,000 votes; but how Mary might have reacted to being referred to as a Briton and as Black is, however, a moot point, for she thought of herself as 'English' and *only a little brown*'. Be that as it may, nothing could stop Britain now setting Mary Seacole's name in stone as a national heroine and cultural icon. But the 2004 vote also, inevitably, provoked a revival of controversy surrounding claims about Mary's nursing skills and medical knowledge, and the level of status that she should rightfully enjoy alongside the traditionally revered icon and founder of women's nursing – Florence Nightingale.

CHAPTER 27

THE MAKING OF A
CULTURAL ICON

From the moment Mary Seacole was voted Greatest Black Briton in 2004 the errors and inaccuracies that had been creeping into her story since the 1980s multiplied exponentially with the electronic age. The explosion of the Internet in that first decade ensured that websites about her sprang up everywhere, all of them drawing on the content of *Wonderful Adventures* without attempting to research further and often repeating and perpetuating each other's mistakes. Over the past twenty years a great deal of inaccuracy, calculated guesswork and downright fantasy has been disseminated about Mary Seacole's true story. Worryingly, some of it has crept into children's textbooks and other educational materials and is in danger of becoming entrenched. Part of the problem lies in the fact that, in general terms, people often trust too much to what the author of a memoir or autobiography tells them about themself. It is a fatal mistake. Every autobiographer likes to be in control of their material; but they often misremember things, forget, embroider and at times are very deliberately economical with the truth. As we have seen, Mary did all of these things, and it is a hazard of which every biographer has to be aware. We suffer also from the enormous disadvantage that the *Wonderful Adventures*, after its very speedy and highly economical canter through Mary's first forty-five years, only in essence covers five years of her life – from her departure for Panama late in 1851 to her return from Crimea in July 1856.

In 2004, *The Guardian* set the misinformation ball rolling with a howler, by announcing that 'A little-known nurse who tended soldiers alongside Florence Nightingale in the Crimean war has been voted the greatest black Briton.'[1] This isn't true as we all know; yet even today some ill-informed sources still talk of Mary nursing at Scutari. Nor can we concede exaggerated claims that she 'saved the lives of thousands of soldiers' or had 'a team of nurses' working with her, or that she 'built a hospital' in Crimea.[2] And although she provided first aid and succour to the wounded, Mary did not go down onto the battlefield under fire and carry them to safety, for the simple reason that by the time she arrived in Crimea the three major battles were over. But she *did* attend the wounded brought up from the siege lines outside Sevastopol, and those on the field *after* the battle of Chernaya in August 1856, not to mention all the unstinting medical help she gave to numberless soldiers who solicited it at her storehouse at Spring Hill.

The other major development in the elevation of Mary Seacole as a cultural icon is the simultaneous intensification of attempts to demote Florence Nightingale. This revisionist attack began in 1999 when Nightingale fans were shocked to hear that at its annual conference, UNISON, the nursing trade union, had voted to remove Nightingale as its figurehead. Among several names tipped to replace her was that of Mary Seacole, seen here in this telling cartoon by Jonty Clark for *BBC History Magazine*.

Those campaigning for this sea-change in nursing tradition felt that, as it entered the twenty-first century, the profession 'should have a more forward-looking image' and concentrate on promoting the valuable contributions of medical staff from ethnic backgrounds, who at the time made up 11 per cent of the NHS workforce. In the subsequent debate, calls were made to 'exorcise the myth of Florence Nightingale'; it was argued that the 'impact of her legacy' as a 'white, English, middle-class Protestant woman' had 'held the nursing profession back too long'. It was time Nightingale's till then inviolable status as the patron of nursing was challenged.[3]

© Jonty Clark Illustration 2005

The suggestion by some admirers of Mary Seacole that she replace Nightingale attracted considerable criticism. True, nursing needed to 'remain alert to old stereotypes' while facing the new challenges of professionalism and multiculturalism, some admitted, and it was time for a change of thinking with regard to what today constitutes true 'nursing'. Some felt that Nightingale's potential defenestration from UNISON was part of a systematic attempt to denigrate her achievements while elevating those of Mary Seacole out of all proportion and beyond their true value. In a nutshell, this attempt to 'turn Mary Seacole into a black Florence Nightingale' was a 'mistaken rewriting of history to fit contemporary narratives'.[4] Major Colin Robins wrote to *The Times* in May 1999, complaining that the plot to demote Nightingale 'smacks of the craziest sort of political correctness'. Mary Seacole, he argued, had worthy instincts but her provision of 'tea and buns' to the soldiers seemed insufficient justification for her elevation to equal sainthood; in other correspondence, Robins alleged that he had found no evidence in contemporary sources of Mary doing anything other than 'running her grocer's shop and providing dinners for officers'.[5] David Starkey offered a similar argument at the time in an article bewailing the inclusion in the *Oxford Dictionary of National Biography* of new entries on what he perceived as inconsequential, minor women – including Mary. It was his contention that in so doing, the editors had 'greatly lowered the bar' in historical and reference writing.[6]

The attempt to remove Nightingale failed; as of her 200th anniversary in May 2020 she was still very much at the heart of UNISON and its nursing ethos. But what would Mary Seacole have thought of this attempt to replace Florence Nightingale with herself, and in so doing turn Nightingale into a casualty of reverse discrimination? In the *Wonderful Adventures*, Mary makes only too clear her admiration and respect for Nightingale, but without in any way conceding that her own medical methods were inferior. For many people today the two women's talents were complementary and not in opposition to each other, and there is room for both of them as inspirational figures. Mary Seacole certainly would not have wished to see Florence Nightingale vilified; nor would she have understood the need to promote herself to the detriment of Nightingale on purely racial grounds. For she well understood that she could not hope to have a place in Britain's white, Imperial meritocracy; she was far too eccentric, too unconventional – and it is precisely that difference that makes her special, if not unique.

For Florence Nightingale, nursing was almost devotional: a mission, an art, a sacred calling. Mary's impulse was utilitarian, practical – 'essentially medically skilled "mothering",' as Alan Eyre has written – and based on her own idiosyncratic brand of folk medicine. It is her approach to hands-on, patient-centred care, with an emphasis on the patient's psychological wellbeing, that has inspired nurses today, but she never put this in any textbook. Meanwhile, Florence Nightingale's *Notes on Nursing*, published in 1859, has never gone out of print and her considerable body of work fills sixteen volumes. This is the monumental achievement of the director of the *Collected Works* project, Dr Lynn McDonald, who has understandably proved to be Nightingale's fiercest defender. But she has also been Mary Seacole's fiercest critic, in particular decrying the use of the word 'nurse' in reference to Mary, simply because she was not a formally trained one and 'never did regular hospital nursing'. This argument makes little sense. Why should that fact be the benchmark for defining someone as a 'nurse' in the looser, humanitarian sense, especially at a time when professionally trained nurses did not yet exist? In the lifetime of both women there were thousands of extremely capable and dedicated women who did the work of domiciliary nurses within the home, caring for sick children and elderly parents – and indeed some of these very same women, such as Eliza Polidori (aunt of the poet Christina Rossetti), who had nursed her ageing parents for many years, were inspired to volunteer to nurse with Nightingale at Scutari.[7]

Traditionally, in the *Oxford English Dictionary* sense of the word, to nurse is to 'foster, tend, cherish a thing'; to 'wait upon or attend to a person who is ill' or to 'perform the duties of a sick nurse'. I would also venture that Mary 'nursed' in the *OED* sense of 'to hold caressingly or carefully in the arms or lap'. There are numerous instances of Mary's hands-on approach to the sick and wounded in the *Wonderful Adventures* and confirmation of this also in news-paper reports and the memoirs of others. McDonald, like several other critics, is uncomfortable with the fact that the multi-skilled Seacole combined entrepreneurship with her nursing and humani-tarian work. Why should the two be irreconcilable? Mary's business venture in Crimea made her the money, while she was there, that enabled her to give free care, food and drink to those who needed it. Unlike Nightingale she did not come from a wealthy and privileged family; she had worked and grafted all her life. Nor did she have any sponsor to fund her charitable work in Crimea, and she returned to England not just out of pocket but deep in debt.

Once the UNISON battle had been won, interest in Mary Seacole gained impetus in the run-up to her bicentenary in 2005, and to coincide with that, Jane Robinson published the first biography of

Mary, not long after the *Oxford Dictionary of National Biography* had finally got round to adding the entry on Mary lamented by David Starkey. (Revised in 2006, this sadly still has several errors.) Meanwhile, after I unveiled the Seacole portrait at the National Portrait Gallery that January, I continued to find out more about the artist and why the portrait had been hidden from view for so many years. Who had owned it and who had then effectively rejected it by concealing it?

From all my subsequent research into the Challen family and discussions with a descendant of a collateral branch, Professor Tom James, I concluded that the painting had never left the Challen family's possession. It had been passed down after Albert Charles's untimely death from TB in 1881 (only three months after that of his famous sitter), to his eldest sister Matilda, who lived in East Hendred in Oxfordshire. When she died in 1943 her niece Dora had inherited her property. On Dora's death, without issue, in 1967, the house clearance people were brought in and, according to Professor James, what didn't end up in a skip was sold off.[8] Somewhere among it all was the Seacole portrait, still hidden from view. In 2002 it turned up at that boot sale, but how it got there and who had had possession of it since 1967 remains an insoluble mystery.

I might have stopped here in my account of the lost portrait, had I not, at a very late stage in the writing of this book, received an extraordinary email from an antiques dealer in Edinburgh. He informed me that some time around the year 2000 he purchased 'a small oil portrait on wood or cardboard' inscribed 'Mary Secole' [*sic*]. The painting was unsigned and in a cheap Victorian frame and, he tells me, 'was not very good', with 'very pronounced impasto under a thick coating of varnish'. He can't remember what he paid for it – maybe £12 – but he sold it on for no more than £30. And no, he couldn't remember where; maybe on eBay. It was a head and shoulders portrait, similar to the Challen in size and in tone, but face on. Just as I began to get excited, he then informed me that a computer malfunction many years ago had caused the photograph he took of it to be lost. There was something 'quite good' about its vivid colours, he said, but the facial anatomy – the 'folds and pouches of elderly flesh' – wasn't as good. Overall, though, 'the handling and subject seemed rather unVictorian'. Might this be the painting put up for sale in 1867 (see page 281)? And might it have been an earlier tryout, by Albert Charles Challen, for the later portrait?[9] Either way, I have yet to come across any other paintings by him. Challen's entire artistic legacy rests on this solitary portrait, now one of the most famous exhibits in the National Portrait Gallery. The total absence of any other extant works is really quite something; it may even be unique in art history. Every time I walk past the gallery and see the banner hanging outside advertising Mary's presence there, I am filled with enormous pride.

The 2005 bicentenary was undoubtedly the turning point in Mary Seacole's posthumous revival, for it was also marked by a Channel 4 documentary, *The Real Angel of the Crimea*, on which I collaborated with producer Paul Kerr. By now, Professor Elizabeth Anionwu, then head of the Mary Seacole Centre for Nursing Practice at Thames Valley University, who had been leading the campaign to promote Mary as a beacon of Black women's nursing, had joined forces with Labour peer Lord Soley in the campaign for a Seacole statue. Suggestions that the statue should occupy the empty fourth plinth in Trafalgar Square once more revived controversy and several other locations were investigated before a site in the grounds of St Thomas Hospital, looking out across the River Thames to the Houses of Parliament, was decided on. Meanwhile, the Seacole controversy once more became heated, when in 2013 then Education Minister Michael Gove announced that he wanted British schoolchildren to focus on 'traditional figures' in British history, such as Churchill and Cromwell, and was considering removing Mary Seacole and Olaudah Equiano from the National Curriculum. This sparked fierce objections; a petition signed by 40,000 people, including several leading Black public figures, was launched in *The Times* under the banner 'Teach Pupils about Great Black Britons'.[10] Gove's assault on diversity in the curriculum failed and, today, even if their parents do not, every school child knows the name of Mary Seacole.[11]

Mary Seacole's place in British history was reaffirmed in 2007 when English Heritage unveiled a blue plaque on the house at 14 Soho Square where she had lived during the writing of her *Wonderful Adventures*. More and more institutions, libraries and university buildings have been named for her since: a Home Office building was named Mary Seacole House in January 2005; a Seacole Building opened at Birmingham's School of Nursing and Midwifery and also a Seacole Library specialising in health education on the same campus. There are now nursing and other awards in Mary's name, notably the Mary Seacole Leadership and Development Awards and the Royal College of Nursing's Mary Seacole Award that funds projects that 'aim to improve the health outcomes of people from black and minority ethnic communities'.[12] The Mary Seacole Trust contributes much to the continued honouring and celebration of Mary's achievements, using her example as 'a source of inspiration for a fair, diverse and inclusive society'.[13] In May 2020, during the Covid-19 pandemic, an NHS Seacole Centre – the first of its kind in England specifically for Covid-19 recovery patients – was opened at the Headley Court Hospital in Leatherhead, Surrey.

The high point of the Mary Seacole Trust's work – in its original 2004 incarnation as the Mary Seacole Memorial Statue Appeal – was the unveiling of the bronze statue of Mary Seacole by sculptor Martin Jennings outside London's St Thomas Hospital on 18 August 2016. This was achieved after many years of vigorous and dedicated fundraising. The final cost of the statue was half a million pounds; the site it occupies was provided at cost by the construction firm McAlpine. The erection of the statue was achieved in the face of objections from the Nightingale Society that the choice of site, on the hallowed ground where Nightingale had established the first Training School for Nurses in 1860, was inappropriate. Others complained that the statue was too large (at three metres, it is taller than Nightingale's statue in Pall Mall) and too imposing for the site and would draw attention away from the nearby Florence Nightingale Museum. But by now nothing could halt the relentless march of Mary Seacole towards secular sainthood, which brought with it one of the downsides of the enormous following she had garnered: a school of Seacole hagiography and uncritical enthusiasm that does her a disservice by seeking to ignore Mary's flaws and human failings and aggrandises her medical contribution beyond its true value. The ultimate accolade of cultural acceptance came with the announcement of a feature film about Mary's exploits in Crimea, made by Racing Green Pictures. In July 2020, Billy Peterson, the film's producer, paid an astonishing £101,000 for one of the copies of the Gleichen bust that came up for auction in Cirencester.[14]

In the meantime, the Albert Challen portrait has become probably the most iconic representation of a Black woman from the Victorian era, and, since my discovery, it has been complemented by a new photographic image of Mary found in a Crimean War album in the library at Winchester College in 2009.

This superb selection of letters, autographs, watercolours, maps and photographs was put together by Lieutenant Colonel Ely Wigram (1801-69) of the Coldstream Guards and was donated to the college in 1916. Among all the male military figures, the album contains images of only two women: Florence Nightingale and Mary Seacole. Mary's oval portrait, signed by her at the bottom, is quite extraordinary and arresting. It bears no photographer's name, but in its style, presentation and sepia colouration it is very reminiscent of the work of the popular Victorian photographer John Mayall, a favourite of Queen Victoria, who took many photographs of celebrities of the day.[15] It probably dates to the early 1870s and may have been taken to coincide with the display of the Gleichen bust of Mary at the Royal Academy exhibition in 1872, for the styling of the hair, the lace collar and the beads that Mary is wearing in both bear a marked similarity. What is so striking about this wonderful photograph is that it brims with character and exudes such warmth and compassion. This, for me, even more than the Challen portrait, is the quintessential Mary Seacole; the Mary that I have held in my imagination through twenty years of research and the writing of this book.

Define her as you will: nurse, doctress, pharmacist, humanitarian, Creole businesswoman, entrepreneur, sutler, philanthropist – or even 'an itinerant trader or "higgler" in the true Afro-Caribbean fashion', as Alan Eyre observed. Whatever definition we choose, the face that gazes out at us here is one for all time, the face of Everywoman. Throughout her life Mary Seacole demonstrated an independence of mind and spirit that bucked every prevailing convention: racial, sexual and social. She fought hard to retain an independent lifestyle as a self-starting, self-supporting woman in a white man's world. What kept her afloat through times of war, hardship and financial difficulty were her irrepressible good humour and optimism. She was an indomitable fighter who never gave in to misfortune or disappointment or despair. Her detractors may continue to denigrate her; her admirers will never cease to idolise her; but if we discard all the tags and labels with which we have tried and failed to define her, we should perhaps remember that it was the soldiers in Crimea who best summed up their beloved Mother Seacole: she was, quite simply, a Good Samaritan. Mary Seacole never allowed herself to be held hostage to bureaucratic rules and stifling regulations, whereas Florence Nightingale spent much of her time in Crimea fighting officialdom. Mary was a free spirit who acted on instinct in all her many enterprises and whose currency was the common language of laughter. Her book is infused with her inimitable good humour, alongside the pain of sickness and the tragedy of war. Humour and laughter are aspects of character that do not spring to mind with Florence Nightingale. Indeed, as Mary told Alexis Soyer when they met in Crimea: 'For my part, my son, I could not live without laughing.'[16] The best medical therapies were not always to be found in textbooks but drawn from hands-on experience; these and Mary's 'particularly West Indian "brand" of Christian love' were the benchmark of her practice.[17] They are reflected in the peerless contribution of Black nurses from the West Indies who followed in her footsteps and who came to Britain to work in the newly established NHS after the Second World War.

At that time the NHS was struggling for lack of staff, and it was estimated that it was 40,000 nurses short. An appeal went out from the British government for nurses and midwives from the Commonwealth to come to Britain and thousands of young women answered the call from Jamaica. A century before them, Mary Seacole had been the first Black nurse to come to the aid of the Mother Country in time of need, and had she been alive in the 1950s she would have been the first on the boat. Her spirit lives on in those dedicated young nurses who saw themselves as 'ambassadors for Jamaica', and who featured in a moving BBC Four documentary made in 2016. One of those interviewed, State Registered Nurse and midwife Beverly Davies, described how her generation of young Jamaican women looked upon nursing as a way of bettering oneself. She spoke with great pride and pleasure about how it felt when she qualified to put on her nurse's cap, her uniform, apron and blue belt with its silver buckle: 'the people respected you for that . . . I was so proud of the scholarship, was so proud of my training, so proud of my patients and how they loved me and the way that I nursed.' Just like Mary Seacole before her, Beverly went that extra mile for those who needed her: 'I wanted to do as I was taught, but with a bit more of me. That's how I nursed, I nursed with a bit more of me.'[18] There truly is no better way of describing Mary Seacole's ethos than that: for she too, unstintingly, and without question, always gave a bit more of herself, and the world is better for her having been in it.

ACKNOWLEDGEMENTS

The acknowledgements for this book stretch back over twenty years and there are many people who during that time helped me in my exploration of Mary Seacole's life and times. I must begin by apologising if I have left anyone out, for in the changeover to a new computer a few years ago I lost many emails from those first years.

My first debt of gratitude must go to those who back in 2002-3 helped me on my way – the members of the Crimean War Research Society, many of whom have stayed with me throughout my long search. I cannot name them all, as so many have been in touch over the years and some sadly have now died, but in particular I owe a huge debt to Douglas Austin, Glenn Fisher, Mike Hargreave-Mawson, Mike Hinton, David Jones, Tony Margrave, Hugh Small, the late Bill Curtis, and the late Keith Smith, for generously sharing information, maps and photographs and for their incomparable knowledge of the war. I must also thank Colin Robins, with whom I have shared a long-standing but chivalrous disagreement on the subject of Mary. Many CWRS members turned out to my talks on Mary and women in the Crimean War and generally have offered unstinting and loyal support to the very long gestation of this project, despite no doubt often wondering if my book would ever get written! When I first started, Norman Gooding of the Orders and Medals Research Society shared valuable insights on the subject of Mary

Seacole's medals; the late Paul Benyon answered many questions on ships and shipping and his Naval Index was invaluable; John Stevenson in Edinburgh was also enormously helpful on the same subject and Douglas Ronald advised me on naval history.

From Jamaica, the late Alan Eyre provided me with valuable insights on Mary and Jamaican Creole society and I shall always value the fortuitous encounter I had with him many years ago at the Florence Nightingale Museum. I am grateful to staff of that Museum for taking an interest in my work on Mary Seacole and for their championing of her contribution to nursing. Steve Porter of the Georgian Society of Jamaica generously helped me with material on locations in Jamaica and the layout and architecture of Kingston; Brett Ashmeade-Hawkins and the members of the Jamaican Colonial Heritage Society on Facebook offered insightful answers to my questions; Ainsley Henriques offered advice on the Jamaican Sephardi Jewish community; Fr Peter Espeut kindly allowed access to the original baptism records in the Roman Catholic archives in Kingston and Shanagaye Grant at the archives in Spanish Town toiled through the Tax Assessments and Poll Tax rolls for me in search of my elusive subject. Jackie Ranston helped me access the rare Belisaro image of the 1843 fire and my thanks to Christopher Issa for permission to reproduce it. My thanks also to Ian Shapiro, the Wellcome Institute, the National Archives and to Times Newspapers Limited Archives, News UK and Ireland Ltd. for permission to quote from sources in their collections.

A large part of this text was written during the second Coronavirus lockdown in the UK from December 2020 to April 2021. This meant that my dream of a research trip to Jamaica was lost and I had to urgently find a surrogate. I simply could not have achieved the breakthroughs in Mary's early life without enlisting the expertise of Jamaica-based genealogist Ann Marie Lazarus, who tolerated an endless barrage of requests and questions from me in England with great good humour.

In England, so many friends, fellow historians and writers have encouraged me to keep going with my Seacole project. I owe a considerable debt first and foremost to Paul Kerr, with whom I worked on the documentary about Mary for Channel 4 in 2005, and with whom I exchanged many emails sharing information and debating all the gaps in Mary's story that we were so desperate to fill. Likewise Keith Atkinson and his wife Nancy, who have shared their fascination with Jamaican genealogy and Nancy's own link to Mary's sister Louisa with me. They have generously hosted me at their home and Keith has been an unfailing and unflagging sounding board for all my theories, questions and frustrations over the Seacole story and has shared his own considerable research database with me. My friend Phil Tomaselli once more responded to eleventh-hour appeals for help in researching military records for the elusive John Grant and shared his incomparable expertise in this area. Anna Erm in Moscow tried hard to find any Russian accounts of Mary Seacole, but much to our mutual disappointment drew a total blank.

In terms of my research on images of Mary, I remain grateful to Peter Funnell, former Curator of Nineteenth Century Portraits at the NPG, and Terence Pepper, former Curator of Photographs, with whom I shared first sight of the Challen painting, and to then director Sandy Nairne, who championed my discovery and the portrait's loan and eventual sale to the NPG. Sarah Moulden at the NPG has since offered helpful insights into the various Seacole images, as too has Jan Marsh, an expert on Black people in nineteenth-century art. Jan put me in touch with Donato Esposito at the V&A who shared his knowledge of Thomas Dewell Scott, the engraver of the front cover of Mary's *Wonderful Adventures*. Tom James in Cheltenham invited me to his home and told me about the James family, a collateral branch of the Challens, and showed me many fascinating documents relating to them and Albert Charles Challen. My friend Paul Frecker, an expert in nineteenth-century photography, has been a wonderful fountain of knowledge on the subject and has helped bring valuable context to the two existing Seacole photographs. Roger Watson, former curator of the Fox Talbot Museum, also answered my photographic queries. Finally, but by no means least, is Jerry Warren, who made it all happen.

Over the years I have been inspired to keep going in my search for Mary Seacole by the work of Clive Soley, Elizabeth Anionwu and the members of the Mary Seacole Statue Appeal in their tireless fundraising. That organisation, newly incarnated as the Mary Seacole Trust, is committed to championing the life, work and achievement of Mary Seacole. Trevor Sterling at the Trust has been a great supporter of my biography, and he and his colleagues do such fine work in drawing attention to the contribution of Black and other ethnic communities to British society and culture. In the Netherlands, Seacole enthusiasts and researchers Corry Staring-Derks and her husband Jeroen Staring, both with a strong background in medicine and science, have done a great deal to keep research on Mary Seacole alive and have been incredibly kind and generous in sharing material with me and offering advice. Corry has written an excellent and detailed introduction to the Dutch reprint of *Wonderful Adventures* with copious endnotes that really deserves to be translated into English. In this regard, I am grateful to my Dutch neighbour Robert Cahn for kindly explaining some passages to me and to John Irons who later provided full translations. In the field of homeopathy, Francis Treuherz and Sue Young shared their knowledge and expertise; I am particularly grateful to Francis for allowing me to spend time at his home trawling through his impressive collection of nineteenth-century Victorian homeopathic books and journals.

Many other friends along the way have at various times been very supportive of my work on Mary, especially when I became discouraged and my energies flagged. My thanks go to David Olusoga, Melisa Tomlin-Kräftner, Jane Wickenden, Celia Brayfield, Susan Ronald, Sue Woolmans, Sharon Mannion, Candace Gahring, Turtle Bunbury, Natasha McEnroe, Christina Zaba, Ruth Marris Macaulay, Audrey Dewjee, Clare Mulley and, more recently, the staff at Brent Libraries and Billy Peterson, CEO of Racing Green Pictures.

During the Coronavirus pandemic my family, albeit sadly at a distance for most of the time, encouraged my work on the Seacole biography, which thanks to being effectively locked up here in West Dorset I wrote in record time. My love and thanks to Pete and Mike, to Chris and Sue down the road from me – who when lockdown allowed provided hot dinners. My daughters Lucy in Banbury and Dani and Wolf and my grandchildren in Austria have offered loving support, despite our separation for most of the writing process.

My agent Caroline Michel at PFD believed in this book as much as I did and totally understood my passion about writing it. I cannot thank her enough for her determination in securing a publishing deal, and I am thrilled that Ian Marshall at Simon & Schuster had the faith to sign *In Search of Mary Seacole*. My editor Frances Jessop responded to my text with sensitivity and enthusiasm and contributed some very helpful suggestions; Victoria Godden ensured a smooth copyedit and Clare Hubbard provided a meticulous proof-read. Through all my struggles, the ups and downs of discoveries and discouragements, the frustrations and disappointments of the research and writing process, my dear friend Lynne Hatwell, to whom this book is dedicated, has been an unfailing cheerleader, whose loving support and many insightful comments on nursing with regard to Mary have meant a great deal.

There remains one final appeal that I must make to all who read this book. As you will have seen, there are many gaps in Mary's story that still need to be filled. Should anyone have any information, especially documentary evidence, that might shed further light on Mary and her life – in Jamaica or in London – and especially any clues about what happened to her daughter Sally, I would be most grateful if they would get in touch: via my website www.helenrappaport.com, or by email info@helenrappaport.com, or through my agents Peters, Fraser & Dunlop, info@pfd.co.uk.

My search for Mary Seacole does not end with this book, for I feel sure that there is more still to be uncovered and I look forward to those emails arriving.

West Dorset, August 2021

BIBLIOGRAPHY

1. JAMAICAN ARCHIVAL SOURCES

Kingston Assessment Roll, Kingston Assessment Book, Kingston
 Capitation Roll: Jamaica Archives, Spanish Town
Roman Catholic Baptism and Marriage records: Roman Catholic
 Archdiocese of Kingston, Jamaica

2. DIGITAL SOURCES FOR JAMAICAN AND BRITISH GENEALOGY

www.jamaicafamilysearch.com
www.ancestry.co.uk
www.findmypast.co.uk
www.geni.com
www.jewishgen.org
www.familysearch.org
www.sog.org.uk Society of Genealogists
www.probatesearch.gov.uk
www.nationalarchives.gov.uk War Office: Printed Annual Army Lists
www.oxforddnb.com *Oxford Dictionary of National Biography* –
 online edition via public libraries

3. DIGITAL SOURCES FOR JAMAICAN HISTORY

Legacies of British Slave-ownership – UCL https://www.ucl.ac.uk/lbs/estate/view/250

Jamaica Almanac – produced annually, selected issues online http://www.jamaicanfamilysearch.com/Samples/Almanacs.htm

Dr Jenny Jemmott, 'The Parish History of St. Elizabeth'. Parish Histories of Jamaica Project, Department of History & Archaeology, University of the West Indies, Mona https://parishhistoriesofjamaica.org/wp-content/uploads/2020/01/The-Parish-History-of-St.-Elizabeth.pdf

Cockpit Country Heritage Survey, Report 2009: https://tinyurl.com/2937ayf6

Former British Colonial Dependencies, Slave Register, 1813-1834: https://www.ancestry.co.uk/search/collections/1129/

Mary Seacole sources online at National Library of Jamaica: https://www.nlj.gov.jm/BN/Seacole_Mary/bio_notes_mseacole.htm

4. NINETEENTH-CENTURY DIGITAL NEWSPAPERS AND MAGAZINES

British Newspaper Archive https://www.britishnewspaperarchive.co.uk/search/advanced

ProQuest newspaper titles not on BL newspaper database, via BL online catalogue: *Guardian, Observer, New York Times, Irish Times, Weekly Irish Times, Scotsman*

Caribbean Newspapers, 1718-1876, at BL Latin American Newspapers, online Series 1 1805-1922 & online Series II, 1822-1922, via BL electronic database

The Times Digital Archive, on Gale.com at BL and most public libraries

www.newspapers.com subscription, available through Ancestry.com

Newspaperarchive.com subscription, essential for the Jamaican *Daily Gleaner*

New Zealand newspaper archive, free online: https://paperspast.natlib.govt.nz/newspapers

Australian newspaper archive, free online: trove.nla.gov.au/search/
    advanced/category/newspapers
American digitised newspapers, free online at Library of Congress:
    https://chroniclingamerica.loc.gov/newspapers/

5. EDITIONS OF *WONDERFUL ADVENTURES OF MRS SEACOLE IN MANY LANDS*

1857: London: James Blackwood; 2nd edn 1858
1857: *Mary Seacole's Avonturen in De West en in De Krim, of het
    belangwekkende leven eener heldin der barmhartigheid, door
    haar zelve verhaald*, Rotterdam: P. C. Hoog
1858: *Aventures et Voyages d'une Créole, Mme Seacole*, à *Panama et
    en Crimée*, Lausanne: Librairie A. Delafontaine / Paris: Grassart
1984: Bristol: Falling Wall Press, with introduction and notes by Ziggi
    Alexander and Audrey Dewjee
1988: Oxford: University Press, with introduction by William Andrews
1994: *Je suis une mal-blanchie: La vie aventureuse d'une cousine de
    l'Oncle Tom, 1805-1881*, Paris: Phébus, 1994
2005: London: Penguin Classics, with introduction and notes by Sarah
    Salih
2007: *Mary Seacole's Avonturen in De West en in De Krim, of het
    belangwekkende leven eener heldin der barmhartigheid, door
    haar zelve verhaald*, Nijmegen: Integraal, 2007, with introduction
    and notes by Corry Staring-Derks

6. JAMAICAN HISTORY AND SOCIETY; DOCTRESSES AND HERBAL MEDICINE

Thesis: Aleric Josephs, 'Mary Seacole: Her Life and Times', MA
    Thesis, Mona: Department of History, University of the West
    Indies, 1985
'An Old Type', *Daily Gleaner*, 27 July 1905
Amphlett, John, *Under a Tropical Sky, A Journal of First
    Impressions of the West Indies*, London: Sampson Low, 1873

Andrade, Jacob, *A Record of the Jews in Jamaica from the English Conquest to the Present Time*, Kingston: Jamaica Times, 1941

Atkinson, Nancy Ffrench, *The Ffrench Connection*, London: privately printed, 2014

Ayensu, E. S., *Medicinal Plants of the West Indies*, Algonac: Reference Publications, 1981

Bailey, Wilma R., 'Geography of Fevers in Early Jamaica', *Jamaican Historical Review*, 10 (Fall 1973): 23-32

Baird, Robert, *Impressions and Experiences of the West Indies and North America in 1849*, London: William Blackwood & Sons, 1850

Barringer, Tim and Wayne Modest (eds), *Victorian Jamaica*, Durham: Duke University Press, 2018

Beckwith, Martha Warren, *Black Roadways: A Study of Jamaican Folk Life*, Chapel Hill: University of North Carolina Press, 1923

Bickell, R., *The West Indies As They Are; Or, A Real Picture of Slavery*, London: J. Hatchard & Son, 1825

Bigelow, John, *Jamaica in 1850: Or, the Effects of Sixteen Years of Freedom on a Slave Colony*, London: George P. Putnam, 1851

Black, Clinton Vane de Brosse, *The Story of Jamaica. From Prehistory to the Present*, London: Collins, 1965

Boa, Sheena, 'Urban Free Black and Coloured Women: Jamaica, 1760-1834', *Jamaican Historical Review*, 18 (1993): 1-6

Brathwaite, Edward, *Development of Creole Society in Jamaica 1770-1820*, New York: Oxford University Press, 1971

Bridges, George Wilson, *The Annals of Jamaica*, 2 vols, London: John Murray, 1827

Brooke, Elisabeth, *Women Healers Through History*, revised and expanded edition, London: Aeon Books, 2020

Bryant, W. C., 'Letters from the Island of Jamaica', *Littell's Living Age*, 24 (1850): 565-7

Buckley, Roger Norman, *The British Army in the West Indies: Society and the Military in the Revolutionary Age*, Gainesville: University Press of Florida, 1998

Bush, Barbara, *Slave Women in Caribbean Society 1650-1838*, Bloomington: Indiana University Press, 1990

Carmichael, Mrs, *Domestic Manners and Social Conditions of the White, Coloured and Negro Population of the West Indies*, London: Whittaker, Treacher & Co., 1833

Chambre, Alan, and William Chambre, *Recollections of West-End Life: With Sketches of Society in Paris, India, &c*, 2, London: Hurst & Blackett, 1858

Cundall, Frank, *Historic Jamaica*, London: West India Committee, 1915

Dancer, Thomas, *The Medical Assistant or Jamaican Practice of Physic*, Kingston: Alexander Aikman, 1801

Du Preez, Michael, and Jeremy Dronfield, *Dr James Barry: A Woman Ahead of Her Time*, London: Oneworld, 2016

Duperly, Adolphe, *Dageurreian Excursions in Jamaica*, Kingston: A. Duperly, 1844

Edmondson, Belinda, '"Most Intensely Jamaican": The Rise of Brown Identity in Jamaica', in Barringer and Modest, *Victorian Jamaica*, 553-76

Eisner, Gisela, *Jamaica 1830-1930: A Study in Economic Growth*, Manchester: Manchester University Press, 1962

'Extracts from the Bishop of Columbia's Journal', *Sixth Annual Report of the Columbia Mission for the Year 1864*, London: Rivingtons, 1865, 9-10

Eyre, Alan, 'Dusky Doctress: A Jamaican Perspective on Mary Grant-Seacole', *Jamaica Journal*, 30: 1-2 (December 2006): 42-9

Faber, Eli, *Jews, Slaves and the Slave Trade: Setting the Record Straight*, New York: New York University Press, 1998

Falconbridge, Anna Maria, *Narrative of Two Voyages to the River Sierra Leone*, Liverpool: Liverpool University Press, 2000 [1794]

Fergusson, William, *Notes and Recollections of a Professional Life*, London: Longman, Brown, Green & Longman, 1846

Fluhr, Nicole, '"Their Calling Me 'Mother' Was Not, I Think, Altogether Unmeaning": Mary Seacole's Maternal Personae', *Victorian Literature and Culture* 34, No. 1 (2006): 95-113

Foulkes, Theodore, *Eighteen Months in Jamaica*, London: Whittaker, Treacher & Arnott, 1833

'Fragments of a Journey to the West Indies and to New Orleans' in W. Ainsworth (ed.), *All Around the World: An Illustrated Record of Voyages, Travels and Adventures in all Parts of the Globe*, III and IV, London: William Collins, Sons & Co, 1866, 229-242

Gosse, Philip Henry, *A Naturalist's Sojourn in Jamaica*, London: Longman, Brown, Green & Longmans, 1851

Graham, J. W., 'Jamaica's Florence Nightingale', *Daily Gleaner*, 4 September 1939

Gunning, Sandra, 'Traveling with Her Mother's Tastes: The Negotiation of Gender, Race, and Location in "Wonderful Adventures of Mrs. Seacole in Many Lands"', *Globalization and Gender* 26, No. 4 (Summer 2001): 949-81

Gurney, Joseph John, *A Winter in the West Indies*, London: John Murray, 1840

Haggerty, Sheryllynne, *Merely for Money? Business Culture in the British Atlantic 1750-1815*, Liverpool: Liverpool University Press, 2012

Hakewill, *A Picturesque Tour of the Island of Jamaica*, London: Hurst & Robinson, 1825

Hart, Marie, 'Jamaica's Florence Nightingale', *Daily Gleaner*, 24 August 1938

Henriques, Fernando, *Jamaica, Land of Woods and Water*, London: MacGibbon & Kee, 1957

——, *Children of Caliban: Miscegenation*, London: Secker & Warburg, 1974

Higgins, Brian T., and Kenneth F. Kiple 'Cholera in Mid-Nineteenth Century Jamaica', *Jamaican Historical Review*, 127 (1991): 31-43

Higman, Barry, *Jamaica Surveyed: Plantation Maps and Plans of the Eighteenth and Nineteenth Centuries*, Kingston: University of West India Press, 1988

Hume, Hamilton, *The Life of Edward John Eyre, Late Governor of Jamaica*, London: Richard Bentley, 1867

Hurwitz, Samuel Justin, *Jamaica: A Historical Portrait*, London: Praeger, 1971

'The Identity of Mrs Seacole: "A Little Yellow Woman"', *Daily Gleaner*, 5 February 1938

Jacobs, H. P., *Sixty Years of Change: 1806-66*, Kingston: Institute of Jamaica, 1973

'The Jamaica Station. From the Journal of a Naval Officer', *United Service Magazine*, 1833, part 1, 203-9

Jamaica ... A Series of Letters Written from Jamaica to a Friend in England, London: n.p., 1842

'Jamaican Proverbs', *Daily Gleaner*, 2 February 1920

Josephs, Aleric, 'Mary Seacole: Jamaican Nurse and Doctress', *Jamaican Historical Review*, 17 (1991): 48-65

——, '"More than a Nurse": Mary Seacole as Wife, "Mother" and Businesswoman', *Jamaica Journal*, 30: 1-2 (2006): 50-5

Kelly, James, *Voyage to Jamaica, and Seventeen Years' Residence in that Island*, London: J. Wilson, 1838

Kerr, Paulette, 'Jamaican Female Lodging House Keepers in the Nineteenth Century', *Jamaican Historical Review*, 18 (1993): 7-17

Lee, Valerie, *Granny Midwives and Black Women Writers: Double Dutched Readings*, New York: Routledge, 1996

Levy, Andrea, *The Long Song*, London: Tinder Press, 2011

Lewis, Matthew, *Journal of a West India Proprietor*, Oxford: Oxford University Press, 1999

Long, Edward, *The History of Jamaica*, 3 vols, London: T. Lowndes, 1774

MacDonald-Smythe, Antonia, 'Trading Places: Market Negotiations in *WAMSML*', in Byfield, Judith A. (ed.), *Gendering the African Diaspora: Women, Culture and Historical Change in the Caribbean and Nigerian Hinterland*, Bloomington: Indiana University Press, 2010, 88-113

M'Mahon, Benjamin, *Jamaican Plantership*, London: Effingham Wilson, 1839

Madden, R. R., *Twelve Months' Residence in the West Indies*, 2 vols, Philadelphia: Carey, Lea & Blanchard, 1835

Mair, Lucille Mathurin, *A Historical Study of Women in Jamaica 1655-1844*, Kingston: University of the West Indies, 2006

Maxwell, James, *Remarks on the Present State of Jamaica*, London: Smith, Elder & Co, 1848

Mercer, Lorraine, 'I Shall Make No Excuse: The Narrative Odyssey of Mary Seacole', *Journal of Narrative Theory* 35, No. 1 (Winter 2005): 1-24

Milne-Home, Mary Pamela Ellis, *Mama's Black Nurse Stories: West Indian Folklore*, Edinburgh: William Blackwood, 1890

Mohammed, Patricia, '"But most of all mi love me browning": The Emergence in Eighteenth- and Nineteenth-Century Jamaica of the Mulatto Woman as the Desired', *Feminist Review* 65, No. 1 (1 June 2000): 22-48

Morais, Herbert M., *The History of the Afro-American in Medicine*, Cornwells Heights: Publishers Agency Inc, 1976

Morris, Michael, *Scotland and the Caribbean, c.1740-1833*, London: Routledge, 2018

'Mrs Seacole: A West Indian Nurse in the Crimea', *The Times*, 24 December 1954

Osborne, John, *Guide to the West Indies, Madeira, Mexico etc.*, London: Simpkin & Marshall, 1845

Pacquet, Sandra Pouchet, 'The Enigma of Arrival: The Wonderful Adventures of Mrs Seacole in Many Lands', *African American Review* 26, No. 4 (1992): 651-63

Patterson, Orlando, *The Sociology of Slavery: An Analysis of the Origins, Development and Structure of Negro Slave Society in Jamaica*, Rutherford: Fairleigh Dickinson University Press, 1967

Phillippo, J. C., 'Cholera in Jamaica in 1850, 51 and 54', lecture given in Kingston February 1887, Kingston: n.p., 1892

Phillippo, James Cecil, *Jamaica Its Past and Present State*, London: John Snow, 1843

——, *The Climate of Jamaica*, London: J. & A. Churchill, 1876

Phillips, T. S., 'Mary Seacole, the Story of a Kingston Girl', in 'Jamaicans Who Have Made Good', Booklet No. 1, Kingston: Institute of Jamaica West India Reference Library, 1932

Pinto, Samantha, 'Civic Desire: Mary Seacole's Adventures in Black Citizenship', in Pinto, *Infamous Bodies: Early Black Women's Celebrity and the Afterlives of Rights,* London: Duke University Press, 2020, 139-72

Pratt, Ann, 'Seven Months in the Kingston Lunatic Asylum and What I Saw There', Kingston: Henderson, Savage & Co., 1860

Radburn, Nicholas, 'Guinea Factors, Slaves Sales, and the Profits of the Transatlantic Slave Trade in Late Eighteenth-Century Jamaica', *William and Mary Quarterly,* 72: 2, 243-86, 2015

Rampini, Charles, *Letters from Jamaica: The Land of Streams and Woods,* Edinburgh: Edmonston & Douglas, 1873

Robinson, Amy, 'Authority and the Public Display of Identity: "Wonderful Adventures of Mrs. Seacole in Many Lands"', *Feminist Studies* 20, No. 3 (Autumn 1994): 537-57

Roughley, *The Jamaica Planters' Guide,* London: Longman, Hurst, Rees, Orme & Brown, 1823

Scott, Michael, *Tom Cringle's Log,* London: Walter Scott Publishing Co., 1834

Senior, Bernard M., *Jamaica as it was, as it is, and as it may be,* London: T. Hurst, 1835

Senior, Olive, *Encyclopedia of Jamaican Heritage,* St Andrew: Twin Guinep Publishers, 2003

Sergeant, Richard, *Letters from Jamaica, on Subjects, Historical, Natural, and Religious,* London: John Mason, 1843

'S.F.' [Sandford Forrest], 'Mrs Mary Seacole', *Daily Gleaner,* 9 February 1938

Shepherd, Verene, '"Dear Mrs Seacole": Groundings with Mary Seacole on Slavery, Gender and Citizenship' – speech delivered at Institute of Jamaica Function to Honour Mary Seacole, 21 November 2005, online at NLJ

——, *Engendering History: Caribbean Women in Historical Perspective,* London: Palgrave MacMillan, 1995

——, *Women in Caribbean History: The British-Colonised Territories,* Kingston: Ian Randle Publishers, 1999

Sheridan, Richard, *Doctors and Slaves: A Medical and Demographic*

History of Slavery in the British West Indies 1680-1834,
   Cambridge: Cambridge University Press, 2009

'Sketches and Incidents from Abroad', number III, *Western Literary
   Messenger*, 12-13 (1849), 209-15

'Sketches of Life and Character in the West Indies. Communicated to
   and edited by, Lord William Lennox', *The Sporting Review*, 30
   (1855): 187-92

Sloane, Sir Hans, *A Voyage to the Islands Madera, Barbados, Nieves, S
   Christophers and Jamaica ...*, Printed by B. M. for the author, 1707

——, *Catalogue of Jamaica Plants*, London, 1696

Stewart, John, *An Account of Jamaica and its Inhabitants. By a
   Gentleman Long Resident in the West Indies*, London: Longman,
   Hurst, Rees and Orme, 1808

Stewart, J., *A View of the Past and Present State of Jamaica*,
   Edinburgh: Oliver & Boyd, 1823

Stewart, Mrs. K., 'Jamaica's Florence Nightingale', *Daily Gleaner*, 29
   August 1939

Sturge, Joseph and Thomas Harvey, *The West Indies in 1837*, London:
   Hamilton Adams & Co., 1838

Tchaprazov, Stoyan, 'A Virtuous Nurse and a Picara: Mary Seacole's
   Self-Characterization in *Wonderful Adventures of Mrs Seacole
   in Many Lands*', in Palavi Rastogi et al., *Before Windrush:
   Recovering an Asian and Black Literary Heritage within Britain*,
   Cambridge Scholars Publishing, 72-87

Thome, James A. & Joseph Horace Kimball, *Emancipation in the West
   Indies: A Six Months' Tour in Antigua, Barbados and Jamaica in
   the Year 1837*, New York: American Anti-Slavery Society, 1839

Traveller's Guide to Madeira and the West Indies, London: G Miller &
   Son, 1815

Trollope, Anthony, *The West Indies and the Spanish Main*, New York:
   Carroll & Graf, 1999 [1860]

Underhill, Edward Bean, *The West Indies: Their Social and Religious
   Condition*, Cambridge: Cambridge University Press, 2010 [1861]

Wade, Barry, 'The Black River: Waterway, Wetlands and a Way of Life',
   Jamaica Journal 17, No. 4 (November 1984, January 1985): 10-23

Wentworth, Trelawney, *The West India Sketch Book*, London: Whittaker & Co., 1834

Williams, Cynric, *A Tour Through the Island of Jamaica*, London: Hunt & Clark, 1826

Wright, Philip, ed., *Lady Nugent's Journal of Her Residence in Jamaica from 1801 to 1805*, Kingston: University of West Indies Press, 2002

7. Panama Isthmus and Railroad during the California Gold Rush

Abbott, William J., *Panama and the Canal in Picture and Prose*, New York: Syndicate Publishing Co., 1913

Bidwell, Charles Toll, *The Isthmus of Panama*, London: Chapman & Hall, 1865

Brodie, Walter, *Pitcairn Island and the Islanders, in 1850*, London: Whittaker & Co., 1851

Bromley, Mrs [Clara Fitzroy Kelly Bromley], *A Woman's Wanderings in the Western World: A Series of Letters Addressed to Sir Fitzroy Kelly, MP*, London: Saunders, Otley & Co., 1861

Burton, Richard Francis, *City of the Saints and Across the Rocky Mountains to California*, London: Longman, 1861

Codman, John, *The Round Trip by Way of Panama through California, Oregon, Nevada, Utah, Idaho and Colorado*, London: GP Putnam's Sons, 1879

Damian, Jessica, 'A Novel Speculation: Mary Seacole's Ambitious Adventures in the New Granada Gold Mining Company', *Journal of West Indian Literature* 16, No. 1 (November 2007): 15-36

Fabens, Joseph Warren, *A Story of Life on the Isthmus*, London: G. Putnam & Co., 1853

Fish, Cheryl, 'Traveling Medicine Chest: Mary Seacole "Plays Doctor" at Colonial Crossroads in Panama and the Crimea', in Fish, *Black and White Women's Travel Narratives*, Gainesville: University Press of Florida, 2004, 65-95

Froebel, Julius, *Seven Years' Travel in Central America, Northern*

Mexico, and the Far West of the United States, London: R. Bentley, 1859

Griswold, Chauncey D., *The Isthmus of Panama and What I Saw There*, New York: Dewitt & Davenport, 1852

Howarth, David, *The Golden Isthmus*, London: Collins, 1966

Hussey, H., *The Australian Colonies ...with a Voyage from Australia to Panama in the Golden Age (1854)*, London: Blackburn & Burt, 1855

Kemble, John Haskell, 'The Panamá Route to the Pacific Coast, 1848-1869', *Pacific Historical Review* 7, No. 1 (March 1938): 1-13

Kennedy, William Robert, *Sporting adventures in the Pacific whilst in command of the 'Reindeer'*, London: Sampson Low, 1876

Lewis, Lancelot S., *The West Indian in Panama: Black Labor in Panama 1850-1914*, Washington: University Press of America, 1980

Liot, W. B., *Panama, Nicaragua and Tehuantepec*, London: Simpkin & Marshall, 1849

Marryat, Frank, *Mountains and Molehills: Recollections of a Burnt Journal*, New York: Harper & Brothers, 1855

Newton, Velma, *The Silver Men: West Indian Migration to Panama 1850-1914*, Kingston: Institute of Social and Economic Research UWI, 1986

'Oran', 'Tropical Journeyings en Route to California', *Harper's New Monthly Magazine*, 16 (1893): 468-71

Otis, F. N., *Illustrated History of the Panama Railroad*, NY: Harper & Brothers, 1861

'Panama as a Home', *All the Year Round*, 9 (1863): 246-7

Pimm, Bedford and Berthold Seeman, *Dottings on the Roadside in Panama, Nicaragua, and Mosquito*, London: Chapman & Hall, 1869

Pyne, Peter, *The Panama Railroad*, Bloomington: Indiana University Press, 2021

Robinson, Tracy, *Fifty Years at Panama, 1861-1907*, New York: Trow Press, 1911

Saunders, Arthur, 'Short History of the Panama Railroad', in *The*

Railway and Locomotive Historical Society Bulletin, 78 (October 1949): 8-44

Schott, Joseph L., *Rails Across Panama: The Story of the Building of the Panama Railroad, 1849-1855*, New York: Bobbs-Merrill, 1967

Seemann, Dr Berthold, *History of the Isthmus of Panama*, Printed and Published by the Star & Herald Panama, 1867

Senior, Olive, *Dying to Better Themselves: West Indians and the Building of the Panama Canal*, revised edition, Kingston: University of West Indies Press, 2014

——, 'The Colon People', *Jamaica Journal* 11, No. 3 (1977): Part I, 62-71

—— ,'The Panama Railway', *Jamaica Journal*, 44 (June 1980): 66-77

Taylor, Bayard, *Eldorado: Adventures in the Path of Empire*, New York: George P., Putnam, 1850

Tomes, R., *Panama in 1855: An Account of the Panama Railroad*, New York: Harper & Brothers, 1855

Woods, Sir Henry, *Spun Yarn From the Strands of a Sailor's Life Afloat and Ashore*, 1, London: Hutchinson, 1924

Wortley, Lady Emmeline Stuart, *Travels in the United States etc., during 1849 and 1850*, London: Richard Bentley, 1851

8. Britain: Victorian Society, Black People in Britain, The Crimean War

Manuscripts:

Calder, William Menzies, asst staff surgeon 49th Regiment, MS Crimean War diary 1855-1856 RAMC/701, Box 137, Wellcome Institute

Cattell, William Daverell, surgeon with 5th Dragoon Guards: TS of memoir 'Bygone Days and Reminiscences by the Way' (no date). RAMC 391/1/1 Box 42, Wellcome Institute

Codrington, General Sir William, letter 11 October 1855, National Army Museum, 1978-08-09

Goulburn Col Edward, letter 2 December 1855, Ian Shapiro collection

Russell, William Howard, diary 1857, Times Newspapers Limited
    Archive and News UK and Ireland Ltd, NRA 19359

Published sources:

*Note: Only major or significant newspaper articles on Mary Seacole
are listed here; others are referenced in the Notes section*

'A Coloured Lady Nurse', *Jewish Chronicle*, 10 August 1855

'A Stir For Seacole', *Punch*, XXXI, 6 December 1856, 221

Alexander, Ziggi, 'Let It Lie Upon the Table: The Status of Black
    Women's Biography in the UK', *Gender & History* 2, No. 1
    (March 1990): 22-33

Anionwu, Elizabeth, 'Scotching three myths about Mary Seacole',
    British Journal of Healthcare Assistants 7, No. 10 (October
    2013): 508-11

Armstrong, Richard Ramsay, *Richard Ramsay Armstrong's Book of
    His Adventures*, Lulu.com, 2009

Astley, Sir John Dugdale, *Fifty Years of My Life*, London: Macmillan
    & Co., 1876

Austin, Dr Douglas, 'The Mary Seacole Funds of 1857 and 1867', *War
    Correspondent* 30, No. 4 (2013): 26-9

——, 'More on the Seacole Fund of 1867', *War Correspondent* 31, No.
    4 (2014): 6

——, 'Mary Seacole's Hut?: "Illustrated London News" and
    Blackwood Sketch', *War Correspondent* 33, No. 1 (2015): 5

——, 'Miss Sally Seacole in a Robertson-Beato Photograph?', *War
    Correspondent* 34, No. 3 (2017): 15-22

——, Letters to the Editor, *History Today* 55, No. 4 (April 2005): 60

Blackwood, Lady Alicia, *Narrative of the Personal Experiences and
    Impressions during a Residence on the Bosphorus throughout the
    Crimean War*, London: Hatchard, 1881

Bolt, Christine, *Victorian Attitudes to Race*, London: Routledge &
    Kegan Paul, 1971

Bostridge, Mark, *Florence Nightingale: The Woman and Her Legend*,
    London: Viking, 2008

——, 'Ministering on Distant Shores', *The Guardian*, 14 February 2004

Brandon, Ruth, *The People's Chef*, Chichester: Wiley, 2004

Buchanan, George, MD, *Camp Life as Seen by a Civilian*, Glasgow: James Maclehose, 1871

Buzzard, Thomas, *With the Turkish Army in the Crimea and Asia Minor*, London: John Muray, 1915

Calthorpe, Somerset, *Letters from Headquarters, Or the Realities of War, by an Officer on the Staff*, London: John Murray, 1856

Coates, Tim, *Delane's War: How front-line reports from the Crimean War brought down the British Government*, London: Biteback, 2009

Cooke, Brian, *The Grand Crimean Central Railway*, Knutsford: Cavalier House, 1997

Douglas, William, *Soldiering in Sunshine and in Storm*, Edinburgh: Adam & Charles Black, 1865

Edwards, Paul and David Dabydeen, *Black Writers in Britain 1760-1890: An Anthology*, Edinburgh: Edinburgh University Press, 1991

Everyday Heroes: Stories of Bravery During the Queen's Reign, 1837-1888, London: Society for Promoting Christian Knowledge, 1888

'Excursion to Sebastopol: British Camp Before Sevastopol, Thursday April 26', *New York Daily Tribune*, 12 June 1855

File, Nigel and Chris Power, *Black Settlers in Britain 1555-1958*, London: Heinemann Educational Publishers, 1981

Fisher, George Smith, *Notes By the Way-Side on A Tour for Health and Recreation, on the Sea, in England, France and Belgium*, New York: Derby & Jackson 1858

Fryer, Peter, *Staying Power: History of Black People in Britain*, London: Pluto Press, 2010

Gerzina, Gretchen, *Black Victorians, Black Victoriana*, Chicago: Rutgers University Press, 2003

Gordon, J. Elise, 'Mary Seacole – A Forgotten Nurse Heroine of the Crimea', *Midwife Health Visitor & Community Nurse* 11, No. 2 (February 1975): 47-50

Griffon, D. P., '"A Somewhat Duskier Skin": Mary Seacole in the Crimea', *Nursing History Review* 6 (1998): 115-27

Hargreaves, Reginald, 'The Lady with the Gamp: A Vignette of Mary Seacole, "Mother of the Crimea",' *Cavalry Journal* XXIX, No. 113 (July 1939): 437-50

'The Hawley Letters', special publication of the Society for Army Historical Research, London, 1970

Hinton, Mike, *Victory Over Disease: Resolving the Medical Crisis in the Crimean War, 1854-1856*, Warwick: Helion and Company, 2019.

——, 'Thomas Day and the Establishment of the British Hotel, aka 'Mrs Seacole's: a new source of information', *The UK Association for the History of Nursing Bulletin* 7, No. 1 (2019): 1-6

'In Re: Seacole and Day. Mrs Seacole in Bankruptcy', *London Evening Standard*, 9 January 1857

James, Tom Beaumont, 'Mary Seacole's Lost Letter', *BBC History Magazine*, October 2010, 53-5.

Jones, Dr David, 'Location of the British Hotel at Spring Hill', *War Correspondent* 30, No. 4 (2013): 23-5

——, 'The Cattle Wharf at Balaclava', *War Correspondent* 32, No. 1 (2014): 23-7

——, *The Crimean War: Then and Now*, Barnsley: Frontline Books, 2017

Jones-Parry, S. H., *An Old Soldier's Memories*, London: Naval & Military Press, 2005

Judd, Catherine, '"A Female Ulysses" – Mary Seacole, Homeric Epic, and the Trope of Heroic Nursing', in Judd, *Bedside Seductions: Nursing and the Victorian Imagination 1830-1880*, New York: St Martin's Press, 1998

Kelly, Christine (ed.), *Mrs Duberly's War: Journal and Letters from the Crimea*, Oxford: Oxford University Press, 2007

Kelly, Gen. Sir Richard Denis, *An Officer's Letters to his Wife during the Crimean War*, London: Elliott Stock, 1902

Kelly, Mrs Tom, *From the Fleet in the Fifties*, London: Hurst & Blackett, 1902

'The Last Days of Sebastopol', *Irish Metropolitan Magazine*, 1 (April-September 1857): 258-9

'The Late Prince Victor of Hohenlohe', *Fortnightly Review*, 58 (1892): 312-14

McDonald, Lyn, 'Florence Nightingale and Mary Seacole: Nursing's Bitter Rivalry', *History Today* 62, No. 9 (2012): 10-16

——, *Mary Seacole: The Making of the Myth*, Toronto: Iguana Books, 2014

——, 'Would the Real Mary Seacole Please Stand Up and Be Recognised?', *War Correspondent* 30, No. 2 (July 2012): 36-8

——, 'Florence Nightingale and Mary Seacole: which is the forgotten hero of health care and why?', *Scottish Medical Journal* 59, No. 1 (February 2014): 67-70

——, 'Mary Seacole and claims of evidence-based practice and global influence', *NursingOpen* 3, No. 1 (January 2016): 5-18

——, 'Florence Nightingale and Mary Seacole on nursing and health care', *Journal of Advanced Nursing* 70, No. 6 (June 2014): 1436-44

Margrave, Tony, 'How and when did Mary Seacole get to the Crimea?', *War Correspondent* 30, No. 2 (July 2012): 13-9

Marsh, Jan (ed.), *Black Victorians: Black People in British Art 1800-1900*, Aldershot: Lund Humphries, 2005

'Mary Seacole', in J. A. Rogers, *The World's Great Men of Color*, Vol. 2, London: Touchstone, 1996 [1947], 262-71

'Mary Seacole in her own words', Bicentenary special, *Nursing Standard* 19, No. 34, 4-10 May 2005

Massie, Alastair, *The National Army Museum Book of the Crimean War: The Untold Stories*, London: Sidgwick & Jackson, 2004

Matthews, L. F., 'Horatio and Emma: A Nelson Mystery', *Essex Review*, 64-5 (1955): 6-8

Mawson, Mike Hargreave, 'Chaplains of the Crimean War', *The War Correspondent*, Part 1, Vol. 20, No. 1 (April 2002): 28-36; Part 2, Vol. 20, No. 2 (July 2002): 34-41

Medical and Surgical History of the British Army which Served in Turkey and the Crimea during the War against Russia in the Years 1854-55-56, 1, London: Harrison & Sons, 1858.

Military Chaplain [Rev. John Boudier], 'Reminiscences of the War in the East', *United Services Quarterly*, Part 1, January 1857, 'The Iron House near the "Col"', 96-99, 102-3

Moore, Henry Charles, *Noble Deeds of the World's Heroines*, London: The Religious Tract Society, 1903

Morris, M O'Connor, *Memini: A Mingled Yarn*, London: Harrison & Sons, 1892

'The Mother of the Regiment', *Punch*, 9 May 1857, 180

'Mother Seacole', letter to the editor, *The Argus* (Melbourne), 10 September 1857

'Noted Men and Women. Mary Seacole the Soldier's Friend', *Eastbourne Gazette*, 12 January 1881

'Our Own Vivandière', *Punch*, XXXII, 30 May 1857, 221

Patterson, Samuel A., 'Mother Seacole', letter to the editor, *The Argus* (Melbourne), 3 September 1857

'Poking Up the Sea-Cole Fire', *Punch*, XXXII, 5 September 1857, 102-3

Poon, Angela, 'Comic Acts of (Be)Longing: Performing Englishness in "Wonderful Adventures of Mrs. Seacole in Many Lands"', *Victorian Literature and Culture* 35, No. 2 (2007): 501-16

Ramdin, Ron, *Mary Seacole*, London: Haus Publishing, 2005

Rappaport, Helen, *No Place for Ladies: The Untold Story of Women in the Crimean War*, London: Aurum Press, 2007

——, 'Florence Nightingale', in Helen Rappaport, *Women Social Reformers*, 2, Santa-Barbara: ABC-Clio, 486-93

——, 'The Invitation That Never Came', *History Today* 55, No. 2 (February 2005): 9-15

——, 'The Lost Portrait', *Jamaica Journal* 30, No. 1-2 (2006): 38-41

Reid, Douglas A., *Memories of the Crimean War*, London: St Catherine Press, 1911

Report of the Sanitary Commission Despatched to the Seat of War in the East 1855-56, London: Harrison & Sons, 1856

Robins, Major Colin, 'Myths Relating to Mary Seacole and Her Work in the Crimean War', *Journal of the Society of Army Historical Research* 84 (2011): 90-1

Robinson, Jane, *Mary Seacole: The Charismatic Black Nurse Who Became a Heroine of the Crimea*, London: Constable, 2005

Robinson, Rod, 'Navvies in the Crimea', *War Correspondent* 3, No. 1 (April 1985): 10-14

Russell, William Howard, *The War: from the Landing at Gallipoli to the Death of Lord Raglan*, London: George Routledge & Company, 1855

— 'The Fall of Sevastopol', dispatch from the Crimea, *The Times*, 27 September 1855

——, 'The British Army. Camp Before Sebastopol, May 3', *The Times*, 15 May 1856

——, 'The Seacole Fund', *The Times*, 11 April 1857

Sala, George, *Things I Have Seen and People I Have Known*, London: Cassell & Co, 1894

Seacole, Mary, letter to Lord Rokeby 25 November 1856, in *Daily News*, 2 December 1856

——, letter to Sir Henry Storks, 1 October 1857, in Staring-Derks, 'New Light on Seacole'

——, letter to *Punch*, 8 May 1857, in 'Our Own Vivandière'

Small, Hugh, *Florence Nightingale, Avenging Angel*, London: Constable, 1998

——, *The Passion of Florence Nightingale*, Stroud: Amberley, 2010

Soyer, Alexis, *A Culinary Campaign by Alexis Soyer*, Lewes: Southover Press, 1995 [1857]

——, *Memoirs of Alexis Soyer with Unpublished Receipts and Odds and Ends of Gastronomy*, London: W. Kent & Co., 1859

Stafford, William Cooke, *England's Battles by Sea and Land*, III, London: London Printing & Publishing Company, 1863

Staring-Derks, Corry, Inleiding [Introduction] and endnotes in Dutch to 2007 edition of *Mary Seacole's Avonturen in de West en in de Krim*

—— and Jeroen Staring, 'Wonderful Adventures of Mrs Seacole in Many Lands: Book Reviews', Nijmegen: Integraal, 2010

——, Corry, Jeroen Staring & Elizabeth Anionwu, 'Mary Seacole: global nurse extraordinaire', *Journal of Advanced Nursing* 71, No. 3 (November 2014): 514-25

——, 'New Light on Seacole', *Nursing Standard* 27, No. 50 (2013): 22-3

Staring, Jeroen, 'Stories about New Avenues to Do Research', Part III, *IJCS* 9, No. 4 (April 2020): 19-25

——, 'Mary Seacole Disclosures', *Impact Factor 3.582 Case Studies Journal* 9, No. 6 (June 2020): 32-44

'A Stir for Seacole', *Punch*, 6 December 1856, 221

Vieth, Frederick, *Recollections of the Crimean Campaign and the Expedition to Kinburn*, Montreal: John Lovell & Son, Limited, 1907

Walvin, James, *The Black Presence: A Documentary History of the Negro in England 1550-1860*, London: Orbach & Chambers, 1971

——, *Black and White, the Negro and English Society*, London: Allen Lane, 1973

West, Shearer, *The Victorians and Race*, London: Ashgate 1996

Young, Sue, 'Mary Jane Seacole (1805-1881) Heroine of the Crimean War', *Homeopathy in Practice* (Spring 2020): 54-6

NOTES

Abbreviations:

AWC   Army Works Corps

BL   British Library

CWRS   Crimean War Research Society

JA   Jamaica Archives & Records Department, Spanish Town

LTC   Land Transport Corps

NLJ   National Library of Jamaica

OMRS   Orders and Medals Research Society

RA   The Royal Archives, Windsor

TNA   The National Archives, Kew

WAMSML   *Wonderful Adventures of Mrs Seacole in Many Lands*

WC   *The War Correspondent*, journal of the Crimean War Research Society

Note: All quotations from WAMSML are from the 1988 Oxford University Press edition

Prologue

1 For the full story of how I discovered the portrait and identified its artist see 'The Lost Portrait', *Jamaica Journal* 30, No. 1-2 (2006): 38-41. It is also available in a slightly edited-down version on my website: https://helenrappaport.com

Chapter 1

1 This is the subtitle of Rampini's book, *Letters from Jamaica*; Maxwell, *Remarks on the Present State of Jamaica*, 5.

2 Foulkes, *Eighteen Months*, 339.

3 Stewart, *View of the Past and Present State of Jamaica*, 12.

4 Foulkes, *Eighteen Months*, 20, 21.

5 *Traveller's Guide to Madeira and the West Indies*, 58-9; Stewart, *View of the Past and Present State of Jamaica*, 13.

6 Stewart, *View of the Past and Present State of Jamaica*, 14.

7 Sergeant, *Letters from Jamaica*, 120-1.

8 Stewart, *View of the Past and Present State of Jamaica*, 14.

9 'Sketches and Incidents from Abroad', 1849, 209.

10 For interesting observations on the 'I was born' convention of the narratives of former enslaved people, see James Olney, '"I Was Born": Slave Narratives, Their Status as Autobiography and as Literature', *Callaloo* 20 (1984): 46-73, especially 52-3.

11 Frederick Douglass, *Narrative of the Life of Frederick Douglass, An American Slave* (New York Classics Modern Library: 2000), 17, xiii.

12 See https://nlj.gov.jm/project/mary-seacole-1805-1881/ and Mary's Wikipedia entry.

13 Harriet Jacobs, *Incidents in the Life of a Slave Girl* (New York: Black & White Classics, 2014), 5.

14 During his work on the documentary, *The Real Angel of the Crimea*, for Channel 4 in 2004, Paul Kerr commissioned searches in the Jamaican baptism registers; Jane Robinson also searched in them at around the same time. Others, myself included, have enlisted the help of genealogists in Jamaica to search the records. I am lucky that my own very determined researcher, Ann Marie Lazarus, finally tracked down Mary's missing baptism when the Coronavirus pandemic prevented my own research trip there.

15 See Mair, *Historical Study of Women in Jamaica*, 269-71. For racial nomenclature see Henriques, *Children of Caliban*, 94-5. Unfortunately records for manumissions do not survive much before 1820. The British Library has an ongoing Endangered Archives Programme to preserve the seventy bound registers of the Manumission of Slaves 1747-1838, but some volumes are missing and others are severely damaged. Other manumission records for 1820-5 can be found at the National Archives, but these are too late for our purposes.

16 See S. F., 'Mrs Mary Seacole'. The writer, Sandford Forrest of Black River, had been born in 1860 at Black River and had lived there since at least the 1900s, as had his father and grandfather before him – at a time when people might well have been still alive who had known of Mary Seacole.

He published a pamphlet on 'The Black River Spa' in 1937. In his letter of 1938 he described how he had recently had the opportunity of clarifying to eminent Jamaica historian Frank Cundall, who also got the place of birth wrong, 'that Mary Seacole originally came from Haughton'.

17 'Between You and Me', *Daily Gleaner*, 21 February 1938.

18 Mair, *Historical Study of Women in Jamaica*, 96.

19 Stewart, *A View of the Past and Present State of Jamaica*, 327; Phillippo, *Jamaica, Its Past and Present State*, 149. Josephs, 'More Than a Nurse', 50.

20 The names of Mary's parents are given in her adult, Roman Catholic baptism, see page 15. See Morris, *Scotland and the Caribbean*, 184-5.

21 Beckwith, *Black Roadways*, 58, 59.

22 For a fascinating discussion of Mary as a 'browning', see Verene Shepherd, 'Dear Mrs Seacole'; *WAMSML* chapter XIX, 188; Aleric Josephs 'Mary Seacole', 48-9.

23 Lloyd, 'Letters from the West Indies', 155; Eyre, 'Dusky Doctress', 43.

24 For 'Free Coloureds' see Ramdin, 2-3; Shepherd, *Women in Caribbean History*, 71-2.

Chapter 2

1 Mary Prince, *The History of Mary Prince* (London: Penguin, 2000), 7. For Nancy Prince, see Ronald G. Walters (ed.), *A Black Woman's Odyssey through Russia and Jamaica*, (Princeton: Markus Wiener Publishers, Princeton, 1995).

2 *WAMSML*, 2.

3 Bush, *Slave Women in Caribbean Society*, 112; Senior, *Encyclopedia of Jamaican Heritage*, 434.

4 Wright, *Lady Nugent's Journal*, 29.

5 See Robinson, *Mary Seacole*, 10-11, where she concedes that this is at best a case of 'informed likelihood'.

6 For James Grant's career see Army Lists 1802-1814. He was promoted to major in 1809. For Major James Grant: see stoppages recorded at Berbice, Demerara 1813-14 in General Muster Books and Pay Lists 1812-1817, TNA, WO12/ 6945. He is probably the same man who died in Edinburgh aged forty on 6 May 1815 not long after being promoted to a lieutenant colonel in the Army. See Calton Old Churchyard, Edinburgh. https://www.findagrave.com/memorial/74712703/james-grant

7 'Statement of the Service of Major John Grant of His Majesty's 2nd West India Regiment, New Providence, 1 February 1810', 25/745/G at TNA.

8 Army List 1785, TNA.

9 See Army List 1809; Deaths section of 1811 Army List and Regimental Officer details in 1810 Army list. For the history of the 2nd West India

Regiment in this period, see Colonel J. E. Caulfield, *100 Years' History of the 2nd West India Regiment 1795 to 1898*, Naval & Military Press, 2009 reprint, 19-33.

10 Information from Army Lists 1794-5, 1802-8, and email correspondence with Phil Tomaselli. John Alexander's brother James, of the 53rd, was killed on campaign in the Netherlands in 1797 and William, of the Scottish Highlanders, at Waterloo in 1815. For information on the family see Ancestry.co.uk. See also 'Services of the 85th Regiment of Foot', *United Services Magazine*, 128, 1872, 513-14. For army wives on campaign, see Don N. Hagist, 'The Women of the British Army in America': http://www.revwar75.com/library/hagist/britwomen.htm

11 Details of John Grant senior can be found on the Gannon family tree on Ancestry: https://www.ancestry.co.uk/family-tree/person/tree/21237334/person/28081131576/facts

12 Jamaica Church of England Parish Register Transcripts 1664-1880, St Catherine Parish BMB 1764-1825, Vol. 2, folio 186; https://www.ucl.ac.uk/lbs/estate/view/2715

13 See *Jamaica Almanac*, 1787, 1801; *Royal Gazette*, 6 July 1811, 25 February 1818. Alexander, James, Robert and Charles Grant were the original partners.

14 Capitation and Assessment Rolls for Kingston, 1792, 1793, 1804, JA.

15 UK British Army and Navy BMD, WO42 G243 Bdle 19, page 377 and page 366, TNA. John Grant senior from Inverness-shire married a Jane Brice.

16 George Eyre-Todd (ed.), *The Autobiography of William Simpson*, RI (London: T. F. Unwin, 1903), 57

17 'Noted Men and Women: Mrs Seacole the Soldier's Friend', *Eastbourne Gazette*, 12 January 1881.

18 Kingston Baptisms 1793-1825, Vol 2, folio 205.

19 Ibid., folio 328.

20 Kingston Baptisms 1793-1825, vol 2 folio 358.

21 *WAMSML*, 2.

22 Josephs, 'Mary Seacole, Her Life and Times', 77-8, notes to 21.

23 Phillips, Thomas S., 'Jamaicans Who Have Made Good', 3; 'Mary Seacole – the first "Red Cross" Nurse', anonymous, undated typescript in NLJ: https://nlj.gov.jm/wp-content/uploads/2017/05/bn_seacole_mj_43.pdf

Chapter 3

1 Falconbridge, *Narrative of Two Voyages*, 135.

2 Wright, *Lady Nugent's Journal*, xxi; John Howard Hinton, *Memoir of William Knibb, Missionary in Jamaica* (London: Houlston & Stone, 1847), 46, 49.

3 Falconbridge, *Narrative of Two Voyages*, 240.

4 Wright, *Lady Nugent's Journal*, 228; Falconbridge, *Narrative of Two Voyages*, 241.

5 Sergeant, *Letters from Jamaica*, 121.

6 Senior, *Jamaica as it Was*, 15-16.

7 Foulkes, *Eighteen Months*, 26-7. See also *Jamaica … A Series of Letters*, Letter II, 21-42. One traveller noted that since the total abolition of slavery was achieved in 1838, 'the number of those who wear shoes has been increasing' – in most of Jamaica they only wore shoes to church on Sundays and holidays.

8 Wright, *Lady Nugent's Journal*, 98.

9 Carmichael, *Domestic Manners*, 75; Phillippo, *Jamaica Its Past and Present State*, 150.

10 Stewart, *A View of the Past and Present State of Jamaica*, 325; Alexander & Dewjee introduction to *WAMSML*, 12.

11 Josephs, 'Mary Seacole', 1991, 50.

Chapter 4

1 See letters to the editor of the *Gleaner*, from E. J. Barry, 2 August 1905, and from Mrs K. Stewart, 29 August 1939. Louisa had rented Blundell Hall well before 1870, as Barry contends; she took up the rental from Grace Blundell's executor and nephew, Henry Franklin, a Kingston attorney, some time between 1855 and Trollope's visit early in 1859.

2 Trollope, *West Indies and the Spanish Main*, 23.

3 Baptisms for Boyden and Bullock on FamilySearch: See *Jamaica Almanac: Return of Proprietors, Properties, etc.* (Parish of Port-Royal: Mountain District, 1816) http://www.jamaicanfamilysearch.com/Members/a/AL15royl.htm

4 See Alexander Barclay, *A Practical View of the Present State of Slavery in the West Indies* (London: Smith, Elder & Company, 1828), 75-6; Williams, *A Tour through the Island of Jamaica*, 173.

5 Kingston Capitation Roll, 1819-1835, 2/6/106, JA. Kingston Burial BMB 1842-1848, Vol 4, folder 358, item 90. In the 1831 Assessment of taxable property in Kingston, 'Mrs Blundell' appears, living in Knight Street.

6 See Faber, *Jews and the Slave Trade*, 117, 120; Radburn, 'Guinea Factors', 16, 17; Haggerty, *Merely for Money?*, 33, 180-1. The Blundell family of Liverpool was headed by Bryan Blundell (1675-1756), a shipmaster and one-time mayor of Liverpool. A Jonathon Blundell in Liverpool had been importing sugar and rum from Jamaica since at least 1763 and invested heavily in the slave trade from 1780. The Rainfords, headed by Samuel Rainford who was based in Kingston, were also from Liverpool and were largely engaged in exporting sugar and pimento from Jamaica and bringing

in enslaved people. The RBR partnership, which had been established in 1779 with Rainford's brother Robert and Jonathon Blundell junior, was brought down in 1804 by its own corruption and mismanagement.

7 Date Tree Hall was apparently built at a cost of $50,000, probably in the late eighteenth century, but the precise date is not known. See *Western Literary Messenger*, XII (1849): 213-14.

8 Haggerty, *Merely For Money?*, 181

9 The Kingston Capitation Tax Rolls refer to both Grace Blundell and 'Mr Blundell' variously at East Street prior to 1844. Grace also owned a property at 12 Knight Street. See Capitation Tax Rolls 2/6/106 1819-35; 2/6/107 1836-43; 2/6/108 1841; 2/6/111 1843; 2/6/112 1844; 2/6/113 1845-6, 1853-7, JA.

10 Gurney, *Winter in the West Indies*, 93; *Jamaica Morning Journal*, 6 September 1842; Sarah E. Fox, *Edwin Octavius Tregelles, Civil Engineer and Minister of the Gospel* (London: Hodder & Stoughton, 1892), 211.

11 Osborne, *Guide to the West Indies*, 76.

12 Boa, 'Urban Free Black and Colored Women', 2; Eisner, *Jamaica 1830 to 1930*, 3.

13 Wentworth, *West India Sketchbook*, 308.

14 Rampini, *Letters From Jamaica*, 18; Lewis, *Journal*, 44.

15 Scott, *Tom Cringle's Log*, 112.

16 Stewart, *View of the Past and Present State of Jamaica*, 17, 19; Madden, *Twelve Months' Residence*, I, 68.

17 Foulkes, *Eighteen Months*, 28. For other lodging house descriptions see also Gosse, *A Naturalist's Sojourn*, 156; Madden, *Twelve Months' Residence*, 68; Scott, *Tom Cringle's Log*, 105-7.

18 Madden, *Twelve Months' Residence*, I, 68-9.

19 Information by email from Professor Alan Eyre, 2002; Kerr, 'Jamaican Female Lodging House Keepers', 12, 16. Kerr's article is a valuable and informative discussion of the lodging-house keepers and the unspoken sexual services they may have offered.

20 Capitation Tax Roll, 1836-1848 2/6/107, JA. 'City and Parish of Kingston', *Jamaica Courant and Public Advertiser*, 22 May 1830.

21 Jamaica Kingston 2383, Claim Details, Associated Individuals and Estates.

22 https://www.ucl.ac.uk/lbs/claim/view/20124; Capitation Tax Roll 2/6/106 1830; 2/6/107 1841, JA.

23 Capitation Tax Roll 2/6/109 1843-7, JA.

24 Phillips, 'Jamaicans Who Have Made Good', 3, 4. In this pamphlet published in 1932, Phillips refers to Blundell Hall as her mother's hotel, this being the common assumption until letters to the *Gleaner* in 1939 clarified that this had not been the case. See Mrs K. Stewart, 'Jamaica's Florence Nightingale', *Gleaner*, 29 August 1939; WAMSML 2, 3.

25 Ibid., 2, 3.

26 *Guide to the Madeiras, Azores, British and Foreign West Indies*, 77.
27 Phillips, 'Jamaicans Who Have Made Good'.

Chapter 5

1 *WAMSML*, 3, 2.
2 Josephs, 'Mary Seacole', 59.
3 Hermi Hyacinth Hewitt, *Trailblazers in Nursing Education: A Caribbean Perspective, 1946-1986* (Kingston: Canoe Press, 2002), 'The Early History of Nursing in Jamaica', 5-6.
4 William Chamberlaine, *A Practical Treatise on the Efficacy of Stizolobium, or Cowhage ... To which is added observations on some other Indigenous Anthelmentics of the West Indies* (London: Darton, Harvey & Co., 1812), 28-9; Roughley, *Jamaica Planters Guide*, 91. Josephs, 'Mary Seacole: Her Life and Times', 38.
5 Long, *History of Jamaica*, Vol. 2, 335.
6 Carola Oman, *Nelson* (London: Naval Institute Press, 1996), 35. Cundall, *Historic Jamaica*, 72. Information from the late Professor Alan Eyre, email 24 April 2003.
7 Frederic Cassidy, *Jamaica Talk: 300 Years of the English Language in Jamaica* (London: Macmillan, 1961), 134.
8 See Josephs, 'Mary Seacole, Jamaican Nurse and Doctress', 57-8.
9 Eyre, 'Dusky Doctress', 44.
10 Ibid. Chlorodyne was not developed until 1848. Phillippo, *Jamaica: Its Past and Present*, 77.
11 Roughley, *Jamaica Planter's Guide*, 92
12 *The New Jamaica Magazine*, 3 April 1799, 208-9.
13 Josephs, 'Mary Seacole, Jamaican Nurse and Doctress', 55.
14 Senior, *Encyclopedia*, 311.
15 *WAMSML*, 60.
16 A useful and insightful description of the various Jamaican herbal remedies can be found in Corry Staring-Derks's detailed introduction to the Dutch edition of *WAMSML*, especially lxix–lxxv.
17 Sheridan, 'Slave Medicine in Jamaica', has a useful list of examples of slave physic and an A-Z list of ingredients. See 10-18; *WAMSML*, 31.
18 See Dancer, *Medical Assistant*, 371-2, 'Index of the prevailing diseases, to which the several country remedies are affixed'.
19 Tom Pocock, *Horatio Nelson* (London: Bodley Head, 1987), 21.
20 For a useful overview, see Josephs, 'Mary Seacole, Jamaican Nurse and Doctress', 1991.

Chapter 6

1 'Sketches of Life and Character ... communicated to Lord William Lennox', *New Sporting Magazine* 30 (1855): 97.

2 *WAMSML*, 4.

3 Ibid.

4 Mair, *Historical Study of Women*, 315, suggests they might have gone as ladies' maids. In her Seacole biography Jane Robinson – 11 and note 24 on 204 – suggested a connection to the Henriques family of Sephardi Jewish West India merchants and that Mary stayed with them in London on these trips. The firm of Henriques Brothers was indeed set up in London but not until the 1840s by the brothers Jacob Quixano (1811-98) and David Quixano (1804-70) from Spanish Town. Mary was close friends with a cousin of theirs, Dr Amos Henriques (1821-80) from Kingston, who later practised in London. But he did not leave Jamaica for England until 1830 and returned to Kingston for several years in the 1840s. We will meet him in Chapter 9.

5 The *Colonial Journal* of 1816, Vol. 1, 618, listed the Jamaica mail as arriving on around the 20th of the month. The packets returned from Port Royal to England on the third Monday after their arrival, in all a round trip of seventeen weeks.

6 *WAMSML*, 4.

7 MacDonald Smythe, 'Trading Places', 88. See also 'Jamaican Proverbs', *Gleaner*, 2 February 1920.

8 Carmichael, *Domestic Manners*, 38.

9 Levy, *The Long Song*, 238-9.

10 *Exeter and Plymouth Gazette*, 4 October 1828. Billy Waters died in the St Giles Workhouse in 1823. See https://www.english-heritage.org.uk/visit/places/portchester-castle/history-and-stories/black-people-in-late-18th-century-britain/

11 *Public Ledger*, 13 May 1825.

12 *WAMSML*, 4-5.

13 See *London National Register*, 17 June 1821; *Register of Shipping for 1819*, London Society of Merchants, Ship-Owners and Underwriters, letter V; *Lloyds List* entries for 1820. For *Volusia*'s sailing, see *Lloyd's List*, 25 November 1825. I am grateful to Tony Margrave of the CWRS for clarification. Captain Raffles is likely to have been related to another Captain Raffles – Benjamin (1793-1811), who was master on several ships sailing the England–West Indies route in the late eighteenth century. Sir Stamford Raffles, founder of Singapore, was his son.

14 *WAMSML*, 5.

15 Ibid.

Chapter 7

1 *WAMSML*, 5.
2 Scott, *Tom Cringle's Log*, I, 201.
3 *WAMSML*, 5.
4 Josephs, 'More Than a Nurse', 50 and note 13, on 55.
5 *WAMSML*, 5.
6 *The Hereford Journal*, 7 December 1786. Why the marriage notice should be published in Hereford is puzzling as there is no other indication of the couple's link to this area.
7 London Metropolitan Archives P93/MRY1/011; all Seacole baptisms for Prittlewell St Mary are to be found at Essex Record Office, Prittlewell Parish Register DP183/1/137. The baptisms can also be found on www.familysearch.org. See also: http://www.essexrecordofficeblog.co.uk/document-of-the-month-august-2015-mystery-baptisms/ Thomas Fowler's career in the East India Company can be tracked in the Register of the Ships of the East India Company.
8 Prittlewell Baptisms, DP183/1/137 and FamilySearch.
9 Overseers Accounts 1782-1798 Essex Records Office DP 183/12/2; see also Matthews, 'Horatio and Emma', 7-8.
10 The names that Thomas and Ann chose for their children are not without significance and in various ways suggest his acknowledgement of and admiration and respect for some of the medical and political personalities of the day:
    Thomas Fowler: for Thomas Fowler MD (1735-1801), physician to the General Infirmary of the County of Hertford, author of several medical papers
    John Henry: for John Henry, Admiral of the Red (1731-1829), a naval commander in the French and American Wars
    Wintringham: for Sir Clifton Wintringham (1710-94), physician to King George III, in 1786 nominated physician-general to the forces
    Anne Fox: for Charles James Fox (1749-1806), Whig statesman and foreign secretary 1782 and 1783
    Elizabeth Caroline Lind: Caroline for Caroline of Brunswick (1768-1821) Princess of Wales; Lind for James Lind MD (1716-94), surgeon and author of the pioneering 'Treatise on the Scurvy' of 1754.
11 Probate 11 July 1881, Principal Probate Registry London.
12 See Matthews, 'Horatio and Emma', and a brief follow-up, 'Nelson Mystery Solved', ibid., Vols 65-6, 6-8.
13 Another version of the story is that local woman Mary Woodward, who had midwifery skills, was also called to attend Emma Hamilton at Southchurch Lawn, a house on the road from Thorpe Bay to Great Wakering to assist Thomas Seacole when Emma went into labour.

According to this version, her brother James Woodward, who had been
one of Nelson's lieutenants at the Battle of the Nile, had arranged this
secret venue for Emma's confinement. See: Karen Bowman, *Essex Girls:
The Scandalous History of the Women of Essex* (Stroud: Amberley
Publishing, 2010) and Greg Lewin, 'Surgeons, Sailors and Smugglers':
http://www.greglewin.co.uk/fh/Miller.php

14 Admiral Lord Nelson, *The Letters of Lord Nelson to Lady Hamilton*,
Vol. 1 (London: Pinnacle Press, 2019), 124; Flora Fraser, *Beloved Emma*
(London: Macmillan, 1994), 304.

15 Despite an extensive search of Nelson biographies and letters, as well as
correspondence with numerous Nelson and Emma biographers – Tom
Pocock, Kate Williams, Flora Fraser, Professor Colin White, John Sugden
among them – over the last eighteen years, I failed to turn up a single
reference to Thomas Seacole in any contemporary sources relating to them.

16 St Mary Burial Register, P85/MRY1/487, London Metropolitan Archives.
Also on ancestry.co.uk.

17 See Return of Land Grants 1805-1824, TNA CO137/162, viewable on www.
jamaicanfamilysearch.com/Members/r/ReturnofLandGrants1805_1824.htm.

18 Cockpit Country Heritage Survey Report, 2009, 87, online.

19 Wade, 'The Black River', 20.

20 John Gordon baptism, B0037 St Elizabeth Parish Register I & II, 1707-
1825, II: 258

21 *Jamaica Almanac* for 1824, 1827, 1839.

22 B0016 Jamaica Parish Register Marriage I & II, 1826-1839, I, fo. 65, no.
92. It is a great pity the licence has not survived as this might have given
more valuable genealogical information.

Chapter 8

1 S[andford] F[orrest], 'Mrs Mary Seacole'.

2 Senior, *Jamaica as it Was*, 5.

3 See 'A Taste of History – Black River, St Elizabeth', Georgian
Society of Jamaica, http://www.georgianjamaica.org/
blog/a-taste-of-history-black-river-st-mary

4 Melsia Kraftner, 'Economic Contributions in Accumulation of Wealth
by Women of Colour in St Elizabeth 1800-1845', abstract; Brathwaite,
Development of Creole Society, 188, 172.

5 Lewis, *Journal of a West India Proprietor*, 36.

6 Jemmott, 'Parish History of St Elizabeth', 68.

7 Senior, *Encyclopedia*, 62, 292.

8 Jemmott, 'Parish History of St Elizabeth', 69-70.

9 The *Jamaica Almanac* can be accessed online at: http://www.
jamaicanfamilysearch.com/Members/al32eliz.htm

10 See Office of Registry of Colonial Slaves and Slave Compensation Commission Records, TNA T71/177 28 June 1832. Legacies of British Slave Ownership: Jamaica St Elizabeth, No. 897 Charles Witton Seacole https://www.ucl.ac.uk/lbs/claim/view/23583 This website is an exceptional contribution to the study of the British slave trade and provides invaluable genealogical data on owners of enslaved people. The equivalent is based on October 2020 figures.
11 Passenger listing, *Evening Post* (New York), 23 February 1837. This sailing was from New York; it is unclear whether Charles Witton took a different boat there from Jamaica. The *Wellington* was completing the crossing in an average of nineteen days.
12 See *Jamaica Watchman*, 11 & 18 August, 8 & 15 September, 20 October 1832.
13 See UCL Legacies of British Slave-ownership website: for Charles Farquharson see https://www.ucl.ac.uk/lbs/person/view/2146644175; for Matthew Farquharson see https://www.ucl.ac.uk/lbs/search/. *Jamaica Almanac* regularly feature the Farquharsons in this period, especially 1820.
14 See TNA ADM 175/97; *Courier*, 9 January 1821; *Edinburgh Advertiser*, 7 April 1826.
15 TNA ADM 175/4/30, 117, 112; 175/6/201, 175//17/97, 196, 269, 261. Email correspondence with Coastguard historian Eileen Stage, April 2003. CUST 47/618/3 W on p. 44.
16 There is extensive press coverage – though Wintringham's name is often misspelled as Wintrington or even given as William and his surname given as Newcole. See *The Times*, 8 January 1840. A full report of Daniel Monaghan's trial, at which he was acquitted, can be found in the *Dublin Evening Mail*, 9 March 1840.
17 *Royal Jamaica Gazette*, 21 March 1840.
18 Ibid.; *WAMSML*, 5-6.; TNA ADM 175/77.
19 S. F., 'Mrs Mary Seacole', *Daily Gleaner*, 9 February 1938.

Chapter 9

1 *WAMSML*, 6.
2 Ibid., 6, 7.
3 Assessment of Taxable Property, Kingston, 1836-1842, 2/6/107. Kingston Dissenter Marriages 1843-1844, Vol. 5 [Wesleyan Methodist], 30 March 1843. Branigan was white and the son of the Irish West India merchant Denny [Daniel] Branigan and his wife Elizabeth. Denny Branigan died of fever in Kingston in 1822.
4 Harry E .Vendryes, 'The James the Founder Fire of 1843', Jamaican radio broadcast, 17 September 1947; *Jamaica Historical Bulletin* 6: 277-82, transcribed at https://jamaica-history.weebly.com/1843.html

5 'James the Founder's, or Matcham's Fire', *Jamaican Historical Society Bulletin* 6: 277-82; this article and a selection of contemporary reports of the fire can be found at: https://jamaica-history.weebly.com/1843.html

6 See note 5 above; 'The Great Kingston Fire of 1843', *Daily Gleaner*, 22 August 1971.

7 The list of fire victims can be found in: 'Votes of Assembly' Appendix No. 44, 'Abstract of Money Expended by the Committee appointed by the Honourable Commissioners of Public Accounts for Relief of Sufferers of the Fire ... etc.', in JA 1B/5/1A/49.

    Mary's account of the fire is in *WAMSML*, 7. Belisario's very useful 1843 lithograph, 'A Diagram of the Burnt District of the City of Kingston', is in Ranston, *Belisario*, 294.

8 'Votes of Assembly' Appendix, No. 44. as above. Elizabeth Lawson at 57 Water Lane appears on page 432.

9 *WAMSML*, 7.

10 Ibid.

11 Assessment of Taxable Property, Kingston, 1848, 2/6/127; 2/6/113 and 114 JA.

12 'An Old Type', *Daily Gleaner*, 27 July 1905.

13 'A Jamaican Veteraness', *Daily Gleaner*, 17 August 1910.

14 Patterson, John, *The Adventures of Captain John Patterson, with Notices of the Officers Etc of the 50th or Queen's Own Regiment, from 1807 to 1821* (London: T & W Boone, 1837), 408, 412, 419.

15 'Dr Hart on Jamaica as a Health Resort', *Daily Gleaner*, 9 November 1897.

16 Major Luke Smyth O'Connor, 1st West India Regiment, 'Leaves From the Tropics', *United Service Magazine*, 1849, part I, 59: 117-18,

17 See birth announcements in *Dundee, Perth & Cupar Advertiser*, 28 July 1846 and 12 May 1848.

18 Eyre, 'Dusky Doctress', 9. This and other residual fragments of knowledge about Mary Seacole that I encountered in my research suggests that some stories have been passed down in Jamaica by people who knew her or knew of her during her lifetime. It is precisely this kind of material that I hope may yet surface.

19 *WAMSML*, 7-8.

20 Ibid., 8.

21 See Robinson, *Mary Seacole*, 181-2.

22 Kingston Roman Catholic Baptismal Book, 108, 1848-51, folio 49. I am most grateful to Fr Peter Espeut for allowing my researcher Ann Marie access to the Archives of the Roman Catholic Archdiocese in Kingston and for all his help in trying to find the missing baptism.

23 *WAMSML*, 8, 9.

24 Extracts from a 'Report on Epidemic Cholera in Newcastle Jamaica',

Medical Times and Gazette, NS, No. 6 (January to June 1853): 572-3. *WAMSML*, 8, 9.

25 Review of Dr Milroy's report on the cholera epidemic in Jamaica 1850-1, in *British and Foreign Medico-Chirurgical Review*, 19 (1857): 79.

26 J. Phillippo, 'Cholera in Jamaica', 15.

27 Review of Dr Milroy's report on the cholera epidemic in Jamaica 1850-1, in *British and Foreign Medico-Chirurgical Review* 19 (1857): 79.

28 *WAMSML*, 9.

29 Ibid.; Phillippo, 'Cholera in Jamaica', 16, 28.

30 Higgins, 'Cholera in Mid-Nineteenth Century Jamaica', 127.

31 Ibid., 43.

32 *WAMSML*, 9.

Chapter 10

1   *WAMSML*, 9, 63; London Principal Probate Registry, 11 July 1881.

2   *WAMSML*, 9.

3   Bromley, *A Woman's Wanderings*, 246; Otis, *Illustrated History*, 16.

4   Schott, *Rails Across Panama*, 86.

5   Otis, *Illustrated History*, 18, 21.

6   Ibid., 21.

7   Senior, 'The Panama Railway', 68; Newton, *Silver Men*, 51.

8   Saunders, 'Short History of the Panama Railroad', 13.

9   Otis, *Illustrated History*, 25.

10 See Senior, 'Panama Railway', 69-72.

11 *WAMSML*, 10, 12.

12 Phillippo, *Climate of Jamaica*, 5-6.

13 *WAMSML*, 10, 11.

14 Otis, *Illustrated History*, 75.

15 *WAMSML*, 11.

16 Ulysses S. Grant, *Personal Memoirs of U. S. Grant* (New York: Charles L. Webster, 1894), 117.

17 See the *Panama Herald*, 14 August 1851: 'It is stated in the New York and New Orleans papers, on very good authority, that the Panama Railroad will be so far completed by the 1st of next month, September, that Steamers may land their passengers at Navy Bay, whence they will be taken ten miles by railroad to Gatune.' In fact the railroad was not opened that far, even by November – but only to Miller's Station, 3 miles on the Aspinwall side of Gatun (17 November 1851). This would suggest that Mary did not arrive on the Isthmus until very late in 1851.

18 Senior, 69; *WAMSML*, 12.

19 Marryat, *Mountains and Molehills*, 15; Wortley, *Travels in the United States* II, 282, 284; Bromley, *Woman's Wanderings*, 242-4; Bayard

Taylor, *El Dorado, or, Adventures in the Path of Empire*, Vol. 1 (London: R. Bentley, 1850), 165-6; Otis, *Illustrated History*, 90. Traveller accounts of the period are extremely vivid and rich in detail on the landscape, vegetation and its wildlife.

20 *WAMSML*, 12-14, 18.

21 Ibid., 13.

22 Ibid.; Mary is quoting from Wordsworth's 1815 poem 'Rob Roy's Grave'.

23 *WAMSML*, 19.

24 Ibid., 15-17.

25 Bromley, *Woman's Wanderings*, 244. *WAMSML*, 17-18.

26 Robinson, *Fifty Years at Panama*, 48; *Guide to the West Indies*, 259-60; 'Crossing the Isthmus of Panama', *Household Words* 6 (1852), 522.

27 Brodie, *Pitcairn's Island and the Islanders, in 1850*, 227-8. In a section (226-31) Brodie describes the hazardous journey across Panama that he made on foot from the Pacific side to Chagres at precisely the same time Mary travelled there.

28 'Panama to Chagres', *North American Miscellany* 2 (1852): 158.

29 *WAMSML*, 21.

30 Ibid., 21-3.

31 Edmund Charles Wendt, *A Treatise on Asiatic Cholera* (New York: William Wood & Co, 1885), 28, 84-5; Grant, *Personal Memoirs of U. S. Grant*, 119; *WAMSML*, 26.

32 *WAMSML*, 24-5.

33 Ibid., 26.

Chapter 11

1 *WAMSML*, 26-7.

2 Ibid., 28-9.

3 Du Preez, *Dr James Barry*, 163-4, 314-15. For the medical careers of the women pioneers Elizabeth Blackwell, Elizabeth Garrett-Anderson and Sophia Jex-Blake, see Helen Rappaport, *Encyclopedia of Women Social Reformers* (Santa Barbara: ABC Clio, 2001).

4 *WAMSML*, 30-1.

5 Ibid., 31-2.

6 Ibid., 33.

7 Ibid., 35.

8 Ibid., 37, 39.

9 Ibid., 40 42 44.

10 Ibid., 40-1.

11 Lola Montez, *Autobiography and Lectures of Lola Montez* (London: James Blackwood, 1860), 51.

12 *WAMSML*, 41.

13 Ibid., 42-3.

14 Ibid., 46-7

15 Ibid., 48.

16 Taylor, *El Dorado*, I, 170.

17 *WAMSML*, 49-50.

18 Taylor, *El Dorado*, I, 172.

19 *WAMSML*, 53

20 Ibid., 57-8. Captain Baynton was based in Southampton with the Royal
    Mail steam packet service that served the West Indies. He is one of the few
    people named in Mary Seacole's memoir who can be identified, thanks
    to the unfortunate loss of a ship, the *Paramamatta*, under his command,
    which was wrecked on the Horseshoe Reef in the Sombrero Channel off
    the Nicobar Islands. The subsequent inquiry was covered in the British
    press; see e.g. *Morning Chronicle*, 12 December 1859. Baynton's full name
    can be found in a letter to the *Daily News*, 11 January 1860.

Chapter 12

1 Sheridan, *Doctors and Slaves*, 10-11; 'Yellow Fever in Jamaica', *Lancet*,
   2, No. 324 (1853).

2 *WAMSML*, 59.

3 'Remedy for Yellow Fever', *Scientific American* 8, No. 49 (August 1853),
   392.

4 *WAMSML*, 59-60.

5 *London Standard*, 3 October 1853.

6 *WAMSML*, 60-1.

7 Ibid., 62.

8 Ibid.

9 For Little Nell's death see: https://madeleineemeraldthiele.wordpress.com/
   2017/04/05/the-death-of-little-nell-from-dickens-the-old-curiosity-shop

10 *WAMSML*, 63.

11 Rathkeale Baptisms, Marriages & Burials, 1742-1905, transcript, ffolliott
    Collection, https://search.findmypast.co.uk/ Confusingly, the London
    papers say Griffith died at Lucea [in Hanover on the northern coast] but
    that is probably where he was stationed before falling ill and being taken
    to Mary's lodging house to be nursed. See *Limerick Chronicle*, 8 October
    1853; *London Standard*, 3 October 1853. Griffith had not long been
    promoted from acting assistant surgeon of the 3rd WI, on 22 October 1852.

12 *WAMSML*, 63-4.

13 Ibid., 64-5,

14 Eyre, 'Dusky Doctress', 10.

15 See Damian, 'A Novel Speculation', 25-6. Damian refers to *The Copy
    of the Prospectus Issued on the Formation of the New Granada Mining*

Company, issued on 16 May 1835, a rare copy of which can be found in the Illingworth Manuscript Collection, Manuscripts Department, Lilly Library, Indiana University at Bloomington.

16 *Sangamo Journal* (Illinois), 19 January 1850; *Morning Chronicle*, 4 May 1852.

17 *Daily News*, 8 December 1853; *Railway Record & Joint Stock Companies Reporter*, 9, 1852, 307. Despite an investment of £180,000 the mine appears to have been abandoned by the end of 1854. See *Observer*, 17 December 1854.

18 *WAMSML*, 66. A 1932 Jamaican source contradicts this and says that Day was 'Mrs Seacole's cousin by her father's side'. Since Mary Seacole's father died when she was very small and his family was far away in Scotland, this seems unlikely. It is more logical to see Day as a connection on the Seacole side in the City of London.

19 One interesting piece of evidence that suggests a business link between the Day firm and the Seacoles is a notice in *John Bull* on 12 March 1826 of the theft of a wooden cash box from the iron safe of Messrs William Day & Company of 95 Gracechurch Street, containing 'many securities, and among them the following Bills and Notes', which includes promissory notes to Day & Co from 'Seacole' 'on Morgan', dated 28 April 1826 for £20. The full implication of this has yet to be ascertained.

20 *Morning Chronicle*, 4 May, and *Daily News*, 3 May 1853. Both carried front-page announcements of the mine and shares for sale.

21 *WAMSML*, 66.

22 Ibid., 68-9.

23 Ibid., 71.

24 Ibid.

25 See Rappaport, *No Place for Ladies*, Chapter 1.

26 *WAMSML*, 73.

27 *London Standard*, 18 October 1854; *Lloyds List*, 19 October 1854.

28 *WAMSML*, 74.

Chapter 13

1 For an interesting article see Yakup Bektas, 'The Crimean War as a technological enterprise', *Royal Society Journal of the History of Science*, 2017 https://royalsocietypublishing.org/doi/10.1098/rsnr.2016.0007

2 See Rappaport, *No Place for Ladies*, 70-4.

3 Queen Victoria to Leopold, King of the Belgians, 13 October 1854, Arthur Benson and Viscount Esher (eds), *Letters of Queen Victoria*, Vol. 3 (London: John Murray, 1907), 50.

4 *WAMSML*, 74.

5 Rappaport, *No Place for Ladies*, 84-6.

6 *The Times*, 12 October 1854.

7 For a useful account of how John Delane, editor of *The Times*, managed the reporting of the war and exposed the shocking lack of medical supplies and staff in the first weeks of the conflict, see Coates, *Delane's War*, Chapter 3: 'Denial'.

8 *The Times*, 19 October 1854.

9 *WAMSML*, 74-5.

10 Ibid., 76.

11 For details of these recruits, see Rappaport, *No Place for Ladies*, 101-2. The original application letters can be found in the National Archives at WO 25/264. But there is no application letter to be found among them from Mary Seacole.

12 Henry Nolan, *History of the War against Russia*, Vol. 4 (London: Virtue, 1856), 705.

13 Rana A. Hogarth, *Medicalizing Blackness: Making Racial Difference in the Atlantic World, 1780-1840* (Chapel Hill: University of North Carolina Press, 2017), 73; Fergusson, *Notes and Recollections*, 63-4.

14 *WAMSML*, 76.

15 Ibid.

16 Ibid., 77.

17 Ibid., 77-8; 137.

18 Ibid., 79.

19 Rappaport, *No Place for Ladies*, 103

20 *WAMSML*, 79.

21 Ibid., 80.

22 Ibid., 80, 81.

23 Ibid., 81-2.

24 Amos Henriques first studied medicine at St Thomas in London in the early 1830s, before travelling to Paris to study for a second medical degree in 1833 and then another in Italy in 1835. He practised medicine in Athens and then was offered a commission to organise medical staff for the Turkish Army, which took him to Constantinople and a period in captivity after the battle of Nezid in 1839. The Turks awarded him the Order of the Medidjie for his services. Henriques travelled in Europe before returning to Jamaica in 1840. But he returned to London in 1847 and spent the remainder of his life there, building a successful practice. He was a fellow of the Royal Medical and Chirurgical Society. See Andrade, *Record of the Jews*, 158-9; *British Homeopathic Review* 24 (1880): 437. https://www.sueyounghistories.com/ 2008-10-10-amos-henriques-1812-1880/

25 See Stichting Maritiem-Historische Databank. https://www.marhisdata. nl/schip?id=8216; *Morning Post*, 15 February 1855; *The Times*, 16 February 1855.

26 *WAMSML*, 82; *Jamaica Almanac*, 1824.

27 The *Hollander*, tonnage 360, horsepower 120, was built in Chester, England and was a three-masted ironclad schooner. The British Admiralty did not officially charter it till 13 May, after which it made four voyages to Crimea with supplies for the army, details of which can be found in the contemporary press. See: Stichting Maritiem-Historische Databank. https://www.marhisdata.nl/schip?id=8216. Information on *Hollander* sailings from John D. Stevenson of The Ships List, email 17 January 2003. See also Tony Margrave, 'How and When Did Mary Seacole Get to the Crimea?' This article concluded that Mary sailed on a different *Hollander* owned by Oppenheim and Company, because considerable confusion had been created by a *Holinder* [*sic*] listed as arriving in Constantinople on 6 March, 'with packages for officers'. Tony Margrave has since revised his original conclusion and, on weighing up the evidence, concludes that this *Holinder* is the Oppenheim-owned *Hollander* out of Liverpool. The Dutch ship of the same name, on which Mary travelled, arrived two days later on 8 March..

28 See *WAMSML*, 12, 36, 39, 45, 57, 70.

Chapter 14

1   See Rappaport, *No Place for Ladies*, 33-4.

2   *WAMSML*, 82, 83.

3   Ibid., 83.

4   Ibid., 83; Elizabeth Charles, *Wanderings Over Bible Lands and Seas* (London: T. Nelson & Sons, 1862), 12, 13.

5   *WAMSML*, 84.

6   This listing was a lucky find made by Crimean War expert Tony Margrave when searching the Maltese press for British Army officers during the period of the war.

7   Information by email from Tony Margrave, 17 and 20 October 2019; additional comments by email from Douglas Austin and Mike Hinton. *Malta Times*, 6 March 1855. This newspaper is only accessible in the National Archives at Kew, ref: TNA CO 163/28. According to Tony Margrave, the Italian language *Il Portafoglio Maltese* for 3 March (also at TNA only) listed a 'Signor C. Keen, Signore Sencold and S. Grand'; email 8 April 2021.

8   *WAMSML*, 85.

9   Russell, *The War: from the Landing at Gallipoli to the Death of Lord Raglan*, 1855, 11.

10 See Elizabeth Charles, *Wanderings over Bible lands and seas* (London: T Nelson & Sons 1862), 16-23; *WAMSML*, 85.

11 *WAMSML*, 85.

12 Forrest's career is well documented in the Army Lists and the *London*

Gazette, a good résumé of which can be found in his detailed and well-referenced Wikipedia entry.

13 *WAMSML*, 85.

14 Ibid., 86.

15 Ibid., 87.

16 For a description of the conditions at Scutari and Nightingale's efforts to improve them, see Rappaport, *No Place for Ladies*, Chapter 7: 'Every Accumulation of Misery'.

17 Ibid., 124-5.

18 Small, *Florence Nightingale*, 88; See also Rappaport, 'Florence Nightingale'.

19 Nightingale to Sidney Herbert, in Brandon, *People's Chef*, 235-6.

20 See Ibid., Chapter 7; for Queen Victoria's efforts, 140-2.

21 *WAMSML*, 87-8.

22 Ibid., 88.

23 Ibid., 88-9.

24 Ibid., 89-90.

25 Ibid., 90-1.

26 See Rappaport, *No Place for Ladies*, 134-5; Bostridge, *Florence Nightingale*, 224; *WAMSML*, 91-2. Mary makes no mention of meeting Lady Alicia, who probably was not accommodated at the washhouse but in the main hospital with the nurses.

27 *WAMSML*, 93. 'Jew Johnny' is mentioned by name again only on *WAMSML*, 113.

28 Ibid., 93. Shipping information from Dr David Jones and Tony Margrave of the CRS.

29 *WAMSML*, 94.

30 For a description, see diary of Fanny Duberly in Christine Kelly (ed.), *Mrs Duberly's War*, 102-3 and 282-3.

31 See Rappaport, *No Place for Ladies*, 132-3.

32 I am grateful to Dr David Jones of the CWRS for drawing my attention to this photograph. See his article 'The Cattle Wharf at Balaclava' and his book *Crimean War: Then and Now*, 70.

33 Queen Victoria and Prince Albert purchased an entire set of Fenton's Crimean photographs. See Sophie Gordon, *Shadows of War: Roger Fenton's Photographs of the Crimea, 1855* (London: Royal Collection Trust, 2017). https://www.rct.uk/collection/themes/publications/shadows-of-war

34 The identity of the ship is uncertain; it was probably a fruit clipper of that name that is recorded as sailing for Balaclava from the London docks on 23 December 1854. See *The Times*, 18 December 1854. The *Nonpareil* left Constantinople for Balaclava on 13 February.

35 'The Harbour of Balaklava – State of the Shipping', *Southern Reporter and Cork Commercial Courier*, 30 August 1855.

36 On page 95 of *WAMSML* Mary alludes merely to Captain H—– of the
    Diamond but he is easily identifiable thanks to the name of the ship.
    Hamilton (1817-92) entered the RN in 1831 and during his service was on
    the West Indies Station, where he probably met Mary Seacole; he retired
    as an admiral in 1877. Boxer's son might have been Lieutenant James
    Michael Boxer (1816-65), who entered the navy in 1827 and was briefly on
    the West Indies station before being invalided out in 1844. Perhaps he had
    fallen sick in Jamaica and Mary had nursed him, hence the acquaintance.

37 'The Harbour of Balaklava – State of the Shipping', *Southern Reporter
    and Cork Commercial Courier*, 30 August 1855; *WAMSML*, 103, 104,
    105.

38 *WAMSML*, 107.

39 Ibid., 104.

40 Ibid., 95; Rappaport, *No Place for Ladies*, 176.

41 Hedley Vicars's 'Walking With God Before Sebastopol, or Reminiscences of
    the late Captain Vicars, 97th Regiment' was published in London in August
    1855, but the only copy of it that appears to have survived was located at
    the British Library and was destroyed by bombing during the Second World
    War. Should any reader ever come across it I would be delighted to hear
    from them. It apparently contains a reference to Mary Seacole.

42 *WAMSML*, 74.

43 See W. H. Russell, *The British Expedition to the Crimea* (London:
    Routledge & Sons, 1877), 198.

44 Mary's aspiration in this regard can be found on page 24 of the memoir
    of the surgeon of the 5th Dragoon Guards, William Daverell Cattell, in
    Wellcome Institute. I am grateful to Dr David Jones for clarifying the
    location of Mary's preferred site for her business.

45 Hinton, 'Thomas Day and the Establishment of the British Hotel', 2.
    Thomas Day's original letter of 23 March 1855 – but sadly missing the
    two enclosures – can be found in Reports & Papers, Quartermaster
    General, Part 3 (1854-56), TNA WO 28/194.

46 Ibid.

47 Ibid.

48 *The Standard*, 8 March 1855; *Waterford News*, 16 March 1855.

49 Ibid., 3.

50 Ibid.

51 *WAMSML*, 102.

Chapter 15

1 *WAMSML*, 97.

2 Calthorpe, *Letters from Headquarters*, 84-5, ix; Reid, *Memories of the
   Crimean War*, 13-14.

3 *WAMSML*, 101.

4 Ibid., 97, 99, 98.

5 *New York Tribune*, 12 June 1855.

6 *Argus* (Melbourne), 4 November 1857.

7 A map published by Captain Frederic Brine in 1857 indicates the close proximity of Major Cox's hut the other side of the railway line from 'Mrs Seacole's. It is reproduced in Jones, 'Location of the British Hotel', 24.

8 Ibid.

9 Ibid.

10 Notes made by Parthenope Nightingale *c*.1857, Claydon House Trust Collection, MS Nightingale 110; quoted in Bostridge, *Florence Nightingale*, 279.

11 Nightingale letter to Sir Harry Verney, 5 August 1870, in Sarah Salih edition of *WAMSML*, 180.

12 For details on the Crimean hospitals, see Hinton, *Victory Over Disease*, 116-17. Nightingale did not have jurisdiction over the various regimental field hospitals within the army camps below Sevastopol, nor that of the Land Transport Corps, near Spring Hill, where Mary regularly visited the sick and wounded.

13 The comments by Nightingale were made to her brother-in-law Sir Harry Verney, when he solicited Nightingale's opinion of Mary Seacole. See Sarah Salih edition of *WAMSML*, 180.

14 Biographical information on Sir John Hall is taken from his online archive listing at the Wellcome Institute, where his papers are lodged at MS.88520. See wellcome.ac.uk/; S. M. Mitra's *Life and Letters of Sir John Hall* (London: Longman's, 1911), regretfully has only a few pages on Hall's early years in Jamaica, including the quotations here on page 8. Mitra makes no mention of Hall's contact with Mary Seacole in Crimea, although in her memoir Mary quotes a letter of commendation given to her by Hall dated 30 June 1856; see *WAMSML*, 129-30. Many of Hall's other papers can be found at the Archives of the Royal Army Medical Corps, RAMC/397/A Early Career 1816-41.

15 *WAMSML*, 99.

16 Ibid., 98, 100. *Lloyd's List* notes HMS *Alarm* sailing from Portsmouth for the West Indies, 20 December 1845. Thereafter it seems to have often been on duty in that area.

17 *The Times*, 26 September 1855.

18 *WAMSML*, 113.

19 *WAMSML*, 108, 109, 112.

20 Calder, diary, 24 August 1855, Rappaport, *No Place for Ladies*, 193, 114-15; Military Chaplain, 'Reminiscences of the War in the East', 96.

21 Day's trading in horses was not revealed until he made a statement at his

and Mary's subsequent bankruptcy hearing. See *The Times*, 6 November 1856; *WAMSML*, 112-13.

22 Information from Dr David Jones; emails, 29 and 30 July 2020; Jones, 'Location of the British Hotel', 23. The photograph of the 'site of the British Hotel' featured in the plates section after page 142 in Jane Robinson's biography is incorrect. This is not the location of Mrs Seacole's but of the Stationary Engines. The 'British Hotel' was one mile away from here to the west.

23 I am grateful to Dr David Jones for drawing my attention to this sketch; email correspondence 30 July 2020.

24 There are numerous descriptions of Mrs Seacole's in contemporary letters and memoirs. See for instance, Russell in *The Times*, 27 September 855; Buchanan, *Camp Life*, 177; Captain Hopton Bassett Scott, letter of 8 October 1855 in Massie, *National Army Museum Book of the Crimean War*, 237; Galt, *Camp and the Cutter*, 65; Military Chaplain, 'Reminiscences of the War in the East'. In his article 'Mary Seacole's Hut', Dr Douglas J. Austin suggests that Mary and Thomas Day possibly also had a warehouse at Kadikoi for the storage of supplies they could not accommodate at Spring Hill.

25 The drawing can be found in Blackwood, *Narrative of the Personal Experiences*, 252. Information on Rev. Hort from Mawson, 'Chaplains of the Crimean War', part I, 35.

26 *WAMSML*, 114; Buchanan, *Camp Life*, 177.

27 Ibid., 116.

28 Ibid., 114-17; Rappaport, *No Place for Ladies*, 182-3

29 *WAMSML*, 118-19.

30 Ibid., 122-3.

31 Ibid., 113, 117, 140.

32 *The Times*, 21 May 1855.

Chapter 16

1 Calder MS diary, 24 August 1855, 114-15; Jones-Parry, *An Old Soldier's Memories*, 159; Letter, 16 June 1855, William Douglas, *Soldiering in Sunshine and Storm*, 1865, p. 198.

2 Calder, MS diary, 24 August 1855, 114-15; George Sala, *Things I Have Seen*, 24; Buchanan, *Camp Life*, 177; *Hawley Letters*, 92.

3 Captain Hopton Bassett Scott, letter 8 October 1855, in Massie, *National Army Museum Book of the Crimean War*, 237.

4 Kelly, *Officer's Letters*, 427; Codrington, letter 11 October 1855, Calder, diary, 24 August 1855, 115.

5 Cattell, 'Bygone Days', 24; Military Chaplain, 'Reminiscences of the War in the East', 96.

6 MS Letter of Colonel Edward Goulburn, 2 December 1855, private collection, courtesy Ian Shapiro; Military Chaplain, 'Reminiscences of the War in the East', 95-6, 102; *Morning Advertiser*, 19 July 1855. See e.g. Thomas Carlyle's 'Occasional Discourse on the Nigger Question' of 1849.

7 'The Crimea', 15 November, *London Evening Standard*, citing Woods. He was, with William Howard Russell of *The Times*, one of the outstanding reporters of the Crimean War. He was unfortunately invalided out by illness in mid-July 1855, but later published a valuable two-volume collection of his reports: *The Past Campaign: A Sketch of the War in the East, from the Departure of Lord Raglan to the Capture of Sevastopol* (London: Longman, Brown, Green, 2 vols, 1855), which was rather eclipsed by the published accounts of the war by W. H. Russell.

8 *WAMSML*, 125.

9 Robinson, 'Navvies in the Crimea', 10, 11.

10 A useful overview of the plight of the men of the LTC can be found in the *Report ... of the Proceedings of The Sanitary Commission ... in The East 1855-1856* (London, 1857). See: Section V, Land Transport Corps, 176-184, and Section VI, Army Works Corps, 184-8.

11 *Report ... of the Proceedings of The Sanitary Commission ... in The East 1855-1856*, as above, 179.

12 Land Transport Corps section, *Medical and Surgical History of the British Army*, 1 (1858), 461. Brine's 1857 *Map of Sevastopol and Surrounding Country showing the Russian Defences, Positions of Allied Armies and their Trenches ...*, TNA, item MPH 1/427, is described in Jones, 'Location of the British Hotel at Spring Hill'.

13 *Illustrated Times*, 6 October 1855.

14 *The Times*, 27 September 1855; *WAMSML*, 125.

15 Calder, letter, 24 August 1855, Rappaport, *No Place for Ladies*, 193.

16 *Morning Advertiser*, 19 July 1855. It is interesting to note that his article was republished in the *Jewish Chronicle* of 10 August, the only such report on Mary in that newspaper. Perhaps Mary's Jewish friend Amos Henriques had passed this to the paper.

17 Kelly, *From the Fleet in the Fifties*, 161-2. The first quotation is from *Henry IV*, I, 3; the second from Rowe, *Jane Shore*, I, 2:
> Think not the good,
> The gentle deeds of mercy thou hast done,
> Shall die forgotten all; the poor, the pris'ner,
> The fatherless, the friendless, and the widow,
> Who daily own the bounty of thy hand,
> Shall cry to heav'n and pull a blessing on thee.

18 Calder, letter, 24 August 1855, 114-15; Rappaport, *No Place for Ladies*, 193; Cattell, 'Bygone Days', 24.

19 See 'Mrs Seacole, A West Indian Nurse in the Crimea'.
20 *WAMSML*, 128-9.
21 'The "Good Samaritan" of the Crimea', *Aberdeen Journal*, 28 May 1856.
22 *WAMSML*, 129-30. For the testimonials see *WAMSML*, 127-32.
23 Ibid., 125-6.
24 *Standard*, 8 October 1855, quoting Woods of the *Morning Herald*. Armstrong, *Richard Ramsay Armstrong's Book*, 191. For Lynn MacDonald's assertions see e.g.:
        http://nightingalesociety.com/author/lynnmcd/
25 For detractors who claim Mary was just a caterer and patronised officers only, see McDonald, *The Making of the Myth*.
26 *Argus* (Melbourne), 4 November 1855.
27 Military Chaplain, 'Reminiscences of the War in the East', 96.
28 Fish, *Black and White Women's Narratives*, 89; 'Our Own Vivandière', *Punch*, 30 May 1857.
29 *Morning Advertiser*, 19 July 55.
30 *The Times*, 27 September 1855; 'Before and after the Assault', *Illustrated Times*, 6 October 1855.
31 Scott, letter, 8 October 1855; Captain Thomas Fanshawe, letter, 12 October 1855, in Fanshawe, *Sebastopol to Dagenham: Crimean War Letters of Captain Thomas Fanshawe* (Barking: Valence House Publications, 2016).
32 *WAMSML*, 145.
33 Tyrrell, *History of the War*, 346.
34 Balaclava, 25th September 1855, Part 1 Quartermaster General, Bundle marked 'Provost Marshall', 29 April 1955-12 June 1856, TNA WO28/193. I am indebted to Glenn Fisher of the CWRS for passing on this valuable reference.
35 Rappaport, *No Place for Ladies*, 191.
36 Quoted in Salih, *WAMSML*, Penguin edition, 180.
37 *Gloucester Journal*, 18 October 1856.
38 Robinson, *Mary Seacole*, 126, quoting MS Nightingale, 110, Claydon House Trust Collection.
39 *WAMSML*, 150.
40 Ibid., 124; Rappaport, 'The Invitation that Never Came'.
41 *WAMSML*, 124; Alfred, Lord Tennyson, 'Victoria: An Ode', dedicated to Queen Victoria in March 1851 was published in a new collected edition of his works. See Hope Dyson, *Dear and Honoured Lady: The Correspondence Between Queen Victoria and Alfred Lord Tennyson* (London: Macmillan, 1969), 31; *WAMSML*, 127.

Chapter 17

1 *WAMSML*, 149; Brandon, *People's Chef*, 228-32; Soyer, *Memoirs*, 258-64

2 See Soyer, *Memoirs*, 258-61.

3 Brandon, *People's Chef*, 245-9.

4 Ibid., 264-5

5 Ibid., 240-1 263-4.

6 Soyer, *Memoirs*, 242; *WAMSML*, 149.

7 *WAMSML*, 149; *Morning Advertiser*, 19 July 1855.

8 *WAMSML*, 143; Soyer, *Culinary Campaign*, 143.

9 *WAMSML*, 149.

10 Soyer, *Culinary Campaign*, 144, 164.

11 Soyer, *Memoirs*, 268.

12 See Robinson, *Mary Seacole*, 154-5.

13 *New York Tribune*, 12 June 1855; see this book page 154.

14 Douglas, *Soldiering in Sunshine and Storm*, 198. Douglas himself had not served in Jamaica so the implication here is that Mary and Sally told him about their life there.

15 Calder, diary, 24 August 1855, 114-15.

16 Armstrong, *Richard Ramsay Armstrong's Book of His Adventures*, 191.

17 See Chapter 10, page 149.

18 The allegation was discovered by Nightingale biographer Mark Bostridge and first mentioned in an article published by him in *The Guardian*; see 'Ministering on Distant Shores'.

19 Ibid. The original document is in Claydon House, MS Nightingale 110, and quoted in Robinson, *Mary Seacole*, 155. Note that Nightingale does *not* name the officer as being 'of the 23rd' as Robinson states. For Henry Bunbury see *Australian Dictionary of Biography*, 1, 1966. https://adb.anu.edu.au/biography/bunbury-henry-william-st-pierre-1846

20 This chapter on Sally and Thomas Bunbury is based on comments and conversations by email over many years with Dr Douglas Austin and with Paul Kerr, producer of the Channel 4 documentary *The Real Angel of the Crimea*, transmitted in 2005. Other information on Bunbury's army career is drawn from Hart's Army List (Ref: PMG3/50 #15), Peter Bunbury (Bunbury family historian in Australia), Turtle Bunbury in Ireland, Ancestry and FindMyPast. For details see Bunbury of Cranavonane: http://www.turtlebunbury.com/family/bunburyfamily_bunburys/bunbury_family_bunburys_cranovonane.html

21 Information from Dr Austin; Bunbury website above; Hart's Army Lists.

22 Thomas Bunbury married Jane Pearse at St James's Westminster, 8 February 1812. She died in the autumn of 1850 in Bath, Somerset.

23 See Legacies of British Slave Ownership: https://www.ucl.ac.uk/lbs/
    person/view/7158

24 *Grenada Free Press*, 30 March 1838. See 'Bow Street', *Reading Mercury*,
    10 August 1839.

25 Morris, *Memini*, 94-7.

26 *Daily News*, 2 May 1856.

27 See *Morning Chronicle*, 2 October 1848. Stonehouse (1818-80) eventually
    was promoted to Lieutenant Colonel. He married in Spanish town in 1850
    and settled in Jamaica.

28 See *Kings County Chronicle*, 6 June 1849: 'Major General Bunbury who
    had been confined to his house ever since his arrival in the island by severe
    indisposition, had so far recovered his usual health as to assume the active
    duties of his command.' If Mary nursed him, did she do so as a live-in
    carer? *Cork Examiner*, 18 December 1850: 'Captain Bunbury, son of the
    General Commanding the Forces, also suffered from the disease [cholera]
    in its incipient stage but is convalescent.'

29 Austin, 'Miss Sally Seacole', 15. Beato and Robertson's work is discussed
    more fully in this article.

30 Ibid.

31 Ibid., 17.

32 See Ebba Almroth, *Sunbeams in My Path*, London: James Nisbet &
    Co, 1900, where Mary Seacole is briefly mentioned on 40; Blackwood,
    Narrative of Personal Impressions, 251-2, 262-3.

33 Austin, 'Miss Sally Seacole', 19.

34 Ibid.

35 Email correspondence with Dr Douglas Austin.

36 Will of Thomas Bunbury PROB 11/2250/ff. 341-2, dated 30 July 1851.

Chapter 18

1   *WAMSML*, 136.

2   *The Times*, 17 March 1855.

3   *WAMSML*, 137, 138.

4   Ibid., 138-40.

5   Seacole & Day, see *WAMSML*, 81; *The Times*, 16 May 1856.

6   *WAMSML*, 139.

7   Ibid., 140, 141.

8   Galt, *Camp and the Cutter*, 75-6; Military Chaplain, 'Reminiscences of
    the War in the East', 96.

9   Timothy Gowing, *A Voice from the Ranks: A Personal Narrative of the
    Crimean Campaign* (Nottingham: privately printed, 1886), 218.

10 *WAMSML*, 152.

11 Ibid., 153.

12 Military Chaplain, 'Reminiscences of the War in the East', 98; see also *The Times*, 4 December 1855, which reported on Mrs Seacole's being hit. Vieth, *Recollections of the Crimean Campaign*, 75-6, describes the terrible carnage after the explosion.

13 Ibid., 156.

14 Ibid., 156, 157, 158.

15 *WAMSML*, 159. Mary only identifies him as 'Col. Y–' but it is clear from the evidence whom she intended.

16 Queen Victoria presented the medals at a ceremony in Hyde Park, 26 June 1857.

17 *WAMSML*, 159.

18 Rappaport, *No Place for Ladies*, 208; 160.

19 *WAMSML*, 161.

20 'Variegated Mourning', *The Sketch*, 53, 14 March 1906, 270. The author's recall of Mary's habit of wearing brightly coloured ribbons in her bonnet was prompted by his dismay at the dourness of the British court, in mourning for King Christian IX.

21 Ibid., 163-4.

22 'The Late Prince Victor of Hohenlohe', *Fortnightly Review* 58 (1892): 314. Count Gleichen (from 1861) took up sculpting after leaving the navy and famously produced a terracotta bust of Mary Seacole in 1871. See Chapter 25.

23 Military Chaplain, 'Reminiscences of the War in the East', 97; *WAMSML*, 164.

24 Ibid., 171; *The Times*, 11 April 1857.

25 *WAMSML*, 165-6.

26 Ibid., 166; 'News of the War: The Crimea', *Lady's Newspaper and Pictorial Times*, 29 March 1856. For the tobacco pouch see Denis Kelly, *An Officer's Letters to his Wife*, 427; for the medallion see 'The Crimea', *Standard*, 24 March 1856, dispatch dated 11 March.

27 *WAMSML*, 169-70.

28 'Mrs Seacole', *The Lancet*, 9 February 1867.

29 'The Last Days of Sebastopol', *Irish Metropolitan Magazine*, 1, April–September 1857, 258-9.

30 *WAMSML*, 171.

31 'The Mother of the Regiment', *Punch*, 2 May 1857; *Argus* (Melbourne), 4 November 1857.

32 Russell, 'The Fall of Sebastopol', *The Times*, 27 September 1855, 10. This extensive dispatch filled four dense pages of *The Times*. It is interesting to note that the mention of Mary, coming as it does at the very end, is thus far more noticeable than if it had been embedded in the main body of the text.

33 See Rappaport, *No Place for Ladies*, 220-1; *WAMSML*, 176.

34 *WAMSML*, 170; 'The Crimea', *London Evening Standard*, 15 November 1855, syndicated from the *Morning Herald*, so written by their special correspondent Woods.

35 *WAMSML*, 173.

36 Ibid., 173, 174.

37 'The Crimea', *Standard*, 15 November 1855. The *Fifeshire Journal* and a couple of other regional papers made a point of extrapolating Woods's piece on Mary as a separate item under the heading 'The Navvy's Friend'. See 22 November 1855.

38 'A Visit to the Camp in Crimea', *St James's Chronicle*, 13 December 1855.

Chapter 19

1 Galt, *Camp and the Cutter*, 75.

2 *WAMSML*, 178.

3 'The Crimea', *London Evening Standard*, 15 November 1855, reproducing dispatch from the special correspondent of the *Morning Herald*. It is not known who Nicholas Woods's replacement was.

4 'Amusement for the Troops', *Liverpool Standard & General Commercial Advertiser*, 20 November 1855.

5 'Letter From the Crimea', *The Times*, 20 December 1855; *Monmouthshire Beacon*, 22 December 1855.

6 'From an Occasional Correspondent', *Daily News*, 2 May 1856. For Mary's description of the various race meetings, see *WAMSML*, 181-2.

7 'Camp Before Sebastopol', *Standard*, 3 March 1856.

8 Soyer, *Culinary Campaign*, 268.

9 See Rappaport, *No Place for Ladies*, 225; Vieth, *Recollections of the Crimean Campaign*, 77-8.

10 *The Zoologist: A Popular Miscellany of Natural History*, Vol. 15 (London: John Van Voorst, 1857), 5603; Mrs Seacole's bustard for sale, *Daily News*, 15 January 1855.

11 *WAMSML*, 185.

12 Military Chaplain, 'Reminiscences of the War in the East', 102-3.

13 'The War in the East', *Morning Post*, 8 January 1856, dispatch dated 24 December 1855.

14 'A Plum-Pudding for Marshal Pélissier', *Essex Standard & General Advertiser*, 1 February 1856.

15 Galt, *Camp and the Cutter*, 75.

16 *WAMSML*, 185.

17 'The Dullness of Facts', *Saturday Review*, 1, 12 January 1856, 183.

18 *WAMSML*, 187.

19 'The Crimea', *Standard*, 29 January 1856.

20 *WAMSML*, 189.
21 'The Crimea', *Standard*, 10 April 1856. The article states that there were doctors 'on hand' – i.e. in the party, hence why Nightingale did not respond warmly to Mary's offer of help.
22 'The Crimea', *Standard*, 22 February 1856, reproducing a dispatch in the *Morning Herald*.
23 'Camp near Headquarters', *Standard*, 21 January 1856, citing *Morning Herald*.
24 'The Crimean War Letters of Colonel William Lygon Pakenham', compiled by William B. Mauk, Part IV, in *War Correspondent* 12, No. 2 (1994): 19.
25 See Vieth, *Recollections of the Crimean Campaign*, 77-80; *WAMSML*, 180.
26 'The "Good Samaritan" in the Crimea', *Aberdeen Journal*, 28 May 1856; 'Camp Before Sebastopol', *Illustrated London News*, 9 February 1856.
27 Calder, MS diary, 24 February 1856.
28 'From an Occasional Correspondent: Camp, Sebastopol', *Daily News*, 2 May 1856; 'The British Army. Camp Before Sebastopol', *The Times*, 15 May 1856.
29 'Movements of the Army in Crimea', *Liverpool Mercury*, 23 June 1856. Hugh Gough, 1st Viscount Gough (1779-1869) may well have already known of Mary Seacole via Thomas Bunbury, for Gough's mother Letitia was a member of the Irish Bunbury family and shared a great-grandfather with the Cranavonane branch. Gough was also a veteran of the Peninsula War in which Bunbury had served. He arrived in Sevastopol on 4 June to distribute the Order of the Bath and left Crimea on the 12th, promising to try to secure the Crimean medal for Mary. But there is no further mention of him or her in this connection.
30 'Military Decorations for Ladies', *The Guardian*, 30 June 1856.
31 *Morning Chronicle*, 11 July 1856.
32 *The Guardian*, 16 May 1856; some of the details of the Seacole & Day trading partnership came to light during their bankruptcy trial in London in November 1856–January 1857.
33 'The British Army', *The Times*, 9 June 1856; 'The Army in the East', *Morning Post*, 9 June 1856; *WAMSML*, 191, 192.
34 Soyer, *Culinary Campaign*, 267.
35 Ibid., 268.
36 *WAMSML*, 196.
37 *London Evening Standard*, 17 July 1856.
38 This useful snippet of information appears in a dispatch headed 'Turkey', in *London Evening Standard*, 31 July 1856.
39 *Morning Chronicle*, 11 July 1856; 'Miscellaneous', *Reynolds's Weekly Newspaper*, 27 July 1856; *Morning Chronicle*, 5 July 1856.

40 *Daily News*, 21 June 1856; *Standard*, 17 July 1856; 'The Last of the Crimea', *Morning Herald*, 4 July 1856.
41 *Cork Constitution*, 8 July 1856.
42 *WAMSML*, 195.
43 *Illustrated London News*, 30 August 1856; see page 185 of this book.
44 Soyer, *Culinary Campaign*, 297.

Chapter 20

1 'Mother Seacole', *Argus* (Melbourne), 3 September 1857; *North British Daily Mail*, 24 July 1856. I am grateful to Tony Margrave for help in identifying this ship. Patterson had served in Crimea as an assistant surgeon with Major General Beatson's Osmanli Irregular Cavalry from February 1856: *Bulletins and Other State Intelligence for the Year 1856*, Part I, London Gazette Office, 1857, 426. In 1859, he was appointed surgeon to the colonial steam sloop HMCSS *Victoria*. See also Patterson, 'Mother Seacole', *The Argus*, 10 September 1857, in which Patterson rued the poor response to his appeal on Mary's behalf.
2 *WAMSML*, 197.
3 Ann can be found on the 1851 census living as a boarder with her brother Charles at 5 York Place, Chelsea, both described as 'fundholders'. See HO107, piece 1473, folio 126, page 2. She died 7 June and was buried at Brompton Cemetery. See: Series Number: Work 97; Piece Number: 77; burial 13508.
4 William James Kent, born 1824, had married Sarah Buckland on 21 October 1848 at All Souls, St Marylebone. See 1861 census, Bow St Mary RG 9; Piece: 303; Folio: 80; Page: 6; GSU roll: 542610.
5 The *Gloucester Journal*, 30 August 1856, confirmed that Mary's address in Tavistock Street was only 'for a short time'.
6 *WAMSML*, 199.
7 Galt, *The Camp and the Cutter*, reviewed in *Morning Post*, 25 August 1856.
8 *Home News for India, China and the Colonies*, 26 August 1856; 'The Dinner to the Guards', *Examiner*, 30 August 1856; see also 'The Banquet to the Guards', *News of the World*, 31 August 1856.
9 'Notes From London', *Gloucester Journal*, 30 August 1856; 'The Dinner to the Guards', *Examiner*, 30 August 1856, which contains an extensive account of the event, singling out Mary Seacole on pages 553-4.
10 'Dinner to the Guards at the Surrey Gardens', *The Globe*, 26 August 1856.
11 *Hereford Times*, 13 September 1856.
12 *The Sun* (London), 22 October 1856.
13 Letter from W. J. Tynan, quoted in *WAMSML*, 194.

14 See Rappaport, 'The Invitation that Never Came', 9-12. For the story of Sarah Forbes Bonetta, see https://helenrappaport.com/queen-victoria/sarah-forbes-bonetta/

15 Rappaport, 'The Invitation that Never Came', 12.

16 'Accident to Madame Seacole', *Caledonian Mercury*, 29 October 1856.

17 For the official listing of the bankruptcy, see London District General Docket Book B/6/100 Jan 1856 to June 1859, Letter S no. 1311, TNA. The first press mention of 'Mrs Seacole's Bankruptcy' was in the *London Evening Standard*, 28 October 1856, and the *Saint James's Chronicle* of the same date. A full enumeration of the Seacole & Day debts can be found in 'Re Seacole and Day – Mrs Seacole in Bankruptcy', *London Evening Standard*, 9 January 1857.

18 'In Re Henry Jones Smith and Benjamin Crane – Unfortunate Trading to the Crimea', *Morning Advertiser*, 13 September 1856.

19 'Re Seacole and Day – Mrs Seacole in Bankruptcy', *London Evening Standard*, 7 November 1856.

20 Ibid.; *Illustrated London News*, 1 November 1856.

21 There is no sign of the drawing in Simpson's Crimean sketchbooks, suggesting it was either removed or done separately, perhaps as a gift for Rev. Stothert.

22 It is clear that Albert Charles Challen, when painting the 1869 portrait, used a degree of artistic licence. Military experts tell me that the medals are not hanging from the correct ribbon bars, which suggests either Mary gaily muddled them up or that Challen had painted them in after the sitting, from memory. For this reason the accuracy of the medals represented in the portrait cannot be relied upon; in addition, there is some division over whether they are full-size medals or dress miniatures. Email correspondence with Mike Hargreave-Mawson; Dr Douglas Austin, email, 11 January 2019.

23 See page 207. See FO 83/697 Foreign Medals Non-Military Awarded to British Subjects 1843-1880. Draft FO letter 17 March 1859. Several documents in FO 83/681 Foreign Orders: Turkey, January-July 1856 repeat the rule about civilian acceptance of a foreign order. See especially Stratford de Redcliffe (British ambassador to Constantinople) to the Earl of Clarendon, 17 April 1856, FO 83/681/453.

24 'The British Army. Camp Before Sebastopol', *The Times*, 16 May 1856.

25 See FO 83/681 Foreign Orders: Turkey, January–July 1856 and especially the draft letter to Stratford de Redcliffe, 20 May 1856 and the FO reply to it.

26 News of Mary's Turkish medal appears to have broken in Crimea in mid-April, when the *Daily News* correspondent noted that she had been 'given a medal for her services to the Turkish troops'. This in turn was reported across the British press, although some papers printed an

abbreviated listing, extrapolated from the original long dispatch of 3 May
by William Howard Russell in *The Times*, in which he specified that 'the
Sultan' himself had sent Mrs Seacole the medal. A *carte de visite* of Mary
Seacole, probably taken for the 1867 Seacole Fund and later reissued in
the 1870s, shows her wearing miniature dress versions of three medals,
but it is impossible to discern which they are. It should be noted that
miniatures were not issued officially and could be purchased at military
outfitters – and even pawn shops – to wear with mess dress, rather than
the heavier and bulkier originals.

Mary clearly had both miniatures and full-size versions of her medals,
as the various images of her attest. At a military display at Aldershot
in 1866 she was described as wearing 'three war medals, the Crimean
medal, *with three clasps*, the Legion of Honour, and the Turkish medal';
see 'Grand Divisional Field Day', *Morning Advertiser*, 29 September
1866. By 1871, when the Gleichen bust was executed, she is wearing
four, and this remains the most accurate representation of the medals in
Mary Seacole's possession at that date. The fact that the Queen's cousin
executed this bust surely serves as confirmation of an official endorsement
of her wearing the medals. According to Norman Gooding of the OMRS
(email correspondence 2003), on the Gleichen bust her necklace obscures
the first medal and its identity is unclear; the central one – the Crimea – is
without clasps and bars (a fact which conflicts with the Aldershot account
above) and the third may be the Al Valore Militare. The star of the
Turkish Medidjie is clearly identifiable below the top three. This suggests
that the fourth medal, whichever one it was, was not awarded till some
time between 1869 and 1871.

When Mary died in May 1881, a brief obituary in the *Daily
Gleaner* in Jamaica confirmed that she 'received English, French,
Russian and Turkish decorations', this fact perhaps confirmed by
her sister Louisa in Kingston. Three of the medals were certainly in
Jamaica by 1895 no doubt as part of Mary's estate inherited by Louisa.
That year, she appears to have presented the medals to the Institute
of Jamaica, along with her copy of the Gleichen bust of Mary and
a watercolour portrait of Mary. According to a letter to the *Daily
Gleaner* ('About Mrs Seacole', 11 December 1916) from Jamaican
historian Frank Cundall, 'the third [medal] could not be recovered
from the debris after the earthquake'. J. A. Rogers's *The World's Great
Men of Color*, 2: 270, published in 1946, confirmed that the Institute
had two of Mary's medals in its collection. Ziggi Alexander and
Audrey Dewjee discussed the provenance of the Seacole medals in their
introduction to the 1984 edition of *WAMSML*, 36. Dutch researchers
Corry Staring-Derks and Jeroen Staring examined the two surviving
full-size medals in the Institute of Jamaica during a research trip in

2006, and confirm that there is no accompanying provenance. At the time, staff at the Institute told them that the third, missing medal was a Russian one, awarded posthumously, but this conflicts with the Jamaican obituary which says Mary had the Russian one at the time of her death. This and the British Crimean and the Sardinian medal all appear to have been lost.

So far, no Seacole researcher, this author included, has been able to get to the bottom of this very vexed question, but see Corry Staring-Derks's discussion of the medals in her Dutch edition of *WAMSML*, *Mary Seacole's Avonturen in de West en in de Krim*, note 11, clxxxvii-viii. Since 2002 I have exchanged numerous emails with members of the CWRS on the subject, most notably Dr Douglas Austin, Tony Margrave and Mike Hargreave-Mawson, to whom I am most grateful for their observations. Norman Gooding of the OMRS also offered me valuable insights and information on the subject; I am grateful also to Jeroen Staring, for email correspondence, 9 February 2021. For a description and images of the various Russian medals awarded during the Crimean War see http://cwrs.russianwar.co.uk/cwrs-R-crimeanmedals.html

27 Staring-Derks, as above; see e.g. Sarah Salih, who in her introduction (xlviii) to the 2005 edition of *WAMSML* noted that she was unable to see the medals during her own research trip. For the argument against Seacole's medals being legitimate, see Lyn McDonald, 'Mary Seacole and claims of evidence-based practice and global influence', 9. There has also been intermittent debate over the past twenty years on the subject in the CWRS journal, the *War Correspondent*.

28 Military Chaplain, 'Reminiscences of the War in the East', 99; Reid, *Memories of the Crimean War*, 13-14.

29 See for example, 'Extracts from the Bishop of Columbia's Journal', 10.

30 One of the first to challenge accusations of fraud made against Mary, and claims that she was 'just a sutler', was Dr Douglas Austin in a letter to the editor of *History Today*. See 'Seacole's Honours', April 2005, 60.

31 An explanation of the Queen's unique position re. awarding medals was sent to me by email by Tony Margrave of the CWRS, 24 June 2003.

32 H. F. J.-T., 'The Crimean Medal', *Journal of the Society for Army Historical Research*, 34 (September 1956): 133-4; in the article the author states that the British Government 'were adamant in refusing the medal to those who ... were not on the roll of a unit of the Expeditionary Force'. Email discussion with Dr Douglas Austin, 4 March 2012.

33 Will of Mary Seacole, Principal Probate Registry, 11 July 1881, No. 564.

34 'In Re Seacole and Day – Mrs Seacole in Bankruptcy', *London Evening Standard*, 9 January 1857. Records of the West Granada or Veraguas Gold & Silver Mining Company are held in the Archive of the Companies

Registration Office, 1844-1951, Folder 3911(OS) & C 686, at the University of California, Berkeley.

35 *Morning Advertiser*, 25 November 1856; *Home News for India, China and the Colonies*, 10 November 1856.

36 Letter of 22 November to the editor, *The Times*, 24 November 1856.

37 Ibid.

38 'A Friend to Merit', 27 November 1856, *Evening Mail*.

39 'To the Editor of the Evening Mail', letter from Lord Rokeby enclosing one from Mary Seacole of 25 November, *Evening Mail*, 1 December 1856.

40 *The Times*, 9 January 1857.

41 *The Sun*, 8 January 1857.

42 *Morning Chronicle*, 31 January 1857.

43 *The Sun*, 8 January 1857. Re India: *London Evening Standard*, 30 January 1857; *The Watchman and Wesleyan Advertiser*, 4 February 1857.

44 *Morning Advertiser*, 27 February, repeated 4 March 1857.

45 'The Seacole Fund', letter from W. H. Russell, *The Times*, 11 April 1857; quotations from this letter on Mary's good works in Crimea are in Chapter 15. For Captain M'Clair see *Era*, 11 January.

46 'Mrs Seacole's Late Partner in the Crimea', letter to the editor, *The Times*, 14 April 1857; W. H. Russell letter to the editor, *The Times*, 15 April 1857.

47 The name is too common to be certain, but on 2 December 1858 *The Age* (Melbourne) published an announcement with regard to a new steam ship postal service – the Australasian and Pacific Company – being set up to operate between Britain, British Columbia, Australia and Panama, of which the 'projector or secretary *pro tem* signs his name as "Thomas Day"'. In *The Times* of 14 September 1858 a Thomas Day had also been mentioned as secretary of this venture, listed at 3 Winchester House, Old Broad Street, EC. With his knowledge of Panama and having travelled a great deal between there and Britain, this does seem the kind of business venture Thomas Day might get involved in, but his name appears only this once in connection with it.

Chapter 21

1 'The Mother of the Regiment', *Punch*, 2 May 1857.

2 'Monthly Catalogue. Poetry', *The Critical Review, or, Annals of Literature*, 36 (1773): 232, 233.

3 The correspondence of the publisher James Blackwood for 1844-74 is held at the Bodleian Library, Special Collections and Western Manuscripts, MSS Eng misc. *c*. 334. Blackwood (1822-1911) was born in Scotland but so far there appears to be no link between him and the more famous Edinburgh publisher, William Blackwood, proprietor of *Blackwood's Edinburgh Magazine*.

4 'Our Own Vivandière', *Punch*, 30 May 1857.

5 A useful note on *Reynolds's* can be found at the British Newspaper Archive https://www.britishnewspaperarchive.co.uk/titles/reynoldss-newspaper

6 14 June 1857, *Reynolds's Weekly Newspaper*: 'A Real Crimean Heroine – Brummagen Heroes'.

7 *WAMSML*, 146, 147.

8 *Literary Gazette*, 4 July 1857, 637.

9 *The Critic*, 15 July 1857; *The Leader*, 22 August 1857; the *Examiner*, 4 July 1857.

10 See John Black Atkins, *The Life of Sir William Howard Russell* (London: John Murray, 1911). Aside from the introduction to *WAMSML* and his wartime dispatches, I drew a total blank on Russell's friendship with Mary Seacole in published sources. There is very little in his archive at News International.

11 See Robinson, *Mary Seacole*, 168. W. J. Stewart (1830-63) published several boys'-adventure type novels in the early 1860s; in May 1863 he was appointed editor of the *Illustrated London News* but died that October at the age of only thirty-three. His last novel, *Picked Up at Sea*, was published posthumously in 1863. See the *Publishers' Circular*, 2 November 1857, 459; ibid., 2 November 1863, 550.

12 W. C. Lubenow, *The Cambridge Apostles, 1820-1914* (Cambridge: Cambridge University Press, 1998), 157. See e.g. Spedding's collected articles as *Reviews and Discussions: Literary, Political, and Historical* (London: C. Kegan Paul, 1879), which has many references to Jamaica. I have not been able to ascertain whether during his time at the Colonial Office he actually went out there, but it is possible. If he did, had he perhaps already met Mary Seacole?

13 It should perhaps be pointed out that no baptism for James Spedding, born 28 June 1808, has come to light and this predates registration of births. There is therefore the faint hope that he might have been baptised with a first name, beginning with a W that he never used. The use of it on the title page of *WAMSML* would thus have acted as a smokescreen to disguise him. The possibility of Spedding's involvement does not quite end with the text, although again, the thesis, I concede, is a tenuous one. He was in fact something of an artist, and drew pencil portraits of several of his Cambridge friends including Tennyson and the poet Edward Fitzgerald. Might he also have drawn the portrait for the front cover of *Wonderful Adventures* that was engraved by Thomas Dewell Scott? It would be logical for Spedding to be enlisted to do the drawing while in Mary's company working on the book, especially given the speed with which it was written and published. There is of course no documentary proof of a link between them,

merely the possibility, after comparing the style of this 1832 drawing of Arthur Henry Hallam by Spedding with the front cover of *Wonderful Adventures*:

14 My thanks to Donato Esposito at the V&A for this valuable identification. He observes that Scott 'appears to be among the first wood engravers to consistently have his name (as an intermediary draughtsman) recorded in a monogram', thus enabling the artist's work, for once, to be identified here; email 20 March 2021.

15 *Morning Post*, 20 August 1857.

16 'Books Recently Published', *London Evening Standard*, 2 July 1857; 'Wonderful Adventures of Mrs Seacole', *Reynolds's Weekly Newspaper*, 19 July 1857; 'Books of the Week', *Examiner*, 4 July 1857; *Kentish Gazette*, 7 July 1857; *Lady's Own Paper*, 1 August 1857.

17 *Kentish Gazette*, 7 July 1857; *Lady's Own Paper*, 1 August 1857; *Illustrated London News*, 25 July 1857.

18 'Wonderful Adventures' review, *The Critic*, 15 July 1857, 321. On American racism see for example *Leicester Journal*, 7 August; *Derbyshire Courier*, 22 August; *Exeter Flying Post*, 27 August 1857.

19 'Literature', *Bristol Mercury*, 1 August 1857.

20 Gordon, 'Mary Seacole', 50.

21 'The Seacole Festival', *Era*, 26 July 1857.

22 *Era*, 26 July 1857.

23 *London Evening Standard*, 28 July 1857.

24 *Reynolds's Weekly Newspaper*, 2 August 1857.

25 *Illustrated London News*, 1 August; *Era*, 2 August 1857.

26 *Illustrated London News*, 1 August 1857; *Era*, 2 August 1857; *Morning Advertiser* 28 July 1857; Russell diary, 27 July 1857.

27 Fisher, *Notes by the Way-Side*, 103.

28 *Reynolds's Weekly Newspaper*, 2 August 1857.

29 'Festival For Mrs Seacole', from suburban correspondent, *Musical World*, 1 August 1857.

30 Discussion of the crisis suffered by Nightingale after her return in 1856 can be found in Hugh Small's excellent studies *Florence Nightingale Avenging Angel* and *The Passion of Florence Nightingale*. Lynn McDonald, 'Seacole and the claim of global influence' has a useful summary of Nightingale's pioneering postwar medical work on 12-14, although she unfairly sets these many incontrovertible and distinguished achievements against Mary's quite different postwar legacy. The comparison is neither valid nor helpful. Mary herself never, in any way, claimed to be Nightingale's equal. It is the subsequent 21st-century hagiographers who have attempted to elevate her quite different medical contribution in order to put her on a par with Nightingale, which does both women a disservice.

31 *Reynolds's Weekly Newspaper*, 2 August 1857. For Australian and NZ reports see e.g. *Lyttleton Times* (NZ), 1 July 1857.

32 *Illustrated London News*, 1 August 1857.

33 'Mrs Seacole and the Royal Surrey Gardens Company', *London Evening Standard*, 20 August 1857.

34 *London Evening Standard*, 24 August 1857; *Morning Post*, 24 August 1857.

35 'Royal Surrey Gardens', 31 August 1857; *The Times*, 28 August 1857; see also Robinson, *Mary Seacole*, 180.

36 *Inverness Courier*, 27 August 1857; *Evening Mail*, 28 August 1857.

37 'Gossip of the Week', *Reynolds's Weekly Newspaper*, 30 August 1857; *Cork Examiner*, 9 September 1857.

Chapter 22

1 'Hospital Nurses in India', letter to the editor of the *Daily News*, 21 September 1857.

2 'Under the Red Cross', *St James' Magazine and United Empire Review*, Vol. 8 (Oct 1871–March 1872): 340-1.

3 Quoted in Ibid.

4 'Hospital Nurses for India', From a Correspondent, *Morning Advertiser*, 2 November 1857.

5 It is extremely fortuitous that Dutch researchers Corry Staring-Derks and Jeroen Staring spotted this letter for sale in a dealer's catalogue and purchased it. Any doubters of Mary's high standard of literacy, and her most elegant and educated hand, should inspect the original in Anionwu, Staring-Derks and Staring, 'New Light on Seacole'. This plus the other extant 1869 MS letter (see pp. 286-7) and her two published letters more than demonstrate Mary Seacole's ability to write her own book.

6 *Morning Advertiser*, 2 February 1858.

7 *Morning Advertiser*, 16 February 1858; *The Sun*, 17 February 1858.

8 *Holborn Journal*, 20 March 1858.

9 See for example 'Reviews of Books. Soyer's Culinary Campaign. M. Soyer and Mrs Seacole', *Reynolds's Weekly Newspaper*, 20 September 1857.

10 *The Camp Life as Seen by a Civilian; Or, Anecdotes, Episodes and Social Incidents of Military Life*, T. W. J. Connolly, 2, 1859, xx; 'The Seacole Ball at Bristol', *Daily News*, 28 December 1857.

11 *The Times*, 28 December 1857; *Era*, 27 December 1857.

12 Rev. Jacob Jongeneel (1831-87) is an interesting personality; a Dutch evangelical who was a professor of history and Dutch literature at Deventer. Mlle Rilliet produced other translations but little is known of her life and work. Corry Staring-Derks and Jeroen Staring have done valuable work in tracking down these editions. Sadly no copies of the Dutch edition by P. C. Hoog survive in the Netherlands, no doubt as the result of bombing damage to the publishing house in Rotterdam during the Second World War. Fortuitously, Staring and Derks discovered one solitary copy of the Dutch translation in the State Library in St Petersburg.

13 Index to Registers of Passport Applications, FO611/7: Seacole, Mary no. 6779, 5 June 1858, at TNA. Information from Phil Tomaselli, email, 19 February 2021.

14 'Promotion of Mrs Seacole', *Morning Chronicle*, 14 June 1858; this small entry was syndicated across thirty-two British newspapers, signifying the continued interest in Mary.

15 *Illustrated London News*, 5 June 1858; 'Death of M. Alexis Soyer', *The Atlas*, 8 August 1858.

16 *Morning Chronicle*, 11 August 1858.

17 'Naval and Military', *Daily News*, 2 February 1859.

18 2 February 1859, *Daily News*: Naval & Military News; *Town Talk*, 26 February 1859.

19 H. H., 'Central American Sketches', I, *Canadian Monthly*, 1875, 233.

20 Trollope, *West Indies and the Spanish Main*, 15.

21 Bigelow, *Jamaica in 1850*, 53, 54, 55, 56.

22 James Linen, 'Island Sketches, Impressions of Jamaica, and of Kingston in particular', *Knickerbocker*, 43 (1854): 374-7.

23 Trollope, *West Indies and the Spanish Main*, 17, 16.

24 Ibid., 23.

25 Grace Blundell died 16 August 1855; her Jamaican will is dated July 1851; B112 Will Books/Original Wills, Liber 127 Fo 93. Résumé at: http://www. jamaicanfamilysearch.com/Members/rbl-bou3.htm

26 *Jamaica Directory and Business Directory 1878*; 'Regina v Nevan Evans', *Colonial Standard and Jamaica Despatch*, 21 March 1860.

27 See letter to the editor from Marie Hart, *Daily Gleaner*, 24 August 1939: Marie recalls 'knowing her sister Louisa Grant who was the proprietress of the then well-known Blundell Hall boarding house ... at the north east corner of East Street and Water Lane. ... The sister [Mary] at that time resided directly opposite.'

28 Sir Alexander Milne, *The Milne Papers*, 2, *The Royal Navy and the American Civil War 1860-1862*, 31.

29 HMS *Imaum* Description Book 1851-1862, ADM 38/8330 TNA. There was a memorial to those who died in the epidemic: https://memorials.rmg.co.uk/m3440/

Because he was based on a British ship, Christopher appears on the census for 1861 at Port Royal; he was now a Boy, 2nd Class. His death is registered in Jamaica Civil Registration index, Ancestry.co.uk. Interestingly, also serving on the *Imaum* in the gun room was a Horatio Henriques, aged twenty-five, also born in Jamaica. He is mentioned in the journal of the ship's Surgeon, Mr Thomas Seccombe, kept during the yellow fever epidemic: ADM 101/229 TNA. The two men were found by chance when searching for Seacoles in the Royal Navy. Were they brothers? The 'Horatio' tempts us to hope there may be a connection with Mary Seacole.

30 Ann Pratt, 'Seven Months in the Kingston Lunatic Asylum', 3, 14, 15; there is a copy of this rare pamphlet in CO 137/350, at TNA. See also Grace Owen, 'Nursing: The Early Years', *Daily Gleaner*, 23 May 1982.

31 Ibid., 18.

32 http://old.skabook.com/foundationska/tag/jamaica-lunatic-asylum/

33 Pratt, 'Seven Months in the Kingston Lunatic Asylum', 18, 19, 20.

34 See 'Official Documents in the Case of Ann Pratt, the Reputed Authoress of a Certain Pamphlet, Entitled "Seven Months in the Kingston Lunatic Asylum and What I Saw There"' (Kingston & Spanish Town: Jordon and Osborn, 1860). This pamphlet is appended to the Pratt document at the same TNA location.

35 'Colonial Hospitals for the Insane', *The Lancet*, 13 October 1860, 363-4. Although the inquiry was extremely limited, it did at least give the impetus for provisions in colonial asylums to be investigated. For an interesting article on the subject see Christienna Fryar, 'The Narrative of Ann Pratt: Life-Writing, Genre and Bureaucracy in a Postemancipation Scandal', *History Workshop Journal* 85 (2018): 265-79.

36 Kingston Burials 1858-71, Vol. 7, fo 422, 315.

Chapter 23

1 'Panama as a Home', *All the Year Round*, 9 (1863): 246 247; Codman, *The Round Trip by Way of Panama*, 14.

2 Richard Francis Burton, *City of the Saints*, 501; Isabel Burton, *The Life of*

Captain Sir Richard F Burton, Vol. 1 (London: Chapman & Hall, 1893), 229.

3 'Camp Followers', *Panama Star and Herald*, 18 March 1862.

4 *Morning Post*, 18 April 1862.

5 *Caledonian Mercury*, 17 January 1863; *Midland Florist and Horticulturist*, Vol. 3 (1859), 136.

6 'Literary and Scientific Institution. Lecture by Rev J Haldane Stewart', *Salisbury and Winchester Journal*, 17 December 1864; Stafford, *England's Battles by Sea and Land*, 154.

7 'A Trip to Vancouver Island and British Columbia', *United Service Magazine*, Vol. 102 (July 1863), 382.

8 Robinson, *Fifty Years at Panama*, 122. There is some discrepancy in Robinson's identification of HMS *Reindeer*, which was not commissioned till October 1866 and sent to the Pacific, by which time Mary was long since back in London. So perhaps he misremembered the name.

9 'Panama as a Home', 248; 'The Island of Taboga', *Panama Weekly Star & Herald*, 22 August 1853; Robinson, *Fifty Years at Panama*, 118-19.

10 'Taboga, Bay of Panama', *Illustrated London News*, 11 January 1868, 45.

11 *Dublin Medical Press*, 4 September 1861; *Cork Examiner*, 29 December 1863.

12 Woods, *Spun Yarn from the Strands of a Sailor's Life*, 147.

13 'Notes of a Pacific Voyage (1863-4) by a Dundee Boy: No. 1', *Dundee Courier and Argus*, 25 August 1864. Part 2 was published on the 29th. Precise dates for the ship's sailings have not been found but the *Benjamin Bangs* arrived back in Ireland at the end of February and was offloading its cargo in Sligo on 10 April 1863. See *Sligo Independent*, 18 April 1863.

14 'Panama as a Home', 248.

15 'Extracts from the Bishop of Columbia's Journal', 9.

16 Ibid., 10.

17 'Jamaica's Florence Nightingale', letter to the editor, *Daily Gleaner*, 29 August 1939. Cooper was also on the Board of Directors of the Standard Life Assurance Company in Jamaica.

18 'Mary Seacole and the Queen of Hawaii', *Jamaican Historical Society Bulletin*, 9-10 (1985): 37.

19 *Addresses to his Excellency Edward John Eyre, Esquire, 1865, 1866* (Kingston: M De Cordova, 1866), 53-4. John Salmon, 64, Louisa M Grant, 62.

20 Storks's arrival reported e.g. in *London Evening Standard*, 30 January 1866.

21 Trollope, *West Indies and the Spanish Main*, 112-13.

22 'Blundle's Hall', letter to the editor of the Kingston *Daily Gleaner*, 6 February 1867.

23 For descriptions of Blundell Hall under Louisa's management in the 1870s, see: Godfrey Turner 'Impressions of Jamaica', *Geographical*

Magazine, 1 September 1874, 243-4; Frank F. Taylor, *To Hell with Paradise: A History of the Jamaican Tourist Industry* (Pittsburgh University Press, 2003), 69; and 'Negro Life in Jamaica' *Harper's Magazine* 44, No. 262 (1872): 559-60.

24 'London Correspondence', *Belfast Newsletter*, 25 January 1867.

25 This article originally appeared in the *Falmouth Post*, a Jamaican newspaper published in Trelawny parish, and was reproduced in the leading new Kingston paper the *Daily Gleaner*. It is the first known mention of Mary in that paper.

26 'The Jamaica Prosecutions', *Reynolds's Weekly Newspaper*, 17 February 1867.

27 *Era*, 22 October 1865.

Chapter 24

1 Henry Haynes Walton, *A Practical Treatise on the Diseases of the Eye* (London: J. & A. Churchill, 1875), 148.

2 Edith Mary 1851; Ada Frances 1853; Ellen Augusta 1856; Herbert William 1858; Florence Seacole 1861. See Civil Registration Births Index.

3 See Phillip A. Nicholls, *Homeopathy and the Medical Profession* (London: Croom Helm, 1988); *Lancet*, 1, 1834-5, 932.

4 'Campaign for a Homeopathic Hospital in the Crimea', *British Journal of Homeopathy* 13, No. 53 (July 1855): 449.

5 A dip into issues of the *British Journal of Homeopathy*, which began in 1854, gives a fascinating insight into the practice during Mary's lifetime. A very useful account of the hospital can be found in 'Lost Hospitals of London' at https://ezitis.myzen.co.uk/homeopathic.html. See also N. Henton, 'A Social History of the (Royal) London Homeopathic Hospital', unpublished thesis at the Wellcome Library.

6 Quoted in *British Journal of Homeopathy* (1859), 502; 21 April 1858 report of dinner at the Willis Rooms, *Illustrated London News* (1858); 'The Prince Consort and his Treatment', *British Journal of Homeopathy* 20 (1862), 1174-5.

7 For a fascinating article on the royals and homeopathy, see Diana Ullman, 'The Royal Medicine: Monarchs' Longtime Love for Homeopathy' https://englishhistoryauthors.blogspot.com/2014/01/the-royal-medicine-monarchs-longtime.html

8 I am grateful to Peter Morrell for valuable notes he emailed to me on this subject back in June 2003; he has written extensively on homeopathy and its history. See http://www.homeoint.org/morrell/articles/index.htm

9 Sue Young provided me with useful background information on this score, in an email of 20 December 2018.

10 *London City Press*, 1 September 1866.

11 *The Owl: A Wednesday Journal of Politics and Society* 1 (18 July 1866): 8. For an interesting perspective of Mary and her methods written by a homeopath, see https://www.sueyounghistories. com/2008-12-16-mary-jane-seacole-1805-1881/

12 *Morning Advertiser*, 27 September 1866; *Army and Navy Gazette*, 22 September 1866.

13 'Grand Divisional Field Day', *Aldershot Military Gazette*, 29 September 1866.

14 Young, 'Mary Jane Seacole (1805-1881)', 55.

15 Ibid.; *Lancet* 1, 1-6 (1867): 255.

16 'To the Editor of the Morning Post', *Morning Post*, 4 February 1867.

17 Reproduced in Alexander & Dewjee edition of *WAMSML*, 237.

18 See letter of Count Gleichen, 25 January 1867, RA PP/VIC/1867/23078.

19 Details of the private anonymous donations by the Queen, Prince of Wales and Duke of Edinburgh are to be found in two letters from Count Gleichen, who was a member of the committee, that are held in the Royal Archives at RA PP/VIC/1867/23078. A full list of donors to the fund can be seen in *The Times* for 2 and 11 March 1867.

20 I am grateful to Paul Frecker, an authority on nineteenth-century photographs for this information. Henry Maull was in business at the addresses on the *carte de visite* of 187A Piccadilly and 62 Cheapside from around 1866, and before that in Piccadilly as Maull & Polyblank from 1856. The photograph is likely to have been reissued with the Maull & Co colophon some time during 1873-8, but I believe it was taken *c*.1866/7 for the Seacole Fund.

21 'Saturday's Sales', *Daily News*, 22, 23 February and 27 March 1867.

22 'The Wandering Thespians', *The Times*, 18 July 1867; *Morning Journal* (Kingston), 29 August 1867, quoting the *Flâneur* of the *Star*.

23 See *Wellington Independent*, 18 & 25 July 1867.

24 Sarah Robinson, *Yarns, Being Sundry Reminiscences* (London: Soldiers' Institute, 1892). This quotation reappeared in 1938 without Robinson being identified as the original source, in a letter from a Major A. C. Whitehorne on the subject of Mary Seacole, published in the *Sunday Times* on 16 January and reproduced in the Jamaican *Daily Gleaner* on 5 February 1938.

25 Alexandra's illness is usually put down to rheumatic fever; more recently, biographer Jane Ridley suggested that she had suffered from 'septic arthritis', a bacterial infection of the joint sometimes linked to gonorrhoea. There are unproven suggestions that Alexandra's promiscuous husband Bertie, Prince of Wales might have infected her. See Jane Ridley, *Bertie: A Life of Edward VII* (London: Chatto & Windus, 2012), 100-2 and Robert S. Pinals, 'Queen Alexandra's Knee', *Journal of Clinical Rheumatology* 22, Vol. 4 (2016): 200-2.

26 'Jamaica's Florence Nightingale', *Daily Gleaner*, 29 August 1939.
27 Unreferenced notes in NLJ, *c.*1951, quoted in Salih introduction to *WAMSML*, xxxix; 'Our London Letter', *Irish Times*, 21 September 1878; 'Recollections of Kingston at Close of Crimean War', *Daily Gleaner*, 21 March 1933.
28 After Queen Victoria's death in February 1901, her youngest daughter Beatrice, who had been her close companion for the last years of the Queen's life, did a most efficient job of editing the 100 or more volumes of her mother's diaries, in so doing eradicating their politically compromising Germanophile comments and any unguarded remarks about John Brown in particular. We can only guess at how much of the original was tampered with, but it is clear that Beatrice either redacted entire undesirable sections or altered them substantially. When she had completed her transcription, she burned the originals.
29 Another example of lost Seacole testimony is that of William Howard Russell. His diaries cover many volumes, and one might expect to find numerous references to his good friend Mary Seacole in them, for they remained in touch after the war. Unfortunately, an inspection of them at the News International Archives reveals that numerous passages have been heavily inked out; others cut from the page, or even the entire page has been torn out. The *Times* archivist suggests that these deletions and the removal of pages probably relate to the use of the diaries by Russell himself for subsequent publication, as he regularly produced books from them, especially for the period from the Crimean War to the American Civil War. For 'Mother Seacole's', see Russell, *Diary in the East During the Tour of the Prince and Princess of Wales*, Vol. 2 (1869), 554.

Chapter 25

1 See 'Gospel Oak Chapel', *Holborn Journal*, 27 June 1868.
2 'Mrs Seacole', *Cork Constitution*, 11 September 1868.
3 Ibid.
4 The Challens lived at Stamford Villas, Kingsland Road, Dalston. Albert Charles's baptism: All Souls St Marylebone. Births and Christenings 15381975, www.ancestry.co.uk
5 1871 England Census, RG 10, piece 589, folio 32, page 14, West Kensington Gardens.
6 Professor Tom Beaumont James of the University of Winchester discovered the letter in 2008 among family papers. See his article: 'Mary Seacole's Lost Letter', *BBC History Magazine*, October 2010, 53-5.
7 Ibid., 54. Albert's parents were George Challen and Hannah Matilda, née James. They were married in 1843, at All Souls, Langham Place.

8   See NPG notes on the Mary Seacole portrait by Jan Marsh, 11 March
    2021. https://www.npg.org.uk/collections/search/portraitExtended/
    mw84190/Mary-Seacole

9   See for example, Marsh, *Black Victorians*.

10 James, 'Mary Seacole's Lost Letter', 54. See Jan Marsh's *Black Victorians*,
    which demonstrates the existence of several portraits of black men as the
    sole subject in the period before 1869 but none of black women.

11 *The Lancet*, 1 October 1870, 484.

12 Florence Nightingale letter to her brother-in-law Sir Harry Verney, 5
    August 1870: Claydon House Trust MS 9004/60, in Salih edition of
    WAMSML, 180; see also Robinson, 189-91.

13 *Morning Advertiser*, 14 December 1870.

14 'Aid for the Wounded', *Portsmouth Times and Naval Gazette*, 27 August
    1870. Mary is in the 'Southsea Visitors Lists' in several issues of this
    paper, see e.g. 3, 7 & 21 September 1870.

15 *Court Journal* quoted in *Liverpool Daily Post*, 12 September 1870.

16 *The Bazaar, Exchange & Mart & Journal of the Household* for 22
    February 1871, 248. There is no sign of Sally living with Mary at Berkeley
    Street on the 1871 census two months later.

17 'The Late Prince Victor of Hohenlohe', 313.

18 'Mrs. Seacole' was exhibit no. 1457. See *Illustrated London News*, 8 June
    1872, 551; 'Sculpture in the Studio', *The Times*, 21 July 1871. 'Count
    Gleichen's Album', 27, Heinz Archive, National Portrait Gallery. It is
    perhaps worth noting that the bust shows Mary wearing what looks
    very much like a necklace of turned coquilla nut beads – and not pearls
    as some have thought, their size being too uniform. These nuts were
    very popular in the West Indies for carving into decorative objects. A
    correspondent has suggested to me that the necklace may have been part
    of a Catholic paternoster, of which examples made from these beads can
    be seen on the web.

19 James R. Creagh, *A Scamper to Sebastopol and Jerusalem* (London: R.
    Bentley & Son, 1873), 225; Robert Arthur Arnold, *From the Levant, the
    Black Sea and the Danube*, Vol. 2 (London: Chapman and Hall, 1868),
    184.

20 'Notification No. 6 Under Law 5 of 1871, Section 10', *Daily Gleaner*,
    1 May 1875 & 4 December 1875; also *London Gazette*, 12 November
    1875, 5399, 5397. *Daily Gleaner*, 29 November 1911.

21 For accounts of Blundell Hall in this period see Atkinson, *The Ffrench
    Connection*.

22 Sir Sibbald David Scott, *To Jamaica and Back* (London: Chapman
    & Hall, 1876), 284; Godfrey Turner, 'Impressions of Jamaica', *The
    Geographical Magazine* 1 (1874), 'Faces at Blundle Hall'.

23 This is confirmed in a letter to the *Gleaner* of 2 August 1905, from an

E. J. Barry of Black River, who wrote to the paper clarifying that Louisa Grant, who had recently died, had not been the owner of Blundell Hall.

24 Information from Keith Atkinson over the course of numerous emails and many years, especially email of 14 March 2021. See Atkinson, *The Ffrench Connection*.

25 It is unclear whether there was already an existing house on the land or whether Mary built one. Corry Staring-Derks was able to locate the title to the property in the Public Record Office at Spanish Town, but the surviving documents in the file date back only to 1917. See Derks, 'Inleiding', ccxxxiv.

26 'Our London Letter', *Irish Times*, 21 September 1878. The rest of the piece, about Mary's Crimean exploits, is full of inaccuracies, but it does at least confirm that she was back in England by September 1878.

27 'Noted Men and Women. Mary Seacole the Soldier's Friend', *Eastbourne Gazette*, 12 January 1881.

28 Will of Mary Seacole, Principal Probate Registry, 11 July 1881, No. 564. Executor William Neilson Farquharson.

29 *Daily Gleaner*, 9 June 1881.

30 'Death of Mrs Seacole' was featured in *Englishwoman's Review*, *Penny Illustrated Paper*, the *London Magnet* and *Daily News* among others. The *Aberdeen Press* headed its feature with 'Death of a Brave Nurse', but perhaps the most fulsome of them all came in the *Fife Free Press & Edinburgh Evening News* with 'Death of a Distinguished Nurse'.

31 This variant appeared on 26 May 1881 in the *Western Times*, *Sheffield Independent* and *South Wales Daily News* among others.

32 'The Late Mrs. Seacole', *The Times*, 24 May 1881.

33 The assessment for death duties is listed in the registers at IR27/419 at TNA; unfortunately it was not possible to access it due to the closure of the archive during the Coronavirus pandemic.

34 Confusingly, Mary refers to both properties as being 'on Staunton Street, formerly Duke Street', but it should be the other way round. Stanton (not Staunton) Street can be seen on old maps as the continuation of Duke Street, north beyond the Parade, and was incorporated into Duke Street in the 1870s. Land registry records for Louisa's property are held at the Public Record Office, Spanish Town, at NS 1, p. 165 and Book 14 NS 1882, 330-1; see Staring-Derks ccxxxv. Email from Jeroen Staring, 14 March 2021. Louisa Grant death certificate, Registrar General's Department, Kingston No AA 5224, issued 21 August 1905.

35 Lady Feodora Gleichen (1861-1922) was a talented sculptor like her father. She died unmarried and without issue and in her will left her jewellery to her sister Helena Emily Gleichen, though made no specific mention of the Seacole pearls. Helena died in 1947, also unmarried and without issue, leaving everything to their third sister Valda, at which

point I gave up searching, for the sake of my sanity. But I often wonder if Feodora is wearing Mary's pearls in this photograph.

36 Amelia and Matilda were born in 1825 and 1823 respectively, the daughters of Jacob Bravo and Frances McLarty. Amelia, who was a sick nurse and lived in Church Street, may have helped Mary nurse sick and convalescent guests at her lodging house. She predeceased Mary in 1878. Matilda was the partner of Captain Joseph Ball Symonette, who sailed the schooner *Maria Luisa* in and around Jamaica. The couple lived in King Street. Mary also left £19. 19s. to 'Mary Ann' Bravo, wife of Phineas Bravo of Kingston. She was born Marian Henriques, of a Sephardi Jewish family in Kingston, as was Phineas Bravo. His brother Alexander Bravo was auditor-general of Jamaica and the first Jew elected to the House of Assembly. Phineas was a magistrate in Kingston and, like Amos Henriques, a member of the Beth Limmud Society. Louisa Cochran remains a mystery, apart from the presence in the Kingston Lunatic Asylum in 1860 – at the same time as Amelia Branigan – of a woman of that name. It may well be that Mary's use of 'cousin' here is in the sense of a much looser family relationship.

37 David Henriques was born in Jamaica in 1850, the son of Armand Henriques and Marian Brandon. He may well be linked to Mary via Rebecca Grant's relationship with Abraham Henriques. By 1876 he had settled at Drumcondra, Dublin, where he worked as a telegraph engineer. He retired to Golders Green in the 1900s and died there in 1926.

38 Florence Seacole marriage: Civil Registration Marriage Index 1837-1915, April quarter, 1883 London 1d 409. Beatrice Tilt birth: Civil Registration Birth Index 1837-1915 January quarter, London 1d 579.

39 Will of Ellen Augusta Watson, Lewes District Probate Registry, 30 January 1925, 205a. Although Alexandra's gift from her father was in

elaborate pendant form, contemporary references to it are as a 'Dagmar brooch'. See e.g *Punch*, in a parody about the new royal baby, 'Afterwards a sudden clutch at his royal mother's Dagmar brooch slightly hurt his hand, but he was delighted when the naughty brooch was well whipped'. 'Prince Baby's Court Circular', *Punch*, 45-8, 19 November 1864, 213. I cannot of course prove that Princess Alexandra gave Mary the brooch for, as explained, the princess's papers were destroyed on her death.

40 They can both be found on the 1911 census at 156 Kennington Park Road, Lambeth, National Archives Series RG14, on www.Ancestry.co.uk.

Chapter 26

1 'Death of Mrs Seacole', *Englishwoman's Review* 25-6 (15 June 1881): 278-9; this was not original to the magazine but a reprint of the *Daily News* obituary.

2 'Death of Prince Hohenlohe', *Daily Gleaner*, 2 February 1892.

3 R. A. Walcott, 'Story of the Life of Mrs Seacole, Remarkable Deeds of a Jamaica Woman. A Name to Remember', *Daily Gleaner*, 27 July 1905. A follow-up letter in the *Gleaner* confirmed that she had never owned Blundell Hall and that her sister Louisa had rented it. See 'Mrs Seacole', letter to the editor, *Daily Gleaner*, 2 August 1905.

4 R. A. Walcott, 'Mrs Mary Seacole', letter to the editor, *The Gleaner* late edition, 27 July 1905.

5 See 'A Jamaican Veteraness', *Daily Gleaner*, 17 August 1910; 'Mary Seacole and the Crimean War', letter to the editor, ibid., 13 November 1916; 'A Noted Jamaican Lady', ibid., 7 December 1916; 'About Mrs Seacole', ibid., 11 December 1916.

6 K. M. Rowley, 'Jamaica's Florence Nightingale: The Odyssey of a Jamaican Brown Lady', *Gleaner Magazine*, 19 August 1939.

7 'The Identity of Mrs Seacole: A Little Yellow Woman', *Daily Gleaner*, 5 February 1938, ex *Sunday Times*; 'Review. Wonderful Adventures of Mrs Seacole', *British Journal of Nursing* 85-6 (June 1937): 165-6. See letters to the *Gleaner*, 9 & 21 February 1938 and 24 & 29 August 1939.

8 Phillips, 'Mary Seacole, the Story of a Kingston Girl'; Rogers, *The World's Great Men of Color*, Vol. 2, 262-71.

9 'Mrs Seacole. A West Indian Nurse in the Crimea'; J. M. Shaftesley, letter to the editor, *The Times*, 16 December 1961, citing the article 'A Coloured Lady Nurse', published 19 July 1855 in the *Morning Advertiser*.

10 Gordon, 'Mary Seacole – A Forgotten Nurse Heroine of the Crimea', 47.

11 Anonymous typescript notes post 1973, 'Mary Seacole – the first "Red Cross" nurse', National Library of Jamaica https://nlj.gov.jm/wp-content/uploads/2017/05/bn_seacole_mj_43.pdf

See also: 'Mary Seacole's grave restored in London', *Daily Gleaner*,

18 December 1973; 'Mary Seacole Honoured in London Ceremony of Reconsecration', *Jamaican Nurse* 13, No. 3 (December 1973): 32-3.

12 See Alexander and Dewjee, Introduction, *Wonderful Adventures*, 40.

13 Matthew Taylor, 'Nurse is greatest Black Briton', *The Guardian*, 10 February 2004. For the names of the Top 10 choices, see http://news.bbc.co.uk/1/hi/uk/3475445.stm

Chapter 27

1 'A Role Model for Us All', *The Guardian*, 11 February 2004.

2 Disappointingly, the 'thousands of soldiers' claim is made on a BBC website https://www.bbc.co.uk/programmes/b0078vq1

3 For a discussion, see 'Lady with the Lamp in the Loony Left Darkness; Political Correctness is about to get rid of Florence Nightingale', *Birmingham Post*, 29 April 1999.

4 'Florence Nightingale, Death of an Icon', *Nursing Times* 95, No. 19 (12 May 1999).

5 'Florence Nightingale redundant?', *The Times*, 3 May 1999; *War Correspondent* 22 (1 April 2004): 3.

6 See 'Should Linda McCartney join Elizabeth I in the revered bible of late great Britons', *Independent* 17 September 2011.

7 For Eliza Polidori see Rappaport, *No Place for Ladies*, 102, 140.

8 James, 'Mary Seacole's Lost Letter', 54. I often wonder if among the items cleared from Dora Challen's house there might have been other letters written by Mary to the Challen family.

9 Private information by email, 17 March 2021.

10 Letter to the editor, *The Times*, 9 January 2013.

11 Unfortunately there are egregious errors in some of the Key Stage 2 material. See in particular a recent BBC history video that shows Mary building a hospital in Crimea and nursing patients there – neither of which happened. https://www.bbc.co.uk/teach/class-clips-video/history-ks2-mary-seacole-ep1/znjtbdm

12 https://www.rcn.org.uk/professional-development/scholarships-and-bursaries/mary-seacole-awards

13 https://www.maryseacoletrust.org.uk/about/

14 https://www.bbc.co.uk/news/uk-england-gloucestershire-53593981

15 My thanks to Paul Frecker, for suggesting this might be the work of Mayall.

16 Soyer, *Culinary Campaign*, 346.

17 Eyre, 'Dusky Doctress', 12.

18 *Black Nurses: The Women Who Saved the NHS*, BBC Four documentary, first transmitted 4 November 2016. I was unfortunately unable to track down Beverly Davies to thank her personally for her wonderful contribution to that programme.

INDEX

Page references in *italics* indicate images.
MS indicates Mary Seacole.